STOCKS FOR THE LONG RUN

Third Edition

STOCKS FOR THE LONG RUN

The Definitive Guide to Financial Market Returns and Long-Term Investment Strategies

JEREMY J. SIEGEL
Russell E. Palmer Professor of Finance
The Wharton School
University of Pennsylvania

McGraw-Hill

New York   Chicago   San Francisco
Lisbon   London   Madrid   Mexico City
Milan   New Delhi   San Juan   Seoul
Singapore   Sydney   Toronto

Library of Congress Cataloging-in-Publication Data

Siegel, Jeremy J.
   Stocks for the long run / Jeremy Siegel. 3rd ed.
      p. cm.
   Includes bibliographical references and index.
   ISBN 0-07-137048-X
   1. Stocks.   2. Stocks—History.   3. Rate of return.   4. Stocks—Rate of return.   I. Title.
HG4661 .S53 2002
332.63'22—dc21

                                             2002002669

McGraw-Hill

A Division of The McGraw·Hill Companies

1 2 3 4 5 6 7 8 9 0 DOC/DOC 0 9 8 7 6 5 4 3 2

ISBN 0-07-137048-X

This book was set in Palatino by North Market Street Graphics.

Printed and bound by R. R. Donnelley & Sons Company.

This publication is designed to provide accurate and authoritative information in regard to the subject matter covered. It is sold with the understanding that neither the author nor the publisher is engaged in rendering legal, accounting, futures/securities trading, or other professional service. If legal advice or other expert assistance is required, the services of a competent professional person should be sought.
         —From a Declaration of Principles jointly adopted by a Committee
         of the American Bar Association and a Committee of Publishers

McGraw-Hill books are available at special quantity discounts to use as premiums and sales promotions, or for use in corporate training programs. For more information, please write to the Director of Special Sales, Professional Publishing, McGraw-Hill, Two Penn Plaza, New York, NY 10121-2298. Or contact your local bookstore.

 This book is printed on recycled, acid-free paper containing a minimum of 50% recycled, de-inked fiber.

CONTENTS

Chapter 12

Stocks and the Business Cycle   203

Chapter 13

World Events That Impact Financial Markets   215

Chapter 14

Reactions of Financial Markets to Economic Data   229

FOREWORD

Some people find the process of assembling data to be a deadly bore. Others view it as a challenge. Jeremy Siegel has turned it into an art form. You can only admire the scope, lucidity, and sheer delight with which Professor Siegel serves up the evidence to support his case for investing in stocks for the long run.

But this book is far more than its title suggests. You will learn a lot of economic theory along the way, garnished with a fascinating history of both the capital markets and the U.S. economy. By using history to maximum effect, Professor Siegel gives the numbers a life and meaning they would never enjoy in a less compelling setting. Moreover, he boldly does battle with all historical episodes that could contradict his thesis and emerges victorious—and this includes the crazy years of the 1990s.

Consequently, I must warn you that his extraordinary skills transform what might have been a dull treatise indeed into a story that is highly seductive. Putting Professor Siegel's program into operation and staying with it for the long run are not the same as reading about the program in a book. His new Chapter 19 in particular focuses a bright light on how often many investors, even the most sophisticated investors, encounter maddening trials and pitfalls in practicing what he preaches.

I frequently recall a brokerage house advertisement from the distant past. The ad pictures three troubled-looking men seated around a table studying a bunch of graphs. A fourth man is reminding the others, "It is always a difficult time to invest." How true! On an emotional level, the challenge is a mighty one, despite the mountains of historical experience. And even with the elegance of the statistical tools and the laws of probability we can apply to that experience, novel and unexpected events are constantly taking investors by surprise. Surprise is what explains the persistent volatility of markets; if we always knew what lay ahead, we would already have priced that certain future into market valuations. The ability to manage the unexpected consequences of our choices and decisions is the real secret of investment success.

Professor Siegel is generous throughout this book in supplying abundant warnings along these lines; in particular, he spares no words as he depicts how temptations to be a short-term investor can overwhelm the need to be a long-term investor. Most of his admonitions, however, relate to the temptation to time or adopt other methods of beating the strategy of buy-and-hold for a diversified equity portfolio. On the basis of my experience, greater danger lurks in the temptation to chicken out when the going is rough and your precious wealth seems to be going down the tubes.

However, remember that the notion of regression to the mean is important in all seasons. Yes, when the going is rough, the happy picture of stocks in the long run may provide comfort and reassurance. By the same token, however, regression to the mean does not sign off when markets are racing far ahead of long-term trends. Hoping that stock prices can soar to the sky—and stay there—is a perilous strategy, even in the most salubrious economic environments.

Indeed, the most powerful part of Professor Siegel's argument is how effectively he demonstrates the consistency of real returns on equities when measured over periods of 20 years or longer. Even the stock returns of Germany and Japan, devastated by World War II, bounced back to challenge the total return of stocks in the United States and the United Kingdom since the 1920s. Indeed, he would be on frail ground if that consistency were not so visible in the historical data and if it did not keep reappearing in so many different guises. Furthermore, he claims that this consistency is the likely outcome of a profit-driven system in which the corporate sector is the engine of economic growth, and adaptability to immense political, social, and economic change is perhaps its most impressive feature. Part 3 of this book, "Economic Environment of Investing," which describes the link between economic activity, the business cycle, inflation, and politics, is the most important part of his story.

In studying this impressive material, however, we must keep in mind that Professor Siegel did not lightly choose *Stocks for the Long Run* as the title of this book. The operative number is 20. Volatility of returns is high in periods of less than 20 years. Figure 2-3, for example, is one of the most revealing graphs in the book. In it we see how badly stocks have fared in the 10-year periods after major market peaks. Spans of 20 years or more after market peaks have been much more encouraging. Professor Siegel's thesis focuses on the *long* run, and he refuses to compromise with it.

Furthermore, we should never forget that all this history tells us what the market did, not what any single investor did, or would do, if the past were to replay itself for us. Few real-world individual portfolios had returns matching what we see here, and I would venture to guess that most portfolios displayed significantly greater volatility in their results. The market is the most broadly diversified portfolio we can find.

Consequently, the owner of a diversified portfolio will never be the center of attraction at a cocktail party, which makes it much less exciting than an actively managed set of investments. However, a diversified portfolio will never be dominated by the dogs either.

When all is said and done, however, the future will always remain hidden from us. The past, no matter how instructive, is always the past. Hence even the wisdom of this insightful volume must be open to constant reexamination and analysis as we move forward in time. Professor Siegel so rightly warns readers of this when he writes that "the returns derived from the past are not hard constants, like the speed of light or gravitation force, waiting to be discovered in the natural world. Historical values must be tempered with an appreciation of how investors, attempting to take advantage of the returns from the past, may alter those very returns in the future." Although the advice set forth in this book very likely will yield positive results for investors, the odds are even higher that uncertainty will forever be your inseparable companion.

Peter Bernstein

PREFACE

I wrote the first edition of *Stocks for the Long Run* with two goals in mind: to document the returns on the major classes of financial assets over the past two centuries and to offer strategies that maximize long-term portfolio growth. My research definitively showed that over long periods of time, the returns on equities not only surpassed those on all other financial assets but also that stock returns were far safer and more predictable than bond returns when measured in terms of purchasing power. I concluded that stocks were clearly the asset of choice for investors seeking long-term growth.

I am both honored and flattered by the tremendous reception that the core ideas of *Stocks for the Long Run* have received. Since the publication of the first edition 8 years ago, I have given hundreds of lectures on the markets and the economy both in the United States and abroad. I have listened closely to the questions that audiences pose, and I have contemplated the many letters, phone calls, and e-mails from readers.

NEW MATERIAL IN THE THIRD EDITION

The unprecedented events of the last several years made the third edition a far more thorough revision than the second. New material has been inserted into almost every chapter, and several chapters have been rewritten completely. Some new topics include a documentation of the unprecedented rise and then fall of the technology stocks and a new approach to calculate the "right" price-earnings (P-E) ratios for growth stocks, a discussion on the trend of global diversification by sector instead of by country, and a new section that documents the rapid growth of exchange-traded funds (ETFs) and other indexed investments.

The extraordinary rise in stock prices over the last decade has caused many people to question the valuation of the market. After a thorough analysis, I conclude that the historical average of 14.5 is no longer appropriate and that a significantly higher ratio is now warranted. However, the implication of this finding, which many investors have not come to grip with, is that future returns on equities are going to be lower than in the past.

Another exciting topic that has been added to this edition is a whole new chapter on behavioral finance, a discipline that rightfully has gained much greater recognition in the finance profession. This chapter is written in a conversational style that is designed to resonate with the anxiety and doubts that virtually all investors (including myself) have experienced at some time during their investing careers. The chapter proposes ways to improve one's investment decisions, as well as strategies that could enhance returns.

The last chapter of the book outlines recommendations to guide investors to construct a well-diversified long-term portfolio. In the first two editions of *Stocks for the Long Run*, I strongly recommended indexation to the major stock market indexes, and that advice has served investors very well. Although I still believe that indexed investments should constitute the core of every investor's long-term portfolio, I have inserted a note of caution. Some indexes, such as the Standard & Poor's (S&P) 500 Stock Index, have become so popular that entry to the index carries with it a price premium that may reduce future returns. This may make it easier for active managers to outperform the S&P 500 Index in the future.

Diversification once again is a theme I advocate as loudly as ever. The countless investors who failed to heed the principles of diversification suffered the worst through the technology crash, the dot-com fiasco, and the Enron debacle. Although a diversified portfolio is hard to maintain when particular stocks and sectors soar in value, those that heed its principles ultimately will enhance their long-run performance.

MARKETS, THE ECONOMY, AND *STOCKS FOR THE LONG RUN*

The Dow Jones Industrial Average was at 3,700 when the first edition of this book was published in May 1994. With interest rates rising rapidly (1994 was by many measures the worst year in the history of the bond market) and stocks already up 60 percent from their October 1990 low, few forecasters predicted further gains for equities. No one expected that just 7 months later stocks would embark on the greatest bull market run in history.

The second edition was published in March 1998 in even more unsettled times. The Dow was at 8,800, and the world stock market had been roiled the previous October by collapse of the Asian markets, which precipitated a record 550-point drop in the Dow and closure of the New York Stock Exchange. A few months after the second edition appeared, the markets were further shaken by collapse of the huge hedge fund Long-Term Capital Management. From July to early September 1998, the Dow fell 20 percent. The trillions of dollars of contracts held by this fund on the verge of bankruptcy threatened the functioning of financial markets, causing an unprecedented intervention by the Federal Reserve to restore liquidity.

Three quick rate cuts by the Fed restored investor confidence. With the uncertainty surrounding Y2K less than 2 years away, few envisioned that October 1998 would begin one of the most spectacular bull markets in history. The technology-laden Nasdaq more than tripled, crossing 5,000 in March 2000. Prices of the world's largest equities surpassed 100 times earnings for the first time in the history of the markets.

Investor optimism was rife. The Internet launched a gold rush that made instant millionaires of many workers in start-up companies who were paid with stock options. John Doerr, a venture capitalist, called the run-up of Internet stocks the largest legal act of wealth creation in world history. And many who missed the first round were lured into a bull market that appeared to ensure profits to all who participated.

This domestic exuberance was matched by a feeling that liberal democracies built on free markets had triumphed as a model for international development. The entire world seemed to stand at the threshold of unprecedented economic growth, where U.S.-based corporations would lead the way. The communications revolution confirmed that the world was getting smaller and that national boundaries were shrinking. Communism had been replaced by democracies in eastern Europe, apartheid was peacefully eliminated in South Africa, and even the Israelis and Palestinians were close to a historic peace accord.

Then it all came crashing down. The Nasdaq, which had peaked in March 2000 at over 5,000, fell by more than 70 percent in the next 18 months. Internet stocks declined even further, and international terrorists launched a successful full-scale attack on the United States. From March 2000 to September 2001, stock values, as measured by the broad Wilshire 5000 Index, fell 40 percent and wiped about $5 trillion from market values.

LESSONS FOR STOCKHOLDERS IN THE NEXT DECADE

Yet the public, once universally regarded as fickle and quick to abandon stocks in difficult times, stuck with equities. There was remarkably little panic selling by investors, and surveys showed that few lost their faith that stocks were still the best long-term investment. If my book played some small part in this newfound tenacity of stock investors, I take great satisfaction.

However, there was another important lesson in *Stocks for the Long*

Run in addition to sticking with stocks. Long-term real returns on equities have averaged about 7 percent per year over all long-term periods. Yet, even counting the bear market of 2000–2001, real returns averaged 11.3 percent per year in the 8 years that my book has been in print. From the beginning of grand bull market in August 1982 through March 2000, real returns averaged 15.6 percent per year. Stock returns in both these periods were significantly above the long-term average.

In the Preface to the second edition, I mentioned my fear that the bull market drove investor expectations too high. Despite the recent bear market, I still believe that many investors have unrealistic expectations of what the stock market can deliver. The lure of short-run gains, the attraction of a "New Economy" paradigm, and the relentless pressure to keep pace with hot sectors and hot stocks caused many investors to abandon their long-term principles. Real returns of 7 percent per year, even though doubling wealth every 10 years, is too slow for many who tasted the spectacular gains made in the last bull market.

But all who strive to be successful investors must exercise patience. In 1937, John Maynard Keynes stated in *The General Theory*, "Investment based on genuine long-term expectation is so difficult today as to be scarcely practicable." Sixty-five years later, long-term investing is as difficult as ever. It is for this reason that *Stocks for the Long Run* remains an important book. Although future stock returns may be diminished from the recent past, there is overwhelming reason to believe that stocks will remain the best investment for all those seeking steady, long-term gains.

Jeremy J. Siegel

A C K N O W L E D G M E N T S

It is never possible to list all the many individuals and organizations that have praised *Stocks for the Long Run* and encouraged me to continue updating past editions. Many who provided me with data for the first two editions of *Stocks for the Long Run* willingly contributed their data for this third edition. I include Lipper Analytical Services and the Vanguard Group for their mutual fund data, Morgan Stanley for their international capital market indexes, and Smithers & Co. for the market-value data. Professors Tim Loughran of Notre Dame and Jay Ritter of the University of Florida also provided me with data and invaluable feedback on the first two editions.

Again, a special thanks goes to my close friend of 35 years, Professor Robert Shiller of Yale University. Since writing *Irrational Exuberance* over 2 years ago, he and I have appeared on many stages together debating the merits of stocks. Despite our differences about whether stock investing will be rewarding over the next 5 to 10 years, we share a common belief that economics has much to say about the right level for stock prices. Although psychological factors may cause the market to deviate substantially from its intrinsic value in the short run, stock values ultimately are determined by economic fundamentals.

My largest debt for this edition of *Stocks for the Long Run* is due to Jeremy Schwartz, a junior at The Wharton School of the University of Pennsylvania. Jeremy not only updated all the charts and tables and provided critical comments on all the chapters, but he also researched and wrote the first draft of Chapter 19 on behavioral finance. Without his efforts, virtually none of the new work in this third edition would have been produced. Shaun Smith, my principal researcher for the first edition, also helped with the analytical material, and Jessica Binder, a Wharton junior, assisted with the material on behavioral finance.

As always, a special thanks goes to the thousands of financial consultants and investment professionals of Merrill Lynch, Morgan Stanley, PaineWebber, Salomon Smith Barney, Prudential Securities, and many other firms who have provided me with invaluable feedback on both editions of *Stocks for the Long Run* in seminars and open forums. These people offered me invaluable opportunities to advance the core concepts of the book as well as expose new research that is included in this edition.

I am particularly indebted to Rittenhouse Financial Services, Inc., of Radnor, Pennsylvania, which has sponsored literally hundreds of my presentations before investors and market professionals throughout the United States and Canada over the past 6 years. We both have an abiding belief in the advantages of long-term equity investment, and Rittenhouse has given me complete freedom to express my views on stocks and the market even if they conflicted with those of the company. I truly value the support of this organization.

Again, I am honored that Peter Bernstein has written a Foreword for this third edition. I strive to attain the clarity that he has achieved in his best-selling books about the history and practice of investing. My editor, Jeffrey Krames of McGraw-Hill, has been one of my biggest fans and has guided this book through both the second and third editions.

A special debt is always owed to one's family when one writes a book. Only those who are close know the total absorption required to produce a work of this magnitude. Despite the effort and the many deadlines, I have managed to spend time with them by combining some of my speaking engagements with family trips. Hopefully, the lessons of this book will enable my family and others to enjoy more leisure time in the future.

STOCKS FOR THE LONG RUN

PART

THE VERDICT OF HISTORY

CHAPTER 1

STOCK AND BOND RETURNS SINCE 1802

I know of no way of judging the future but by the past.

PATRICK HENRY, 1775[1]

"EVERYBODY OUGHT TO BE RICH"

In the summer of 1929, a journalist named Samuel Crowther interviewed John J. Raskob, a senior financial executive at General Motors, about how the typical individual could build wealth by investing in stocks. In August of that year, Crowther published Raskob's ideas in a *Ladies' Home Journal* article with the audacious title, "Everybody Ought to Be Rich."

In the interview, Raskob claimed that America was on the verge of a tremendous industrial expansion. He maintained that by putting just $15 a month into good common stocks, investors could expect their wealth to grow steadily to $80,000 over the next 20 years. Such a return—24 percent per year—was unprecedented, but the prospect of effortlessly amassing a great fortune seemed plausible in the atmosphere of the 1920s bull mar-

---

[1] Speech in Virginia Convention, March 23, 1775.

ket. Stocks excited investors, and millions of people put their savings into the market seeking a quick profit.

On September 3, 1929, a few days after Raskob's ideas appeared, the Dow Jones Industrial Average hit a historic high of 381.17. Seven weeks later, stocks crashed. The next 34 months saw the most devastating decline in share values in U.S. history.

On July 8, 1932, when the carnage was finally over, the Dow stood at 41.22. The market value of the world's greatest corporations had declined an incredible 89 percent. Millions of investors' life savings were wiped out, and thousands of investors who borrowed money to buy stocks were forced into bankruptcy. America was mired in the deepest economic depression in its history.

Raskob's advice was ridiculed and denounced for years to come. It was said to represent the insanity of those who believed that the market could rise forever and the foolishness of those who ignored the tremendous risks inherent in stocks. Indiana's Senator Arthur Robinson publicly held Raskob responsible for the stock crash by urging common people to buy stock at the market peak.[2] In 1992, 63 years later, *Forbes* magazine warned investors of the overvaluation of stocks in its issue headlined, "Popular Delusions and the Madness of Crowds." In a review of the history of market cycles, *Forbes* fingered Raskob as the "worst offender" of those who viewed the stock market as a guaranteed engine of wealth.[3]

Conventional wisdom holds that Raskob's foolhardy advice epitomizes the mania that periodically overruns Wall Street. However, is this verdict fair? The answer is decidedly no. If you were to calculate the value of the portfolio of an investor who followed Raskob's advice, patiently putting $15 a month into stocks, you would find that his or her accumulation would exceed that of someone who placed the same money in Treasury bills after less than 4 years! After 20 years, his or her stock portfolio would have accumulated to almost $9,000, and after 30 years, over $60,000. Although not as high as Raskob had projected, $60,000 still represents a fantastic 13 percent return on invested capital, far exceeding the returns earned by conservative investors who switched their money to Treasury bonds or bills at the market peak. Those who never bought stock, citing the great crash as the vindication of their caution, eventually

---

[2]Irving Fisher, *The Stock Market Crash and After* (New York: Macmillan, 1930), p. xi.
[3]"The Crazy Things People Say to Rationalize Stock Prices," *Forbes*, April 27, 1992, p. 150.

found themselves far behind investors who had patiently accumulated equity.[4]

John Raskob's infamous prediction illustrates an important theme in the history of Wall Street. This theme is not the prevalence of foolish optimism at market peaks; rather, it is that over the last century, accumulations in stocks have always outperformed other financial assets for the patient investor. Even such calamitous events as the great stock crash of 1929 did not negate the superiority of stocks as long-term investments.

FINANCIAL MARKET RETURNS FROM 1802

This chapter analyzes the returns on stocks and bonds over long periods of time in both the United States and other countries. This two-century history is divided into three subperiods. In the first subperiod, from 1802 through 1870, the United States made a transition from an agrarian to an industrialized economy, comparable with the "emerging markets" of Latin America and Asia today.[5] In the second subperiod, from 1871 through 1925, the United States became the foremost political and economic power in the world.[6] The third subperiod, from 1926 to the present, contains the 1929–1932 stock collapse, the Great Depression, and the postwar expansion. The data from this period have been analyzed extensively by academics and professional money managers and have served as a benchmark for historical returns.[7] Figure 1-1 tells the story. It depicts the total return indexes for stocks, long- and short-term bonds, gold, and commodities from 1802 through 2001. *Total returns* means that all returns, such as interest and dividends and capital gains, are automatically reinvested in the asset and allowed to accumulate over time.

---

[4]Raskob succumbed to investors in the 1920s who wanted to get rich quickly by devising a scheme by which investors borrowed $300, adding $200 of personal capital, to invest $500 in stocks. Although in 1929 this was certainly not as good as putting money gradually in the market, even this plan beat investment in Treasury bills after 20 years.

[5]A brief description of the early stock market is found in Appendix 1. The stock data during this period are taken from Schwert (1990), although I have inserted my own dividend series. G. William Schwert, "Indexes of United States Stock Prices from 1802 to 1987," *Journal of Business* 63(1990):399–426.

[6]The stock series used in this period are taken from Cowles indexes as reprinted in Shiller (1989). Robert Shiller, *Market Volatility* (Cambridge, MA: M.I.T. Press, 1989). The Cowles indexes are capitalization-weighted indexes of all New York Stock Exchange stocks and include dividends.

[7]The data from the third period are taken from the Center for Research in Stock Prices (CRSP) capitalization-weighted indexes of all New York stocks and, starting in 1962, American and Nasdaq stocks.

FIGURE   1–1

Total Nominal Return Indexes, 1802–2001

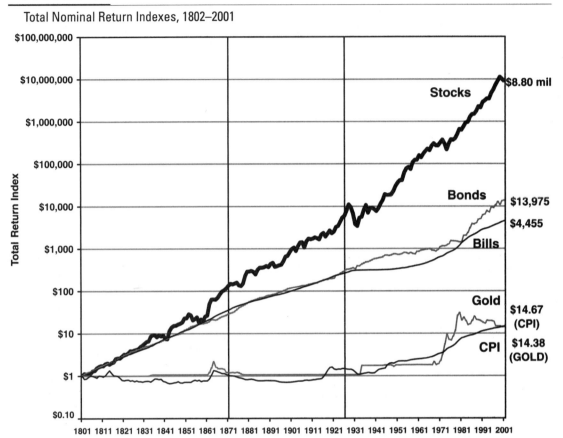

It can be easily seen that the total return on equities dominates all other assets. Even the cataclysmic stock crash of 1929, which caused a generation of investors to shun stocks, appears as a mere blip in the stock return index. Bear markets, which so frighten investors, pale in the context of the upward thrust of total stock returns. One dollar invested and reinvested in stocks since 1802 would have accumulated to nearly $8.80 million by the end of 2001. This sum can be realized by an investor holding the broadest possible portfolio of stocks in proportion to their market value and does not depend on how many of these companies survive or not.[8]

By extension, the preceding analysis indicates that $1 million invested and reinvested during these 200 years would have grown to the

---

[8]Analysis of the survivorship issue in computing returns is discussed in Chapter 3.

incredible sum of $8.80 trillion by the end of 2001, nearly 70 percent of the entire capitalization of the U.S. stock market!

One million dollars in 1802 is equivalent to roughly $15 million in today's purchasing power. This was certainly a large, though not over-whelming, sum of money to the industrialists and landholders of the early nineteenth century.[9] However, total wealth in the stock market, or in the economy for that matter, does not accumulate as fast as the total return index. This is so because investors consume most of their dividends and capital gains, enjoying the fruits of their past saving.

It is rare for anyone to accumulate wealth for long periods of time without consuming part of his or her return. The longest period of time investors typically plan to hold assets without touching principal and income is when they are accumulating wealth in pension plans for their retirement or in insurance policies that are passed on to their heirs. Even those who bequeath fortunes untouched during their lifetimes must realize that these accumulations often are dissipated in the next generation. The stock market has the power to turn a single dollar into millions by the forbearance of generations—but few will have the patience or desire to let this happen.

HISTORICAL SERIES ON BONDS

Bonds are the most important financial assets competing with stocks. Bonds promise fixed monetary payments over time. In contrast to equity, the cash flows from bonds have a maximum monetary value set by the terms of the contract and, except in the case of default, do not vary with the profitability of the firm.

The bond series shown in Figure 1-1 are based on long- and short-term government bonds, when available; if not, similar highly rated securities were used. Default premiums were removed from all interest rates in order to obtain a comparable series over the entire period.[10]

Figure 1-2 displays the interest rates on long- and short-term bonds, called *bills*, over the 200-year period. Interest-rate fluctuations during the nineteenth and twentieth centuries remained within a narrow range. But from 1926 to the present, the behavior of both long- and

---

[9]Blodget, an early nineteenth-century economist, estimated the wealth of the United States at that time to be nearly $2.5 billion, so $1 million would be only about 0.04 percent of the total wealth. S. Blodget, Jr., *Economica: A Statistical Manual for the United States of America*, 1806 edition, p. 68.

[10]See Jeremy Siegel, "The Real Rate of Interest from 1800–1990: A study of the U.S. and U.K.," *Journal of Monetary Economics* 29(1992):227–252, for a detailed description of the process by which a historical yield series was constructed.

FIGURE 1–2

U.S. Interest Rates, 1800–2001

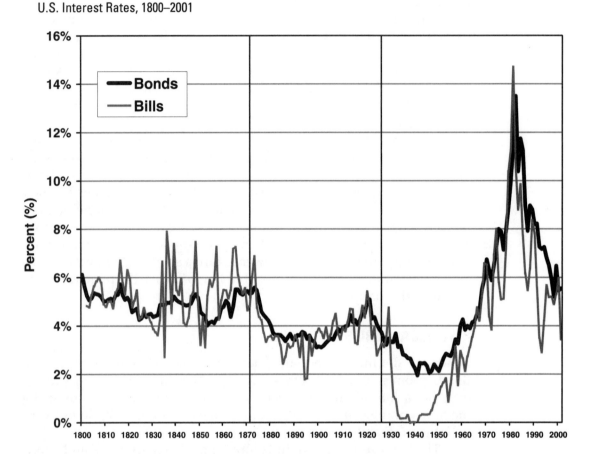

short-term interest rates changed dramatically. During the Great Depression of the 1930s, short-term interest rates fell nearly to zero, and yields on long-term government bonds fell to a record-low 2 percent. In order to finance record wartime borrowings, the government maintained low rates during World War II and the early postwar years. Deposit rates also were kept low by strict limits (known as Regulation Q[11]) imposed by the Federal Reserve on bank deposit rates through the 1950s and 1960s.

The 1970s marked an unprecedented change in interest-rate behavior. Inflation reached double-digit levels, and interest rates soared to

---

[11]Regulation Q was a provision in the Banking Act of 1933 that imposed ceilings on interest rates and time deposits.

heights that had not been seen since the debasing of continental currency in the early years of the republic. Never before had inflation been
so high for so long.

The public clamored for government action to slow rising prices.
Finally, by 1982, the restrictive monetary policy of Paul Volcker, chairman of the Federal Reserve System since 1979, brought inflation and interest rates down to more moderate levels. One can see that the level of
interest rates is closely tied to the level of inflation. Understanding the
returns on fixed-income assets therefore requires knowledge of how the
price level is determined.

THE PRICE LEVEL AND GOLD

Figure 1-3 depicts consumer prices in the United States and the United
Kingdom over the past 200 years. In each country, the price level at the
end of World War II was essentially the same as it was 150 years earlier.
Since World War II, however, the path of inflation changed dramatically.
The price level rose almost continuously over the past 55 years, often
gradually but sometimes at double-digit rates, as in the 1970s. Excluding
wartime, the 1970s witnessed the first rapid and sustained inflation ever
experienced in U.S. history.

The dramatic changes in the recent inflationary trend should not
come as a surprise. During the nineteenth and early twentieth centuries,
the United States, the United Kingdom, and the rest of the industrialized
world were on a gold standard. As described in detail in Chapter 11, a
gold standard restricts the supply of money and hence the inflation rate.
From the Great Depression through World War II, however, the world
shifted to a paper money standard. Under a paper money standard,
there is no legal constraint on the issuance of money, so inflation is subject to political as well as economic forces. Price stability depends on the
ability of the central banks to limit the supply of money and control the
inflationary policies of the federal governments.

The chronic inflation that the United States and other developed
economies have experienced since World War II does not mean that the
gold standard was superior to the current paper money standard. The
gold standard was abandoned because of its inflexibility in the face of economic crises, particularly the banking collapse of the 1930s. The paper
money standard, if administered properly, can avoid the banking panics
and severe depressions that plagued the gold standard. However, the cost
of this stability is a bias toward chronic inflation.

F I G U R E   1–3

U.S. and U.K. Price Indexes, 1800–2001 (1800 = $1)

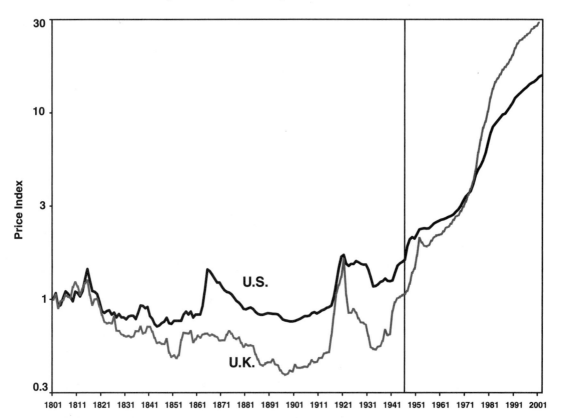

It is not surprising that the price of gold has followed the trend of overall inflation closely over the past two centuries. The price of gold soared to $850 per ounce in January 1980, following the rapid inflation of the preceding decade. When inflation was brought under control, the price of gold fell. One dollar of gold bullion purchased in 1802 was worth $14.38 at the end of 2001. That is actually less than the change in the overall price level! In the long run, gold offers investors some protection against inflation but little else. Whatever hedging property precious metals possess, these assets will exert a considerable drag on the return of a long-term investor's portfolio.[12]

[12]Ironically, despite the inflationary bias of a paper money system, well-preserved paper money from the early nineteenth century is worth many times its face value on the collectors' market, far surpassing gold bullion as a long-term investment. An old mattress found containing nineteenth-century paper money is a better find for the antique hunter than an equivalent sum hoarded in gold bars!

TOTAL REAL RETURNS

The focus of every long-term investor should be the growth of purchasing power—monetary wealth adjusted for the effect of inflation. Figure 1-4 shows the growth of purchasing power, or total real returns, in the same assets that were graphed in Figure 1-1: stocks, bonds, bills, and gold. These data are constructed by taking the dollar returns and correcting them by the changes in price level shown in Figure 1-3.[13]

[13]Total returns are graphed on a ratio, or logarithmic, scale. Economists use this scale to graph virtually all long-term data because equal vertical distances anywhere in the chart represent equal percentage changes in return. As a result, a constant slope represents a constant after-inflation rate of return.

FIGURE 1–4

Total Real Return Indexes, 1802–2001

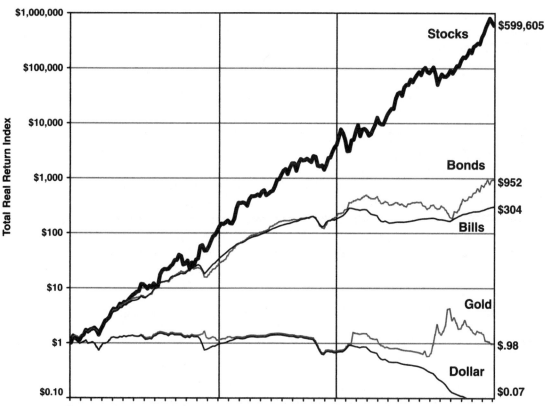

The growth of purchasing power in equities not only dominates all other assets but also shows remarkable long-term stability. Despite extraordinary changes in the economic, social, and political environments over the past two centuries, stocks have yielded between 6.6 and 7.0 percent per year after inflation in all major subperiods.

The wiggles on the stock return line represent the bull and bear markets that equities have suffered throughout history. The long-term perspective radically changes one's view of the risk of stocks. The short-term fluctuations in the stock market, which loom so large to investors when they occur, are insignificant when compared with the upward movement of equity values over time.

In contrast to the remarkable stability of stock returns, real returns on fixed-income assets have declined markedly over time. In the first and even second subperiods, the annual returns on bonds and bills, although less than those on equities, were significantly positive. Since 1926, however, and especially since World War II, fixed-income assets have returned little after inflation.

INTERPRETATION OF RETURNS

Long-Period Returns

Table 1-1 summarizes the annual returns on U.S. stocks over the past two centuries.[14] The shaded column represents the real after-inflation, compound annual rate of return on stocks. The real return on equities has averaged 6.9 percent per year over the past 200 years. This means that purchasing power has, on average, doubled in the stock market every 10 years. If past trends persist, inflation averages 3 percent, and equities offer a 7 percent real return, this would translate into a 10.2 percent per year nominal or money return on stocks.

Note the extraordinary stability of the real return on stocks over all major subperiods: 7.0 percent per year from 1802 through 1870, 6.6 percent from 1871 through 1925, and 6.9 percent per year since 1926. Even

---

[14]The dividend yield for the first subperiod has been estimated by statistically fitting the relation of long-term interest rates to dividend yields in the second subperiod, yielding results that are closer to other information we have about dividends during the period. See Walter Werner and Steven Smith, *Wall Street* (New York: Columbia University Press, 1991), for a description of some early dividend yields. See also recent papers by William Goetzmann and Phillipe Jorion, "A Longer Look at Dividend Yields," *Journal of Business* 68(4)(1995):483–508, and by William Goetzmann, "Patterns in Three Centuries of Stock Market Prices," *Journal of Business* 66(2)(1993):249–270.

T A B L E   1–1

Annual Stock Market Returns, 1802–2001

Comp = compound annual return
Arith = arithmetic average of annual returns
Risk = standard deviation of arithmetic returns
All Data in Percent (%)

		Total Nominal Return			Nominal Capital Appreciation			Div Yld	Total Real Return			Real Capital Appreciation			Real Gold Retn	Consumer Price Inflation
		Comp	Arith	Risk	Comp	Arith	Risk		Comp	Arith	Risk	Comp	Arith	Risk		
Periods	1802-2001	8.3	9.7	17.5	3.0	4.4	17.5	5.2	6.9	8.4	18.1	1.6	3.2	17.9	0.0	1.4
Periods	1871-2001	9.0	10.6	18.5	4.2	5.8	18.3	4.6	6.8	8.5	18.8	2.1	3.8	18.6	-0.1	2.0
Major Sub-Periods	I 1802-1870	7.1	8.1	15.5	0.7	1.8	15.5	6.4	7.0	8.3	16.9	0.6	1.9	16.6	0.2	0.1
Major Sub-Periods	II 1871-1925	7.2	8.4	15.7	1.9	3.1	16.1	5.2	6.6	7.9	16.8	1.3	2.7	17.1	-0.8	0.6
Major Sub-Periods	III 1926-2001	10.2	12.2	20.3	5.8	7.8	19.6	4.1	6.9	8.9	20.3	2.7	4.6	19.6	0.4	3.1
Post-War Periods	1946-2001	11.6	12.8	16.8	7.5	8.7	16.2	3.8	7.1	8.6	17.4	3.2	4.6	16.8	-0.3	4.1
Post-War Periods	1946-1965	13.1	14.3	19.5	8.2	9.2	18.7	4.6	10.0	11.4	18.7	5.2	6.5	18.1	-2.7	2.8
Post-War Periods	1966-1981	6.6	8.3	17.2	2.6	4.3	16.6	3.9	-0.4	1.4	17.1	-4.1	-2.4	16.7	8.8	7.0
Post-War Periods	1982-1999	17.3	18.0	12.5	13.8	14.5	12.4	3.1	13.6	14.3	12.6	10.2	10.9	12.6	-4.9	3.3
Post-War Periods	1982-2001	14.1	15.0	14.9	10.9	11.8	14.4	2.9	10.5	11.5	14.7	7.4	8.3	14.3	-4.8	3.2

since World War II, during which all the inflation that the United States has experienced over the past 200 years occurred, the average real rate of return on stocks has been 7.1 percent per year. This is virtually identical to the preceding 125 years, which saw no overall inflation. This remarkable stability of long-term real returns is a characteristic of *mean reversion,* a property of a variable to offset its short-term fluctuations so as to produce far more stable long-term returns.

The long-term stability of these returns is all the more surprising when one reflects on the dramatic changes that have taken place in our society during the last two centuries. The United States evolved from an agricultural to an industrial economy and now to a postindustrial service- and technology-oriented economy. The world shifted from a gold standard to a paper money standard. And information, which once took weeks to cross the country, can now be transmitted instantaneously and broadcast simultaneously around the world. Yet, despite mammoth changes in the basic factors generating wealth for shareholders, equity returns have shown an astounding persistence.

Short-Period Returns

The long-term stability of real equity returns does not deny that short-term returns can be quite variable. In fact, there are a number of periods when stock returns differ from their long-term average. Samples of such episodes after World War II are reported at the bottom of Table 1-1.

The bull market from 1982 through 1999 gave investors an after-inflation return of 13.6 percent per year, which is nearly double the historical average. However, the superior equity returns over this period have barely compensated investors for the dreadful stock returns realized in the preceding 15 years, from 1966 through 1981, when the real rate of return was –0.4 percent. In fact, during the 15-year period that preceded the current bull market, stock returns were more below their historical average than they have been above their average during the 1982–1999 great bull market run.

The bull market since 1982 has brought stocks back from the extremely undervalued state that they reached at the beginning of the 1980s. Certainly the superior performance of stocks over the last decade is extremely unlikely to persist, but this does not necessarily imply that stock returns over the next decade must be below average in order to offset the bull market from 1982. Chapter 7 will analyze future returns on stocks in light of the great bull market of the past two decades.

REAL RETURNS ON FIXED-INCOME ASSETS

As stable as the long-term real returns have been for equities, the same cannot be said of fixed-income assets. Table 1-2 reports the nominal and real returns on both short- and long-term bonds over the same time periods as in Table 1-1. The real return on bills has dropped precipitously from 5.1 percent in the early part of the nineteenth century to a bare 0.7 percent since 1926, a return only slightly above inflation.

The real return on long-term bonds has shown a similar pattern. Bond returns fell from a generous 4.8 percent in the first subperiod to 3.7 percent in the second and then to only 2.2 percent in the third. If the returns from the last 75 years were projected into the future, it would take nearly 33 years to double one's purchasing power in bonds and over 100 years to do so in Treasury bills in contrast to the 10 years it takes in stocks.

The decline in the average real return on fixed-income securities is striking. In any 30-year period beginning with 1889, the average real rate of return on short-term government securities has exceeded 2 percent only three times. Since the late nineteenth century, the real return on

TABLE 1-2

Fixed-Income Returns, 1802–2001

Comp = compound annual return
Arith = arithmetic average of annual returns
Risk = standard deviation of arithmetic returns
All Data in Percent (%)

			Long-Term Governments						Short-Term Governments					Consumer Price Inflation
		Coupon Rate	Nominal Return			Real Return			Nominal Rate	Real Return				
			Comp	Arith	Risk	Comp	Arith	Risk		Comp	Arith	Risk		
Periods	1802-2001	4.8	4.9	5.1	6.3	3.5	3.9	8.9	4.3	2.9	3.1	6.1		1.4
	1871-2001	4.7	4.9	5.1	7.5	2.8	3.2	9.1	3.8	1.7	1.9	4.6		2.0
Major Sub-Periods	I 1802-1870	4.9	4.9	4.9	2.8	4.8	5.1	8.3	5.2	5.1	5.4	7.7		0.1
	II 1871-1925	4.0	4.3	4.4	3.0	3.7	3.9	6.4	3.8	3.2	3.3	4.8		0.6
	III 1926-2001	5.2	5.3	5.7	9.5	2.2	2.7	10.7	3.9	0.7	0.8	4.1		3.1
Post-War Periods	1946-2001	6.0	5.5	6.0	10.7	1.3	1.9	11.5	4.9	0.6	0.7	3.3		4.1
	1946-1965	3.1	1.6	1.7	7.1	-1.2	-1.0	8.1	2.0	-0.8	-0.7	2.1		2.8
	1966-1981	7.2	2.5	2.8	12.3	-4.2	-3.9	13.2	6.9	-0.2	-0.1	2.4		7.0
	1982-1999	8.4	12.0	12.8	14.4	8.4	9.3	14.2	6.3	2.9	2.9	1.8		3.3
	1982-2001	8.1	12.0	12.8	13.8	8.5	9.3	13.6	6.1	2.8	2.8	1.7		3.2

bonds and bills over any 30-year horizon has seldom matched the average return of 4.5 to 5 percent reached during the first 70 years of our sample. From 1880, the real return on long-term bonds over every 30-year period has never reached 4 percent, and it exceeded 3 percent during only 17 such periods.

You have to go back more than 1½ centuries to the period from 1831 through 1861 to find any 30-year period where the return on either long- or short-term bonds exceeded that on equities. The dominance of stocks over fixed-income securities is overwhelming for investors with long horizons.

THE FALL IN FIXED-INCOME RETURNS

Although the returns on equities have fully compensated stock investors for the increased inflation since World War II, the returns on fixed-income securities have not. The change in the monetary standard from gold to paper had its greatest effect on the returns of fixed-income assets. It is clear that the buyers of long-term bonds in the 1940s, 1950s, and early 1960s did not recognize the inflationary consequences of the change in monetary regime. How else can you explain why investors voluntarily purchased 30-year bonds with 3 and 4 percent coupons, ignoring a government policy that was determined to avoid deflation and in fact favored inflation?

However, there must have been other reasons for the decline in real returns on fixed-income assets. Theoretically, the unanticipated inflation of the postwar period should have had a significantly smaller effect on the real return on short-term bonds such as Treasury bills. This is so because short-term rates may be reset frequently to capture expected inflation. As noted previously, however, the decline in the real return on short-term bonds actually exceeded the decline in the real return on long-term bonds.

Another explanation for the fall in bond returns is investors' reactions to the financial turmoil of the Great Depression. The stock collapse of the early 1930s caused a whole generation of investors to shun equities and invest in government bonds and newly insured bank deposits, driving their return downward. Finally, many investors bought bonds because of the widespread (but incorrect) prediction that another depression would follow the war.

However, it was not just the risk preferences of investors that kept fixed rates low. The Federal Reserve actively supported the bond market through much of the 1940s to keep the government's interest expense low. This support policy was abandoned in 1951 because it led to interest rates that were inconsistent with one of the Fed's primary goals of maintaining low inflation.

And finally, one should not ignore the transformation of a highly segmented market for short-term instruments in the nineteenth century into one of the world's most liquid markets. Treasury bills satisfy certain fiduciary and legal requirements that no other asset can match. The premium paid for these services, however, has translated into a meager return for investors.

EQUITY PREMIUM

Whatever the reasons for the decline in the real return on fixed-income assets over the past century, it is almost certain that the real returns on bonds will be higher on average in the future than they have been over the last 70 years. As a result of the inflation shock of the 1970s, bondholders have incorporated a significant inflation premium in the coupon on long-term bonds. In most major industrialized nations, if inflation does not increase appreciably from current levels, real returns of about 2 to 3 percent will be realized from government bonds whose nominal rate is between 5 and 6 percent. These projected real returns are not much lower than the 3½ percent average compound real return on U.S. long-term government bonds over the past 200 years. Moreover, they are comparable with the yields of the newly floated inflation-linked bonds issued by the U.S. Treasury in 1997.

The excess return for holding equities over short-term bonds is referred to as the *equity risk premium*, or simply the *equity premium*, and is plotted in Figure 1-5.[15] The equity premium, calculated as the difference

[15]For a rigorous analysis of the equity premium, see Jeremy Siegel and Richard Thaler, "The Equity Premium Puzzle," *Journal of Economic Perspectives* 11(1)(Winter 1997):191–200.

FIGURE 1–5

Equity Risk Premium (30-Year Compound Annual Moving Average, 1831–2001)

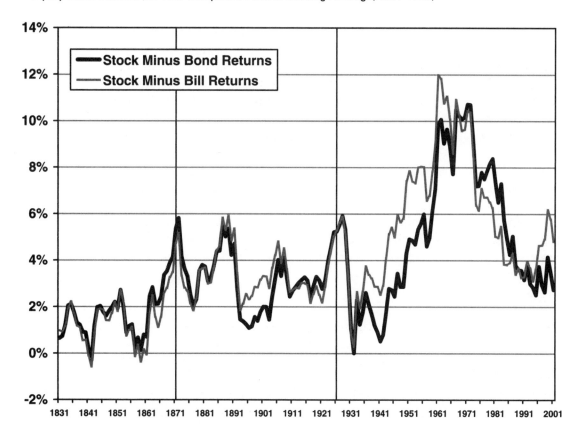

in 30-year compound annual real returns on stocks and bills, averaged
1.9 percent in the first subperiod, 3.4 percent in the second subperiod,
and 6.5 percent since 1926.

The abnormally high equity premium since 1926 is certainly not
sustainable. It is not a coincidence that the highest 30-year average equity return occurred in a period marked by very low real returns on
bonds. Since firms finance a large part of their capital investment with
bonds, the low cost of obtaining such funds increased returns to shareholders. The 1930s and 1940s marked an extremely undervalued period
for equities and overvalued period for government bonds, leading to
unusually high returns for stocks and low returns for bonds. As stocks
and bonds become more correctly priced, the equity premium certainly
will shrink. Chapter 7 will discuss the equity premium and its implications for future returns in more detail.

INTERNATIONAL RETURNS

Some economists have maintained that the superior returns to equity are
a consequence of choosing data from the United States, a country that has
been transformed from a small British colony to the world's greatest economic power over the last 200 years.[16] However, equity returns in other
countries also have substantially outpaced those on fixed-income assets.

Figure 1-6 displays the total real stock return index for the United
States, the United Kingdom, Germany, and Japan from 1926 to the present.[17] It is striking that the cumulative real returns on German and U.K.
stocks over the 76-year period from 1926 through 2001 come so close to
those of the United States. The compound annual real returns on stocks
in each of these three countries are all within about 1 percentage point of
each other.

The collapse of Japanese stocks during and after World War II was
far greater than occurred in its defeated ally, Germany. In Japan, the
breakup of the *Zaibatsu* industrial cartel, the distribution of its shares to
the workers, and the hyperinflation that followed the war caused a 98
percent fall in the real value of equities.[18]

---

[16]See S. J. Brown, W. N. Goetzmann, and S. A. Ross, "Survival," *Journal of Finance* 50(1995):853–873.
[17]The German returns are obtained from Gregor Gielen, *Können Aktienkurse Noch Steigen? Langfristige Trendanalyse des deutschen Aktienmarktes* (Berlin: Gabler, 1994). British returns are from Shiller (1989) and updated from various sources.
[18]T. F. M. Adams and Iwao Hoshii, *A Financial History of the New Japan* (Tokyo: Kodansha Interna-tional, 1972), p. 39.

FIGURE 1–6

International Real Stock Returns in the United States, Germany, the United Kingdom, and Japan, 1926–2001

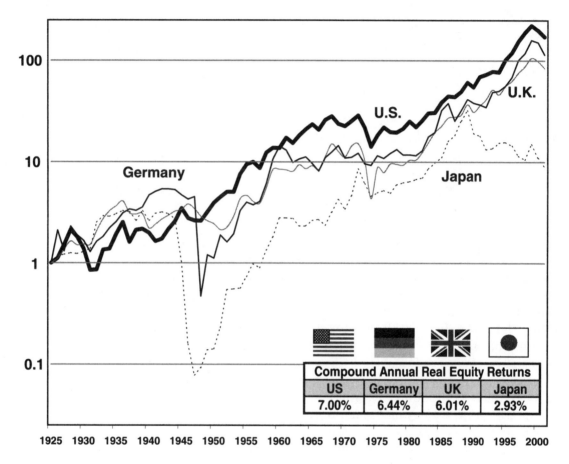

Compound Annual Real Equity Returns			
US	Germany	UK	Japan
7.00%	6.44%	6.01%	2.93%

Despite the collapse of the equity market, Japanese stocks regained almost all the ground they lost to the Western countries by the end of the 1980s. From 1948 through 1989, the real return on the Japanese market has exceeded 10.4 percent per year, nearly 50 percent higher than the U.S. market. Even including its recent bear market, Japan's real equity returns since 1926 have been 2.9 percent per year. Moreover, because the yen has appreciated in real terms relative to the dollar, the average annual real-dollar returns in the Japanese market have been 3.15 percent per year. Measured in *any* currency, the real returns in *every* one of these major countries from 1926 through 2001 have exceeded the real returns on fixed-income assets in *any* of these countries.

Germany

Despite the fact that World War II resulted in a 90 percent drop in real German equity prices, investors were not wiped out. Those who patiently held equity were rewarded with tremendous returns in the postwar period.[19] By 1958, the total returns for German stocks had surpassed its prewar level. In the 12 years from 1948 through 1960, German stocks rose by over 30 percent per year in real terms. Indeed, from 1939, when the Germans invaded Poland, through 1960, the real returns on German stocks nearly matched those in the United States and exceeded those in the United Kingdom. Despite the devastation of the war, the recovery of German markets powerfully attests to the resilience of stocks in the face of seemingly destructive political, social, and economic forces.

United Kingdom

Over the long run, the returns on British equities are almost as impressive as those in the American market. In contrast to the U.S. experience, the greatest stock decline in Great Britain occurred in 1973 and 1974, not the early 1930s. In 1973–1974, rampant inflation as well as political and labor turmoil caused the British market to lose over 70 percent of its value. The capitalization of the British market fell to a measly $50 billion. This is less than the market value of many individual Internet stocks during the height of the dot-com mania in 1999–2000 or the yearly profits of the OPEC oil-producing nations, whose increase in oil prices contributed to the decline in share values.[20]

In fact, the OPEC nations could have purchased a controlling interest in every publicly traded British corporation in the 1970s with less than 1 year's oil revenues! It is lucky for the British that they did not. The British market has increased dramatically since the 1974 crash and has outstripped the dollar gains in all other major world markets. Again,

---

[19]Of course, not everyone in Germany was able to realize the German postwar miracle. The stock holdings of many who resided in the eastern sector, controlled by the Soviet Union, were totally confiscated. Despite reunification with West Germany, many of these claims were never recovered.
[20]"The défi Opec" (no author), *The Economist*, December 7, 1974, p. 85. OPEC stands for "Organization of Petroleum Exporting Countries," a cartel that attempts to regulate the supply of oil.

these rewards went to those who held onto British stocks through this crisis.

Japan

Despite Japan's recent bear market, the postwar rise in Japanese stocks is quite remarkable. The Nikkei Dow Jones Stock Average, patterned after the U.S. Dow Jones Average and containing 225 stocks, was first published on May 16, 1949. The day marked the reopening of the Tokyo Stock Exchange, which had been officially closed since August 1945. On the opening day, the value of the Nikkei was 176.21—virtually identical to the U.S. Dow Jones Industrials at that time. By December 1989, the Nikkei soared to nearly 40,000, more than 15 times that of the Dow. Japan's bear market brought the Nikkei below 10,000 following the terrorist attacks in September 2001, just above the level reached by the American Dow. On February 1, 2002, the Nikkei closed at 9,791, below the Dow for the first time in 45 years.

However, comparing U.S. and Japanese Dow indexes overstates the extent of the Japanese decline. The gain in the Japanese market measured in *dollars* far exceeds that measured in *yen*. The yen was set at 360 to the dollar 3 weeks before the opening of the Tokyo Stock Exchange—a rate that was to hold for more than 20 years. Since then, the dollar has fallen to about 130 yen. In dollar terms, therefore, the Nikkei climbed to over 100,000 in 1989 and is currently over 30,000, three times its American counterpart, despite the great bear market that has enveloped Japan in the past decade.

Foreign Bonds

The story for foreign countries remains the same as that of the United States: Stocks dominate bonds over all long-term periods. The postwar hyperinflation, when the yen was devalued from 4 to the dollar to 360 to the dollar, wiped out Japanese bondholders. However, nothing compares with the devastation experienced by German bondholders during the 1922–1923 hyperinflation, when the reichsmark was devalued by more than 10 billion to one. All German fixed-income assets were rendered worthless, yet stocks, which represented claims on real land and capital, weathered the crisis.

Figure 1-7 summarizes the return on international bonds as well as stocks. The superiority of stocks to fixed-income investments over the

FIGURE 1–7

International Total Real Stock and Bond Returns, 1802–2001

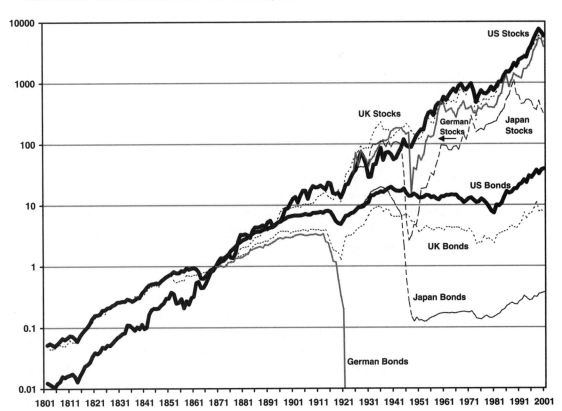

long run is indisputable. Stocks not only outperform bonds on the basis
of return but also display far greater stability of purchasing power.

CONCLUSION

Over the past 200 years, the compound annual real return on a diversified portfolio of common stock is nearly 7 percent in the United States
and has displayed a remarkable constancy over time. The reasons for the
persistence and long-term stability of stock returns are not well understood. Certainly the returns on stocks depend on the quantity and quality of capital, productivity, and the return to risk taking. However, the
ability to create value also springs from skillful management, a stable
political system that respects property rights, and the capacity to provide value to consumers in a competitive environment. Swings in in-

vestor sentiment resulting from political or economic crises can throw stocks off their long-term path, but the fundamental forces producing economic growth enable equities to regain their long-term trend. Perhaps this is why long-term stock returns have displayed such stability despite the radical political, economic, and social changes that have affected the world over the past two centuries.

The superior returns to equity over the past two centuries might be explained by the growing dominance of nations committed to free-market economics. Who might have expected the triumph of market-oriented economies 50 or even 30 years ago? The robustness of world equity prices in recent years might reflect the emergence of the golden age of capitalism—a system in ascendancy today but whose fortunes could decline in the future. Yet, even if capitalism declines, it is unclear which assets, if any, will retain value. In fact, if history is any guide, government bonds in our paper-money world may fare far worse than stocks in any political or economic upheaval. As the next chapter shows, the risks in bonds actually outweigh those in stocks over long horizons.

APPENDIX 1: STOCKS FROM 1802 TO 1871

The first actively traded U.S. stocks, floated in 1791, were two banks: the Bank of New York and the Bank of the United States.[21] Both offerings were enormously successful and were quickly bid to a premium. However, they collapsed the following year when Alexander Hamilton's assistant at the Treasury, William Duer, attempted to manipulate the market and precipitated a crash. It was from this crisis that the antecedents of the New York Stock Exchange were born on May 17, 1792.

Joseph David, an expert on the eighteenth-century corporation, claimed that equity capital was readily forthcoming not only for every undertaking likely to be profitable but, in his words, "for innumerable undertakings in which the risk was very great and the chances of success were remote."[22] Although over 300 business corporations were chartered by the states before 1801, fewer than 10 had securities that traded on a regular basis. Two-thirds of those chartered before 1801 were connected with transportation: wharves, canals, turnpikes, and bridges. However,

---

[21]The oldest continuously operating firm is Dexter Corp., founded in 1767, a Connecticut maker of special materials; the second is Bowne & Co. (1775), which specializes in printing; the third is CoreStates Financial Corp., founded in 1782 as the First National Bank of Pennsylvania; and the fourth is the Bank of New York Corp., founded in 1782, which was involved in the successful 1791 stock offering with the Bank of the United States that eventually was involved in the crash of 1792.
[22]Werner and Smith (1991), p. 82.

the important stocks of the early nineteenth century were financial institutions: banks and, later, insurance companies. Banks and insurance companies held loans and equity in many of the manufacturing firms that, at that time, did not have the financial standing to issue equity. The fluctuations in the stock prices of financial firms in the nineteenth century reflected the health of the general economy and the profitability of the firms to whom they lent. The first large nonfinancial venture was the Delaware and Hudson Canal, which issued stock in 1825 and also became an original member of the Dow Jones Industrial Average 60 years later. In 1830, the first railroad, the Mohawk and Hudson, was listed, and for the next 50 years, railroads dominated trading on the major exchanges.

APPENDIX 2: ARITHMETIC AND GEOMETRIC RETURNS

The average arithmetic return r_A is the average of each yearly return. If r_1 to r_n are the n yearly returns, $r_A = (r_1 + r_2 \ldots + r_n)/n$. The average geometric or compound return r_G is the nth root of the product of 1-year total returns minus 1. Mathematically, this is expressed as $r_G = [(1 + r_1)(1 + r_2) \ldots (1 + r_n)]^{1/n} - 1$. An asset that achieves a geometric return of r_G will accumulate to $(1 + r_G)^n$ times the initial investment over n years. The geometric return is approximately equal to the arithmetic return minus one-half the variance σ^2 of yearly returns, or $r_G \approx r_A - \tfrac{1}{2}\sigma^2$.

Investors can be expected to realize geometric returns only over long periods of time. The average geometric return is always less than the average arithmetic return except when all yearly returns are exactly equal. This difference is related to the volatility of yearly returns.

A simple example demonstrates the difference. If a portfolio falls by 50 percent in the first year and then doubles (up 100 percent) in the second year, "buy and hold" investors are back to where they started, with a total return of zero. The compound or geometric return r_G, defined earlier as $(1 - 0.5)(1 + 1) - 1$, accurately indicates the zero total return of this investment over the 2 years.

The average annual arithmetic return r_A is +25 percent = (−50 percent + 100 percent)/2. Over 2 years, this average return can be turned into a compound or total return only by successfully "timing" the market, specifically increasing the funds invested in the second year and hoping for a recovery in stock prices. Had the market dropped again in the second year, this strategy would have been unsuccessful and would have resulted in lower total returns than achieved by the buy-and-hold investor.

CHAPTER 2

RISK, RETURN, AND PORTFOLIO ALLOCATION

As a matter of fact, what investment can we find which offers real fixity or certainty income? . . . As every reader of this book will clearly see, the man or woman who invests in bonds is speculating in the general level of prices, or the purchasing power of money.

IRVING FISHER, 1912[1]

MEASURING RISK AND RETURN

Risk and return are the building blocks of finance and portfolio management. Once the risk and expected return of each asset are specified, modern financial theory can determine the best portfolio for the investor. However, the risk and return on stocks and bonds are not physical constants, like the speed of light or gravitational force, waiting to be discovered in the natural world. Historical values must be tempered with an appreciation of how investors, attempting to take advantage of the returns from the past, can alter those very returns in the future.

---

[1]Irving Fisher et al., *How to Invest When Prices Are Rising* (Scranton, PA: G. Lynn Sumner & Co., 1912), p. 6.

In finance, the problems of estimating risk and return do not come from a lack of sufficient data. Daily prices on stocks and bonds go back more than 200 years, and monthly data on some agricultural and industrial prices go back much further. However, the overwhelming data do not guarantee accuracy in estimating these parameters because you can never be certain that the underlying factors that generate asset prices have remained unchanged. You cannot, as in the physical sciences, run controlled experiments, holding all other factors constant while changing the value of the variable in question. As Nobel laureate Paul Samuelson is fond of saying, "We have but one sample of history."

Yet you must start with the past in order to understand the future. Chapter 1 demonstrated that over the long run, not only have the returns on fixed-income assets lagged substantially behind equities, but also, because of the uncertainty of inflation, fixed-income returns can be quite risky. In this chapter you shall see that this uncertainty makes portfolio allocations crucially dependent on the investor's planning horizon.

RISK AND HOLDING PERIOD

For many investors, the most meaningful way to describe risk is by portraying a worst-case scenario. Figure 2-1 displays the best and worst real returns for stocks, bonds, and bills from 1802 over holding periods ranging from 1 to 30 years. Note how dramatically and rapidly the heights of the bars, which measure the difference between best and worst returns, decline for equities compared with fixed-income securities when the holding period increases.

Stocks unquestionably are riskier than bonds or bills in the short run. In every 5-year period since 1802, however, the worst performance in stocks, at −11 percent per year, has been only slightly worse than the worst performance in bonds or bills. Moreover, for 10-year holding periods, the worst stock performance actually has been *better* than that for bonds or bills.

For 20-year holding periods, stocks have never fallen behind inflation, whereas bonds and bills once fell as much as 3 percent per year behind the rate of inflation. A 3 percent annual loss over 20 years will wipe out almost half the purchasing power of a portfolio. For 30-year periods, the worst annual stock performance remained comfortably ahead of inflation by 2.6 percent per year, which is just below the average 30-year return on fixed-income assets.

It is very significant that stocks, in contrast to bonds or bills, have never offered investors a negative real holding period return yield over

F I G U R E   2–1

Maximum and Minimum Real Holding Period Returns, 1802–2001

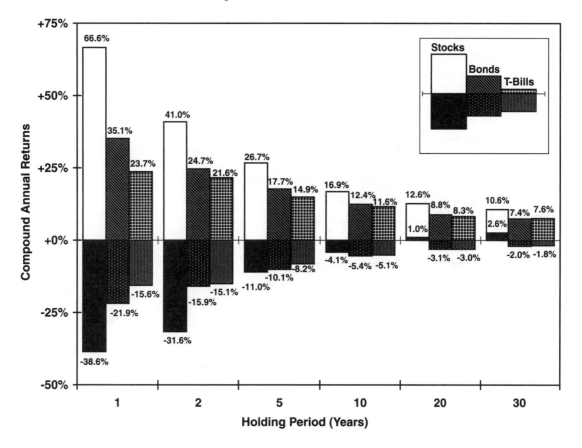

periods of 17 years or more. Although it might appear to be riskier to ac-cumulate wealth in stocks rather than in bonds over long periods of time, precisely the opposite is true: The safest long-term investment for the preservation of purchasing power clearly has been a diversified portfolio of equities.

Table 2-1 shows the percentage of times that stock returns outper-form bond or bill returns over various holding periods. As the holding period increases, the probability that stocks will outperform fixed-income assets increases dramatically. For 10-year horizons, stocks beat bonds and bills about 80 percent of the time; for 20-year horizons, it is over 90 percent of the time; and for 30-year horizons, it is virtually 100 percent of the time.

TABLE 2–1

Holding Period Comparisons: Percentage of Periods When Stocks Outperform Bonds and Bills

Holding Period	Time Period	Stocks Outperform Bonds	Stocks Outperform T-Bills
1 Year	1802-2001	61.0	61.5
	1871-2001	60.3	64.1
2 Year	1802-2001	65.3	65.3
	1871-2001	65.6	69.5
5 Year	1802-2001	70.9	74.0
	1871-2001	74.0	77.1
10 Year	1802-2001	80.1	80.1
	1871-2001	82.4	84.7
20 Year	1802-2001	91.7	94.5
	1871-2001	95.4	99.2
30 Year	1802-2001	99.4	97.1
	1871-2001	100.0	100.0

As noted in Chapter 1, the last 30-year period in which bonds beat stocks ended in 1861, at the onset of the U.S. Civil War. This is a point worth remembering, considering that market commentators frequently point to rising interest rates, especially on long-term government securities, as a negative influence on equity prices. This suggests that investors may do better in bonds than in stocks. Yet never in the past 150 years has a buyer of a newly issued 30-year government bond who held it to maturity achieved greater gains than an investor who held a diversified portfolio of common stocks over the same period.[2]

Although the dominance of stocks over bonds is readily apparent in the long run, it is more important to note that over 1- and even 2-year periods, stocks outperform bonds or bills only about 3 out of every 5

---

[2]In October 2001, the Treasury announced that it was temporarily suspending new issues of all 30-year bonds, including standard and inflation-indexed bonds. Because of the impending scarcity, this has pushed their prices up and corresponding yield downward.

years. This means that in nearly 2 out of every 5 years a stockholder will fall behind the return on Treasury bills or bank certificates. The high probability in the short run of underperforming bonds and bank accounts is the primary reason why it is so hard for many investors to stay in stocks.[3]

INVESTOR HOLDING PERIODS

Some investors question whether holding periods of 10 or 20 or more years are relevant to their planning horizon. Yet these long horizons are far more relevant than most investors recognize. One of the greatest mistakes that investors make is to underestimate their holding period. This is so because many investors think about the holding periods of a particular stock, bond, or mutual fund. But the holding period that is relevant for portfolio allocation is the length of time the investors hold *any* stocks or bonds, no matter how many changes are made among the individual issues in their portfolio.

Figure 2-2 shows the average length of time that investors hold financial assets based on gender and the age at which they *begin* purchasing such assets. It is assumed that individuals accumulate savings during their working years in order to build sufficient assets to fund their retirement, which normally occurs at age 65. After age 65, retirees live off the funds derived from both the returns and sale of their assets. It is also assumed that investors either plan to exhaust all their assets by the end of their expected life span or plan to retain one-half of their retirement assets at the end of their expected life span as a safety margin or for bequests.

Under either assumption, Figure 2-2 shows that individuals who begin accumulating assets in their thirties will hold financial assets for 40 years and more. Even investors who begin accumulating assets near retirement will have a holding period of up to 20 years or more. It should be noted that the life expectancy for males is now about 82 years; for females, more than 86 years; and for either spouse, about 90 years. Many retirees will be holding assets for 20 years or longer. In addition, if the investor works beyond age 65, which is increasingly common, or plans to leave a large percentage of assets as a bequest, the average holding period is even longer than those indicated in Figure 2-2.

---

[3]Chapter 19 analyzes investors' aversion to taking losses, no matter how small, and how this affects portfolio performance.

FIGURE 2–2

Average Holding Period Based on Age 65 Retirement and Normal Life Expectancy
(M = Male, F = Female)

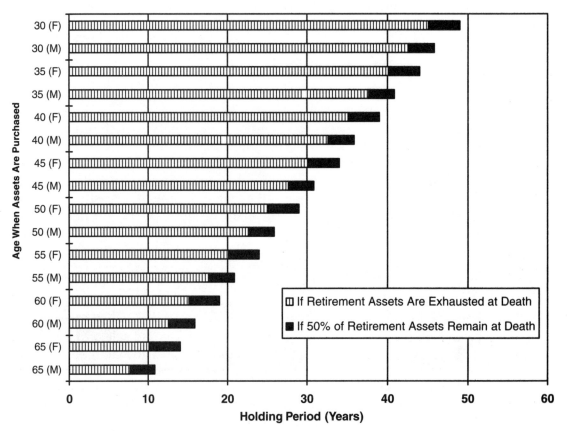

INVESTOR RETURNS FROM MARKET PEAKS

Many investors, although convinced of the long-term superiority of equity, believe that they should not invest in stocks when stock prices appear at a peak. However, this is not true for the long-term investor. Figure
2-3 shows the after-inflation total return over 10-, 20-, and 30-year holding periods after the six major stock market peaks of the last century.[4]

Even from major stock market peaks, the wealth accumulated in
stocks is more than four times that in bonds and more than five times that

---

[4]These peaks are June 1901, September 1906, September 1929, February 1937, April 1946, and December 1968.

FIGURE 2–3

Average Total Real Returns after Major Twentieth-Century Market Peaks ($100 Initial Investment)

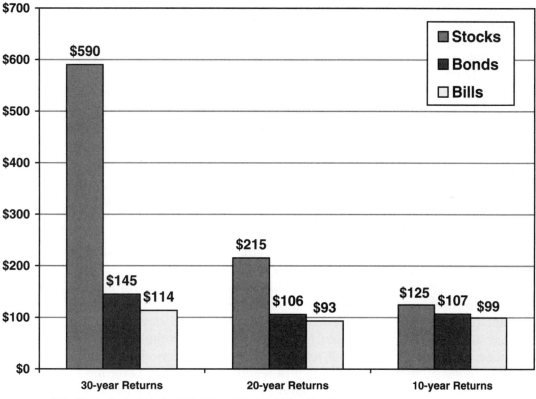

Major Market Peaks include 1901, 1906, 1915, 1929, 1937, 1946, 1968

in Treasury bills if your holding period is 30 years. If your holding period is 20 years, stocks beat bonds by about 2:1. At 10-year holding periods, stocks still have a slight advantage over fixed-income assets measured from market peaks. Moreover, these results follow from stock purchases made at the worst possible time. Unless investors believe there is a high probability that they will need to liquidate their savings over the next 5 to 10 years to maintain their living standard, history has shown that there is no compelling reason for long-term investors to significantly reduce a diversified portfolio of stocks, no matter how high the market seems.

Of course, if investors can identify peaks and troughs in the market, they can outperform the buy-and-hold strategy that is advocated in this book. Needless to say, however, few investors can do this. And even if an

investor sells stocks at the peak, this does not guarantee superior returns. As difficult as it is to sell when stock prices are high and everyone
is optimistic, it is more difficult to buy at market bottoms, when pessimism is widespread and few people have the confidence to venture
back into stocks.

A number of "market timers" boasted how they yanked all their
money out of stocks before the 1987 crash. However, many did not get
back into the market until it had already passed its previous highs. Market timers may get satisfaction from having sold before market declines,
but by not knowing when to reenter the market, they realize inferior returns to those investors who never try to time the market cycles.

STANDARD MEASURES OF RISK

The risk of holding stocks and bonds depends crucially on the holding
period. Figure 2-4 displays the risk—defined as the standard deviation
of average real annual returns—for stocks, bonds, and bills based on the
historical sample of nearly 200 years. This is the measure of risk used in
portfolio theory and asset allocation models.

As noted previously, stocks are riskier than fixed-income investments over short-term holding periods. However, once the holding period increases to between 15 and 20 years, the standard deviation of
average annual after-inflation returns becomes lower than the standard
deviation of average bond or bill returns. Over 30-year periods, equity
risk falls to less than three-fourths that of bonds or bills. As the holding
period increases, the standard deviation of average stock returns falls
nearly twice as fast as that of fixed-income assets.

It has been determined mathematically how fast the risk of average
annual returns should decline as the holding period lengthens if asset returns follow a random walk.[5] A *random walk* is a process where future returns have no relation to and are completely independent of past
returns. The broken bars in Figure 2-4 show the decline in risk predicted
under the random walk assumption.

However, the historical data show that the random walk hypothesis cannot be maintained and that the risk of stocks declines far faster
than predicted when the holding period increases. This is a direct result
of the mean reversion of equity returns described in Chapter 1.

---

[5]In particular, the standard deviation of average returns falls as the square root of the length of the
holding period.

FIGURE 2–4

Risk for Average Real Return over Various Holding Periods, 1802–2001 (Historical Risk versus Risk Based on Random Walk Hypothesis)

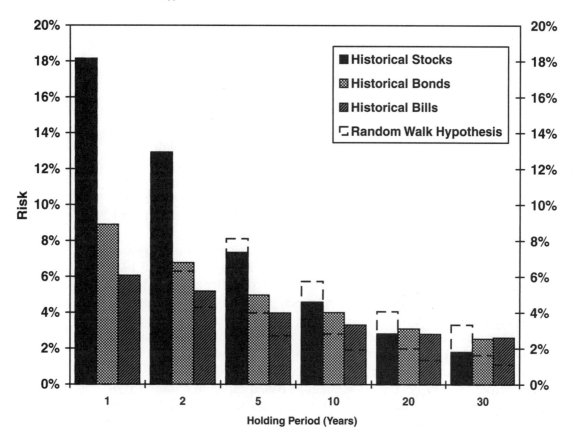

The risk of fixed-income assets, on the other hand, does not fall as fast as random walk theory predicts. This slow decline of the standard deviation of average annual real returns in the bond market is a manifestation of mean aversion of bond returns.[6] *Mean aversion* means that once an asset's return deviates from its long-run average, there is an increased chance that it will deviate further rather than return to more normal levels. Mean aversion certainly was characteristic of both the Japanese and German bond returns depicted in Figure 1-6. Once infla-

---

[6]See John Y. Campbell, Yeung Lewis Chan, and Luis M. Viceira, "A Multivariate Model of Strategic Asset Allocation," working paper, September 2000, for the implications of bond mean aversion in portfolio choice.

tion begins to accelerate, the process becomes cumulative, and bond-holders have no chance of making up losses to their purchasing power. In contrast, stockholders, who hold claims on real assets, rarely suffer a permanent loss due to inflation.

CORRELATION BETWEEN STOCK AND BOND RETURNS

Even though the average return on bonds falls short of the return on stocks, bonds still may serve to diversify a portfolio and lower overall risk. This will be particularly true if bond and stock returns are nega-tively correlated. The correlation coefficient, which ranges between −1 and +1, measures the degree to which asset returns are correlated with the returns of the rest of the portfolio; the lower the correlation coeffi-cient, the better the asset is for portfolio diversification. Assets with neg-ative correlations are particularly good diversifiers. As the correlation coefficient between the asset and portfolio returns increases, the diversi-fying quality of the asset declines.

Figure 2-5 shows the correlation coefficient between annual stock and bond returns for four subperiods between 1926 and 2001. From 1926 through 1966, the correlation was slightly positive, indicating that bonds were good diversifiers for stocks. From 1967 through 1989, the correla-tion coefficient jumped to +0.34, and from 1990 through 1997, the corre-lation increased further to +0.55. This means that the diversifying quality of bonds diminished markedly from 1926 through 1997.

There are good economic reasons why the correlation became more positive from 1970 to 1997. Under the gold-based monetary standard of the 1920s and early 1930s, bad economic times were associated with falling commodity prices. Therefore, when the real economy was sink-ing and the stock market declined, as occurred during the Great Depres-sion of the 1930s, the real value of government bonds rose.

Under a paper-based monetary standard, bad economic times are more likely to be associated with inflation, not deflation. This is so be-cause the government often attempts to offset economic downturns with expansionary monetary policy. This policy results in inflation and ac-companies a declining real economy, such as occurred during the 1970s. The negative short-term effects of inflation on equity returns are detailed in Chapter 11.

However, Figure 2-5 also shows that since 1998 there has been a dramatic reversal in the short-term correlation between stock and bond prices. In fact, over that period, stock prices have been significantly *neg-atively* correlated with government bond prices. The reason for this

FIGURE 2–5

Correlation Coefficient between Monthly Stock and Bond Returns

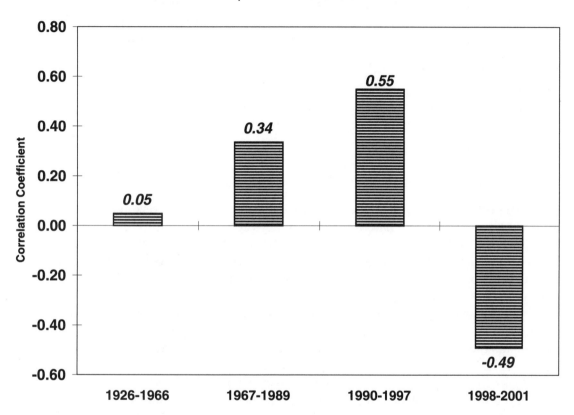

change comes from an understanding of international events. Since 1997, the world markets were roiled by economic and currency upheavals originating in Asia that spread to the rest of the world.[7] The collapsing currency markets, combined with falling commodity prices, had an eerie resemblance to the 1930s, when deflation ruled, and government bonds were the only appreciating assets. As a result, international investors fled to the U.S. government securities market when turmoil hit equities. Long-term U.S. government bonds became safe havens for investors fearing a meltdown in the stock market.[8]

---

[7]The causes and consequences of these events are discussed in Chapter 10.
[8]Short-term Treasury securities such as bills often have enjoyed safe-haven status. Rising bond prices in a tumultuous equity market also occurred during the October 19, 1987 stock market crash, but much of the rise then was predicated on the (correct) belief that the Federal Reserve would lower short-term interest rates.

This tendency for investors to hide in long-term U.S. Treasury issues when equities experienced sudden declines persisted despite the recovery in the U.S. and Asian economies. As a result, U.S. Treasury issues have become excellent short-term diversifiers of equity risk, a property that bids up their price and down their yield. However, it is still an open question whether in the long run the positive correlation between stocks and bonds will return as fears of deflation fade. The premium now enjoyed by Treasury issues generated by investors seeking short-term safe havens means that government bonds are now even *less* desirable to long-term investors seeking to balance risk and return within their portfolios.

EFFICIENT FRONTIERS[9]

Modern portfolio theory describes how investors may alter the risk and return of a portfolio by changing the mix between assets. Figure 2-6, based on the 200-year history of stock and bond returns, displays the risks and returns that result from varying the proportion of stocks and bonds in a portfolio over various holding periods ranging from 1 to 30 years.

The square at the bottom of each curve represents the risk and return of an all-bond portfolio, whereas the cross at the top of each curve represents the risk and return of an all-stock portfolio. The circle in the middle of each curve indicates the minimum risk achievable by combining stocks and bonds. The curve that connects these points represents the risk and return of all blends of portfolios from 100 percent bonds to 100 percent stocks. This curve, called the *efficient frontier*, is the heart of modern portfolio analysis and is the foundation of asset allocation models.

Investors can achieve any combination of risk and return along the curve by changing the proportion of stocks and bonds. Moving up the curve means increasing the proportion in stocks and correspondingly reducing the proportion in bonds. As stocks are added to the all-bond portfolio, expected returns increase and risk decreases, a very desirable combination for investors. However, after the minimum risk point is reached, increasing stocks will increase the return of the portfolio, but only with extra risk.

The slope of any point on the efficient frontier indicates the risk-return trade-off for that allocation. By finding the points on the longer-term efficient frontiers that have a slope equal to the slope on the 1-year

[9]This section, which contains some advanced material, can be skipped without loss of continuity.

FIGURE 2–6

Risk-Return Trade-Offs for Various Holding Periods, 1802–2001

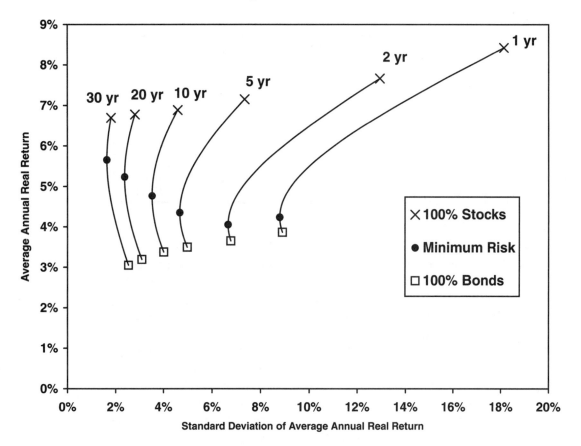

frontier, one can determine the allocations that represent the same risk-return trade-offs for all holding periods.

RECOMMENDED PORTFOLIO ALLOCATIONS

Table 2-2 indicates the percentage of an investor's portfolio that should be invested in stocks based on standard portfolio models incorporating both the risk tolerance and the holding period of the investor.[10] Four

---

[10]The 1-year proportions (except minimum risk point) are arbitrary and are used as benchmarks for other holding periods. Choosing different proportions as benchmarks does not change the following results qualitatively.

TABLE 2–2

Portfolio Allocation: Percentage of Portfolio Recommended in Stocks Based on All Historical Data

Risk Tolerance	Holding Period			
	1 year	5 years	10 years	30 years
Ultraconservative (Minimum Risk)	8.1%	23.3%	39.5%	71.4%
Conservative	25.0%	40.6%	60.1%	89.7%
Moderate	50.0%	63.1%	87.2%	114.9%
Risk Taking	75.0%	79.8%	108.3%	136.5%

classes of investors are analyzed: the ultraconservative investor who demands maximum safety no matter the return, the conservative investor who accepts small risks to achieve extra return, the moderate risk-taking investor, and the aggressive investor who is willing to accept substantial risks in search of extra returns.

The recommended equity allocation increases dramatically as the holding period lengthens. Based on the 200 years of historical returns on stocks and bonds, ultraconservative investors should hold nearly three-quarters of their portfolios in stocks over 30-year holding periods. This allocation is justified because stocks are safer than bonds in terms of purchasing power over long periods of time. Conservative investors should have nearly 90 percent of their portfolios in stocks, whereas the analysis indicates that moderate and aggressive investors should have over 100 percent in equity. Borrowing or leveraging an all-stock portfolio can achieve this allocation, although investors would do quite well to hold 100 percent of their long-term portfolios in stocks.

Given these striking results, it might seem puzzling why the holding period almost never has been considered in portfolio theory. This is so because modern portfolio theory was established when the academic profession believed in the random walk theory of security prices. As noted earlier, under a random walk, the *relative* risk of various securities does not change for different time frames, so portfolio allocations do not depend on the holding period. The holding period becomes a crucial issue in portfolio theory when the data reveal mean reversion of stock returns.[11]

INFLATION-INDEXED BONDS

Until recently, there was no asset in the United States whose return was guaranteed against changes in the price level. Both stocks and bonds are risky when uncertain inflation is taken into account. In January 1997, however, the U.S. Treasury issued the first government-guaranteed inflation-indexed bond. The coupons and principal repayment of this inflation-protected bond are increased automatically when the price level rises, so bondholders suffer no loss of purchasing power when they receive the coupons or final principal. Since any and all inflation is compensated, the interest rate on this bond is a *real*, or inflation-adjusted, interest rate.

At the end of 2001, the interest rate on the 10-year inflation-indexed bond was about 3.5 percent. Although this is less than one-half the historical return on equity, these bonds are a very attractive alternative for investors who do not want to assume the risks inherent in stocks but fear loss of purchasing power through inflation. In fact, in 23 percent of all 10-year periods from 1926, stocks have fallen short of a 3.5 percent real return.

Figure 2-7 replicates the efficient frontier for the 10-year holding period and includes the risk and return possibilities achieved by adding inflation-indexed securities.[12] Investors can attain any risk and return trade-off along the straight line connecting the risk-free asset at the tangency to the efficient frontier. The point of tangency is the optimal mix of the risky assets in the portfolio.

---

[11]For an excellent review of this literature, see Luis M. Viceira and John Y. Campbell, *Strategic Asset Allocation: Portfolio Choice for Long-Term Investors* (New York: Oxford University Press, 2002). Also see Nicholas Barberis, "Investing for the Long Run When Returns Are Predictable," *Journal of Finance* 55(2000):225–264. Paul Samuelson has shown that mean reversion will increase equity holdings if investors have a risk aversion coefficient greater than unity, which most researchers find is the case. See Paul Samuelson, "Long-Run Risk Tolerance When Equity Returns Are Mean Regressing: Pseudoparadoxes and Vindications of 'Businessmen's Risk'," in W. C. Brainard, W. D. Nordhaus, and H. W. Watts (eds.), *Money, Macroeconomics, and Public Policy* (Cambridge, MA: MIT Press, 1991), pp. 181–200. See also Zvi Bodie, Robert Merton, and William Samuelson, "Labor Supply Flexibility and Portfolio Choice in a Lifecycle Model," *Journal of Economic Dynamics and Control* 16(3)(July–October 1992):427–450. Bodie et al. have shown that equity holdings can vary with age because stock returns can be correlated with labor income.

[12]The material in this section can be skipped without loss of continuity.

FIGURE 2–7

Optimal Portfolio Allocation with Inflation-Linked Bonds (10-Year Holding Period)

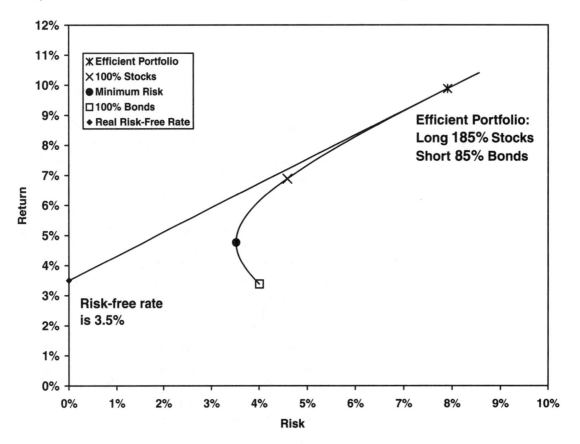

The addition of inflation-indexed securities makes standard nominal bonds even less attractive. Based on historical data, the optimal portfolio of risky assets is 185 percent stocks and –85 percent bonds![13] This means that an investor should sell (or "short") nominal bonds, using the proceeds to buy stocks or the indexed-linked bond. Historical data indicate that standard nominal bonds are completely dominated by stocks and inflation-indexed bonds. The failure of nominal bonds to provide long-term protection against uncertain inflation effectively excludes them from a long-term portfolio on the basis of historical risk and return data.

---

[13]This does not necessarily mean that you should buy more equities when the inflation-linked bond is considered than earlier when it was not. Depending on risk aversion, the inflation-linked bond could dominate a conservative investor's portfolio.

CONCLUSION

No one denies that in the short run stocks are riskier than fixed-income assets. In the long run, however, history has shown that this is not the case. The inflation uncertainty that is inherent in the paper money standard that the United States and the rest of the world have adopted indicates that *fixed income* does not mean "fixed purchasing power." Despite the dramatic gains in price stability seen over the past decade, there is still much uncertainty about what a dollar will be worth two or three decades from now. Historical evidence indicates that we can be more certain of the purchasing power of a diversified portfolio of common stocks 30 years hence than we can of the final payment on a 30-year U.S. government bond.

3

STOCK INDEXES

It has been said that figures rule the world.
JOHANN WOLFGANG GOETHE, 1830

MARKET AVERAGES

"How's the market doing?" one stock investor asks another.

"It's having a good day—it's up over 70 points."

For most of the past 100 years, no one would ask, "What's up 70 points?" Everyone knew the answer: the Dow Jones Industrial Average, the most quoted stock average in the world. This index, popularly called the Dow, was so renowned that the news media often called the Dow "the stock market." Furthermore, one of the most popular investment strategies, known as the "dogs of the Dow," is based on the stocks in this index and is described in Chapter 19. No matter how imperfectly this index describes the movement of share prices—and virtually no money manager would peg his or her performance to it—the Dow was the way that virtually all investors thought of the stock market.

Not any longer, however. Because of the technology boom of 1999–2000, another exchange, the Nasdaq, an automated electronic market begun in 1971, became the most exciting venue to trade stocks. Large and extremely fast-growing technology companies such as Microsoft, Intel, Cisco Systems, Oracle, Sun Microsystems, and others easily overtook issues traded on the New York Stock Exchange (NYSE) as the volume leaders. Even after the technology bubble ended, Nasdaq stocks dominated the list of most active issues.

The Nasdaq Composite Index became a proxy for technology stocks and captured the imaginations of traders and investors alike. In fact, the Nasdaq became so important that the Dow, for the first time in its over 100-year history, ventured off the "Big Board," as the New York Stock Exchange was called, and selected two Nasdaq stocks—Microsoft and Intel—to join its venerable group of 30 select stocks in 1999. We shall examine the Nasdaq in more detail later in this chapter, but first let us describe the world's oldest and most venerable average.

THE DOW JONES AVERAGES

Charles Dow, one of the founders of Dow Jones & Co., which also publishes *The Wall Street Journal*, created the Dow Jones averages in the late nineteenth century. On February 16, 1885, he began publishing a daily average of 12 stocks (10 rails and 2 industrials) that represented active and highly capitalized stocks. Four years later, Dow published a daily average based on 20 stocks—18 rails and 2 industrials.

As industrial and manufacturing firms succeeded railroads in importance, the Dow Jones Industrial Average was created on May 26, 1896 from the 12 stocks shown in Table 3-1. The old index created in 1889 was reconstituted and renamed the Rail Average on October 26, 1896. In 1916, the Industrial Average was increased to 20 stocks, and in 1928, the number was expanded to 30. The Rail Average, whose name was changed in 1970 to the Transportation Average, is composed of 20 stocks, as it has been for over a century.

The early Dow stocks were centered on commodities: cotton, sugar, tobacco, lead, leather, rubber, etc. Six of the 12 companies have survived in much the same form, but only one—General Electric (GE), which boasts the world's highest market value—has both retained its membership in the Dow Jones Industrial Average and not changed its name.[1]

Almost all the original Dow stocks thrived as large and successful firms, even if they did not remain in the index (see the chapter Appendix for details). The only exception is U.S. Leather Corp., which was liquidated in the 1950s. Shareholders received $1.50 plus one share of Keta Oil

---

[1]Chicago Gas Company, an original member of the 12 Dow stocks, became People's Energy, Inc., and was a member of the Dow Jones Utilities Average until May 1997.

TABLE 3–1

Firms in the Dow Jones Industrial Average

1896	1916	1928	2001		
			Dow Companies	Price Wght	Mkt-Value Wght
American Cotton Oil	American Beet Sugar	Allied Chemical	Alcoa Inc	2.45%	0.87%
	American Can	American Can	American Express Co	2.46%	1.38%
American Sugar	American Car &	American Smelting	AT&T Corp	1.28%	1.91%
	Foundry	American Sugar	Boeing Co	2.62%	0.88%
American Tobacco		American Tobacco	Caterpillar Inc	3.55%	0.51%
	American Locomotive	Atlantic Refining	Citigroup Inc	3.50%	7.57%
Chicago Gas	American Smelting	Bethlehem Steel	Coca-Cola	3.26%	3.41%
		Chrysler	Disney	1.47%	1.26%
Distilling & Cattle Feeding	American Sugar	General Electric	DuPont	2.95%	1.27%
	American Tel & Tel	General Motors	Eastman Kodak	2.01%	0.25%
		General Railway Signal	Exxon Mobil	2.72%	7.81%
General Electric	Anaconda Copper	Goodrich	General Electric	2.81%	11.73%
	Baldwin Locomotive	International Harvester	General Motors	3.34%	0.78%
		International Nickel	Hewlett-Packard	1.49%	1.21%
Laclede Gas	Central Leather	Mack Trucks	Home Depot	3.46%	3.41%
		Nash Motors	Honeywell Int'l	2.29%	0.78%
National Lead	General Electric	North American	Intel	2.27%	6.39%
	Goodrich	Paramount Publix	IBM	8.35%	6.04%
		Postum, Inc.	International Paper	2.76%	0.56%
North American	Republic Iron & Steel	Radio Corp.	Johnson & Johnson	4.03%	5.16%
	Studebaker	Sears, Roebuck	JP Morgan Chase	2.50%	2.07%
		Standard Oil (N.J.)	McDonald's Corp	1.82%	0.98%
Tennessee	Texas Co.	Texas Corp.	Merck	4.10%	3.92%
	U.S. Rubber	Texas Gulf Sulphur	Microsoft	4.60%	10.42%
Coal & Iron		Union Carbide	Minn Mining & Mfg	8.05%	1.33%
	U.S. Steel	U.S. Steel	Philip Morris	3.20%	2.92%
	Utah Copper	Victor Talking Machine	Procter & Gamble	5.50%	2.99%
U.S. Leather Pfd.	Westinghouse	Westinghouse Electric	SBC Communications	2.74%	3.87%
		Woolworth	United Technologies	4.42%	0.87%
U.S. Rubber	Western Union	Wright Aeronautical	Wal-Mart Stores	3.99%	7.46%

& Gas, a firm acquired earlier. In 1955, however, the president, Lowell Birrell, who later fled to Brazil to escape U.S. authorities, looted Keta's assets. Shares in U.S. Leather, which in 1909 was the seventh-largest corporation in the United States, became worthless.

COMPUTATION OF THE DOW INDEX

The original Dow Jones averages were simply the sum of the prices of the component shares divided by the number of stocks in the index. However, this divisor had to be adjusted over time to prevent jumps in the index when there were changes in the companies that constituted the average and stock splits. In January 2002, the divisor was about 0.1445, so a 1-point rise in any Dow stock caused the average to increase by about 7 points.[2]

The Dow Jones Industrial Average is a *price-weighted index*, which means that the prices of the component stocks are added together and then divided by the number of firms in the index. As a result, proportional movements of high-priced stocks in the Dow have a much greater impact than movements of lower-priced stocks regardless of the size of the company. A price-weighted index has the property that when a component stock splits, the split stock has a reduced impact on the average, and all the other stocks have a slightly increased impact.[3]

Price-weighted indexes are unusual because the impact of a firm's price on the index has nothing to do with the relative size of the company. This is in stark contrast to a capitalization-weighted index, such as Standard & Poor's 500 Index, which is described later in this chapter. As of December 2001, the 30 Dow stocks were valued at $3.5 trillion, which is about 25 percent of the capitalization of the entire U.S. market. Of the 10 largest U.S.-based capitalization stocks, all but Pfizer and AIG are in the Dow Jones Industrial Average. However, not all the Dow stocks are large. Three Dow stocks are not even in the top 100: International Paper, Caterpillar, Inc., and the smallest, Eastman Kodak, which is ranked below 300 and has about 2 percent of the market value of GE, which is the largest component.

Long-Term Trends in the Dow

Figure 3-1 plots the monthly high and low of the Dow Jones Industrial Average from its inception in 1885, corrected for changes in the cost of living. The inset shows the Dow Jones Industrial Average uncorrected for inflation.

A trend line and a channel are created by statistically regressing the Dow on a time trend. The upper and lower bounds are 1 standard devi-

---

[2]The procedure for computing the Dow Jones averages when a new (or split) stock is substituted is as follows: The component stock prices are added up before and after the change, and a new divisor is determined that yields the same average as before the change. Because of stock splits, the divisor generally moves downward over time, but the divisor could increase if a higher-priced stock is substituted for a lower-priced one in the average.

[3]Before 1914, the divisor was left unchanged when a stock split, and the stock price was multiplied by the split ratio when computing the index. This led to rising stocks having greater weight in the average, something akin to value-weighted stock indexes today.

FIGURE 3-1

The Real Dow Jones Industrial Average, February 1885–December 2001 (in 2001 Dollars)

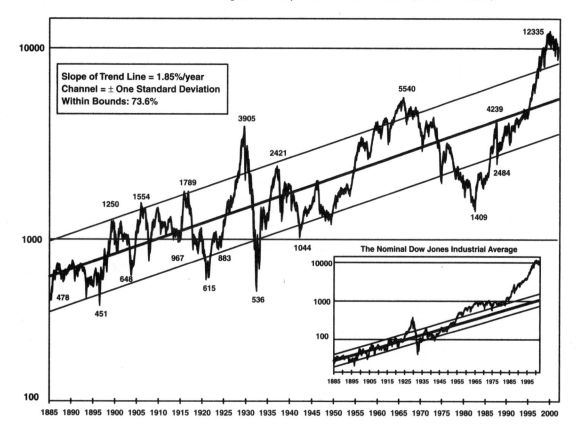

ation, or 50 percent, above and below the trend. The slope of the trend line, 1.85 percent per year, is the average compound rate at which the Dow stocks have appreciated, excluding inflation, since 1885. The Dow Jones Industrial Average, like most other popular averages, does not include dividends, so the change in the index greatly understates the total return on the Dow stocks. Since the average dividend yield on stocks was about 4.6 percent during this time, the total annual real compound return on the Dow stocks was 6.5 percent over this period, very close to the long-term real stock return reported in Chapter 1.

The inflation-corrected Dow has stayed within the channel about three-quarters of the time. When the Dow broke out of the channel to the upside, as it did in 1929 and again in the mid-1960s, stocks subsequently suffered poor short-term returns. Likewise, when stocks penetrated the channel on the downside, they subsequently experienced superior short-term returns.

Use of Trend Lines to Predict Future Returns

Using channels and trend lines to predict future returns, however tempting, can be misleading. Long-standing trends have been broken in the past. Uncorrected for inflation, the Dow Jones Industrial Average broke and stayed above the trend line in the mid-1950s, as shown in the inset of Figure 3-1. This is so because inflation, caused by the shift to a paper money standard, propelled nominal stock prices justifiably above their previous, noninflationary trend. Those who used trend-line analysis and who failed to analyze stock prices in real, instead of nominal, terms would have sold in 1955 and *never* reentered the market.[4]

One reason why the upper channel on the long-term real Dow now might be permanently penetrated is that stock indexes record only capital appreciation and therefore understate total returns, which include dividends. The magnitude of understatement has increased in recent years as firms have paid an ever-lower fraction of their earnings as dividends. Instead, management has chosen to use retained earnings to boost the price of shares, which subjects investors to a lower tax than dividends. This means that there has been an increase in capital gains, which are represented in stock indexes, and a decrease in dividends, which are not.

VALUE-WEIGHTED INDEXES

Standard & Poor's Index

Although the Dow Jones Industrial Average was published in 1885, it certainly was not a comprehensive index of stock values since it covered at most 30 stocks. In 1906, the Standard Statistics Co. was formed, and in 1918, it began publishing the first index of stock values based on each stock's performance weighted by its capitalization, or market value. This technique is now recognized as giving the best indication of the overall market and is used almost universally in establishing market benchmarks. In 1939, Alfred Cowles, founder of the Cowles Foundation for Economic Research, constructed indexes of stock values back to 1871

---

[4]For a related situation where a long-standing benchmark was broken because of inflation, see the first section of Chapter 6, "An Evil Omen Returns."

that consisted of all stocks listed on the NYSE using Standard & Poor's market-weighting techniques.

The Standard & Poor's Stock Price Index began in 1923 and in 1926 became the Standard & Poor's Composite Index containing 90 stocks. The index was expanded to 500 stocks on March 4, 1957 and became the S&P 500 Index. At that time, the value of the S&P 500 Index comprised about 90 percent of the value of all NYSE-listed stocks. The 500 stocks contained exactly 425 industrials, 25 railroads, and 50 utility firms. Until Standard & Poor's Corporation changed its guidelines in 1988, the companies listed in each industry were restricted to these numbers.

A base value of 10 was chosen for the average value of the S&P 500 Index from 1941 to 1943 so that when the index was first published in 1957, the average price of a share of stock (which stood between $45 and $50) was approximately equal to the value of the index. An investor at that time could easily identify with the changes in the S&P 500 Index because a 1-point change approximated the price change for an average stock.

The S&P 500 Index does not contain the 500 largest stocks, nor are all the stocks in the index U.S.–based corporations. For example, Warren Buffett's Berkshire Hathaway, which is considered a holding company, is not in the S&P 500 Index, whereas Royal Dutch Petroleum and Unilever, both large Dutch-based firms, are included. On the other hand, the S&P 500 Index has a few firms that are quite small, representing companies that have fallen in value and have yet to be replaced. As of December 2001, the total value of all S&P 500 companies was about $10.5 trillion, but this only constituted about 80 percent of the value of all stocks traded in the United States, significantly less than 40 years ago when the index comprised almost 90 percent of the market.

Nasdaq Index

On February 8, 1971, a revolutionary innovation occurred in the trading of stocks. On that date, an automated quotation system called *Nasdaq* (for National Association of Securities Dealers Automated Quotations) provided up-to-date bid and asked prices on 2,400 leading over-the-counter (OTC) stocks, as they were then called. Formerly, quotations for these unlisted stocks were submitted by the principal trader or by brokerage houses that carried an inventory. Now Nasdaq linked the terminals of more than 500 market makers nationwide to a centralized computer system.

In contrast to Nasdaq, stocks traded on the NYSE or the American Stock Exchange (AMEX) are assigned to a single specialist, who is charged with maintaining an orderly market in that stock. Nasdaq revolutionized the way quotes were disseminated and made these issues far more attractive to both investors and traders.

At the time that Nasdaq was created, it was clearly more prestigious to be listed with an exchange (and preferably the NYSE) than to be traded on Nasdaq. Nasdaq stocks tended to be small or new firms that had gone public recently or did not meet the listing requirements of the larger exchanges. However, many young technology firms found the computerized Nasdaq system a natural home. Many, such as Intel and Microsoft, chose not to migrate to the "Big Board," as the NYSE was termed, even when they qualified.

The Nasdaq Index, which is a capitalization-weighted index of all stocks traded on the Nasdaq, was set at 100 on the first day of trading in 1971. It took almost 10 years to double to 200 and another 10 years to reach 500 in 1991. It reached its first major milestone of 1,000 in July 1995.

As the interest in technology stocks grew, the rise in the Nasdaq Index accelerated, and it doubled its value to 2,000 in just 3 years. In the fall of 1999, the technology boom sent the Nasdaq into orbit. The index increased from 2,700 in October 1999 to its peak of 5,048.62 on March 10, 2000.

The increase in popularity of Nasdaq stocks resulted in a tremendous increase in volume on the exchange. In 1971, volume on the Nasdaq was a small fraction of that on the NYSE. By 1994, share volume on the Nasdaq exceeded that on the NYSE, and 5 years later, dollar volume on the Nasdaq surpassed the NYSE as well.[5]

No longer was Nasdaq the home of small firms waiting to qualify for Big Board membership. By 1998, capitalization of the Nasdaq already exceeded that of the Tokyo Stock Exchange. At the market peak in March 2000, the total market value of firms traded on the Nasdaq reached nearly $6 trillion, more than half that of the NYSE and more than any other stock exchange in the world. At the peak, Nasdaq's Microsoft and Cisco had the two largest market valuations in the world, and Nasdaq-listed Intel and Oracle also were among the top 10. Despite the decline in the Nasdaq Index and the subsequent bear market, the list of most active stocks is still dominated by Nasdaq-listed stocks.

Although there is a lively rivalry between the Nasdaq and the NYSE, most investors are not concerned about what exchange a stock is listed on. Small stocks may be better served by having a specialist provide liquidity, but bid-ask spreads may be lower on active stocks under the Nasdaq

---

[5]There is admittedly some double counting of volume in the Nasdaq dealer system.

market-maker system. Institutions have their own ways of dealing with big blocks of stock no matter what exchange the stock is listed on.

Wilshire 5000 and Russell Indexes

The largest comprehensive index of U.S. firms, the Wilshire Total Market Index (formerly called the Wilshire 5000), was founded in 1974 and now includes 6,148 firms.[6] Figure 3-2 shows the size and total market capitalization of the stocks in this index. The top 500 firms, which closely

---

[6]There are nearly 10,000 listed stocks on U.S. exchanges, excluding some 20,000 "penny stocks" that are traded infrequently.

FIGURE 3–2

Wilshire Total Market Index (6,148 Stocks Valued at $11,727 Trillion as of October 31, 2001)

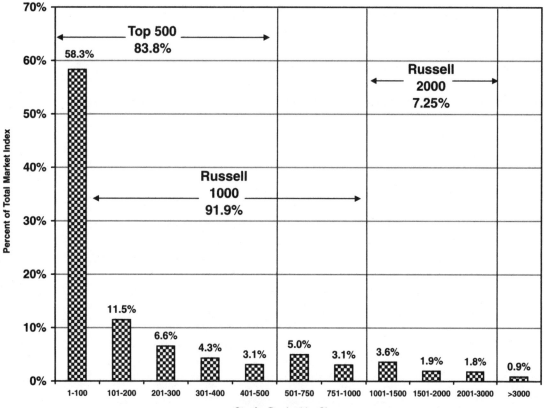

match the S&P 500 Index,[7] constitute roughly 84 percent of the total value of the Wilshire Index. The top 1,000 firms in market value, called the Russell 1000 and published by the Frank Russell Co., comprise 92 percent of the total value of equities. The Russell 2000 contains the next 2,000 largest companies and an additional 7 percent of the market value of the total index. The Russell 3000, the sum of the Russell 1000 and 2000 indexes, comprises almost the entire value of U.S. stocks. The remaining 3,148 firms that are in the Wilshire Index but not in the Russell 3000 constitute less than 1 percent of the total value of U.S. equity.

WORLDWIDE RANK OF INDIVIDUAL FIRMS

In January 2002, GE, at $406 billion, had the world's highest market capitalization. Microsoft, Exxon Mobil, Pfizer, and Citigroup follow. Nippon Telephone and Telegraph, which for years reigned supreme as the world's most valuable company, fell to 33d on the world list since its privatization by the Japanese government in 1987. Its spin-off, NTT Mobile Communications Network (known as DoCoMo) is ranked 11th, and the combination of the two units would be in the top five firms worldwide. AT&T, for many years the world's largest corporation before NTT took over, has fallen to 46th place worldwide. However, this is so because of the court-ordered divestiture of the "Baby Bells" in 1993 and the many spin-offs AT&T has shed over the years. If we include these firms with AT&T, the total capitalization of "Ma Bell," as America's most popular and widely owned stock was once called, would be over $600 billion today, making it the world's largest firm.[8]

TRANSFORMATION OF S&P 500 INDEX

The history of large corporations reflects the history of industrial America. In 1909, U.S. Steel was by far the largest American corporation, with assets approaching $2 billion. It was followed by Standard Oil Company, which was only one-fifth the size of U.S. Steel, American Tobacco, International Mercantile Marine (later U.S. Lines), and International Harvester (now Navistar).

---

[7]Royal Dutch Petroleum and Unilever, which are in the S&P 500 Index, are not in the Wilshire or Russell indexes. Berkshire Hathaway also is not in either.

[8]In mid-2001, the world's largest private corporation, in terms of sales, is Exxon Mobil ($232 billion) followed closely by Wal-Mart. General Motors, Ford, and DaimlerChrysler are ranked numbers 3, 4, and 5, respectively, although they have far lower market value.

Table 3-2 lists the 20 largest corporations in terms of market value in the S&P 500 Index in 1964 and 2001. It is fascinating to see the change in composition of this benchmark index. Despite the perception that large companies are, through mergers and acquisitions, becoming ever more dominant in corporate America, the truth is quite the opposite. There is a clear tendency for the largest companies to represent a smaller fraction of the market value of all stocks. The top five firms constituted more than 28 percent of the market value of the index in 1964, but this declined to less than 15 percent in 2001.

Only one company that made the top 5 in 1964, Standard Oil of New Jersey, is on the list today. In 1964, 8 of the top 20 firms were oil and energy companies, and that sector comprised 17.6 percent of the S&P 500 Index. Today, there is only one energy company, Exxon Mobil, and the

T A B L E 3–2

The Top 20 Companies in the S&P 500 Index

1964			2001		
Company	% of Mkt Cap S&P 500	Mkt Cap (Billions $)	Company	% of Mkt Cap S&P 500	Mkt Cap (Billions $)
AT&T	9.1	$35.1	**General Electric**	3.9	$408.0
General Motors	7.3	$28.2	**Microsoft**	3.4	$352.2
Standard Oil of NJ	5.0	$19.3	**Pfizer**	2.6	$271.5
IBM	3.7	$14.3	Citigroup	2.5	$254.9
Texaco	3.1	$12.0	Exxon Mobil	2.5	$259.6
DuPont	2.9	$11.2	**Wal-Mart**	2.4	$248.8
Sears Roebuck	2.5	$9.7	AIG	2.0	$211.5
General Electric	2.2	$8.5	**Intel**	1.9	$201.0
Gulf	1.6	$6.2	IBM	1.9	$198.5
Eastman Kodak	1.4	$5.4	**Johnson & Johnson**	1.8	$185.3
Std Oil of California	1.4	$5.4	America Online	1.6	$163.7
Socony Mobil	1.2	$4.6	**Cisco Systems**	1.4	$144.6
Royal Dutch	1.1	$4.2	**Merck**	1.4	$145.9
Union C&C	1.0	$3.9	Verizon Communications	1.3	$133.6
Shell	0.9	$3.5	**SBC Communications**	1.3	$131.4
Procter & Gamble	0.9	$3.5	**Coca-Cola**	1.2	$121.9
General T&T	0.8	$3.1	**Tyco International**	1.1	$111.0
Std Oil of Indiana	0.8	$3.1	**Home Depot**	1.0	$107.9
MMM	0.8	$3.1	**Bristol-Myers**	1.0	$108.3
Ford Motor	0.7	$2.7	**Philip Morris**	1.0	$103.3
Top 20	48.4	$186.9	Top 20	37.1	$3,862.8
S&P 500	100.0	$386.2	S&P 500	100.0	$10,400.0

Boldface Denotes Growth Stocks (High Market-to-Book Ratios)

sector's weight in the index has dropped to 6.7 percent. On the other hand, four drug firms occupied the 2001 list, and health care comprises 15 percent of the market weight of the index today, whereas in 1964 there were no health care firms in the top 20, and the entire sector had a meager 2.3 percent weight in the index.

Of course, the new technology giants Intel and Microsoft, which went public in 1971 and 1986, now are among the top 10 most valuable firms in the United States. Information technology comprises about 17 percent of the index compared with one-third that level in 1964. However, the biggest gainers have not been technology companies but rather financial companies, which were less than 1 percent of the index in 1964 but now are almost 20 percent, with two firms, Citigroup and AIG, in the top 20.

There also has been a massive shift from cyclic stocks to growth stocks. Today, 15 of the top 20 stocks in the S&P 500 Index are growth stocks, which is in sharp contrast to 1964, when only 5 such firms were on the list. Chapter 8 will examine the characteristics of growth and value stocks in detail.

RETURN BIASES IN STOCK INDEXES

Many of the companies that were in the S&P 500 Index in 1964 are not there today because they were either absorbed by merger or declined in value and were removed. Some of the firms in the small stock indexes, such as those in the Russell 2000, either graduate into large-cap indexes, are absorbed by other firms, or decline and fall from even this small stock index.

Because these indexes are updated constantly, some investors believe there are biases in these popular size-based indexes so that over time investors can expect the return from these indexes to be higher than what can be achieved in the overall market.

However, this is not the case. It is true that the strongest stocks will stay in the S&P 500 Index, but this index misses the powerful upside move of many small and midsized issues. For example, Microsoft was not added to the S&P 500 Index until June 1994, 8 years after going public. While small stock indexes are the incubators of some of the greatest growth stocks, they also contain those "fallen angels" that have dropped out of the large-cap indexes and are headed downward.

An index is not biased if it can be replicated or matched by an investor. To replicate an index, the dates of additions to and deletions from the index must be announced in advance so that new stocks can be bought and deleted stocks can be sold. This is particularly important for issues that enter into bankruptcy: The postbankruptcy price (which may be zero) must be factored into the index. It should be noted that all the major stock indexes, such as Standard & Poor's, Dow Jones, and Russell, can be replicated by investors.[9] For this reason, there is no statistical reason for capitalization-based indexes to be biased.

APPENDIX: WHAT HAPPENED TO THE ORIGINAL 12 DOW JONES INDUSTRIALS?

Two stocks (GE and Laclede) retained their original names (and industries); five (American Cotton, American Tobacco, Chicago Gas, National Lead, and North American) became large public companies in their original industries; one (Tennessee Coal and Iron) was merged into the giant U.S. Steel; and two (American Sugar and U.S. Rubber) went private—both in the 1980s. Surprisingly, only one (Distilling and Cattle Feeding) changed its product line (from alcoholic beverages to petrochemicals, although it still manufactures ethanol), and only one (U.S. Leather) liquidated. Here is a rundown of the original 12 stocks (market capitalizations as of January 2002):

American Cotton Oil became Best Food in 1923, Corn Products Refining in 1958, and finally, CPC International in 1969—a major food company with operations in 58 countries. In 1997, CPC spun off its corn-refining business as Corn Products International and changed its name to Bestfoods. Bestfoods was acquired by Unilever in October 2000 for $20.3 billion. Unilever (UN), which is headquartered in The Netherlands, has a current market value of $32.4 billion.

American Sugar became Amstar in 1970, went private in 1984, and now manufactures, markets, and distributes portable electric power tools.

American Tobacco changed its name to American Brands (AMB) in 1969 and to Fortune Brands (FO) in 1997, a global consumer products holding company with core businesses in liquor, office products, golf equipment, and home improvements. The current market value is $5.8 billion.

Chicago Gas became People's Gas Light and Coke Co. in 1897 and then People's Energy Corp., a utility holding company, in 1980.

---

[9]The original Value Line Index of 1,700 stocks, which was based on a geometric average of the changes in the individual stocks, was biased downward. This eventually led Value Line to abandon the geometric average in favor of an arithmetic one, which could be replicated.

People's Energy Corp (PGL) has a market value of $1.3 billion and was a member of the Dow Jones Utility Average until May 1997.

Distilling and Cattle Feeding became American Spirits Manufacturing and then Distiller's Securities Corp. Two months after the passage of prohibition, the company changed its charter and became U.S. Food Products Corp. and then National Distiller's and Chemical. The company became Quantum Chemical Corp. in 1989, a leading producer of petrochemicals and propane. Nearing bankruptcy, it was purchased for $3.4 billion by Hanson PLC, an Anglo-American conglomerate. It was spun off as Millennium Chemicals (MCH) in October 1996. The current market value is $820 million.

General Electric (GE), founded in 1892, is the only original stock still in the Dow Jones Industrials. GE is a huge manufacturing and broadcasting conglomerate that owns NBC and CNBC. Its market value of $413 billion is the highest in the world.

Laclede Gas (LG) changed its name to Laclede Group, Inc., and is a retail distributor of natural gas in the St. Louis area. The market value is $460 million.

National Lead (NL) changed its name to NL Industries in 1971 and manufactures titanium dioxide and specialty chemicals. The market value is $770 million.

North American became Union Electric Co. (UEP) in 1956, providing electricity in Missouri and Illinois. In January 1998, UEP merged with Cipsco (Central Illinois Public Service Co.) to form Ameren (AEE) Corp. The market value is $5.8 billion.

Tennessee Coal and Iron was bought out by U.S. Steel in 1907 and became USX-U.S. Steel Group (X) in May of 1991. In January 2002, the company changed its name to U.S. Steel Corp. U.S. Steel has a market value of $1.6 billion.

U.S. Leather, one of the largest makers of shoes in the early part of the twentieth century, liquidated in January 1952, paying its shareholders $1.50 plus stock in an oil and gas company that was to become worthless.

U.S. Rubber became Uniroyal in 1961 and was taken private in August of 1985.

CHAPTER 4

THE IMPACT OF TAXES ON ASSET RETURNS

In this world nothing is certain but death and taxes.

BENJAMIN FRANKLIN[1]

The power to tax involves the power to destroy.

JOHN MARSHALL[2]

For all long-term investors, there is only one objective—maximum total real return after taxes.

JOHN TEMPLETON[3]

John Templeton's objective, to maximize total real return after taxes, must be considered in all investment strategies. And stocks are very well suited to this purpose. In contrast to fixed-income investments, a significant portion of the return from stocks comes from capital appreciation,

---

[1]Letter to M. Leroy, 1789.
[2]*McCulloch v. Maryland*, 1819.
[3]Excerpts from *The Templeton Touch*, by William Proctor, quoted in *Classics*, edited by Charles D. Ellis (Homewood, IL: Dow Jones–Irwin, 1989), p. 738.

which is treated favorably by the tax code. Taxes are not paid until a gain is realized, and such gains almost always have been subject to a lower tax rate. Thus, in addition to having superior before-tax returns, stocks also have a tax advantage over bonds.

HISTORICAL TAXES ON INCOME AND CAPITAL GAINS

Figure 4-1a plots the marginal tax rate on dividend and interest income for investors at three income levels: the tax rate of an investor in the highest tax bracket, the tax rate for an investor with a real income of $150,000 in today's dollars, and the tax rate for an investor with a real income of $50,000. Figure 4-1b plots the tax rate on capital gains income. You can see the volatility in marginal tax rates for the high-income investor, whereas the tax rate on capital gains has remained far more stable. A history of the tax code applicable to stock investors is provided in the Appendix at the end of this chapter.

A TOTAL AFTER-TAX RETURNS INDEX

In Chapter 1 I presented a total returns index for stocks, bonds, bills, and gold. In this chapter I will calculate a range of after-tax returns on these assets under various tax rates. Figure 4-2 presents the effect of taxes on total real returns. The upper line of the stock range represents the before-tax real stock return, identical to the one in Figure 1-4. This return would be applicable to tax-exempt individuals or institutions. The lower line of the stock range in Figure 4-2 assumes that investors pay the highest tax rate on dividend, interest, and capital gains income, with no deferral of capital gains taxes. The shaded range shows the range of total returns from zero to the highest marginal tax rate. This chapter considers only federal taxes; no state, local, or estate taxes are included.

The difference between before- and after-tax total return is striking. Total before-tax real stock returns accumulate to $599,605, whereas after-tax accumulations are about $25,020—less than ¹⁄₂₀ the before-tax accumulation. A return range is also displayed for the accumulations on Treasury bonds, as well as the total return from municipal bonds, which are exempt from federal taxes. Since municipal bond interest rates generally are lower than the interest paid by federal government bonds (called Treasuries), the total return on municipal bonds is lower than that on Treasuries for an untaxed investor but higher than the return on Treasuries for most taxable investors.

FIGURE 4-1

Federal Tax Rates, 1913–2001

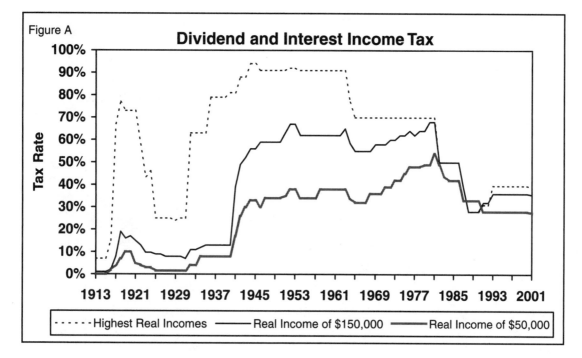

Figure A

Dividend and Interest Income Tax

- - - - - Highest Real Incomes   ——— Real Income of $150,000   ——— Real Income of $50,000

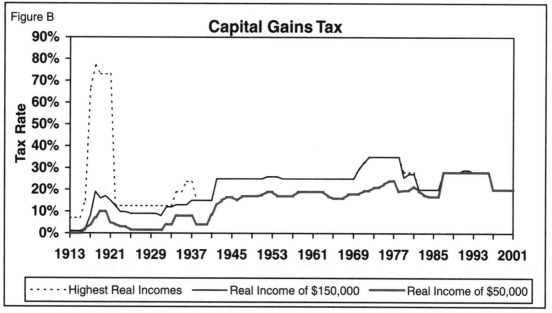

Figure B

Capital Gains Tax

- - - - - Highest Real Incomes   ——— Real Income of $150,000   ——— Real Income of $50,000

FIGURE 4–2

After-Tax Real Return for Various Federal Tax Brackets, 1802–2001

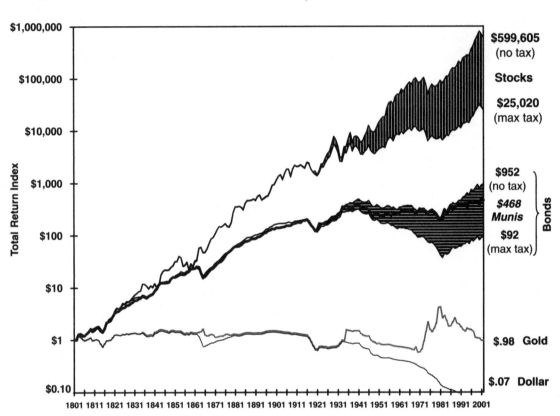

Table 4-1 displays the historical real after-tax returns for four tax brackets. Since 1913, when the federal income tax was instituted, the after-tax real return on stocks has ranged from 6.5 percent for untaxed investors to 2.8 percent for investors in the maximum bracket who do not defer their capital gains. For taxable bonds, the real annual return falls from 1.8 to –0.8 percent, and for bills from 0.5 to –2.4 percent. Municipal bonds have yielded a 1.1 percent annual real return since the income tax was instituted.

Despite the debilitating effect of taxes on equity accumulation, taxes cause the greatest damage to the returns on fixed-income investments. On an after-tax basis, an investor in the top tax bracket who put $1,000 in Treasury bills at the beginning of 1946 would have $151 after taxes and after inflation today, a *loss* in purchasing power of more than

TABLE 4–1

After-Tax Real Asset Returns, 1802–2001: Compound Annual Rates of Return (%)*

		Stocks Tax Bracket				Bonds Tax Bracket				Bills Tax Bracket				Muni Bds	Gold	CPI
		$0	$50K	$150K	Max	$0	$50K	$150K	Max	$0	$50K	$150K	Max			
Period	1802-2001	6.9	6.0	5.6	5.2	3.5	2.8	2.6	2.3	2.9	2.4	1.9	1.6	3.1	0.0	1.4
	1871-2001	6.8	5.4	4.9	4.2	2.8	1.8	1.5	3.5	1.8	1.0	0.3	-0.3	2.2	-0.1	2.0
	1913-2001	6.5	4.5	3.7	2.8	1.8	0.4	-0.1	-0.8	0.5	-0.6	-1.6	-2.4	1.1	-0.3	3.3
Major Sub-Periods	I 1802-1870	7.0	7.0	7.0	7.0	4.8	4.8	4.8	4.8	5.1	5.1	5.1	5.1	5.0	0.2	0.1
	II 1871-1925	6.6	6.5	6.4	6.2	3.7	3.7	3.6	3.4	3.2	3.1	3.0	2.7	3.4	-0.8	0.6
	III 1926-2001	6.9	4.6	3.8	2.9	2.2	0.5	-0.1	-0.7	0.7	-0.6	-1.7	-2.3	1.3	0.4	3.1
Post-War Periods	1946-2001	7.1	4.3	3.4	2.8	1.3	-0.8	-1.4	-1.9	0.7	-1.1	-2.6	-3.3	0.7	-0.3	4.1
	1946-1965	10.0	7.0	5.2	3.8	-1.2	-2.0	-2.7	-3.5	-0.8	-1.5	-2.3	-2.7	-0.6	-2.7	2.8
	1966-1981	-0.4	-2.2	-3.0	-3.3	-4.2	-6.1	-7.0	-7.5	-0.2	-3.0	-5.2	-6.1	-1.0	8.8	7.0
	1982-1999	13.6	9.4	9.1	9.1	8.4	4.9	4.5	4.4	2.9	0.8	-0.8	-1.7	2.7	-4.9	3.3
	1982-2001	10.5	7.1	6.9	6.8	8.5	5.1	4.7	4.6	2.8	0.8	-0.7	-1.6	3.5	-4.8	3.2

*Federal Income Tax Only. Assume 1-year holding period for capital gain portion of return.

85 percent. Such an investor would have turned $1,000 into over $4,660 by buying stocks, a 350 percent increase in purchasing power.

In fact, for someone in the highest tax bracket, short-term Treasury bills have yielded a negative after-tax real return since 1871, even longer if state and local taxes are taken into account. In contrast, top-bracket investors would have increased their purchasing power in stocks 233-fold over the same period.

THE BENEFITS OF DEFERRING CAPITAL GAINS TAXES

Many investors assume that capital gains are beneficial solely because of the favorable rates at which such gains have been taxed. However, lower capital gains tax rates are not the only advantage of investing in appreciating assets. Taxes on capital gains are paid only when the asset is sold, not as the gain is accrued. The advantage of this tax deferral is that assets accumulate at the higher before-tax rates rather than the after-tax rates of return.

In fact, for long-term investors, the advantage of tax deferral is about equal to that of lower rates. For example, take two investments, one yielding 10 percent per year in taxable income and the other yielding 10 percent in capital gains. For an untaxed investor, both investments would yield identical returns. However, assume that an individual is in the 30 percent tax bracket and that the capital gains tax rate is 20 percent. The after-tax yield on the taxable asset is 7 percent per year. If the investor realizes capital gains every year, his or her yield would be 8 percent per year. However, if the investor waits for 30 years before realizing the capital gains, the after-tax return jumps to 9.24 percent per year, not far from the return of an untaxed investor.

From a tax standpoint, there should be a clear preference for investors to receive capital gains over dividend income. However, many investors still prefer to receive a steady flow of dividends rather than obtaining funds from selling stock. These investors show a desire to preserve capital and consume the income generated from the investment. Under our current tax system, however, one pays a high price for this preference.

INFLATION AND THE CAPITAL GAINS TAX

In the United States, capital gains taxes are paid on the difference between the cost of an asset and the sale price, with no adjustment made for inflation. An investor must pay taxes on any gain in price, whether or not he or she has realized any *real* gain. This means that an asset that appreciates by less than the rate of inflation—meaning that the investor has lost purchasing power—nevertheless will be taxed on sale. Figure 4-3 displays the after-tax real rate of return for various inflation rates and various holding periods under the current tax system.[4]

Even if the nominal appreciation of stock prices includes the rate of inflation, as our long-term evidence suggests, the tax code has a dramatic impact on investors' realized after-tax real return. For even moderate inflation of 3 percent, an investor with a 5-year average holding period suffers a 50-basis-point (hundredths of a percentage point) reduction in average real after-tax return compared with the after-tax return if the rate of inflation were zero. If the inflation rises to 6 percent, the loss of return is more than 94 basis points.

---

[4]Figure 4-3 assumes a total real return of 7 percent (real appreciation of 5 percent and a dividend yield of 2 percent) and tax rates of 20 and 28 percent, respectively, on capital gains and dividend income. If inflation is 3 percent, the total return on stocks will be 10 percent in nominal terms.

FIGURE   4–3

Real After-Tax Returns and Inflation (Assume 2 Percent Dividend Yield, 5 Percent Real Capital Appreciation, 20 Percent Capital Gains Rate, and 28 Percent Dividend Tax Rate)

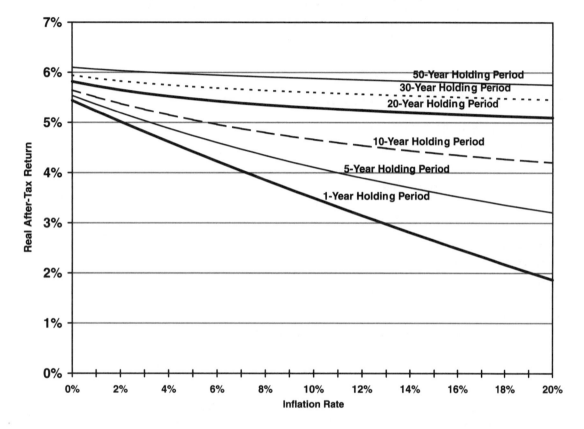

The inflation tax has a far more severe effect on realized after-tax real returns when the holding period is short than when it is long. This is so because the more frequently an investor buys and sells assets, the more frequently the government can capture the nominal capital gains tax. However, even for very long-term investors, inflation cuts into real returns. And the tax effect is more serious if stocks have been sheltered in a tax-deferred account, for in this case funds taken out are taxed at the ordinary income tax rate.

There is considerable support, both inside and outside of government, to make some adjustment for inflation in the capital gains tax. In 1986, the U.S. Treasury proposed the indexation of capital gains, but this provision was never enacted into law. In 1997, the House of Representatives included capital gains indexation in its tax law, but it was removed by House-Senate conferees under threat of a presidential veto. Under such plans, investors would pay taxes only on that portion of the gain (if any) that exceeded the increase in the price level over the holding period of the asset. Inflation indexation of the capital gains tax would have a very positive effect on realized returns. Alternatively, however, if the central bank can keep inflation low, this would nullify the "inflation tax" on capital gains.

INCREASINGLY FAVORABLE TAX FACTORS FOR EQUITIES

In recent years there have been some very favorable tax developments for stocks. They are:

1. Low inflation
2. Low capital gains tax
3. Greater portion of stock return in capital gains and less in dividend income

Table 4-2 summarizes how each of these favorable developments influences a stockholder's after-tax return. In the preceding section we described how low inflation increases the real return to stockholders by reducing the effective tax on capital gains. For an upper-middle-income shareholder with a 3-year average holding period, every 1 percentage point reduction in the rate of inflation increases the average after-tax real

T A B L E   4–2

Increase in After-Tax Real Returns from Declines in Various Tax Factors, 1950–2001: Investor with $150,000 Real Taxable Income

Tax Factors	Average Level 1950-2001	Level 2001	Increase in After-Tax Return (BPS)	
			Per Percentage Point Shift	Total
Inflation Rate	4.0%	2.5%	24	36
Capital Gains Tax	26.4%	20.0%	10	62
Dividend Yield	3.6%	1.2%	22	52
Dividend Tax Rate	52.4%	39.1%	1.3	16
After-Tax Real Return (Excluding Dividend Tax)	2.79%	4.19%	140*	
After-Tax Real Return (Including Dividend Tax)	2.79%	4.35%	156	

*Does not add because of interaction effects.

return by 24 basis points. The average rate of inflation in the United States since 1950 has been 4.0 percent. Over the last 5 years it has been 2.5 percent. The lower inflation therefore has increased after-tax real returns of shareholders by 37 basis points.

The average capital gains tax over the postwar period has been 26.4 percent. In 2001, the capital gains tax rate was 20 percent, the lowest level since 1941. Every percentage point reduction in the capital gains tax increases the after-tax real return of investors by 10 basis points. If we take the current capital gains tax at 20 percent, this means that the after-tax real return for the taxable shareholder is 62 basis points higher compared with the postwar average.[5]

The third favorable development is the transformation of taxable dividends into lightly taxed capital gains. As will be discussed in Chapter 6, a firm can choose to use its earnings to pay dividends, to reinvest in the firm, or to buy back its shares. Paying dividends exposes investors to the highest tax bracket. By reinvesting earnings or buying back shares, the firm can generate capital gains, which, as we have seen, are taxed at a preferential rate. Every 1 percentage point reduction in the dividend yield that is transformed into capital gains increases the real return of stockholders by 22 basis points. The average postwar dividend yield has been 3.6 percent, and currently it is 1.2 percent. If we assume that the 2.4 percent difference is fully reinvested in the company to generate further capital gains, this means that the lower dividend yield has increased the after-tax real return of shareholders by 52 basis points.

Combined, these three favorable factors have increased the after-tax return from an average of 2.79 percent from 1950 through 2001 to 4.19 percent in 2001, an increase of 140 basis points.[6]

In addition to the preceding changes that primarily affect stock returns, marginal tax rates on income also have declined substantially in recent years. The average marginal tax rate for an upper-income investor since 1950 was 52.4 percent, and in 2001 it fell to 39.1 percent. Each percentage point decline in the marginal tax rate increases after-tax real returns by 1.3 basis points, so the cumulative change has added 16 basis points to the return. Since the change in the income tax rate influences the return from all assets, the impact of the reduction in the dividend tax is broken out from the other factors.

---

[5] If the new 18 percent capital gains tax bracket is considered, this will raise real after-tax returns by 81 basis points.

[6] The total effect is slightly less than the sum due to interaction terms.

The bottom line is that the changes in the effective marginal capital gains tax rate, inflation, and dividend yield have raised the after-tax real return from 2.79 to 4.19 percent. If the income tax rate is considered, the after-tax real return has further increased to 4.35 percent. These are substantial changes and will boost the justifiable price-to-earnings (P-E) ratio of the market from its historical levels. The impact of these favorable developments on the equilibrium P-E ratio of the market will be discussed in Chapter 7.

STOCKS OR BONDS IN TAX-DEFERRED ACCOUNTS?

The most important saving vehicle for many individuals is their tax-deferred account (TDA), such as a Keogh, Individual Retirement Account (IRA), 401(k), or similar plan. Many investors hold most of their stocks (if they hold any at all) in their tax-deferred account, whereas they hold primarily fixed-income assets in their taxable accounts.

Yet many financial advisors recommend that investors do exactly the opposite. They rightly claim that stocks will realize the capital gains tax advantage only if they are held in taxable accounts. This is so because when a tax-deferred account is cashed out at retirement, an individual pays ordinary income tax on the entire withdrawal, regardless of how much of the accumulation has been realized through capital gains and how much through dividend income.

As a result, these advisors assert that you should hold stocks in a taxable account where the lower capital gains tax can be enjoyed and bonds in a tax-deferred account where interest can be shielded from taxes. Because of the recent reduction in capital gains tax rates, advisors claim that these recommendations become even more imperative.

The preceding counsel, however, ignores two important factors. First, it is virtually impossible not to realize some capital gains over time in a stock portfolio. Even index funds must buy and sell stock to match the index and satisfy redemptions. Furthermore, nonindex funds often realize quite a few capital gains in their attempts to maximize their return. Thus sheltering realized capital gains in a tax-deferred account could be very important.

Second, although the government taxes your capital gains from stocks at ordinary rates in a TDA, the government also shares more of the downside risk. If you realize a capital loss in a taxable account, the government limits your ability to offset this loss against ordinary income. However, when funds are withdrawn from a tax-deferred account, the full withdrawal is treated as taxable income, so all losses effectively become deductible from taxable income.

When all the factors are considered, it is better for most investors to hold stocks in their TDAs rather than in their taxable accounts. This is particularly true if they do not have sufficient savings both to fund a TDA with bonds and to buy stocks in a taxable account. It is important to fund your TDA to its maximum level, even if you have to borrow to do so. However, it rarely pays to borrow just to hold stocks in your taxable account while you fund the TDA with bonds.

If you buy more stock than the maximum allowed contribution to the TDA, then you should put the higher-yielding stock in your TDA, where the dividend income is sheltered from taxes, and keep the low-dividend stock in your taxable account. For example, income-oriented mutual funds, which tend to pay higher dividends, should be put into a TDA, whereas growth-oriented funds, with low dividends, should be placed in the taxable account. Individual stocks or specialized funds that have high-dividend yields, such as utilities and real estate investment trusts, make good candidates for TDAs. However, do not overbuy these stocks just to shelter dividend income because doing so would make your portfolio unbalanced. Make sure to diversify across the broadest base of stocks to maximize return for the lowest possible risk.

CONCLUSION

Tax planning is important to maximize returns from financial assets. Because of favorable capital gains tax rates and the potential to defer realizing those gains, stocks hold a significant tax advantage over fixed-income assets. These advantages have risen in recent years as the capital gains tax has been reduced, inflation has remained low, and firms have repurchased shares to enhance capital gains and to avoid highly taxed dividend income. These favorable developments have increased the after-tax return of equities by about 1½ percentage points relative to the average return of the preceding 50 years.

Despite the favorable tax advantages to equities, it is still advantageous to accumulate equities in TDAs and shield the dividends and capital gains from taxes as long as possible. If investors hold stocks both in taxable and tax-deferred accounts, it is advantageous to accumulate the higher-yielding stocks and funds that are traded frequently and generate capital gains in the TDAs. Low-dividend stocks that are going to be held for long periods of time and index funds that generate little capital gains should be held in taxable accounts. Smart tax planning can make the superior returns available in stocks even more attractive.

APPENDIX: HISTORY OF THE TAX CODE

Federal income tax was first collected under the Revenue Act of 1913, when the Sixteenth Amendment to the U.S. Constitution was ratified. Until 1921, no tax preference was given to capital gains income. When tax rates were increased sharply during World War I, investors refrained from realizing gains and complained to Congress about the tax consequences of selling their assets. Congress was persuaded that such "frozen portfolios" were detrimental to the efficient allocation of capital, and so in 1922, a maximum tax rate of 12.5 percent was established on capital gains income. This rate became effective when taxable income reached $30,000, which is equivalent to about $240,000 in today's dollars.

In 1934, a new tax code was enacted that for the first time excluded a portion of capital gains from taxable income. This exclusion allowed middle-income groups, and not just the rich, to enjoy the tax benefits of capital gains income. The excluded portion of the gain depended on the length of time the asset was held; there was no exclusion if the asset was held for 1 year or less, but the exclusion was increased to 70 percent if the asset was held more than 10 years. Since marginal tax rates ranged up to 79 percent in 1936, the effective maximum tax on very long-term gains was reduced to about 24 percent.

In 1938, the tax code was amended again to provide for a 50 percent exclusion of capital gains income if an asset was held for more than 18 months, but in no case would the tax exceed 15 percent on such capital gains. The maximum rate on capital gains income was raised to 25 percent in 1942, but the holding period was reduced to 6 months. Except for a 1 percent surtax that raised the maximum rate to 26 percent during the Korean War, the 25 percent rate held until 1969.

In 1969, the maximum tax rate on capital gains in excess of $50,000 was phased out over a number of years so that, ultimately, the 50 percent exclusion applied to all tax rates. Since the maximum rate on ordinary income was 70 percent, this meant that the maximum tax rate on capital gains rose to 35 percent by 1973. In 1978, the exclusion was raised to 60 percent, which lowered the effective maximum tax rate on capital gains to 28 percent. When the maximum tax rate on ordinary income was reduced to 50 percent in 1982, the maximum tax rate on capital gains was again reduced to 20 percent.

In 1986, the tax code was altered extensively to reduce and simplify the tax structure and ultimately eliminate the distinction between capital gains and ordinary income. By 1988, the tax rates for both capital gains and ordinary income were identical, at 33 percent. For the first time since 1922, there was no preference for capital gains income. In 1990, the top rate was lowered to 28 percent on both ordinary and capital gains income. In 1991, a slight wedge was reopened between capital gains and ordinary income: The top rate on the latter was raised to 31 percent, whereas the former remained at 28 percent. In 1993, President Clinton raised tax rates again, increasing the top rate on ordinary income to 39.6 percent while keeping the capital gains tax unchanged. In 1997, Congress lowered the maximum capital gains tax to 20 percent for assets held more than 18 months and the following year returned to the 12-month capital gains period. Starting in 2001, investors could take advantage of a new 18 percent top capital gains rate for assets held at least 5 years. In 2001, President George W. Bush and a Republican Congress passed a tax law phasing in lower marginal tax rates and phasing out the estate tax, but no change in the capital gains tax was enacted.

5

CHAPTER

PERSPECTIVES ON STOCKS AS INVESTMENTS

The "new-era" doctrine—that "good" stocks (or "blue chips") were sound investments regardless of how high the price paid for them— was at the bottom only a means of rationalizing under the title of "investment" the well-nigh universal capitulation to the gambling fever.
BENJAMIN GRAHAM AND DAVID DODD, 1934[1]

Investing in stocks has become a national hobby and a national obsession. . . . To update Marx, it is the religion of the masses.
ROGER LOWENSTEIN, 1996[2]

It was a seasonally cool Monday evening on October 14, 1929, when Irving Fisher arrived at the Builders' Exchange Club at 2 Park Avenue in New York City. Fisher, a professor of economics at Yale University and the most renowned economist of his time, was scheduled to address the monthly meeting of the Purchasing Agents Association (PAA).

---

[1]Benjamin Graham and David Dodd, *Security Analysis* (New York: McGraw-Hill, 1934), p. 11.
[2]Roger Lowenstein, "A Common Market: The Public's Zeal to Invest," *Wall Street Journal*, September 9, 1996, p. A11.

Fisher, the founder of modern capital theory, was no mere aca-demic. He actively analyzed and forecast financial market conditions, wrote dozens of newsletters on topics ranging from health to invest-ments, and created a highly successful card-indexing firm based on one of his own patented inventions. Despite hailing from a modest background, his personal wealth in the summer of 1929 exceeded $10 million.[3]

Members of the PAA and the press crowded into the meeting room. Fisher's speech was designed mainly to defend investment trusts, the forerunner of today's mutual funds. However, the audience was most eager to hear his views on the stock market.

Investors had been nervous since early September when Roger Babson, businessman and market seer, predicted a "terrific" crash in stock prices.[4] Fisher had dismissed this pessimism, noting that Babson had been bearish for some time. However, the public sought to be reas-sured by the great man who had championed stocks for so long.

The audience was not disappointed. After a few introductory re-marks, Fisher uttered a sentence that, much to his regret, became one of the most quoted phrases in stock market history: "Stock prices have reached what looks like a permanently high plateau."[5]

On October 29, two weeks to the day after Fisher's speech, stocks crashed. Fisher's "high plateau" turned into a bottomless abyss. The next 3 years witnessed the most devastating market collapse in his-tory. Like Neville Chamberlain's proud claim that the "agreement" Adolph Hitler signed in Munich in September 1938 guaranteed "peace in our time," Fisher's prediction about the stock market stands as a memorial to the folly of great men who failed to envision impending disaster.

After the crash, Fisher's reputation was shattered. It made little dif-ference that he had correctly forecast the rising bull market in the 1920s, rightly emphasized the importance of the Federal Reserve in creating a favorable economic climate, and properly defended investment trusts, the forerunners of today's mutual funds, as the best way that the public could participate in the stock market.

While Fisher may not have predicted the crash that October evening, he did in fact point out that the increase in stock prices at the time largely stemmed from a rise in earnings. Fisher noted, "Time will

---

[3]Robert Loring Allen, *Irving Fisher: A Biography* (Cambridge, MA: Blackwell, 1993), p. 206.
[4]*Commercial and Financial Chronicle*, September 7, 1929.
[5]"Fisher Sees Stocks Permanently High," *New York Times*, October 16, 1929, p. 2.

tell whether the increase will continue sufficiently to justify the present high level. I expect that it will."[6]

Time eventually did justify stock levels in 1929. But the time frame was far longer than Irving Fisher or anyone else, for that matter, believed. The truth that stocks were in fact better investments after their prices had dropped from their highs held no interest for investors. The proven long-term superiority of equity investing, which served as the rationale during the stock market advance, was roundly ignored as investors dumped stocks regardless of their intrinsic value.

EARLY VIEWS OF STOCK INVESTING

Throughout the nineteenth century, stocks were deemed the province of speculators and insiders but certainly not conservative investors. It was not until the early twentieth century that researchers came to realize that stocks, as a class, might be suitable investments under certain economic conditions. At that time, Irving Fisher himself maintained that stocks would indeed be superior to bonds during inflationary times but that common shares likely would underperform bonds during periods of declining prices.[7] This view of stock returns became the conventional wisdom of the early twentieth century.

Edgar Lawrence Smith, a financial analyst and investment manager of the 1920s, exploded this popular conception. Smith was the first to demonstrate that accumulations in a diversified portfolio of common stocks outperformed bonds not only in times of rising commodity prices but also when prices were falling. Smith published his studies in 1925 in a book entitled *Common Stocks as Long-Term Investments*. In the Introduction, he stated:

> These studies are a record of a failure—the failure of facts to sustain a preconceived theory. [The theory] . . . that high-grade bonds had proved to be better investments during periods of . . . [falling commodity prices].[8]

By examining stock returns back to the Civil War, Smith found not only that stocks beat bonds whether prices were rising or falling but also that there was a very small chance that you would have to wait a long time (which he put at 6 years and, at most, 15 years) before having an opportunity to liquidate your stocks at a profit. He concluded:

---

[6]*New York Times*, October 16, 1929, p. 2.
[7]Irving Fisher, *How to Invest When Prices Are Rising* (Scranton, PA: G. Lynn Sumner & Co., 1912).
[8]Edgar L. Smith, *Common Stocks as Long-Term Investments* (New York: Macmillan, 1925), p. v.

We have found that there is a force at work in our common stock holdings which tends ever toward increasing their principal value. . . . [U]nless we have had the extreme misfortune to invest at the very peak of a noteworthy rise, those periods in which the average market value of our holding remains less than the amount we paid for them are of comparatively short duration. Our hazard even in such extreme cases appears to be that of time alone.[9]

Smith's conclusion was right not only historically but also prospectively. It took just over 15 years to recover the money invested at the 1929 peak, following a crash far worse than Smith had ever examined. And since World War II, the recovery period for stocks has been better than Smith's wildest dreams. The longest it has ever taken since 1945 to recover an original investment in the stock market (including reinvested dividends) was the 3½-year period from December 1972 to June 1976.

INFLUENCE OF SMITH'S WORK

Smith wrote his book at the onset of one of the greatest bull markets in our history. Its conclusions caused a sensation in both academic and investing circles. The prestigious weekly, *The Economist*, stated, "Every intelligent investor and stockbroker should study Mr. Smith's most interesting little book, and examine the tests individually and their very surprising results."[10]

Irving Fisher saw Smith's study as a confirmation of his own long-held belief that bonds were overrated as safe investments in a world with uncertain inflation. Fisher summarized the new findings as follows:

It seems, then, that the market overrates the safety of "safe" securities and pays too much for them, that it underrates the risk of risky securities and pays too little for them, that it pays too much for immediate and too little for remote returns, and finally, that it mistakes the steadiness of money income from a bond for a steadiness of real income which it does not possess. In steadiness of real income, or purchasing power, a list of diversified common stocks surpasses bonds.[11]

Smith's ideas quickly crossed the Atlantic and were the subject of much discussion in Great Britain. John Maynard Keynes, the great

---

[9]*Ibid.*, p. 81.

[10]"Ordinary Shares as Investments," *The Economist*, June 6, 1925, p. 1141.

[11]From the Foreword by Irving Fisher in Kenneth S. Van Strum, *Investing in Purchasing Power* (New York: Barron's, 1925), p. vii. Van Strum, a writer for *Barron's* weekly, followed up and confirmed Smith's research.

British economist and originator of the business cycle theory that became the accepted paradigm for generations, reviewed Smith's book
with much excitement. Keynes stated:

> The results are striking. Mr. Smith finds in almost every case, not only
> when prices were rising, but also when they were falling, that common
> stocks have turned out best in the long-run, indeed, markedly so. . . .
> This actual experience in the United States over the past fifty years af-
> fords prima facie evidence that the prejudice of investors and investing
> institutions in favor of bonds as being "safe" and against common
> stocks as having, even the best of them, a "speculative" flavor, has led to
> a relative over-valuation of bonds and under-valuation of common
> stocks.[12]

Money managers also were quick to realize the impact of Smith's
work. Hartley Withers wrote the following in *The London Investors Chronicle* and *Money Market Review*:

> Old-fashioned investors and their old-fashioned advisers have so long
> been in the habit of looking on all holdings of ordinary shares or common
> stocks as something rather naughty and speculative, that one feels a cer-
> tain amount of hesitation in even ventilating the view that is now rapidly
> gaining acceptance that ordinary shares, under certain conditions, are re-
> ally safer than . . . [bonds], even though the latter may be of the variety
> which is commonly called "gilt-edged."[13]

Smith's writings were published in such prestigious journals as the
Review of Economic Statistics and the *Journal of the American Statistical Association*.[14] Further research confirmed his results. Smith acquired an international following when Siegfried Stern published an extensive study
of returns in common stock in 13 European countries from the onset of
World War I through 1928. Stern's study showed that the advantage of
investing in common stocks over bonds and other financial investments
extended far beyond America's financial markets.[15]

---

[12]J. M. Keynes, "An American Study of Shares versus Bonds as Permanent Investments," *The Nation
& The Athenaeum*, May 2, 1925, p. 157.
[13]Quoted by Edgar Lawrence Smith in *Common Stocks and Business Cycles* (New York: William-
Frederick Press, 1959), p. 20.
[14]Edgar Lawrence Smith, "Market Value of Industrial Equities," *Review of Economic Statistics* 9(January 1927):37–40, and "Tests Applied to an Index of the Price Level for Industrial Stocks," *Journal of
the American Statistical Association* (Suppl., March 1931):127–135.
[15]S. Stern, *Fourteen Years of European Investments, 1914–1928* (London: The Bankers' Publishing Co.,
1929).

COMMON STOCK THEORY OF INVESTMENT

The research demonstrating the superiority of stocks became known as the *common stock theory of investment*.[16] Smith himself was careful not to overstate his findings. He wrote:

> *Over a period of years* the principal value of a *well-diversified holding* of common stocks of *representative* corporations in essential industries tends to increase in accordance with the operation of compound interest. . . . Such stock holding may be relied upon *over a term of years* to pay an average income return on such increasing values of something more than the average current rate on commercial paper.[17]

Yet Chelcie C. Bosland, a professor of economics at Brown University in the 1930s, claimed that the common stock theory often was misused to justify any investment in stocks no matter what the price. Bosland stated:

> The purchase of common stocks after 1922 was more likely to result in profit than in loss. Even though this was largely a cyclical up-swing, many believed that it was a vindication of the theory that common stocks are good long-term investments. Participation in this profit-making procedure became widespread. The "boom psychology" was everywhere in evidence. No doubt the "common stock theory" gave even to the downright speculator the feeling that his actions were based upon the solid rock of scientific finding.[18]

A RADICAL SHIFT IN SENTIMENT

The glorious days of common stocks did not last, however. The crash pushed the image of stocks as safe and fundamentally sound investments into the doghouse and with it the credibility of Smith's contention that stocks were the best long-term investments. Lawrence Chamberlain, an author and well-known investment banker, stated, *"Common stocks, as such, are not superior to bonds as long-term investments, because primarily they are not investments at all. They are speculations."*[19]

The common stock theory of investment was attacked from all angles. In 1934, Benjamin Graham, an investment fund manager, and

---

[16] Chelcie C. Bosland, *The Common Stock Theory of Investment: Its Development and Significance* (New York: Ronald Press, 1937).

[17] Smith (1927), p. 79, emphasis added.

[18] Bosland (1937), p. 4.

[19] Lawrence Chamberlain and William W. Hay, *Investment and Speculations* (New York: Henry Holt & Co., 1931), p. 55, emphasis his.

David Dodd, a finance professor at Columbia University, wrote the book *Security Analysis*, which became the bible of the value-oriented approach to analyzing stocks and bonds. Through its many editions, this book has had a lasting impact on students and market professionals alike.

Graham and Dodd clearly blamed Smith's book for feeding the bull market mania of the 1920s by proposing plausible-sounding but fallacious theories to justify the purchase of stocks. They wrote:

> The self-deception of the mass speculator must, however, have its element of justification. . . . In the new-era bull market, the "rational" basis was the record of long-term improvement shown by diversified common-stock holdings. . . . [There is] a small and rather sketchy volume from which the new-era theory may be said to have sprung. The book is entitled *Common Stocks as Long-Term Investments* by Edgar Lawrence Smith, published in 1924.[20]

POSTCRASH VIEW OF STOCK RETURNS

As the news spread about all the people who lost their life savings in the market, the notion that stocks could still beat other financial assets sounded ludicrous. In the late 1930s, Alfred Cowles III, founder of the Cowles Commission for economic research, constructed capitalization-weighted stock indexes back to 1871 of all stocks traded on the New York Stock Exchange. Cowles examined stock returns including reinvested dividends and concluded:

> During that period [1871–1926] there is considerable evidence to support the conclusion that stocks in general sold at about three-quarters of their true value as measured by the return to the investor.[21]

Yet Cowles placed the blame for the crash of 1929 squarely on the shoulders of the government, claiming that increased taxation and government controls drove stock prices downward.

As stocks slowly recovered from the depression, their returns seemed to warrant a new look. In 1953, two professors from the University of Michigan, Wilford Eiteman and Frank P. Smith, published a study of the investment returns on all industrial companies with trading volume over 1 million shares in 1936. By regularly purchasing these 92 stocks without any regard to the stock market cycle (a strategy called *dol-*

---

[20]Benjamin Graham and David Dodd, *Security Analysis*, 2d ed. (New York: McGraw-Hill, 1940), p. 357.

[21]Alfred Cowles III and associates, *Common Stock Indexes 1871–1937* (Bloomington, IN: Pricipia Press, 1938), p. 50.

lar cost averaging), they found that the returns over the next 14 years, at 12.2 percent per year, far exceeded those of fixed-income investments. Twelve years later they repeated the study using the same stocks they used in their previous study. This time the returns were even higher, despite the fact that they made no adjustment for any of the new firms or new industries that had surfaced in the interim. They wrote:

> If a portfolio of common stocks selected by such obviously foolish methods as were employed in this study will show an annual compound rate of return as high as 14.2 percent, then a small investor with limited knowledge of market conditions can place his savings in a diversified list of common stocks with some assurance that, given time, his holding will provide him with safety of principal and an adequate annual yield.[22]

Many people dismissed the Eiteman and Smith study because it did not include the great crash of 1929–1932. However, in 1964, two professors from the University of Chicago, Lawrence Fisher and James H. Lorie, examined stock returns through the stock crash of 1929, the Great Depression, and World War II.[23] Fisher and Lorie concluded that stocks offered significantly higher returns (which they reported at 9.0 percent per year) than any other investment medium during the entire 35-year period, 1926–1960. They even factored taxes and transaction costs into their return calculations and concluded:

> It will perhaps be surprising to many that the returns have consistently been so high. . . . The fact that many persons choose investments with a substantially lower average rate of return than that available on common stocks suggests the essentially conservative nature of those investors and the extent of their concern about the risk of loss inherent in common stocks.[24]

Ten years later, Roger Ibbotson and Rex Sinquefield published an even more extensive review of returns in an article entitled "Stocks, Bonds, Bills, and Inflation: Year-by-Year Historical Returns (1926–74)."[25] They acknowledged their indebtedness to the Lorie and Fisher study and confirmed the superiority of stocks as long-term investments. Their summary statistics, which are published annually in yearbooks, are

---

[22]Wilford J. Eiteman and Frank P. Smith, *Common Stock Values and Yields* (Ann Arbor: University of Michigan Press, 1962), p. 40.
[23]"Rates of Return on Investment in Common Stocks," *Journal of Business* 37(January 1964):1–21.
[24]*Ibid.*, p. 20.
[25]*Journal of Business* 49(January 1976):11–43.

quoted frequently and often have served as the return benchmarks for the securities industry.[26]

THE CULT OF EQUITIES

The findings of Ibbotson and Sinquefield were first published in the teeth of the worst bear market since the Great Depression. Because of the war in Vietnam, surging inflation, and the OPEC oil embargo, real stock returns were negative from the end of 1966 through the summer of 1982. However, as the Federal Reserve (Fed) successfully squeezed out inflation and interest rates fell sharply, the stock market began its greatest bull market in August 1982. From a level of 790, the Dow began to shoot skyward, surging past 1,000 to a new record by the end of year.

Few people thought the trend would last. In 1992, *Forbes* warned investors in a cover story entitled "The Crazy Things People Say to Rationalize Stock Prices" that stocks were in the "midst of a speculative buying panic" and cited Raskob's foolish advice to invest at the market peak in 1929.[27]

Yet other investors took the correct view of the markets. Robert Foman, president and chairman of E.F. Hutton, proclaimed in October 1983 that we are "in the dawning of a new age of equities" and boldly predicted that the Dow Jones Average could hit 2,000 or more by the end of the decade.

However, even Foman was too pessimistic. Except for the great stock crash of October 1987, which is documented in Chapter 16, stocks marched steadily upward, and the Dow broke 3,000 just before Saddam Hussein invaded Kuwait in August 1990. The Gulf War and a real estate recession precipitated a second bear market, but this one, like the crash in 1987, was short-lived.

Iraq's defeat in the Gulf War ushered in one of the most fabulous decades in stock market history. The world witnessed the collapse of Communism and a diminished threat of global conflict. The transfer of resources from military expenditures to domestic consumption enabled the United States to experience increased economic growth and low inflation. The interests of Americans turned inward, and the postwar baby

---

[26]*Stocks, Bonds, Bills, and Inflation Yearbooks, 1983–1997* (Chicago: Ibbotson and Associates).
[27]William Baldwin, "The Crazy Things People Say to Rationalize Stock Prices," *Forbes*, April 27, 1992, pp. 140–150.

boomers became preoccupied with career enhancement and retirement security.

The Dow Jones Industrial Average quickly scaled 3,000 in March 1991. After a successful battle against inflation in 1994, the Fed eased interest rates, and the Dow subsequently moved above 4,000 in early 1995. *Business Week,* when the Dow was at 4,300, defended the durability of the bull market against professional skepticism in an article on May 15, 1995, entitled "Dow 5,000? Don't Laugh." The Dow quickly crossed that barrier by November and then reached 6,000 eleven months later.

By late 1995, the persistent rise in stock prices caused many analysts to sound the alarm. Michael Metz of Oppenheimer, Charles Clough of Merrill Lynch, and Byron Wein of Morgan Stanley expressed strong doubts about the underpinnings of the rally. In September 1995, David Shulman, chief equity strategist for Salomon Brothers, wrote an article entitled "Fear and Greed" that compared the current market climate with that of similar stock market peaks in 1929 and 1961. Shulman claimed intellectual support was an important ingredient in sustaining bull markets, noting Edgar Smith's and Irving Fisher's work in the 1920s, the Fisher-Lorie studies in the 1960s, and my *Stocks for the Long Run* in the 1990s. Shulman's own long-term studies, based on dividend growth, reinforced his long-term bearish views on stocks.[28]

By 1996, price-earnings (P-E) ratios on the Standard & Poor's (S&P) 500 Index reached 20, considerably above its average postwar level. More warnings were issued. Roger Lowenstein, a well-known author and financial writer, asserted in the *Wall Street Journal:*

> Investing in stocks has become a national hobby and a national obsession. People may denigrate their government, their schools, their spoiled sports stars. But belief in the market is almost universal. To update Marx, it is the religion of the masses.[29]

Floyd Norris, lead financial writer for the *New York Times,* echoed Lowenstein's comments by penning an article in January 1997 entitled "In the Market We Trust."[30] Henry Kaufman, the Salomon Brothers guru whose pronouncements on the fixed-income market frequently rocked bonds in the 1980s, declared that "the exaggerated financial euphoria is increasingly conspicuous" and cited assurances given by the optimists

---

[28]Three months later, in December 1995, Shulman capitulated to the bullish side, claiming that his long-time emphasis on dividend yields was incorrect.
[29]Roger Lowenstein, "A Common Market: The Public's Zeal to Invest," *Wall Street Journal,* September 9, 1996, p. A1.
[30]Floyd Norris, "In the Market We Trust," *New York Times,* January 12, 1997.

equivalent to Irving Fisher's utterance that stocks had reached a permanently high plateau.[31]

Warnings of the end of the bull market did not just emanate from Wall Street, however. Academicians increasingly were investigating this unprecedented rise in stock values. Robert Shiller of Yale University and John Campbell of Harvard University wrote a scholarly paper showing that the market was significantly overvalued and presented this research to the Board of Governors of the Federal Reserve System in early December 1996.[32]

With the Dow surging past 6,400, Alan Greenspan, chairman of the Federal Reserve, issued a warning in a speech before the annual dinner for the American Enterprise Institute in Washington on December 5, 1996. He asked, "How do we know when irrational exuberance has unduly escalated asset values, which then become subject to unexpected and prolonged contractions as they have in Japan over the past decade? And how do we factor that assessment into monetary policy?"

His words had an electrifying effect, and the phrase *irrational exuberance* became the most celebrated utterance of Greenspan's tenure as Fed chairman. Asian and European markets fell dramatically as his words were flashed across computer monitors, and Wall Street opened dramatically lower. However, investors quickly regained their balance, and stocks closed in New York with only moderate losses.

From there it was onward and upward, with the Dow breaking 7,000 in February 1997 and 8,000 in July. Even *Newsweek*'s cautious cover story, "Married to the Market," depicting a Wall Street wedding between America and a bull, did nothing to quell investor optimism.[33]

The market became an ever-increasing preoccupation of middle- and upper-income Americans. Business books and magazines proliferated, and the all-business cable news stations, particularly CNBC, drew huge audiences. Television sets in bars, airports, and other public places invariably were tuned to an all-business network. Electronic tickers and all-business stations were shown in lunchrooms, bars, and lounges of the major business schools throughout the country. Cruise ships and resorts in

---

[31]Henry Kaufman, "Today's Financial Euphoria Can't Last," *Wall Street Journal,* November 25, 1996, p. A18.

[32]Robert Shiller and John Campbell, "Valuation Ratios and the Long-Run Stock Market Outlook," *Journal of Portfolio Management* 24(Winter 1997):11–26.

[33]*Newsweek*, April 27, 1998. Cover stories about the stock market in major newsweeklies often have been poorly timed. *BusinessWeek*'s cover article, "The Death of Equities," on August 13, 1979, occurred 14 years after the market had peaked and 3 years before the beginning of the greatest bull market in stocks.

some of the world's most isolated locations were sure to carry all-financial stations. Air travelers could view up-to-the-minute Dow and Nasdaq averages flying 35,000 feet above sea level as they were flashed from monitors on phones anchored to the backs of the seats in front of them.

Adding impetus to the already surging market, technology spread not only stock quotations but also financial information faster and further than ever before. Internet service providers such as AOL allowed investors to stay in touch with markets and their portfolios from anywhere in the world. Whether it was from Internet chat rooms, financial Web sites, or e-mail newsletters, investors found access to a plethora of information at their fingertips. CNBC became so popular that major investment houses made sure that all their brokers watched the station on television or their desktop computers so that they could be one step ahead of clients calling in with breaking business news.

THE TECHNOLOGY BOOM

The bull market in stocks appeared impervious to financial and economic shocks. The first wave of the Asian crisis, the causes of which are detailed in Chapter 10, sent the market down a record 554 points on October 27, 1997, and closed trading temporarily. However, this did little to dent investors' enthusiasm for stocks.

The following year, new shocks hit the market. The Russian government defaulted on its bonds, and Long-Term Capital Management, considered the world's premier hedge fund, was entangled in speculative positions measured in the *trillions* of dollars that they could not trade. Markets seized up, and the Fed facilitated a rescue of the fund in order to resuscitate financial markets. These events sent the Dow down almost 2,000 points, but the Fed action and three quick interest-rate cuts sent the market soaring again. On March 29, 1999, the Dow closed above 10,000 and then went on to a record close of 11,722.98 on January 14, 2000.

The real action was not in the Dow stocks, however, but on the Nasdaq. The once sleepy over-the-counter market in unlisted stocks soared to preeminence with the public's fascination with computers, the Internet, mobile communications, and networking firms. Volume on the Nasdaq eclipsed that of the New York Stock Exchange as investors feverishly traded shares in Cisco, Sun Microsystems, Oracle, JDS Uniphase, and other companies that were scarcely in existence a decade earlier. The heated pace of trading centered on Internet stocks, where a dot-com index of 24 online firms soared from 142 in November 1997 to a high of 1,350 on March 10, 2000.

The date March 10, 2000, marked the peak not only of the Nasdaq but also of many Internet and technology stock indexes. When investment in technology unexpectedly slowed, the third and most severe of the post-1982 bear markets took hold. The Nasdaq Index subsequently fell by 70 percent, and Internet stocks lost all their spectacular gain in the next 12 months. The feverish interest in the market began to fade. The number of investment clubs, which had reached 35,000 by year 2000, declined, as did the audience for financial news networks such as CNBC.[34]

LEGACY OF THE BULL MARKET

Despite the turmoil in the technology sector and the sharp slowdown in economic growth, most investors claim to retain their faith in stocks as the best long-term investments. The mantra of the common investor in the 1990s was "Buy the dips." This behavior was motivated by experience that showed that market sell-offs were indeed ideal times for investors to commit more to the market. Small investors, as indicated by mutual fund flows, were more steadfast in their faith in equities during the 1990s than many professional investors.

However, perhaps the most lasting legacy of the 1990s was the near unanimity of ordinary investors that stocks were the best long-run investment. Even the crash of technology stocks did little to dent investor enthusiasm. Data collected by Robert Shiller of Yale University confirmed that despite the market decline in 2001, 91 percent of investors believed that stocks were the best long-term investment. This is hardly different from the 97 percent that Shiller found during the bull market of 1999–2000.[35]

Despite the steadfast faith in the market, the bear market of 2000–2001 has raised doubts in many minds about the desirability of holding the overwhelming proportion of a portfolio in stocks. Has the continued popularity of the stock market planted the seeds of its own destruction? Have investors sent equity prices so high that they cannot in the future possibly match their superior historical returns? The answer to these questions must come from an understanding of how stock prices influence their future returns. This is the topic of our next chapter.

---

[34] As one bar owner colorfully put it, "People are licking their wounds, and they don't want to talk about stocks anymore. It's back to sports, women, and who won the game." Paul Sloan, "The Craze Collapses," *US News and World Report Online*, November 30, 2000.

[35] Data collected by the Yale School of Management under the direction of Robert Shiller.

PART

2

VALUATION, FUTURE STOCK RETURNS, AND STYLE INVESTING

SOURCES AND MEASURES OF STOCK MARKET VALUE

Even when the underlying motive of purchase [of common stocks] is mere speculative greed, human nature desires to conceal this unlovely impulse behind a screen of apparent logic and good sense.

BENJAMIN GRAHAM AND DAVID DODD, 1940[1]

AN EVIL OMEN RETURNS

In the summer of 1958, an event of great significance took place for those who followed long-standing indicators of stock market value. For the first time in history, the interest rate on long-term government bonds exceeded the dividend yield on common stocks.

BusinessWeek noted this event in an August 1958 article entitled "An Evil Omen Returns," warning investors that when yields on stocks approached those on bonds, a major market decline was in the offing.[2] The stock market crash of 1929 occurred in a year when stock dividend yields fell to the level of bond yields. The stock crashes of 1907 and 1891

---

[1]"The Theory of Common-Stock Investment," *Security Analysis*, 2d ed. (New York: McGraw-Hill, 1940), p. 343.
[2]*BusinessWeek*, August 9, 1958, p. 81.

also followed episodes when the yield on bonds came within 1 percent of the dividend yield on stocks.

As Figure 6-1 indicates, prior to 1958, the yearly dividend yield on stocks had always been higher than long-term interest rates, and most analysts thought that this was the way it was supposed to be. Stocks were riskier than bonds and therefore should command a higher yield in the market. Under this reasoning, whenever stock prices went too high and brought dividend yields down to that of bonds, it was time to sell.

However, things did not work this way in 1958. Stocks returned over 30 percent in the 12 months after dividend yields fell below bond yields and continued to soar into the early 1960s. There were good economic reasons why this famous benchmark fell by the wayside. Inflation increased the yield on bonds to compensate lenders for rising prices,

FIGURE 6–1

Dividend and Nominal Bond Yields, 1871–2001

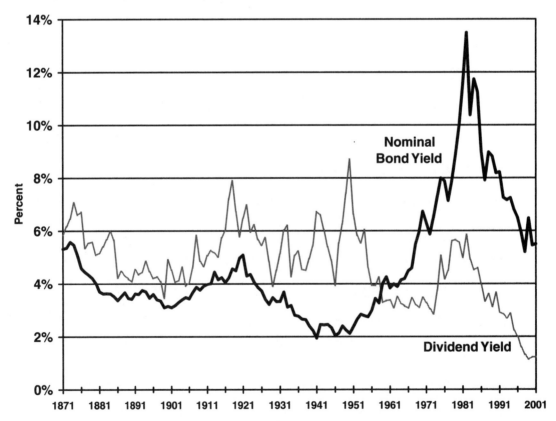

whereas investors regarded stocks as the best investment to protect against the eroding value of money. As early as September 1958, *BusinessWeek* noted that "the relationship between stock and bond yields was clearly posting a warning signal, but investors still believe inflation is inevitable and stocks are the only hedge against it."[3]

Yet many on Wall Street were still puzzled by the "great yield reversal." Nicholas Molodovsky, vice president of White, Weld & Co. and editor of the *Financial Analysts Journal*, observed:

> Some financial analysts called . . . [the reversal of bond and stock yields] a financial revolution brought about by many complex causes. Others, on the contrary, made no attempt to explain the unexplainable. They showed readiness to accept it as a manifestation of providence in the financial universe.[4]

Imagine value-oriented investors who pulled all their money out of the stock market in August of 1958 and put it into bonds, vowing never to buy stocks again unless dividend yields rose above those on high-quality bonds. Such investors would still be waiting to get back into stocks. After 1958, stock dividend yields never again exceeded those of bonds. Yet, from August 1958 onward, overall stock returns overwhelmed the returns on fixed-income securities over any long-term period.

Benchmarks for valuation are valid only as long as economic institutions do not change. The chronic postwar inflation, resulting from the switch to a paper money standard, changed forever the way investors judged the yields on stocks and bonds. Investors who clung to the old ways of valuing equity never participated in the greatest bull market for stocks in history.

VALUATION OF CASH FLOWS FROM STOCKS

The fundamental sources of stock valuation are the dividends and earnings of firms. In contrast to a work of art—which can be bought both for an investment and for its viewing pleasure—stocks have value only because of the potential cash flows that investors receive. These cash flows can come from any distribution (such as dividends or capital gains realized on sale) that stockholders expect to receive from their share of ownership of the firm, and it is by forecasting and valuing

---

[3]"In the Markets," *BusinessWeek*, September 13, 1958, p. 91.
[4]"The Many Aspects of Yields," *Financial Analysts Journal* 18(2)(March–April 1962):49–62.

these expected future cash flows that one can judge the investment value of shares.[5]

The value of any asset is determined by the discounted value of all expected future cash flows. Future cash flows from assets are *discounted* because cash received in the future is not worth as much as cash received in the present. The reasons for discounting are (1) the innate *time preferences* of most individuals to enjoy their consumption today rather than wait for tomorrow, (2) *productivity*, which allows funds invested today to yield a higher return tomorrow, and (3) *inflation*, which reduces the future purchasing power of cash received in the future. These factors also apply to both stocks and bonds and are the foundation of the theory of interest rates. A fourth reason, which applies primarily to the cash flows from equities, is the *uncertainty* associated with the magnitude of future cash flows.

SOURCES OF SHAREHOLDER VALUE

For the equity holder, the source of future cash flows is the earnings of firms. Earnings are the cash flows that remain after the costs of production are subtracted from the sales revenues of the firm. The costs of production include labor and material costs, interest on debt, corporate taxes, and allowance for depreciation.

Earnings create value for shareholders by the:

- Payment of cash dividends
- Repurchase of shares
- Retirement of debt
- Investment in securities, capital projects, or other firms

If a firm repurchases its shares (known as *buybacks*), it reduces the number of shares outstanding and thus increases future *per-share* earnings. If a firm retires its debt, it reduces its interest expense and therefore increases the cash flow available to shareholders. Finally, earnings that are not used for dividends, share repurchases, or debt retirement are referred to as *retained earnings*. Retained earnings may increase future cash flows to shareholders if they are invested productively in securities, capital projects, or other firms.

---

[5] There might be some psychic value to holding a controlling interest above and beyond the returns accrued. In such a case, the owner values the stock more than minority shareholders.

Some people argue that shareholders most value stocks' cash dividends. But this is not necessarily true. In fact, from a tax standpoint, share repurchases are superior to dividends. Cash dividends are taxed at the highest marginal tax rate to the investor; share repurchases, however, generate capital gains that can be realized at the shareholder's discretion and at a lower capital gains tax rate. Recently, there have been an increasing number of firms who engage in share repurchases. As will be discussed in the next chapter, the shift from dividends to share repurchases is one factor that has raised the valuation of some equities.

Others might argue that debt repayment lowers shareholder value because the interest saved on the debt retired generally is less than the rate of return earned on equity capital. They also might claim that by retiring debt, they lose the ability to deduct the interest paid as an expense (the interest tax shield).[6] However, debt entails a fixed commitment that must be met in good or bad times and, as such, increases the volatility of earnings that go to the shareholder. Reducing debt therefore lowers the volatility of future earnings and may not diminish shareholder value.[7]

Many investors claim that the fourth factor, the reinvestment of earnings, is the most important source of value, but this is not always the case. If retained earnings are reinvested profitably, value surely will be created. However, retained earnings may tempt managers to pursue other goals, such as overbidding to acquire other firms or spending on perquisites that do not increase the value to shareholders. Therefore, the market often views the buildup of cash reserves and marketable securities with suspicion and frequently discounts their value.

If the fear of misusing retained earnings is particularly strong, it is possible that the market will value the firm at less than the value of its reserves. Great investors, such as Benjamin Graham, made some of their most profitable trades by purchasing shares in such companies and then convincing management (sometimes tactfully, sometimes with a threat of takeover) to disgorge their liquid assets.[8]

---

[6]Whether debt is a valuable tax shield depends on whether interest rates are bid up enough to offset that shield. See Merton H. Miller, "Debt and Taxes," Papers and Proceedings of the Thirty-Fifth Annual Meeting of the American Finance Association, Atlantic City, NJ, September 16–18, 1977, *The Journal of Finance* 32(2)(May, 1977):261–275.

[7]Meeting interest payments also may be a good discipline for management and reduce the tendency to waste excess profits. See Michael Jensen, "The Takeover Controversy: Analysis and Evidence." In John Coffee, Louis Lowenstein, and Susan Rose-Ackerman (eds.), *Takeovers and Contests for Corporate Control* (New York: Oxford University Press, 1987).

[8]Benjamin Graham, *The Memoirs of the Dean of Wall Street* (New York: McGraw-Hill, 1946), Chap. 11.

One might question why management would not employ assets in a way to maximize shareholder value, since managers often hold a large equity stake in the firm. The reason is that there may exist a conflict between the goal of the shareholders, which is solely to increase the return on the company's shares, and the goals of management, which may include prestige, control of markets, and other objectives. Economists recognize the conflict between the goals of managers and shareholders as *agency costs*, and these costs are inherent in every corporate structure where ownership is separated from management. Payment of cash dividends or committed share repurchases often lowers management's temptation to pursue goals that do not maximize shareholder value.

In recent years dividend yields have fallen to 1½ percent, less than one-third of their historic average. The major reasons for this are the tax disadvantage of dividends and the increase in employee stock options, where capital gains and not dividends figure into option value. Nevertheless, dividends historically have served the function of showing investors that the firms' earnings were indeed real. Recent concerns about aggressive accounting policies and the integrity of earnings following the Enron debacle may bring back this once-favored way of delivering investor value.[9]

DOES THE VALUE OF STOCKS DEPEND ON DIVIDENDS OR EARNINGS?

Management determines its dividend policy—the fraction of earnings it will pay out to shareholders—by evaluating many factors, including the tax differences between dividend income and capital gains, the need to generate internal funds to retire debt or invest, and the desire to keep dividends relatively constant in the face of fluctuating earnings. Since the price of a stock depends primarily on the present discounted value of all expected future dividends, it appears that dividend policy is crucial to determining the value of the stock.

However, this is not generally true. It does not matter how much is paid as dividends and how much is reinvested *as long as* the firm earns the same return on its retained earnings that shareholders demand on its stock.[10] The reason for this is that dividends not paid today are reinvested by the firm and paid as even larger dividends in the future.

---

[9]Jeremy J. Siegel, "The Dividend Deficit," *Wall Street Journal*, February 13, 2002, p. A20.
[10]This ignores differential taxation between capital gains and dividend income that favors reinvestment. This is explored in Chapter 4.

Of course, management's choice of dividend payout ratio, which is the ratio of cash dividends to total earnings, does influence the timing of the dividend payments. The lower the dividend payout ratio, the smaller the dividends will be in the near future. Over time, however, dividends will rise and eventually will exceed the dividend path associated with a higher payout ratio. Moreover, assuming that the firm earns the same return on investment as the investors require from its equity, the present value of these dividend streams will be identical no matter what payout ratio is chosen.

Note that the price of the stock is always equal to the present value of all future *dividends* and not the present value of future earnings. Earnings not paid to investors can have value only if they are paid as dividends or other cash disbursements at a later date. Valuing stock as the present discounted value of future earnings is manifestly wrong and greatly overstates the value of a firm.[11]

John Burr Williams, one of the greatest investment analysts of the early part of last century and author of the classic *The Theory of Investment Value*, argued this point persuasively in 1938. He wrote:

> Most people will object at once to the foregoing formula for valuing stocks by saying that it should use the present worth of future earnings, not future dividends. But should not earnings and dividends both give the same answer under the implicit assumptions of our critics? If earnings not paid out in dividends are all successfully reinvested at compound interest for the benefit of the stockholder, as the critics imply, then these earnings should produce dividends later; if not, then they are money lost. Earnings are only a means to an end, and the means should not be mistaken for the end.[12]

LONG-TERM EARNINGS GROWTH AND ECONOMIC GROWTH

Since stock prices are the present value of future dividends, it would seem natural to assume that economic growth would be an important factor influencing future dividends and hence stock prices. However, this is not necessarily so. The determinants of stock prices are earnings and dividends on a *per-share* basis. Although economic growth may influence *aggregate* earnings and dividends favorably, economic growth does not necessarily increase the growth of per-share earnings or dividends. It is earnings per share (EPS) that is important to Wall Street be-

---

[11]Firms that pay no dividends, such as Warren Buffett's Berkshire Hathaway, have value because their assets, which earn cash returns, can be liquidated and disbursed to shareholders in the future.
[12]John Burr Williams, *The Theory of Investment Value* (Cambridge, MA: Harvard University Press, 1938), p. 30.

cause per-share data, not aggregate earnings or dividends, are the basis of investor returns.

The reason that economic growth does not necessarily increase EPS is because economic growth requires increased capital expenditures and this capital does not come freely. Implementing and upgrading technology requires substantial firm investment. These expenditures must be funded either by borrowing in the debt market (through banks or trade credit or by selling bonds) or by floating new shares. The added interest costs and the dilution of profits that this funding involves place a burden on the firm's bottom line.

Can earnings increase without increasing capital expenditures? In the short run, this may occur, but the long-run historical evidence suggests that it will not. One of the signal characteristics of long-term historical data is that the level of the capital stock—the total value of all physical capital such as factories and equipment, as well as intellectual capital, that has accumulated over time—has grown in proportion to the level of aggregate output. In other words, a 10 percent increase in output requires a 10 percent increase in the capital stock.

Many investors believe that investment in productivity-enhancing technology can spur earnings growth to permanently higher levels. However, "cost-saving investments," frequently touted as a source of increasing profit margins, only temporarily affect bottom-line earnings. As long as these investments are available to other firms, competition will force management to reduce product prices by the amount of the cost savings, and extra profits will quickly be competed away. In fact, capital expenditures often are undertaken not necessarily to *enhance* profits but rather to *preserve* profits when other firms have adopted competitive cost-saving measures.

Table 6-1 shows the summary statistics for dividends per share, earnings per share (EPS), and stock returns from 1871 through Septem-

TABLE 6–1

Long-Term Growth of GDP, Earnings, and Dividends, 1871–2001

	Real GDP Growth	Real Per-Share Earnings Growth	Real Per-Share Dividend Growth	Dividend Yield*	Payout Ratio*
1871-2001	3.91%	1.25%	1.09%	4.54%	58.75%
1871-1945	4.51%	0.66%	0.74%	5.07%	66.78%
1946-2001	3.11%	2.05%	1.56%	3.53%	51.91%

* Denotes median.

ber 2001. The data show that real per-share earnings growth over the entire 130 years has been a paltry 1.25 percent, considerably below the nearly 4 percent growth rate of real gross domestic product (GDP). Because of the funding requirement, EPS growth does not match aggregate economic growth over the long run.

The data also show that the acceleration of earnings growth since World War II is associated with the drop in the dividend yield. Greater retained earnings allow firms to buy back shares and reinvest for growth. John Williams' contention that dividends withheld today spur earnings growth in the future is strongly supported by the data.

HISTORICAL YARDSTICKS FOR VALUING THE MARKET

Many yardsticks have been used to evaluate whether stock prices are overvalued or undervalued. Most of these measure the market value of the shares outstanding relative to economic *fundamentals* such as earnings, dividends, book value, or some economic aggregate, such as GDP or total replacement cost of the capital stock. Stock prices often are said to be "too high" if they exceed the average value over time.

Yet such a comparison begs the question: Have the historical valuation measures been consistent with the return shareholders should expect from equities? As indicated in Chapters 2 and 3, there is strong evidence that stocks have provided investors excessive returns based on their long-term risk-return profile, suggesting that, on average, they have been undervalued throughout history. Therefore, higher valuations could be justified as investors recognize the superior returns on stocks and bid their prices up relative to earnings or dividends.

The Price-to-Earnings Ratio

The most basic and fundamental yardstick for valuing stocks is the *price-earnings (P-E) ratio.* The P-E ratio is simply the ratio of the price of a share of stock to the annual EPS and measures how much an investor is willing to pay for a dollar's worth of current earnings.

The single most important variable determining the P-E ratio of an individual stock is the expectation of future earnings growth. If investors believe that earnings growth is going to accelerate, they will pay a higher price relative to current earnings than if they expect earnings to stagnate or decline. However, earnings growth is not the only variable influencing the P-E ratio. P-E ratios are also influenced by other factors, such as interest rates, risk attitudes of investors, taxes, and liquidity, among others.

The P-E ratio of the entire market is determined by dividing the total market value of all stocks by the aggregate earnings of all stocks. This market P-E ratio, which is shown in Figure 6-2, moved into all-time high ground in the year 2001, reaching a level more than twice its historical average value of 14.5 calculated since 1870.[13]

However, peaks in the P-E ratio are not always bad omens for investors. If a sharp drop in earnings causes the P-E ratio to spike upward, such as occurred in the 1894, 1921, 1938, and 1990–1991 recessions, real returns following these spikes have averaged a robust 9.7 percent annually over the subsequent 5 years. These returns are high because sharp

---

[13] The earnings are taken to be the last 12 months of reported earnings on the Standard & Poor's (S&P) 500 Stock Index or a like group of stocks.

FIGURE 6–2

Historical P-E Ratios Based on Last 12 Months Reported Earnings, 1871–2001

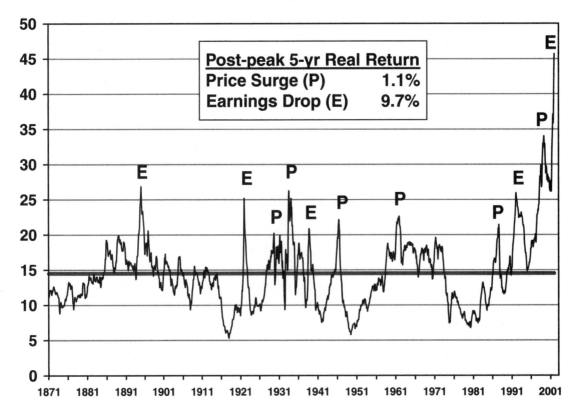

declines in earnings always have been temporary, caused by recessions or other special circumstances, and earnings as well as stock prices have rebounded subsequently. Nevertheless, the P-E ratio associated with the 2000–2001 recession is so high that investors should not expect above-average returns to prevail.

When surges in stock prices cause P-E ratios to rise, as occurred in September 1929, July 1933, June 1946, November 1961, and August 1987, 5-year future real returns have averaged only 1.1 percent. Surging stock prices often reflect undue optimism about future earnings growth. When faster earnings growth is not realized, stock prices fall, and returns suffer. Certainly the P-E spike that occurred in late 1999 and early 2000 accurately foretold poor future returns.

The P-E Ratio and Future Stock Returns

Although the P-E ratio can be a very misleading indicator of future stock returns in the short run, in the long run, the P-E ratio is a very useful predictor. The reasons may be understood by analyzing how stock and bond returns are calculated.

The *current yield* of a bond is measured as the ratio of the interest received over the price paid and is a good measure of future return if the bond is not selling at a large premium or discount to its maturity value. A similar computation can be made for stocks by computing the *earnings yield*, which is the EPS divided by the price. The earnings yield is the inverse of the P-E ratio.

Since the underlying assets of a firm are real, the earnings yield is a *real*, or inflation-adjusted, return. Over time, inflation will raise the cash flows from the underlying assets, and the assets themselves will appreciate in value. This contrasts with the *nominal* return earned from fixed-income assets, where all the coupons and the final payment are fixed in money terms and do not rise with inflation.

The long-run data bear out the contention that the earnings yield is a good long-run estimate of real stock returns. Figure 6-2 shows that the average P-E ratio of the market over the past 130 years has been 14.45, so the average earnings yield on stocks has been 1/14.45, or 6.8 percent. This earnings yield exactly matches the 6.8 percent real return on equities from 1871 taken from Table 1-1.

As noted earlier, there are limitations to using the P-E ratio to predict future short-term stock returns. For example, future returns will be higher than predicted by the earnings yield if the economy is emerging from a recession. And in the short run, there are many other sources of market movement, such as changes in interest rates or the risk premium demanded by stockholders.

EARNINGS DEFINITIONS AND CONTROVERSY

Reported and Operating Earnings

Although computation of the P-E ratio appears straightforward, it is not. The "earnings" that appears in the denominator of this well-known ratio are not a well-defined concept, and depending on whom you ask, you may get different definitions and standards for the measurement of earnings.

The earnings used in Figure 6-2 are determined by "generally accepted accounting principles" (GAAP) and are formulated by the Financial Accounting Standards Board (FASB), a private, nongovernmental organization created by the Securities and Exchange Commission (SEC) in 1973 to govern standards used in financial reports. The SEC officially recognizes these standards as authoritative. The earnings calculated with these standards, referred to as *reported earnings*, are released to shareholders on a quarterly basis.

However, the FASB also allows firms to flag unusual or extraordinary expenses and revenues when reporting earnings. Consideration of these extraordinary items is important for investors to determine the ongoing earnings that firms are capable of delivering. Since the value of a stock depends on projecting earnings into the far future, it is of prime interest for stockholders to judge those components of the earnings stream which are permanent and those which are temporary. For example, if the P-E ratio of a stock is 20, then a permanent change in earnings will have 20 times the impact on the stock price. However, if a change in earnings is considered to occur only once because of extraordinary circumstances and long-term earnings and cash flow expectations remain unchanged, the stock price should not be affected significantly.

Firms often use the term *operating earnings* to represent their ongoing revenues and expenses adjusted for any one-time occurrences that may distort the normal reported earnings. Unfortunately, the term *operating earnings* is not defined by GAAP, and without any established standards, firms have complete discretion over what revenues and expenses they consider extraordinary in their calculation of operating earnings. Firms often exclude restructuring charges, investment gains and losses, inventory write-offs, expenses associated with mergers and spin-offs, depreciation of goodwill, and many other items to arrive at a number that, in their judgment, represents the ongoing or operating earnings of the firm.

Before 1989, firms rarely excluded special items from reported earnings. From 1970 to 1990, reported earnings were only 2 percent lower than operating earnings. However, the 1990–1991 recession marked a turning point. Many firms engaged in major restructurings and discontinued unprofitable operations, writing off a significant fraction of fixed assets and the corresponding expenses involved with such restructuring programs.

These charges caused a very large drop in reported earnings, but Wall Street greeted these write-offs enthusiastically. Investors reasoned that firms finally acknowledged losing divisions, and this was very positive for the company going forward. Investors' favorable reactions encouraged firms to continue the practice of writing off restructuring and other charges that they deemed one-time expenses. Since 1991, the average difference between operating and reported earnings has been 12 percent, six times higher than previously. The difference was especially large during the 1990–1991 and 2001–2002 recessions.

The debate about the proper earnings measure by which to judge the value of a firm does not end with the firm's choice of what to include or exclude in operating earnings. The use of options to compensate workers, very common in technology firms, generally results in an undercounting of employee expenses and an overreporting of net income. It is true that technology firms generally expense all research and development costs, and there is a good argument that some of these costs should be capitalized and written off over time. However, an exhaustive Merrill Lynch study of the technology industry done in 2000 concluded that, on the whole, industry profits were overstated by about 25 percent using the common procedures to report income.[14]

Aggregate Earnings Estimates

When Wall Street estimates future earnings, it invariably estimates operating earnings because analysts cannot predict when a firm will take special charges. When estimating earnings for a large group of stocks, such as the Standard & Poor's (S&P) 500 Index, two different methods are employed. The first is simply to add up the individual estimates of the firms in the index. This is referred to as the *bottom-up earnings esti-*

---

[14]Gary Scheineman, Steven Milunovich, and Lisa Liu, "Quality of Technology Earnings," Merrill Lynch & Company Global Securities Research and Economics Group, June 19, 2001.

mate. The second method of estimating aggregate earnings, called the *top-down estimate,* is formulated by economists who forecast such macro-economic variables as GDP, unemployment, and interest rates and fit these forecasts to past trends in aggregate earnings. These two estimates can differ significantly.

The bottom-up estimates derived from individual analysts' fore-casts are almost always too high. This may be so because analysts rely heavily on management's assessment of future profitability and such estimates often are overly optimistic. In January 2002, the top-down estimate for aggregate S&P 500 earnings for the upcoming year was more than 20 percent above the bottom-up estimate.

Unless the economy is in a period of unusually high earnings growth, the bottom-up earnings estimate is usually reduced over time. The top-down estimate is frequently more realistic, but this estimate may miss new cost-saving and productivity-enhancing measures that firms are taking that are not observable in the past data. Investors should use each estimate to frame a range of future aggregate earnings, realizing that unforeseen events such as occurred in 2001 often cause earnings estimates to miss by a wide margin.

Earnings Quality and Returns

With creative earnings management becoming more prevalent, one must look ever more closely at earnings quality. There is evidence that firms with high earnings quality have better returns than firms with low earnings quality. One way to measure the quality of earnings is by examining a firm's *accruals,* which are defined as the difference in accounting earnings and cash flows. A firm with high accruals could be one that is manipulating its earnings, and this could be a warning sign of bad times to come. Alternatively, a firm that has low accruals and shows no signs of earnings manipulation could be signaling continued strength and prosperity.[15]

BOOK VALUE, MARKET VALUE, AND TOBIN'S Q

The *book value* of a firm is the value of a firm's assets minus its liabilities, evaluated at historical costs. However, the use of aggregate book value as a measure of the overall value of a firm is severely limited because book value uses *historical* prices and thus ignores the effect of changing

---

[15] K. Chan et al., "Earnings Quality and Stock Returns," NBER Working Paper No. 8308, May 2001.

prices on the value of the assets or liabilities. If a firm purchased a plot of land for $1 million that is now worth $10 million, examining the book value will not reveal this. Over time, the historical value of assets becomes less reliable as a measure of current market value.

To help correct these distortions, James Tobin, a professor at Yale University and a Nobel laureate, adjusted the book value for inflation and computed the "replacement cost" of the assets and liabilities on the balance sheet.[16] He developed a theory that indicated that the "equilibrium" or "correct" market price of a firm should equal its assets minus liabilities adjusted for inflation. If the aggregate market value of a firm exceeds the cost of capital, it would be profitable to create more capital, sell shares to finance it, and reap a profit. If the market value falls below the replacement cost, then it would be better for a firm to dismantle and sell its capital or stop investment and cut production.

Tobin designated the ratio of the market value to the replacement cost with the letter Q and indicated that its ratio should be unity if the stock market were valued properly. The historical values of *Tobin's Q*, as the theory has become known, are shown in Figure 6-3a. The ratio has fluctuated between a high of 1.83 in 1999 and a low of 0.33 in 1920, with the average being 0.72.

In 1999, Andrew Smithers and Stephen Wright of the United Kingdom published a book, *Valuing Wall Street*,[17] that maintained that Tobin's Q was the best measure of value and that the U.S. market (as well as the U.K. and many other European markets) was extremely overvalued by this criterion. There are some who maintain that Q generally should be less than unity because older capital is not as productive as newly installed capital.[18] If this is true, then the market was even more overvalued in the late 1990s.

However, there are critics of the Q theory. Capital equipment and structures lack a good secondary market, and hence there is no realistic way to value much of the physical capital stock. The inability to value intellectual capital is perhaps a more significant drawback. Microsoft has a book value of about $50 billion but a market value seven times as large. In fact, the value of most technology firms is composed of their intellectual capital.

---

[16]"A General Equilibrium Approach to Monetary Theory," *Journal of Money, Credit, and Banking* 1(February 1969):15–29.

[17]Andrew Smithers and Stephen Wright, *Valuing Wall Street* (New York: McGraw-Hill, 2000).

[18]This is also because in equilibrium the marginal productivity of capital should be equated with the cost of new capital, whereas the stock market measures the average productivity of both old and new capital.

FIGURE 6–3

Market Value, Replacement Cost, and GDP

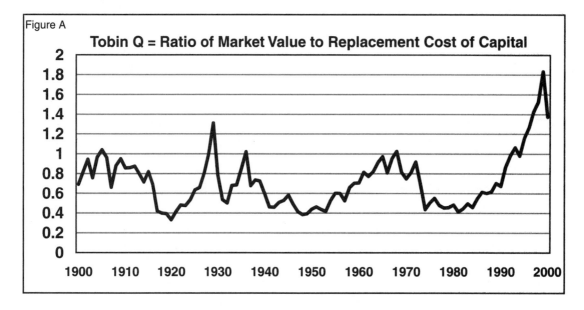

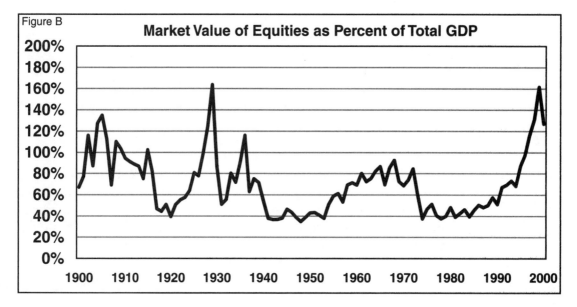

Smithers maintains that the existence of intellectual capital should not be used to justify any gap between book and market value. Although firms may own trademarks and patents, they do not own the entrepreneurs, engineers, or other employees who generate ideas. As long as there is a competitive labor market, human factors of production must be paid their market value, just as physical capital. The stock options lavished on employees during the technology boom of the late 1990s to keep key personnel from being bid away by other firms are an example of this.

This point is well taken, but some firms are more successful than others at creating and maintaining productive groups of talented individuals. Often employees can create more firm value by working together than they can by working separately, and other firms may not be able to create the same creative environment. The ability of the United States to draw talent from the rest of the world may create shareholder value in excess of the cost of hiring these workers.[19]

It may be that in the very long run the market value of the tangible and intangible capital must equal the cost of reproducing it. However, book value is a construct of the past; market value derives from prospective earnings and looks to the future. These prospective earnings more accurately establish the basis of stock valuation than the historical costs at which the firms purchased these assets.

MARKET VALUE RELATIVE TO GDP

GDP is a more familiar benchmark to compare with aggregate market value of equity than is book value. GDP, despite its shortcomings, is universally regarded as the best measure of the overall output in the economy. It would be reasonable to assume that the market valuations of firms should bear some relation to that output. Figure 6-3*b* shows the ratio of the market value of stocks to GDP since 1900.

The ratio of the market value of equity to GDP can both theoretically and empirically exceed 1. Equity valuation is a balance-sheet item, whereas GDP is an annual flow. Many firms have capital that far exceeds their annual sales, so it is not at all unusual for the value of an economy's capital to be greater than its output.

More important, however, equity capital is only a part of total capital. Both debt and equity finance the capital stock, and the ratio between them changes over time. In the 1990s, as interest rates fell, many firms re-

---

[19]Of course, one can reply that for every firm that creates a more productive environment, there is one that creates an unsuccessful one and ends up overpaying and wasting intellectual resources.

TABLE 6–2

Summary Market Statistics for Various Countries (Market Value/GDP, P-E Ratio, Dividend Yield, December 2001)

Statistic	U.S.	Japan	Germany	Britain	Hong Kong	Switzerland	Italy
MV/GDP*	117%	68%	82%	185%	382%	366%	70%
P-E**	29.9	64.4	52.2	33.3	15.1	16.2	17.1
Div. Yld.**	1.81%	0.84%	3.14%	2.91%	2.81%	1.27%	2.08%

* Data for Market Value/GDP for December 31, 2000.
**P-E and Dividend Yield based on last 12 months of earnings and dividends.

tired high-coupon bonds and reduced their leverage, a process called *deleveraging*. Deleveraging increases the value of equity and decreases the value of debt but leaves the total value of the firm unchanged. As the market has risen, more firms have become public companies. This will increase the market value of stocks even if the total value of firms, public and private, remains unchanged.

Moreover, the ratio of market capitalization to GDP differs widely among countries. Multinational firms may be headquartered in a particular country, but their sales span the globe. As international trade increases, it should not be surprising if market value shows less and less relation to the GDP of any one country. Table 6-2 shows that the market value of shares traded in Hong Kong are almost 400 percent of its GDP, whereas in Italy and Japan the ratio is only about 70 percent. Yet Hong Kong had the lowest average P-E ratio and the third highest dividend yield of these seven countries. The variation between countries results from large differences in the leverage and the fraction of firms that are traded publicly.[20]

THE FED MODEL OF MARKET VALUATION

In early 1997, in response to increasing concern by Federal Reserve Chairman Alan Greenspan about the impact of the rising stock market on the economy, three researchers from the Federal Reserve (Fed) produced a paper entitled "Earnings Forecasts and the Predictability of

---

[20] One ratio that has very little meaning is the ratio of a stock index such as the S&P 500 Index or the Dow Jones Industrials to GDP or, for that matter, to any economy-wide variable. Stock indexes report the average prices of individual shares of common stock, not the value of such stock. Over time, the number of shares can rise or fall depending on the dividend and buyback policies of firms.

Stock Returns: Evidence from Trading the S&P."[21] This paper documented the remarkable correspondence between the earnings yield on stocks and the 30-year government bond rate. The *earnings yield* on stocks was defined as an estimate of the current operating earnings of the S&P 500 Index (as reported by I/B/E/S, a service that collects and processes analysts' estimates of earnings) divided by the value of the S&P 500 Index. The earnings yield (which is the inverse of the well-known P-E ratio) is the current return that a corporation earns on a dollar invested in its stock.

Greenspan's testimony in his semiannual address to Congress that year suggested that the central bank regarded the stock market as overvalued whenever this earnings yield fell below the bond rate and undervalued whenever the reverse occurred. Greenspan's analysis showed that the market was most overvalued in August 1987, just before the record October 1987 stock market crash, and most undervalued in the early 1980s, when the great bull market began.

The basic idea behind this Fed model is that bonds are the chief alternative for stocks in investors' portfolios. The return on a bond can be termed the *interest yield*. The return on stock is termed the *earnings yield*. When the interest yield rises above the earnings yield, stock prices fall because investors shift their portfolio from stocks to bonds. On the other hand, when the interest yield falls below the stock yield, investors move into stocks, boosting their prices.

Institutions have been using the relation between interest yields and stock yields to determine their asset allocations for many years. What is unique about the Fed model is that it directly compares these two yields rather than just noting a correlation between them. As Figure 6-4 shows, the Fed model appears to have worked fairly well since 1970. When interest rates fell, stocks rallied to bring the earnings yield down, and the opposite occurred when interest rates rose.

What is surprising is that this relation holds despite the fact that stocks and bonds are very different assets. Bonds, especially government bonds, have ironclad guarantees to pay a specified number of dollars over time. However, stocks have the advantage of being real assets, assets that will rise over time with the price level. The reason why the Fed model works is that the market rates these two advantages as approximately of equal value when inflation is an important factor.

---

[21] Joel Lander, Athanasios Orphanides, and Martha Douvogiannis, "Earnings Forecasts and the Predictability of Stock Returns: Evidence from Trading the S&P," Federal Reserve, January 1997. It refers to an earlier version that was presented in October 1996.

FIGURE 6–4

Fed Model of Stock Market Valuation (1926–2001)

There is no question that both bonds and stocks do badly when inflation increases. Bond prices fell in the late 1960s and 1970s because rising inflation forced interest rates up to offset the depreciating value of money. Stocks fell during that period for many reasons. Inflation was accompanied by an increase in energy costs, poor productivity growth, and poor monetary policy. All these factors depressed stock prices. In addition, the U.S. tax code does not index depreciation of firms' assets or investors' capital gains to inflation. Therefore, inflation depresses corporate profits and real stock returns. Finally, inflation increases uncertainty and raises the threat of central bank tightening of money policy to halt rising consumer prices. This is also negative for stocks.[22]

Paul Volcker, chairman of the Fed before Greenspan, set the stage for interest rates to fall as he slammed on the monetary breaks in 1979 and subsequently broke inflation. Falling interest rates boosted both stock and bond prices as economic growth increased. Thus the 1980s and 1990s were good decades for both stocks and bonds as inflation declined from its record high levels.

However, both history and theory suggest that the Fed model breaks down when inflation is very low or when consumer prices are stagnant and deflation threatens. In such circumstances, bonds (especially risk-free government bonds) will do very well, but stocks returns will be ambiguous. Figure 6-4 shows that before inflation became a major concern, there was absolutely no relation between the interest yield on bonds and the earnings yield on stocks.

Given that interest rates and inflation have now shrunk to their lowest levels in four decades, stock investors should be wary of using the Fed model. Stocks still will welcome any Fed reduction in interest rates, but declines in long-term government bond rates often signal strong deflationary or recessionary forces. It will be harder under these circumstances for firms to raise their output prices to cover costs. Deflation undermines firms' pricing power, and this cuts into profit margins. Moreover, because it is extremely difficult for firms to negotiate nominal wage cuts, deflation increases real wage costs and reduces profits. Thus nominal assets such as bonds will shine under deflation, whereas real assets often suffer.

Unless inflation heads upward again, it is unlikely that the tight correlation experienced over the past two decades between these two yields will continue. In a low-inflation world, pricing power and earnings potential will dominate stock valuations, whereas bonds will be valued for their ability to hedge deflationary risk. Rising and falling interest rates still will be very important determinants of stock prices in the very short run (see Chapter 14), but long-run patterns are apt to diverge as investors recognize the fundamental differences in the assets.

WHAT DO THESE VALUATION MEASURES SHOW?

Despite the controversies among academics and practitioners about which of the preceding measures is better for valuing the market, the

---

[22]Chapter 11 discusses why stocks are pure short-term hedges against inflation.

truth is that with the exception of the Fed model, they tell a similar story. Figure 6-5 shows four measures of valuation of the U.S. stock market: (1) Tobin's Q, (2) the market-value-to-GDP ratio, (3) stock prices divided by smoothed earnings, and (4) a simple measure of the market's deviation from a long-term trend line.

I have shown that the P-E ratio is a better predictor of returns when one excludes episodes of earnings volatility and concentrates on longer-run earnings trends. Calculating the P-E ratio from a 5-year average period of earnings is one way to improve the valuation measure. The market's deviation from a long-term trend line, which closely matches the other three, illustrates that bull and bear markets drive all these measures. Fundamentals move very slowly in comparison with stock prices, and so a simple measure of price deviation from a long-term trend captures virtually all the movements of these valuation series.

FIGURE 6–5

Measures of Market Valuation

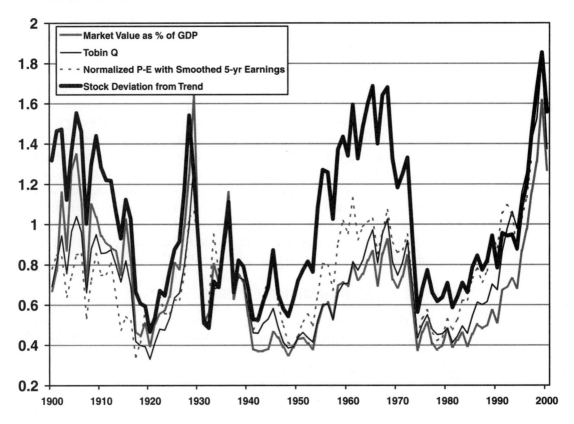

It is truly remarkable how similar all these measures look. The first three give the same message: Relative to economic fundamentals, the level of the stock market reached in 2000 was extremely high, and in the past these valuations have been followed by lower stock returns. The fourth measure tells us that high prices, relative to trend, have been followed by lower prices no matter what the economic fundamentals.

Figure 6-5 looks ominous, but so did Figure 6-1, when in 1958, for the first time in history, dividend yields decisively fell below the interest rates on government bonds. The greatest secular bull market in history followed that episode. Can the market continue its upward momentum, or will history reassert itself and bring stock prices downward? That is the question we shall investigate in the next chapter.

CHAPTER

7

THE GREAT BULL MARKET, THE NEW ECONOMY, THE AGE WAVE, AND FUTURE STOCK RETURNS

The term "new economy" has become, beginning in 2000, a fad in itself. It appears suddenly as a new name for our hopes and for economic progress due to recent technological advances, notably the Internet, and for our reasons to think that the future growth prospects are ever so brilliant.

ROBERT SHILLER[1]

The great bull market of 1982 through 1999 witnessed the largest increase in total real stock returns in U.S. history. Despite the fact that real per-share earnings more than doubled, real stock prices increased nearly sixfold. By year 2000, the valuation of the stock market relative to every traditional measure of firm value—earnings, dividends, sales, book value, and replacement cost—had reached historic highs.

As the market soared in the 1990s, many investors rationalized the exorbitant stock returns as consistent with the United States entering a

---

[1]Robert Shiller, *Irrational Exuberance* (New York: First Broadway Books, 2000), p. 249.

new era of rapid technological change that would generate ever-rising corporate profits and stock prices. Even Merrill Lynch published a report in February 2000 claiming that the new economy called for "creative" valuation models because the Internet unleashed a new alignment between businesses and humanity's innate need to create.[2] By March 2000, 6 out of the top 20 most valuable firms in the United States had price-earnings (P-E) ratios in excess of 100, a level no other large stock had ever before reached.

Despite the crash of technology stocks, the recession, and the terrorist attacks of 2001, stock prices, on average, remained very high relative to earnings and dividends. Given the extraordinary increase in the stock market over the past two decades, investors are right to ask: "Do future returns on equities have any chance of matching the 7 percent average real return that stocks have yielded through history?"

THE NEW ECONOMY AND EARNINGS GROWTH

In the 1990s, the term *New Economy* became synonymous with rapid technological and structural change. Many investors see the New Economy as a profit bonanza not only for the companies producing the hardware and software needed to implement technological advances but also for firms that would benefit from the cost-saving opportunities such technologies afforded. Optimists maintained that the earnings downturn in 2000 and 2001, which caused such havoc in the technology sector, would be viewed as just a small hiccup in a much brighter future.

The problem is that there is little historical evidence that periods of more rapid technological progress have had any *permanent* impact on either earnings growth or stock prices. The decade of the 1990s contained the longest economic expansion in U.S. history, yet real per-share earnings increased at an annual rate of only 4.64 percent. Furthermore, future profit growth is constrained by overall economic growth; it makes little sense to project 10 to 12 percent long-term earnings growth in an economy that is barely growing at one-third that rate.

CORPORATE PROFITS AND NATIONAL INCOME

Examining long-run data on national income and corporate profits demonstrates the limit to the growth rate of earnings. Figure 7-1 dis-

---

[2]Merrill Lynch Global Fundamental Equity Research Department, New York, February 14, 2000.

FIGURE 7–1

Profits Relative to National Income,* 1929–2001

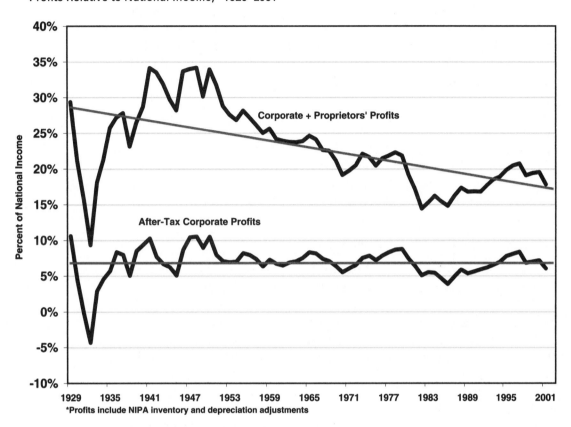

*Profits include NIPA inventory and depreciation adjustments

plays the ratio of after-tax corporate profits and after-tax profits plus proprietors' income or noncorporate business profits to national income over the past 70 years. The corporate profits ratio has fluctuated from a high of 10.60 percent in 1929 to a low of –4.33 percent in 1932, and in year 2000, it stood just a shade above the long-term average of 6.8 percent, before falling in the 2001 recession.

Although both these ratios fluctuate with the business cycle, it should be apparent that neither could grow faster than national income in the long run. If this occurred, it would imply that the owners of capital would receive an ever-increasing portion of the economic pie, and therefore, labor would receive an ever-shrinking portion. Such a development would be a recipe for social unrest and raise calls for government action to redress such a trend.

Therefore, limits on real gross domestic product (GDP) growth put a lid on long-term profit growth. For example, if real economic growth is 3 percent, long-term corporate profits could not grow by more than 3 percent per year after inflation.

Now it is true that real *per-share earnings* could grow faster or slower than 3 percent depending on whether firms are net buyers of shares (through buybacks financed by retained earnings that are not needed to fund capital expenditures) or net issuers of shares (through follow-on equity offerings, employee stock options plans, etc.). Recent evidence suggests that from 1995 through 2000 corporations have been net purchasers of shares. The shrinkage in the number of shares has added between 1 and 1½ percent annually to per-share earnings (PSE) growth.[3] Therefore, with the economy growing at 3 percent, the upper limit on real long-term PSE growth, which is the sum of real growth plus the reduction in the number of shares outstanding, would be 4½ percent.

This limit on real PSE growth also puts a limit on the rate of return shareholders can expect from equity. The real rate of return on equity is the sum of the real appreciation rate on stocks plus the dividend yield. If the P-E ratio remains constant, the real appreciation rate on stock is identical to the rate of growth of real PSE.[4] I indicated that 4½ percent is a reasonable cap on long-run PSE growth. Since the dividend yield in 2001 is 1½ percent, the long-run real return on equity under these assumptions is, at most, 6 percent.

Even if real GDP growth accelerates to a New Economy rate of 4 percent, this will not provide much of a permanent boost, if any, to stock prices. As noted in Chapter 6, increased growth must be financed with increased capital expenditures that reduce future cash flows to shareholders. Furthermore, increased growth puts upward pressure on real interest rates as both firms and consumers vie for funds in the capital market.[5] Increased real interest rates will put downward pres-

---

[3]See Nellie Liang and Steven Sharpe, "Share Repurchases and Employee Stock Options and Their Implications for S&P 500 Share Retirements and Expected Returns," working paper, Federal Reserve Board, November 1999.

[4]The expression rate of return on stock equals rate of dividend growth (which in the long run equals earnings growth) plus dividend yield is sometimes called the *Gordon model*, although it was first derived by John B. Williams. See M. J. Gordon and E. Shapiro, "Capital Equipment Analysis: The Required Rate of Profit," *Management Science* 3(October 1956):102–110.

[5]At the height of the technology boom in March 2000, the real return on U.S. government inflation-indexed bonds rose to 4½ percent, fully 1 percentage point higher than a year earlier (or a year later). This depressed the price of nontechnology issues.

sure on stock prices as bonds compete more effectively for investors' dollars.

PROFITS IN THE NEW ECONOMY

The conclusions reached earlier do not refute the claim that new technological advances in computers, communications, and robotics, among others, will increase operating efficiencies of firms greatly. However, the profits generated through increased efficiency often prove transitory. As long as the sources of those efficiency gains are not proprietary and can be replicated and used by other firms, the excess profits will be competed away quickly in the form of lower prices. History shows that the ultimate beneficiary of technological change is always the *consumer*— not the firm—through lower prices for goods and services.

Certainly some firms will be able to increase their PSE by creating brand names, establishing trademarks and patents, exploiting global markets, and implementing efficiency gains that cannot be matched by others. However, there are always those firms at the opposite end of the spectrum which have overexpanded capacity, overpaid for resources, and wasted capital. In a competitive economy—and few can deny that the future world economy will be extremely competitive—excess profits will be quite short-lived.

All this does not deny that in the *short run* earnings can grow faster or slower than national income. Over a business cycle, accelerated economic growth will increase earnings at a rapid rate as firms use spare capacity and spread fixed costs over a larger revenue base. Similarly, a recession lowers profits because firms must spread the costs of production, especially those fixed costs for resources that are underused in a recession, over a smaller level of output. Indeed, recessions often expose inefficiencies that have accumulated during the prosperous years, forcing cost-cutting measures and boosting efficiency in the long run. Nevertheless, when prosperity returns, the long-term constraints on earnings growth detailed earlier will resurface quickly.

FACTORS RAISING THE VALUATION RATIOS

Even if earnings growth does not increase in the future, there are several favorable factors that do justify higher valuation ratios for the stock market as we enter the new millennium. And there is good reason to believe that many of these factors may be expected to persist over some time.

As noted in Chapter 2, historically stocks have been undervalued assets, delivering much higher returns than should be expected considering their long-term risk. One possible explanation for the rise in stock prices in the late 1990s is that stocks have been bid up because the investing public has finally recognized the superiority of equities as long-term investments.

However, the past decade has not been the only period when investors recognized the superiority of common stocks as long-term investments. In the 1920s and again in the late 1960s, investors bid up stock prices only to be hammered first by the Great Depression of the 1930s and then by the record high interest rates and inflation of the 1970s. Is there any reason to believe that investor optimism at the turn of this century is better founded?

More Stable Economy

I believe so. There is undeniable evidence that the economy *has* become more stable over time, and this should benefit stock prices. Although governments have not been able to eliminate the business cycle (and probably never will), policymakers are able to avoid the sharp swings in real output and inflation that in the past made stocks far riskier investments.

Examine Figure 7-2, which displays the changes in U.S. industrial production since 1884. One can see a major reduction in economic volatility over time, particularly after the Great Depression and again following 1980. Furthermore, by examining industrial production alone, one ignores the importance of the highly stable service sector that has become an ever-increasing fraction of overall GDP.[6]

One could counter that if the real economy is more stable, why has there not been a trend toward more stable stock returns? As I shall show in Chapter 16, the volatility of equity returns has remained relatively stable over time. Part of the reason for this is that firms have taken advantage of the increased economic stability by leveraging their equity stake. More important, however, greater economic stability means that labor income has become more predictable and workers can be persuaded to put a larger share of their savings into riskier assets such as equities.[7] A more

---

[6]There is some debate over the exact causes of this reduced volatility, but suffice it to say that better monetary policy and the shift of the mix of economic production to the less volatile service sector from the volatile industrial sector played a significant role.

[7]See John Heaton and Deborah Lucas, "Portfolio Choice in the Presence of Background Risk," *Economic Journal* 110(January 2000):1–26.

FIGURE 7–2

Monthly Percentage Change in Industrial Production, 1884–2001

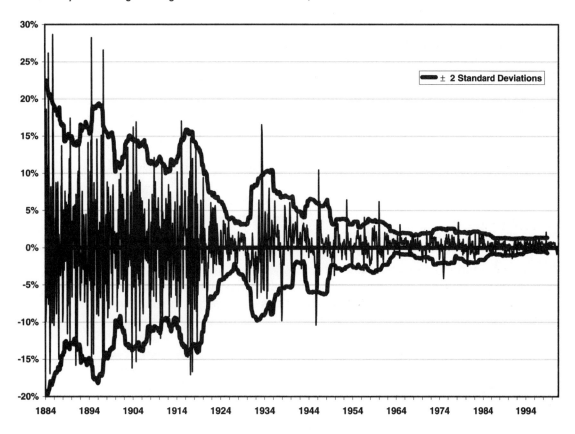

Transactions Costs

The collapse in stock transaction costs is another development that undoubtedly has increased the demand for equities. Chapter 1 confirmed that the real return on equity as measured by stock indexes was about 7 percent in the nineteenth century as well as the twentieth century. However, over the nineteenth century and the early part of the twentieth century, it was extremely difficult, if not impossible, for an investor to replicate the stock returns calculated from these stock indexes.

Charles Jones of Columbia University has documented stock trading costs over the last century.[8] These costs include both the fees paid to brokers and the bid-asked spread, or the difference between the buying and selling costs, for stocks. His analysis shows that the average one-way cost to either buy or sell a stock has dropped from over 1 percent of value traded as late as 1975 (before deregulation of brokerage fees) to under 0.18 percent today.

The fall in transactions costs suggests that the price of obtaining and maintaining a diversified portfolio of common stocks, which is necessary to replicate index returns, easily could have cost from 1 to 2 percent per year over much of the nineteenth and twentieth centuries. Because of these costs, investors in the earlier years purchased fewer stocks and were less diversified, thereby assuming more risk than implied by stock averages. Alternatively, if investors attempted to diversify completely, their real returns could have been as low as 5 percent per year after deducting transactions costs.

The collapse of transactions costs over the past two decades means that stockholders now can obtain a completely diversified portfolio at an extremely low cost.[9] It has been well established that liquid securities, i.e., assets that can be sold quickly and at little cost on short notice in the public market, command a premium over illiquid securities. Through most of the past two centuries, stocks were far less liquid than today and therefore sold at a significant discount to such safe and liquid assets as government bonds. As stocks become more liquid, their valuation relative to earnings and dividends should rise.[10]

Taxes

Another positive factor influencing stock returns over the last half century is the development of a very favorable tax structure for equities. Taxes have an impact on valuations because a considerable (and increasing) part of a stock's return is realized through capital gains, and taxes on those gains are set at substantially lower levels than the rates on other capital returns such as bond interest or rental income. The current 20 percent maximum capital gains tax rate matches the lowest

[8]Charles M. Jones, "A Century of Stock Market Liquidity and Trading Costs," working paper, June 2000.
[9]The cost of some index funds for even small investors is only 0.2 percent per year. See Chapter 20.
[10]John B. Carlson and Eduard A. Pelz, "Investor Expectations and Fundamentals: Disappointment Ahead?" Federal Reserve Bank of Cleveland, *Economic Commentary*, May 1, 2000.

post-World War II tax rate, and the new 18 percent maximum capital gains tax instituted in 2001 on assets held over 5 years is the lowest since 1941.[11]

Firms have been taking advantage of the low capital gains tax rate by reducing dividend payouts and using the funds either to buy back shares or to fund capital expenditures. Both these actions generate future capital gains for shareholders. In the year 2000, the *dividend-payout ratio* of corporations—the ratio of dividends paid to earnings—fell to an all-time low of 32 percent partly in response to the increasing desire of investors to obtain tax-preferred income.

A further favorable tax-related development is a low rate of inflation. Most aspects of our tax code are now indexed to inflation—tax brackets, exemptions, standard deductions, etc.—but capital gains are not. Inflation therefore adds a second layer of tax on equities—a tax on the *nominal* as well as the *real* appreciation on stocks. The lower inflation that marked the late 1990s reduced the effective capital gains tax on equities.

The changes in tax treatment of stock returns have been very important in boosting the after-tax return on equities and are described in detail in Chapter 4. The reductions in the capital gains tax, the dividend-payout ratio, and the inflation rate have added about 1½ percentage points to the after-tax return of upper-middle-income investors compared with the average levels of these variables over the past 50 years.[12]

New Justified P-E Ratios

What do all these favorable developments mean for the stock market? First, they mean that the average historical P-E ratio of 14 or 15 is no longer appropriate in today's market. In Chapter 4 I calculated how much changes in taxes and inflation altered the after-tax real rate of return of investors. If we assume that investors bid stock prices up or down in response to changing taxes and inflation to obtain the same *after-tax* real return, we can calculate how shifts in these variables affect

---

[11]See Chapter 4 for details on historical tax rates. It is true that federal income taxes were much lower (or nonexistent) before World War II. However, the lower capital gains tax opens a wedge that favors stocks over other forms of capital.
[12]See Table 4-2. Ellen McGrattan and Edward Prescott, "Is the Stock Market Overvalued?" working paper, Federal Reserve Bank of Minneapolis, November 2000, provides another tax-motivated argument for high stock prices. These authors claim that the high and growing fraction of stocks held in tax-exempt form boosts their after-tax yield and stock price.

FIGURE 7–3

Actual and Justified P-E Ratios, 1950–2001

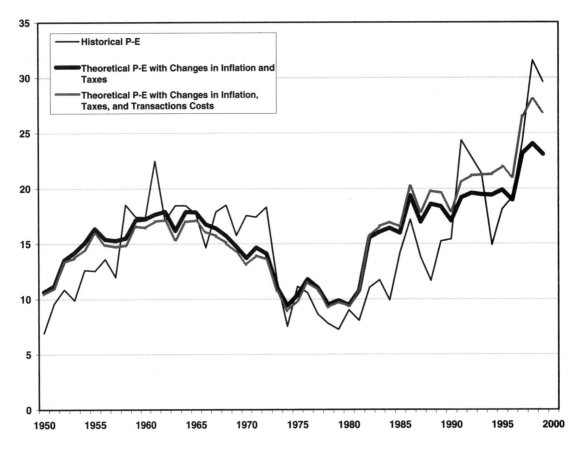

the P-E ratio.[13] This is shown in Figure 7-3. If in addition we incorporate the fall in transactions costs, the justified P-E ratio is further increased.

Figure 7-3 also shows that these factors—taxes, inflation, and transactions costs—can explain the major movements of the market's P-E ratio over the past 50 years. One can see that the justified P-E ratio rises

---

[13]Assume that $R_t(T_t, P_t)$ equals the *before-tax* rate of return, dependent on tax parameters T and stock price level P at time t. If we assume that P changes as the tax parameters T change so that the *after-tax* real rate of return $r_t(T_t, P_t)$ is a constant r^* (which depends on the long-run growth characteristics and time preferences of the economy), then the valuation level P_t is a function of T_t and r^* (see McGrattan and Prescott, 2000).

to the low 20s excluding changes in transactions costs and to the high 20s including the fall in transactions costs.

It is true that the assumption that investors demand the same after-tax real return whenever taxes and inflation change is quite strong and may overstate their impact on the P-E ratio. Nevertheless, Figure 7-3 does not include other factors likely to boost P-E ratios, such as the greater stability of the economy or the increased demand for stocks generated by the investing public's recognition of the superior returns to equity. As a result, I feel that the future P-E ratio on the market should be higher than the historical average. An average P-E ratio for the market in the low 20s is fully warranted as long as inflation stays low and tax policy remains favorable.

THE EQUITY PREMIUM

Over the past 200 years, the average compound rate of return on stocks over safe long-term government bonds—the *equity premium*—has been almost 3½ percent. Since 1926, the premium has averaged almost 5 percent. In 1985, at the onset of this great bull market and well before taxes, transactions costs, and inflation turned so favorable for stocks, economists Rajnish Mehra and Ed Prescott published a paper entitled, "The Equity Premium: A Puzzle."[14] In their work they showed that given the standard models of risk and return that economists had developed over the years, one could not explain the large gap between the returns on equities and fixed-income assets found in the historical data. They claimed that economic models predicted that either the rate of return on stocks should be lower or the rate of return on fixed-income assets should be higher or both. In fact, according to their studies, an equity premium as low as 1 percent or less could be justified.[15]

Mehra and Prescott were not the first to believe that the equity premium derived from historical returns was too large. Fifty years earlier, Professor Chelcie Bosland of Brown University stated that one of the consequences of the spread of knowledge of superior stock returns in the 1920s would be a narrowing of the equity premium:

---

[14]Rajnish Mehra and Edward C. Prescott, "The Equity Premium: A Puzzle," *Journal of Monetary Economics* 15(March 1985):145–162.

[15]Mehra and Prescott used Cowles Foundation data going back to 1872. In their research, they did not even mention the mean reversion characteristics of stock, which would have shrunk the equity premium even more.

Paradoxical though it may seem, there is considerable truth in the statement that widespread knowledge of the profitability of common stocks, gained from the studies that have been made, tends to diminish the likelihood that correspondingly large profits can be gained from stocks in the future. The competitive bidding for stocks which results from this knowledge causes prices at the time of purchase to be high, with the attendant smaller possibilities of gain in the principal and high yield. The discount process may do away with a large share of the gains from common stock investment and returns to stockholders and investors in other securities may tend to become equalized.[16]

James Glassman, a syndicated financial writer, and economist Kevin Hassett took this argument one step further in a book published in 1999 entitled *Dow 36,000*. Citing the results from my book, *Stocks for the Long Run*, that the after-inflation returns on equities are at least as safe as those on bonds over long periods of time, they claim that the equity premium should be zero and that this should send the Dow Jones Industrials soaring to 36,000![17]

To come up with such an extreme result, Glassman and Hassett ignored some salient contrary evidence. Although stocks may be as safe as or safer than nominal bonds at long horizons, stocks cannot be safer than the new government inflation-indexed bonds. Since inflation-indexed bonds are now yielding about 3.5 percent (and rose temporarily to almost 4.5 percent during the stock market peak in March 2000), it stands to reason that investors must expect stocks to yield more than this.

But how much more should stocks yield than inflation-indexed bonds is an open question. If the equity premium were 1 percent, as Mehra and Prescott estimated, forward-looking real stock returns would be only 4½ percent given a 3½ percent return on inflation-indexed securities. Could the higher valuation of equity in recent years bring equity returns down to a level consistent with Mehra and Prescott's analysis?

FUTURE EQUITY RETURNS

In Chapter 6 I pointed out that in the long run the historical real return on stocks of nearly 7 percent closely matched the average earnings yield, which is 1 divided by the average P-E ratio. I also have shown in this

---

[16]Chelcie C. Bosland, *The Common Stock Theory of Investment* (New York: Ronald Press, 1937), p. 132.
[17]Over the period they examined, the real bond return was 2.9 percent, so they asserted that the forward-looking real stock returns should fall to that level. To generate such a low return, they calculated that the P-E ratio of the market should rise immediately to 100, resulting in a Dow Jones Industrial Average of 36,000.

chapter that the favorable economic factors justify a P-E ratio in the low 20s, which corresponds to an earnings yield of between 4 and 5 percent.

Is it possible that forward-looking real equity returns can be as low as 4 to 5 percent? Most certainly, but there are a number of favorable factors that make this forecast too pessimistic.

The formula that relates the real returns on equity to the earnings yield depends on the market value of capital equaling its replacement cost. When the market value of equity exceeds the replacement cost of capital (Tobin's Q is greater than 1), such as existed in 2001, the earnings yield provides an underestimate of future returns.[18] This occurs because higher equity prices allow for a smaller offering of new shares to fund capital expenditures. Furthermore, with the sharp drop in the cost of information and communications technology, the overall cost of productivity-enhancing capital investment has declined markedly. This leaves firms with more funds to buy back shares or increase dividends.

One of the reasons for the collapse of technology prices is the *over-investment* in many technology areas, particularly networking and telecommunications. Although this overinvestment has been extremely painful for the firms *producing* such technology, it is ultimately favorable to firms *using* this technology. The excess supply of capital lowers funding costs and increases future shareholder returns. This is not unlike the aftermath of the railroad mania that hit the United Kingdom in the 1840s and produced a tremendous overbuilding of rail lines. After the prices collapsed, the cheaper and faster transportation brought many benefits to the Victorian economy.[19]

Furthermore, the United States is still viewed in the global economy as the center for entrepreneurship and the incubator of new technology. Financial and intellectual capital are flowing into the United States from abroad because the openness and flexibility of the U.S. economy are seen as a magnet for the types of firms that will spur growth in this new century. This flow is enhanced because the economic policies of many developing countries do not promote stability or entrepreneurship. There is a large and growing flow of funds from abroad seeking safe haven, a factor that boosts U.S. equity prices.

---

[18]The general formula relating the earnings yield to the expected return on equity r is $r = EY + g(1 - RC/MV)$, where EY is the earnings yield (inverse of the P-E ratio), and RC/MV is the ratio of the replacement cost of capital to the market value. As long as $RC/MV < 1$, then $r > EY$. See Thomas K. Philips, "Why Do Valuation Ratios Forecast Long-Run Equity Returns?" *Journal of Portfolio Management* (Spring 1999):39–44.

[19]See Edward Chancellor, *The Devil Take the Hindmost* (New York: Farrar, Straus and Giroux, 1999), Chap. 5.

Finally, there is still room in the short run for U.S. corporate profits to grow without distorting the returns to capital and labor. I noted in the discussion of Figure 7-1 that the share of corporate profit relative to national income was at or slightly above its historical average in the year 2000. However, given the shift toward a corporate form of ownership and away from partnerships and sole proprietorships, one might have expected the corporate profit share to increase. Yet it did not, and as Figure 7-1 illustrates, the total return to capital, including corporate profits and proprietors' incomes, has had a declining trend. As a result, *total* capital income does not appear especially high, and this leaves corporate profits with some room to grow before impinging significantly on the share of labor income in our national accounts.

These positive factors should boost the future real return on equities to about 6 percent, somewhat lower than the long-run average but above the 4½ percent return calculated from a market P-E ratio in the low 20s. This means that the future equity premium is likely to be in the range of 2 to 3 percent, about one-half the level that has prevailed over the past 70 years.

TERRORISM

September 11, 2001, shattered the illusion that the United States or any of the major developed countries of the world would not be a target of a major terrorist strike.[20] An increase in the terrorist threat has two major economic effects. First, the composition of U.S. output will be tilted toward increased military and security expenditures designed to defend our domestic and international interests. These expenditures will reduce productivity growth because, for firms, security is considered an input into the production process and not included in GDP.[21] Increased security thus will raise the price and lower the quantity of final output produced.

Immediately after the terrorist attacks, capital began flowing to industries that supply private and public security services. Even though their output may not find its way into GDP, their market values increased. In general, *security-using* firms will lose earnings that *security-producing* firms will gain.

The second effect of the terrorist attacks is to raise the level of uncertainty and hence the equity premium. Much of our economy is pred-

---

[20]The short-term impact of these strikes on the financial markets is described in Chapter 13.

[21]In contrast, security provided by government, as well as increased security purchases that consumers make, is included in GDP.

icated on the ability to predict the demands of consumers. Since it requires several years to construct hotels and jetliners, if consumers suddenly shift their demands away from traveling and tourism, the value of this capital will suffer dramatically. Unpredictable consumer demands mean that less capital will be devoted to industries that require substantial investment. This also may lead to an increase in the equity risk premium because the unpredictability of corporate profits may cause investors to require a higher return on equity capital.

However, it is very hard to quantify the increase in the equity risk premium, if there is any, arising from the terrorism menace. The United States has lived under substantial threats before. The world was threatened with a potential nuclear holocaust from the time the Soviet Union developed the atomic bomb in August 1949 until the end of the 1980s when the Soviet Union collapsed. And the height of this threat occurred in the late 1950s and early 1960s, a decade that witnessed strong economic growth and robust stock prices. The increased need for security certainly reduces consumer welfare, but its effect on stock market valuation is ambiguous.

THE AGE WAVE

To some forecasters, all the issues mentioned earlier are small potatoes compared with what is going to hit asset markets over the next generation. These prognosticators claim that a demographic phenomenon called the *age wave* eventually will crest and drown stockholders as surely as it sent stock prices soaring in the last decade.[22]

The story goes like this: The baby boomer generation, born between 1946 and 1964, is rapidly accumulating assets in anticipation of their retirement needs. Their highest saving years occur when they are in their forties and fifties, with the mortgage paid off (or nearly so) and children well on their way to finishing college. Many are hoping to prepare for their retirement by accelerating their tax-exempt contributions to Individual Retirement Accounts (IRAs), 401(k) plans, and Keogh plans.

So far the markets have been good to the boomers. Stock and bond returns in the 1980s and 1990s have been far above the norm and have left many with substantial assets despite the 2000–2001 bear market. With their retirement nest eggs in place, many are projecting a life of leisure.

---

[22]The book by Harry Dent, *The Great Boom Ahead* (New York: Hyperion, 1994), popularized these ideas.

The only problem is that when it comes time for them to cash in their assets, they cannot eat their stock or bond certificates. Assets can be turned into purchasing power only if there are buyers willing to give up their consumption so that sellers can enjoy theirs. In the past, the younger generation, when reaching middle age, usually has had sufficient purchasing power to buy its parents' assets. This time, however, the situation is very different. There are not nearly enough generation Xers (the generation born in the late 1960s and 1970s) with sufficient wealth to absorb the baby boomers' substantial portfolios of stocks and bonds at current prices. The age wave of baby boomers in the developed world is depicted in Figure 7-4a.

The looming problem of the baby boomer population is reminiscent of an old Wall Street story. A broker recommends that his client buy a small speculative stock with good earning prospects. The investor purchases the stock, accumulating thousands of shares at ever-rising prices. Patting himself on the back, he phones his broker, instructing him to sell all his shares. His broker snaps back, "Sell? Sell to whom? You're the only one who has been buying the stock!"

The cry, "Sell? Sell to whom?" might haunt the baby boomers in the next century. Who are the buyers of the trillions of dollars of baby boomer assets? The generation that has swept politics, fashion, and the media in the last half of the twentieth century has produced an age wave

FIGURE 7–4

World Population Trends and Pension Flows

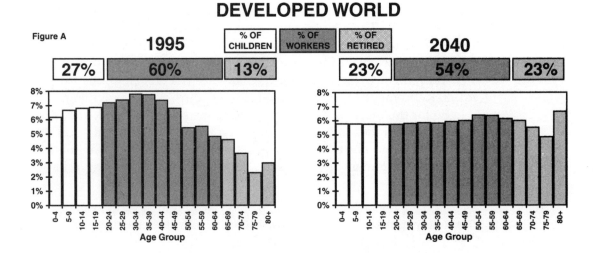

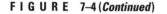

FIGURE 7–4 (Continued)

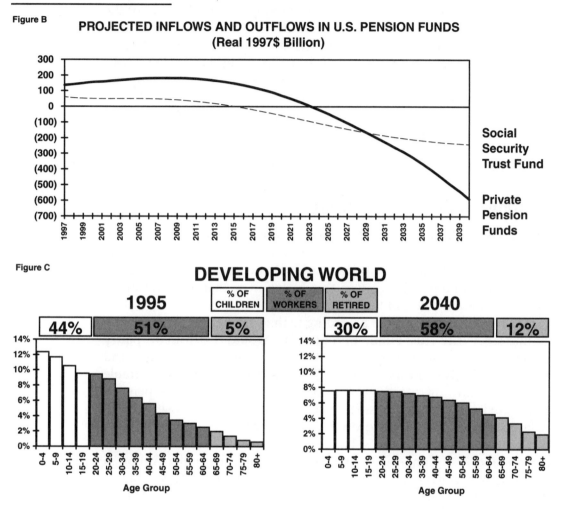

Figure B

PROJECTED INFLOWS AND OUTFLOWS IN U.S. PENSION FUNDS
(Real 1997$ Billion)

Figure C

DEVELOPING WORLD

that threatens to drown in financial assets. The consequences could be disastrous not only for the baby boomer's retirement but also for the economic health of the entire population.

John Shoven of Stanford University and Sylvester Scheiber of the Wyatt Company have projected the accumulation and distribution of baby boomer assets into the next century.[23] Their data, as well as those of

[23]John Shoven and Sylvester Scheiber, "The Consequences of Population Aging on Private Pension Fund Saving and Asset Markets," in *Public Policy Towards Pensions*, A Twentieth Century Fund Book (Cambridge, MA: MIT Press, 1997), Chap. 7, pp. 219–245.

the Social Security Trust Fund, are displayed in Figure 7-4*b*. The net inflow of pension assets, which has contributed to the bull market of the 1990s, becomes a net outflow by 2018 in the Social Security Trust Fund and 10 years later for all private pension plans.

The insufficiency of the Social Security Trust Fund to cover its obligations has garnered much publicity and has led to proposals to supplement the fund with private savings. The big picture indicates that the main threat to the baby boomers is not whether the trust fund contains government or private assets but that there is not enough buying power to absorb the sale of *any* asset. The massive distribution of stocks and bonds portends soaring interest rates and falling security prices.

SOLUTIONS TO THE AGE WAVE CRISIS

Is there a potential solution to this age wave crisis? Yes, there are several. The first is to rely on more rapid economic growth. One can compensate for the dearth of numbers of generation Xers who follow the baby boomers by making all generation Xers better off so that they are able to buy the abundant assets of the baby boomers.

It may be surprising, but according to the very figures published by the Social Security Trust Fund, if productivity would rise from the paltry 1½ percent rate assumed by the trustees to 3½ percent, the trust fund would be fully funded for the next 75 years. There are no comparable figures on how increased growth would influence private pension funds, but it is certain that absorption of the baby boomers' assets would be far greater if productivity growth were higher.[24]

However, pitching one's hat entirely on increased productivity growth to solve the long-run age wave problem is clearly risky. Although most economists have raised their long-term productivity projections to 2½ percent, few believe that productivity growth can be boosted to 3½ percent over long periods of time.

Therefore, it is unlikely that U.S. growth alone can solve the crisis. A solution most likely will involve the world economy. As Figure 7-4*c* indicates, the age wave is strictly a phenomenon of the developed world. The developing world, such as India, Indonesia, Africa, and Latin

---

[24]Maintaining that higher productivity growth is good for stock prices may seem to contradict my earlier comments that higher productivity in the past has not led to higher and faster earnings growth. However, in this case we are looking over a much longer period and trying to ameliorate the age mismatch that threatens the value of retirement assets. If the population of the generation Xers is insufficient to absorb the baby boomers' assets, making them better off will help increase their buying power.

America, has experienced ever-increasing population growth. Over the next half-century, workers aged 20 to 65 will decline from 60 percent of the population to 54 percent in the developed world, whereas in the faster-growing developing countries, the percentage of such workers is predicted to rise from 51 to 58 percent.[25]

The developing world can emerge as one answer to the age mismatch of the industrialized economies. If their progress continues, they will sell goods to the baby boomers and thereby acquire the buying power to purchase their assets. In the 1990s, the developed world is many times richer than the developing world and is providing it with capital to develop its industries and infrastructures. As the economies of the developing world grow, their people will increase their standards of living and levels of saving. If this occurs, the developing nations will pay off their debts, acquire ownership of their own capital, and eventually buy a significant stake in the assets of the developed world.

This scenario does not depend on developing nations becoming as rich as the developed countries, but it is critically dependent on the continued integration of world economies. Protectionism, import restrictions, or other impediments to the free flow of goods, services, and capital among countries would sharply curtail the ability of the world economy to undertake these massive asset transfers. A permanent slowdown in growth of the developing economies will have sharply negative implications for all the world's capital markets.

CONCLUSION

It is not difficult to point to the positive factors that have pushed equity prices higher over the past two decades. Reductions in inflation, the increased stability of the overall economy, and the sharp drop in transactions costs all point to a higher level of stock valuation.

Furthermore, a low capital gains tax and the shift from dividends to capital gains have boosted stock prices. Clearly, changing political winds can alter the favorable taxation equities now enjoy. However, with baby boomers taking the political reins for the next several decades, they are apt to be very protective of their gains in the equity market. Finally, the age wave may not be a long-term negative for the stock market as long as productivity and population trends in the rest of the world are taken into account.

---

[25]The data come from United Nations, *The Sex and Age Distribution of the World Populations,* rev. ed. (New York: United Nations, 1994).

However, the economic factors that increase stock prices have their cost. The very factors that boost stock prices—less uncertainty, higher liquidity, more favorable taxes, and lower transaction costs—make it less likely that stocks will be able to achieve their historical long-run returns. From P-E ratios of 15, stocks easily should achieve the 7 percent real return that has been their historical norm. However, from P-E ratios in the low 20s, which I believe are justified by these favorable circumstances, future real returns on stocks could be 1 to 2 percentage points lower.

Furthermore, given the terrorist attacks of September 2001, it would be premature to say that the world in the future will be free of events that can shock investors. Although policymakers are more adept at avoiding economic disasters (such as depressions and double-digit inflation), future biological, chemical, or nuclear terrorism; the collapse of globalization; or even the proliferation of uncontrollable computer viruses could send equity prices spiraling downward. Fear incites human action far more urgently than does the impressive weight of historical evidence.

However, even if equity prices do fall back to lower levels, there is a silver lining for investors. One should remember that the best historical returns for stocks often have emerged from past economic crises when investors became overly bearish about the earnings prospects of firms. Although bear markets cause considerable short-term pain, they ultimately benefit the younger and longer-term investors who can buy and accumulate equities at discounted prices. Although stocks may not match their impressive returns of the past, all the evidence still indicates that equities will significantly outperform fixed-income investments over the long run.

CHAPTER 8

LARGE STOCKS, SMALL STOCKS, VALUE STOCKS, GROWTH STOCKS

Security analysis cannot presume to lay down general rules as to the "proper value" of any given common stock. . . . The prices of common stocks are not carefully thought out computations, but the resultants of a welter of human reactions.

BENJAMIN GRAHAM AND DAVID DODD[1]

OUTPERFORMING THE MARKET

What factors can investors use to choose individual stocks with superior returns? Earnings, dividends, cash flows, book values, capitalization, and past performance, among others, have been suggested as important criteria to find stocks that will beat the market.

Yet finance theory has long maintained that if capital markets are efficient, in the sense that known valuation criteria are already factored into stock prices, analyzing these fundamentals will not improve returns. The only characteristic yielding higher returns is higher risk, and the correct measure of risk is the sensitivity of a stock's return to the

---

[1]"Price-Earnings Ratios for Common Stocks," in *Security Analysis,* 2d ed. by Benjamin Graham and David Dodd (New York: McGraw-Hill, 1940), p. 530.

overall market, which is known as *beta*.[2] Beta can be estimated from historical data and represents the risk to an asset's return that cannot be eliminated in a well-diversified portfolio. Risk that can be eliminated through diversification (called *diversifiable* or *residual risk*) does not warrant a higher return.

Unfortunately, beta has not been very successful at explaining the differences among the historical returns of individual stocks or groups of stocks. In 1981, Rolf Banz, a graduate student at the University of Chicago, investigated the returns on stocks using the database provided by the Center for Research in Security Prices (CRSP). He found that small stocks systematically outperformed large stocks, even after adjusting for risk as defined within the framework of the capital asset pricing model.[3]

RISKS AND RETURNS IN SMALL STOCKS

Table 8-1 shows the compound annual return from 1926 through September 2000 on stocks listed on the New York Stock Exchange, the American Stock Exchange, and the Nasdaq, sorted into deciles according to their market capitalization. The top two deciles, or the top 20 percent of all firms, containing firms with over \$4.14 billion in market value, are often called *large-cap stocks* and comprise most of the Standard & Poor's (S&P) 500 Stock Index. Deciles 3 through 5, with market capitalizations ranging between \$840 million and \$4.14 billion, are called *mid caps;* deciles 6 through 8 (\$192.6 million to \$840 million) are called *low* (or *small*) *caps;* and the smallest 20 percent (below \$192.6 million) are called *micro caps.*[4]

The compound annual return on the smallest decile of stocks is about 6½ percentage points above the largest decile, and the risk of these small stocks is also higher. Yet the nondiversifiable risk, called *beta*, is not

---

[2]Greek letters have long been used in mathematics to designate the coefficients of regression equations. Beta, the second coefficient, is calculated from the correlation of an individual stock's return with the market. The first coefficient estimated is the average historical return on the stock and is termed *alpha*.

[3]R. Banz, "The Relationship Between Return and Market Value of Common Stock," *Journal of Financial Economics* 9(1981):3–18. Further research has shown that the excess returns on small stocks apply to foreign markets as well, especially Japan. For an excellent discussion of international returns, see Gabriel Hawawini and Don Keim, "The Cross Section of Common Stock Returns: A Review of the Evidence and Some New Findings," working paper, Wharton School, University of Pennsylvania, May 1997.

[4]These dollar ranges are based on the September 2000 values and will vary with the level of the overall market.

TABLE 8-1

Long-Term Returns of NYSE/AMEX/Nasdaq Stocks Ranked by Size, 1926–2000 (B = billion, M = million)

Size Decile	Geometric Return	Annual Risk	Beta	Largest Firm in Decile, Sept. 2000	Total Capitalization of Decile, Sept. 2000
Largest	10.26%	19.0%	0.91	$524.35 B	$11,757 B
2	11.32%	22.7%	1.04	$10.34 B	$1,797 B
3	10.59%	24.5%	1.09	$4.14 B	$865 B
4	11.52%	27.6%	1.13	$2.18 B	$547 B
5	11.32%	30.1%	1.16	$1.33 B	$400 B
6	11.31%	30.2%	1.18	$840.0 M	$287 B
7	10.99%	32.5%	1.24	$537.7 M	$222 B
8	11.27%	34.7%	1.28	$333.4 M	$138 B
9	12.59%	38.8%	1.34	$192.6 M	$117 B
Smallest	16.71%	49.3%	1.42	$84.5 M	$74 B

high enough for the smaller capitalization stocks to justify their extra return. Some analysts maintain that the superior historical returns on small stocks are compensation for the higher transaction costs of acquiring or disposing of these securities. This means that there may be an extra return for illiquidity, and recent research appears to support the idea that liquidity is an important factor in determining individual stock returns.[5] Yet, for long-term investors who do not trade small stocks, transactions costs should not be of great importance. The reasons for the excessive returns to small stocks are difficult to explain from an efficient markets standpoint.

TRENDS IN SMALL STOCK RETURNS

Although the historical return on small stocks has outpaced that of large stocks since 1926, the magnitude of the small stock premium has waxed and waned unpredictably over time. Figure 8-1 compares the returns on small stocks with those of the S&P 500 Stock Index over the past 75 years.[6]

---

[5]See Lubos Pastor and Robert Stambaugh, "Liquidity Risk and Expected Stock Returns," working paper, August 2001.
[6]The small stock index is the bottom quintile (20 percent) size of the NYSE stocks until 1981, then the performance of Dimensional Fund Advisors (DFA) Small Company Fund from 1982 through 2000, and then the Russell 2000 Index for 2001.

FIGURE 8–1

Small Stocks and S&P 500 Returns, 1926–2001 (Including and Excluding 1975–1983)

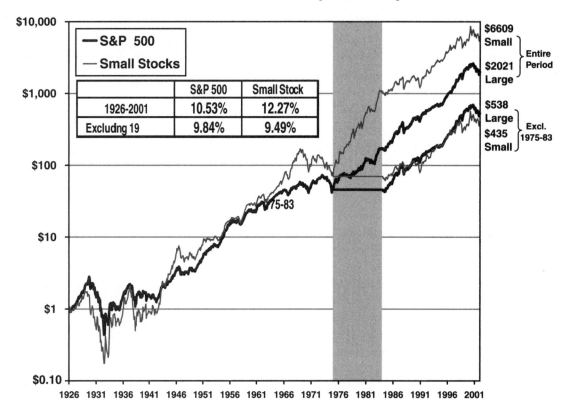

Small stocks recovered smartly from their beating during the Great Depression but still underperformed large stocks from the end of World War II until almost 1960. In fact, the cumulative total return on small stocks (measured by the bottom quintile of market capitalization) did not overtake that of large stocks once between 1926 and 1959. Even by the end of 1974, the average annual compound return on small stocks exceeded that of large stocks by only about 0.5 percent per year, not nearly enough to compensate most investors for their extra risk and trading costs.

However, between 1975 and the end of 1983, small stocks exploded. During these years, small stocks averaged a 35.3 percent compound annual rate of return, more than double the 15.7 percent return on large stocks. Total returns on small stocks during these 9 years exceeded 1,400 percent.

After 1983, small stocks hit a long dry period and underperformed large stocks. In fact, Figure 8-1 shows that if the 9-year period from 1975 through 1983 is eliminated, the total accumulation in large stocks over the entire period from 1926 through 2001 is more than 20 percent greater than that in small stocks.

What caused the tremendous performance of small stocks during the 1975–1983 period? First, at the beginning of the period, the United States was recovering from the worst economic slowdown since the Great Depression, and small stocks typically do well coming out of recessions. Second, the OPEC oil price increases during the period slammed many of the largest U.S. firms, such as the steel and motor companies, whose production processes were not energy efficient. And finally, pension and institutional managers, who had held only large-cap stocks found themselves attracted to smaller stocks following the collapse of the "nifty fifty," large growth stocks that were so popular in the preceding bull market. The enactment of the Employee Retirement Income Security Act (ERISA) by Congress in 1974 made it far easier for pension funds to diversify into small stocks, boosting their holdings of these issues.[7]

In 1975, investors were able to find many undervalued stocks among these smaller issues. By 1983, however, many of these small stocks had become overpriced and significantly underperformed large stocks in subsequent years. When 1975–1983 is removed from the historical data, small stocks go from outperforming large stocks by 1.74 percent per year to underperforming large stocks by 0.35 percent.

To test how truly unique 1975–1983 was, computer simulations were performed that randomized the series of historical returns and then removed the large and small stock returns for the 9-year period when small stocks did their best. Reversals of this magnitude that actually occurred in the data are very rare and occurred in just 7 percent of the simulations performed.

The instability of small stock returns does not mean that an investor should avoid these firms. Stocks not in the S&P 500 Index constitute about one-quarter of the total market value of stocks. As I shall show in Chapter 20, there may be evidence that the huge trend toward indexing may be a drag on the returns to large-cap indexes in the future. However, as I shall show below, there is some very strong evidence that certain groups of small stocks perform significantly better than others.

---

[7]Some people maintain that the fall in tax rates was partially responsible for the small stock surge. However, tax rates on dividend income actually fell more than the capital gains tax rate, which should have favored the larger stocks that had a higher dividend yield.

VALUE-BASED CRITERIA

Price-to-Earnings (P-E) Ratios

Market capitalization is not the only factor influencing returns. In the late 1970s, Sanjoy Basu, building on the work of S. F. Nicholson in 1960, discovered that stocks with low price-to-earnings (P-E) ratios have significantly higher returns than stocks with high P-E ratios.[8]

This would not have surprised Benjamin Graham and David Dodd, who in their classic 1934 text, *Security Analysis,* argued that a necessary condition for investing in common stock was a reasonable ratio of market price to average earnings. They stated:

> Hence we may submit, as a corollary of no small practical importance, that people who habitually purchase common stocks at more than about 16 times their average earnings are likely to lose considerable money in the long run.[9]

Yet even Benjamin Graham must have felt a need to be flexible on the issue of what constituted an excessive P-E ratio. In their second edition, written in 1940, the same sentence appears with the number 20 substituted for 16 as the upper limit of a reasonable P-E ratio.[10] I discuss the types of P-E ratios that are justified in today's economy in the next chapter.

Price-to-Book Ratios

Price-earnings ratios are not the only value-based criterion for buying stocks. A number of academic papers, beginning with Dennis Stattman's in 1980 and culminating in the paper by Eugene Fama and Ken French in 1992, have suggested that price-to-book ratios may be even more significant than P-E ratios in predicting future cross-sectional stock returns.[11]

Like P-E ratios, Graham and Dodd considered book value to be an important factor in determining returns. More than 60 years ago, they wrote:

---

[8]S. F. Nicholson, "Price-Earnings Ratios," *Financial Analysts Journal* (July–August 1960):43–50; S. Basu, "Investment Performance of Common Stocks in Relation to Their Price-Earnings Ratio: A Test of the Efficient Market Hypothesis," *Journal of Finance* 32(June 1977):663–682.

[9]Benjamin Graham and David Dodd, *Security Analysis* (New York: McGraw-Hill, 1934), p. 453.

[10]Graham and Dodd (1940), p. 533.

[11]D. Stattman, "Book Values and Expected Stock Returns," unpublished MBA honors paper, University of Chicago, 1980; E. Fama and K. French, "The Cross Section of Expected Stock Returns," *Journal of Finance* 47(1992):427–466.

[We] suggest rather forcibly that the book value deserves at least a fleeting glance by the public before it buys or sells shares in a business undertaking. . . . Let the stock buyer, if he lays any claim to intelligence, at least be able to tell himself, first, how much he is actually paying for the business, and secondly, what he is actually getting for his money in terms of tangible resources.[12]

VALUE AND GROWTH STOCKS

Stocks that exhibit low price-to-book and low price-to-earnings ratios are often called *value stocks*, whereas those with high P-E and price-to-book ratios are called *growth stocks*. Prior to the 1980s, value stocks often were called *cyclic stocks* because low P-E stocks often were found in industries whose profits were tied closely to the business cycle. With the growth of style investing, equity managers who specialized in these stocks were uncomfortable with the *cyclic* moniker and greatly preferred the term *value*.

Value stocks are concentrated in oil, motor, finance, and most utilities, whereas growth stocks are concentrated in the high-technology industries such as drugs, telecommunications, and computers. Of the 10 largest U.S.-based corporations at the end of 2001, 7 can be regarded as growth stocks (GE, Microsoft, Pfizer, Wal-Mart, Intel, IBM, and Johnson & Johnson), whereas only 2 (Exxon Mobil and Citigroup) are value stocks; AIG can go either way depending on the criteria used for selection.

Table 8-2 summarizes the compound annual returns on stocks from 1963 through 2000 ranked on the basis of both capitalization and book-to-market ratios. These tables appear to confirm Graham and Dodd's emphasis on value-based investing. Historical returns on value stocks have surpassed those of growth stocks, and this outperformance is especially true among smaller stocks. The smallest value stocks returned 23.26 percent per year, the highest of any of the 25 categories analyzed, whereas the smallest growth stocks returned only 6.41 percent, the lowest of any category. As firms become larger, the difference between the returns on value and growth stocks becomes much smaller. The largest value stocks returned 13.59 percent per year, whereas the largest growth stocks returned about 10.28 percent.

One theory about why growth stocks have underperformed value stocks is behavioral: Investors get overexcited about the growth prospects

---

[12]Graham and Dodd (1934), pp. 493–494.

TABLE 8–2

Compound Annual Returns by Size and Book-to-Market Ratio (July 1963–December 2000)

Entire Period		Size Quintiles				
		Small	2	3	4	Large
Book-to-Market Quintiles	Value	23.26%	15.94%	17.44%	16.18%	13.59%
	2	20.40%	15.23%	14.60%	15.18%	11.27%
	3	18.03%	13.96%	14.75%	11.39%	11.02%
	4	12.87%	11.99%	11.83%	10.37%	12.13%
	Growth	6.41%	5.15%	5.93%	10.71%	10.28%

Excluding 1975-83		Size Quintiles				
		Small	2	3	4	Large
Book-to-Market Quintiles	Value	16.90%	10.27%	12.80%	12.40%	11.11%
	2	13.85%	9.96%	10.56%	11.88%	9.09%
	3	11.54%	8.62%	9.64%	7.99%	8.90%
	4	5.43%	6.71%	6.57%	6.86%	11.60%
	Growth	-0.76%	0.13%	1.41%	8.64%	10.24%

of firms with rapidly rising earnings and bid them up excessively. "Storybook stocks" such as Intel or Microsoft, which in the past provided fantastic returns, capture the fancy of investors, whereas firms providing solid earnings with unexciting growth rates are neglected. This behavioral theory is discussed further in Chapter 19. Another more economically based reason is that value stocks have higher dividends, and dividends are taxed at a higher rate than capital gains. As a result, value stocks must have higher returns to compensate for their higher taxability. However, tax factors cannot explain the wide spreads between small value and growth stocks.

The differences in the return between large growth and large value stocks appears to wax and wane over long cycles. Growth stocks gained in the late 1960s and peaked in December 1972, when the "nifty fifty," which are analyzed in Chapter 9, hit their highs. When investors dumped the nifty fifty, growth stocks went into a long bear market relative to value stocks. One of the reasons for this was the surge in oil stocks, which are classified as value stocks, when OPEC caused petroleum prices to soar. From 1982 onward, growth stocks gained relative to value stocks, soaring in the technology boom of 1990–2000, only to fall again when the euphoria subsided. In fact, large growth stocks have outperformed large value stocks in about half the years since 1963. Another surprising result, which will be discussed in Chapter 18, is that a large part of the difference between the returns on large value and growth stock returns takes place in the month of January.[13]

BARRA, Inc., a California-based stock research firm, has divided the firms in the S&P 500 Stock Index into two groups of growth and value stocks with equal value on the basis of the firm's market-to-book ratio.[14] Figure 8-2 shows the ratio of the cumulative return on these two large capitalization growth and value indexes since December 31, 1974, when the indexes were first formulated. On the basis of capital appreciation alone, growth stocks, with an 11.06 percent annual return, beat value stocks by 0.31 percent over this 37-year period. However, these value stocks have dividend yields that are about 2 percentage points above that of growth stocks. When the dividend yields are included to find total cumulative returns, value stocks' return of 15.65 percent per year outperforms growth stocks by about 1.9 percent.

However, for taxable investors, the difference between the cumulative returns on S&P growth and value stocks has been very slight over the past 27 years. Since the tax on dividend income has been far higher than that on capital gains income during most of the period, the average annual return for a taxable investor in the upper-middle-income bracket has been 10.72 percent in value stocks and 10.03 percent in growth stocks, a difference of only 0.69 percent.[15]

Furthermore, the unprecedented volatility of growth stocks relative to value stocks in recent years has played havoc with historical data. For someone who began investing in 1975, the technology bubble of the late 1990s sent after-tax growth returns higher than after-tax value returns

---

[13]See Tim Loughran, "Book-to-Market Across Firm Size, Exchange, and Seasonality: Is There an Effect?" *Journal of Financial and Quantitative Analysis* 32(September 1997):249–268.

[14]Since growth stocks tend to have higher market capitalizations, in late 2001 the growth index had 146 firms, and the value index had 354 firms.

[15]This assumes that the growth investor keeps his or her stocks an average of 3 years. For longer holding periods, the difference between growth and value stock returns becomes even smaller.

FIGURE 8–2

Ratio of Cumulative Growth Returns to Cumulative Value Returns in S&P 500 Stocks, 1975–2001

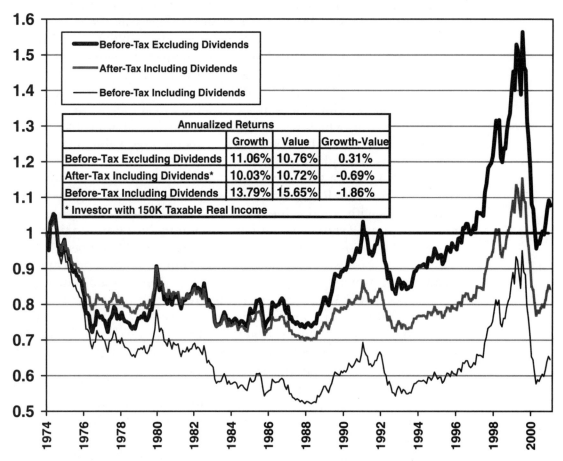

Annualized Returns			
	Growth	Value	Growth-Value
Before-Tax Excluding Dividends	11.06%	10.76%	0.31%
After-Tax Including Dividends*	10.03%	10.72%	-0.69%
Before-Tax Including Dividends	13.79%	15.65%	-1.86%
* Investor with 150K Taxable Real Income			

from September 1999 through September 2000. Once the bubble popped, however, growth stock returns fell back below those of value stocks very quickly.

It should be noted that beginning the growth and value series in 1975 is very favorable for value stocks. Large value stocks crushed large growth stocks from 1975 through 1977, when soaring oil prices sent the price of oil and resource firms (which are always ranked as value stocks) skyrocketing. Since August 1982, when the great bull market began, cumulative returns for growth and value investors have been almost identical, even after the growth stock collapse of 2000–2001.

NATURE OF GROWTH AND VALUE STOCKS

When examining growth and value stocks, investors should keep in mind that these designations are not inherent in the products the firms make or the industries they are in. The terms depend solely on the market value of the firm relative to some fundamental variable, such as earnings, book value, etc.

Therefore, the stock of a producer of technology equipment, which is considered to be an industry with high growth prospects, actually could be classified as a value stock if it is out of favor with the market and sells for a low book-to-market ratio. Alternatively, the stock of an automobile manufacturer, which is a relatively mature industry with limited growth potential, could be classified a growth stock if its stock is in favor. In fact, over time, many stocks go through value and growth designations as their market price fluctuates.

This means that the literature showing value stocks beating growth stocks may not imply any more than that stocks become priced too high or low because of unfounded optimism or pessimism and eventually will return to true economic value. It definitely does not mean that industries normally designated as growth industries will underperform those designated as value industries. There is no question that investors always should be concerned with valuation, no matter which stocks they buy. In the next chapter I shall talk about the long-term returns of individual growth stocks that caught the fancy of investors in the early 1970s and during the great 1999–2000 technology boom.

DIVIDEND YIELDS

Another favorite value-based criterion for choosing stocks is dividend yields. Research by Krishna Ramaswamy and Robert Litzenberger more than 20 years ago established the correlation between dividend yield and subsequent returns.[16] More recent studies by James O'Shaughnessy have shown that from the period 1951–1996, the 50 highest dividend-yielding stocks had a 1.5 percent higher annual return among large capitalization stocks.[17] Chapter 19 also will confirm that a strategy based on

---

[16]See Robert Litzenberger and Krishna Ramaswamy, "The Effects of Personal Taxes and Dividends on Capital Asset Prices: Theory and Empirical Evidence," *Journal of Financial Economics* (1979):163–195.

[17]James O'Shaughnessy, *What Works on Wall Street,* rev. ed. (New York: McGraw-Hill, 1998), pp. 143–156.

the highest yielding stocks in the Dow Jones Industrial Average outperformed the market.

The correlation between the dividend yield and return can be explained in part by taxes. As has been discussed in Chapter 4, dividends
receive no tax preference, whereas capital gains offer investors favorable
tax treatment. Thus stocks with higher dividend yields must offer higher
before-tax returns to compensate shareholders for the tax differences. It
also should be noted that most current studies, like O'Shaughnessy's,
exclude utility stocks, which as a group have by far the highest dividend
yield but have vastly underperformed the market over the past decade.

DISTRESSED FIRMS

Despite the higher returns provided by value-based firms, there is one
class of stocks, those of distressed firms, that has achieved some of the
highest returns of all. Many distressed firms have negative earnings and
zero or negative book value and pay no dividends. Research has shown
that as the ratio of book value or earnings to price declines, so does the
return. However, when book value or earnings turn negative, the price
of the stock becomes so depressed that the future returns soar.

This same discontinuity is also found with dividend yields. As
noted earlier, the higher the dividend yield, the higher is the subsequent
return. However, firms that pay no dividend at all have among the highest subsequent returns.

The superior returns to non-dividend-paying stocks were first recognized in a book entitled *Investing in Purchasing Power* by Kenneth S.
Van Strum, a financial writer of the 1920s. Van Strum set out to confirm
Edgar Lawrence Smith's study of a year earlier that proclaimed the superiority of stocks as long-term investments.

Expecting to find such superior performance only in investment-
grade stocks, Van Strum was surprised to find quite the opposite. In one
of his studies, he analyzed what would happen if the common stock investor purchased only stocks of companies that had no dividends and
that were priced under $50 per share, which at that time were viewed as
low-priced speculative stocks. He concluded:

> This group [no dividends and price under $50 per share] of low-priced
> common stocks not only permitted the stock investor to maintain his pur-
> chasing power intact, but also showed the best results of any investment
> made in the entire group of studies.[18]

---

[18]Kenneth S. Van Strum, *Investing in Purchasing Power* (New York: Barron's, 1925), p. 232.

In fact, Irving Fisher stated in the Foreword of Van Strum's book, "This result [the best performance of non-dividend-paying stocks] is as surprising as any among the many surprising results of this investigation."[19] Recent analysis shows that Van Strum's findings persist today.

Most stocks that have negative earnings or negative book values have experienced very adverse financial developments and have become severely depressed. Many investors are quick to dump these stocks when the news gets very bad. This often drives the price down below the value justified by future prospects. Few investors seem able to see the light at the end of the tunnel or cannot justify—to themselves or to their clients—the purchase of such stocks under such adverse circumstances.

INITIAL PUBLIC OFFERINGS

Initial public offerings (IPOs) always have fascinated investors. New companies are launched with enthusiasm and hope that they can turn into the next Microsoft or Intel. The large demand for IPOs means that most IPOs will "pop" in price after they are released into the secondary market, offering investors who bought the stock at the offering price immediate gains. For this reason, many investors seek to obtain as many shares in IPOs as possible, so underwriting firms ration the shares to brokerage firms and institutional investors. A study by *Forbes* magazine of the long-term returns on IPOs from 1990 to 2000 showed that investing in IPOs at their *offering* price beat the S&P 500 Index by 4 percent per year.[20]

However, many investors forget that most IPOs utterly fail to live up to their promise after they are issued. A study by Tim Loughran and Jay Ritter followed every operating company (almost 5,000) that went public between 1970 and 1990.[21] Those who bought at the market price on the first day of trading and held the stock for 5 years reaped an average annual return of 11 percent. Those who invested in companies of the same size on the same days that the IPOs were purchased gave investors a 14 percent annual return. And these data do not include the IPO price collapse in 2001.

---

[19]*Ibid.*, p. vii.
[20]Scott DeCarlo, "A Decade of New Issues," *Forbes,* March 5, 2001.
[21]Jay Ritter, "The Long Run Performance of IPOs," *Journal of Finance* 46(1)(March 1991):3–27; Tim Loughran and Jay Ritter, "The New Issue Puzzle," *Journal of Finance* 50(1)(March 1995):23–51. Data updated by author.

In the 1980s, the average first-day return on IPOs was 7 percent. This return more than doubled to 15 percent from 1990 to 1998. However, during the Internet stock bubble of 1999–2000, the average first-day return catapulted to 65 percent. The most spectacular IPO was VA Linus, a software company that went public on December 9, 1999, at $30 per share and closed at $239.25 on the first day after reaching $320 during the day. In December 2001, the stock traded under $3.00 after reaching a low of 76 cents the previous September.

Market valuations of Internet-related IPOs reached extreme valuations during the height of the mania. In February 1990, when Cisco Systems was floated, the market value after the first day was $287 million. Cisco had reported last-12-month sales at $69.7 million and profits of $13.9 million. Nearly a decade later, in October 1999, both Sycamore Networks and Akamai Technologies went public with market values of about $14 billion each and annual sales of $11 million and $1.3 million, respectively. However, the top prize for initial valuation goes to Corvis Corp., a networking firm that went public on July 28, 2000, and had a market value of $28.7 billion after the first day of trading, although it had never made a single dollar of sales and had a $72 million loss in the preceding 12 months. In December 2001, Corvis' price was $2.50 after reaching $108 at the end of the first week of trading.

The lessons from the IPO market are clear. If you can get an IPO at the offering price, it is often (but not always) a great buy. But do not hold on! The subsequent performance almost always disappoints.

INVESTMENT STRATEGY

"Style investing," where money managers rotate between small and large and value and growth stocks, is all the rage on Wall Street. Historical data seem to imply that small stocks outperform large stocks and value stocks outperform growth stocks.

Yet the historical returns on these investment styles may not represent their future returns at all. The superior performance of small stocks over large stocks depends crucially on whether the 1975–1983 period is included. Furthermore, the superior performance of value stocks over growth stocks may not be inherent to the industry they are in but merely reflect fluctuations in investor enthusiasm about certain sectors.

All of this implies that the average investor will do best by diversifying into all stock sectors. Trying to catch styles as they move in and out of favor not only is difficult but also is quite risky and costly. Hot sectors or investment styles can lull investors into a trap. When a sector reaches an extreme valuation level, such as the technology issues did at the end of the last bull market, reducing its allocation will improve your returns. The next chapter indicates how an investor could have used the lessons of history to avoid getting caught in the technology bubble.

CHAPTER 9

VALUATION OF GROWTH AND TECHNOLOGY STOCKS

The meaning of life is creative love, loving creativity. And loving creativity may explain why tech stocks are high and going higher. The Internet revolution is allowing for creativity like never before, perhaps putting more of us in touch with the meaning of life.

MERRILL LYNCH
GLOBAL FUNDAMENTAL EQUITY RESEARCH DEPARTMENT
FEBRUARY 14, 2000

The turn of the millennium was an extraordinary event. Not only did an orgy of midnight celebrations roll across the globe to greet the turn of the calendar, but the world also was caught up in one of the most astonishing speculative markets in history. In financial centers around the globe, technology issues advanced steadily to new highs. Despite widespread fears that the strike of midnight on December 31, 1999, would cause massive disruptions because computers would not be able to turn the clock from 1999 to 2000, Y2K passed without a hitch. The world embraced the twenty-first century.

Confidence in the stock market appeared well-founded. The longest economic boom in U.S. history produced a heady mix of excitement and optimism. Newspapers headlined the accelerating growth of productivity, near-record-low unemployment rates, and the greatest bull market in history.

Rising prosperity and the end of the cold war made it appear that there were no major ideological divides remaining. The developed world basked in the certainty that free markets and democracy were the only viable models for economic progress and that it was only a matter of time before the peoples of all other nations agreed. Socialism, communism, fascism, dictatorships, and faith-based republics were historical curiosities and detours on the road to a world that respected individuals' personal and economic freedoms and engaged in expanding global enterprise.

The communications revolution captured everyone's imagination. The number of mobile phones exploded, and their price fell to the point where many people abandoned their traditional landline connections. As fees on domestic and international long-distance calls plummeted, our globe appeared to contract to the point where borders and even nations seemed no longer to matter.

In this shrinking world, the Internet was born. And it would fundamentally change the way people communicated. Up-to-date information was available instantly online from a burgeoning number of Web sites. Personal Web pages allowed individuals and businesses to display any information to anyone anywhere in the world. Instant-messaging systems enabled costless real-time communication worldwide. E-mail became a popular and even preferred means of communication for many firms as well as individuals.

Excitement about this technology led to extraordinary valuations of any firm even tangentially involved with the Internet. Certainly brokerage houses and the media fed the stock-buying mania, but it was the investors themselves, through Internet chat rooms and online trading, who generated much of the enthusiasm surrounding this new and fascinating medium.

Many people believed (or feared) that online selling would put traditional retailers (referred to as *bricks-and-mortar retailers*) out of business. In October 1999, the market value of eToys, Inc., an online toy retailer, was more than double Toys"R"Us, the world's largest bricks-and-mortar toy retailer that owned more than 1,600 stores worldwide. In April 1999, the online book retailer Amazon.com had a market value that was almost *10 times* the combined market value of its two greatest bricks-and-mortar competitors, Barnes & Noble and Borders, that each operated over 1,000 bookstores worldwide. In that same month, Priceline.com, a company that sells cheap airline tickets over the Web, had a peak market value that was more than one-half the entire equity of the U.S. airline industry.

Although the prices of Internet stocks seemed nonsensical, many of the leading brokerage firms and investment houses sought to justify these valuations by almost metaphysical reasoning, illustrated by the Merrill Lynch statement at the beginning of this chapter. However, the more serious money was being funneled into the profitable technology firms that set the stage for the Internet revolution.

After the pure Internet stocks peaked in 1999, investor interest shifted to what was known as the "backbone" of the Internet. Financial advisors reminded their clients that during the California gold rush of 1848, very few of the thousands of miners who were drawn by tales of gold nuggets as large as melons made any money. However, those who *supplied* the miners with pick axes, clothing, and other gear most certainly did. Thus, as the pure dot-com companies faded, investors rushed to those companies that facilitated the Internet—networking and storage companies, software manufacturers, and firms pioneering wireless communications.

In March 2000, the Nasdaq Market Index soared to over 5,000, almost four times its level 18 months earlier. Table 9-1 lists technology stocks that had a market value over $90 billion in that peak month. Twelve of the 20 largest U.S. firms by market value were technology firms, and 6 had

T A B L E   9–1

Large-Cap Stocks with P-E Ratios in Excess of 100, March 7, 2000

Company	Market Value Rank	Market Value $bil	Price-Earnings Ratio	Past 5-yr EPS Growth (%)	IBES Est. 5-yr EPS Growth (%)
Cisco	2	452	148.4	37.6	29.5
AOL Time Warner	6	232	216.3	84.2	31.5
Oracle	8	211	152.9	28.3	24.9
Nortel Networks	12	167	105.6	45.3	20.7
Sun Microsystems	13	149	119.0	29.4	21.1
EMC Corp	17	130	115.4	31.9	31.1
JDS Uniphase	27	99	668.3	57.0	44.0
QUALCOMM	30	91	166.8	93.8	37.3
Yahoo!	31	90	623.2	443.8	55.9
Sum/Average		1,621	157.5	49.7	27.9

price-earnings (P-E) ratios in excess of 100. QUALCOMM, Yahoo!, and JDS Uniphase rounded out the list. For the first time in U.S. history firms in the top 20 ranking sold at a triple-digit P-E ratio.[1]

As can be seen from Table 9-1, the past earnings growth of these new technology firms was truly remarkable, and analysts believed that their future growth would remain extremely high. Investors should have asked two questions before buying these stocks. First, were these stocks reasonably priced *if* analysts' earnings projections were realized, and second, were these earnings projections realistic?

THE NIFTY FIFTY OF THE 1970s

To answer the two questions just posed, it is useful to go back to a similar episode of investor infatuation with growth stocks that took place nearly 30 years earlier. That episode consisted of a group of high-flying growth stocks that soared in the early 1970s only to come crashing to earth in the vicious 1973–1974 bear market. After these stocks fell, they were held up as examples of unwarranted optimism about the capacity of growth stocks to continue to generate rapid and sustained earnings growth.

The "nifty fifty," as these stocks were called, was a group of premier growth stocks, such as Xerox, IBM, Polaroid, and Coca-Cola, that became institutional darlings in the early 1970s. All these stocks had proven growth records, continual increases in dividends (virtually none had cut its dividend since World War II), and high market capitalizations. This last characteristic enabled institutions to load up on these stocks without significantly influencing the price of their shares.

Many investors did not seem to find 40, 50, and even 60 times earnings at all an unreasonable price to pay for the world's preeminent growth companies, although many of these stocks sold for barely half that price just a few years earlier. Five years after the nifty fifty peaked, *Forbes* magazine commented on the phenomenon:

> What held the Nifty Fifty up? The same thing that held up tulip-bulb prices in long-ago Holland—popular delusions and the madness of crowds. The delusion was that these companies were so good it didn't matter what you paid for them; their inexorable growth would bail you out.
>
> Obviously the problem was not with the companies but with the temporary insanity of institutional money managers—proving again that

---

[1] Table 9-1 was the basis for my article, "Big Cap Stocks Are a Sucker's Bet," that appeared in the *Wall Street Journal* on March 14, 2000.

stupidity well-packaged can sound like wisdom. It was so easy to forget that probably no sizable company could possibly be worth over 50 times normal earnings.[2]

However, was this assessment fair? To determine whether these stocks were worth their price, I traced the subsequent performance of the nifty fifty stocks as identified by Morgan Guaranty Trust, one of the largest managers of equity trust assets.[3] These stocks are listed in Table 9-2, along with their 1972 P-E ratios and subsequent earnings growth. The product lines of these stocks included drugs, computers and electronics, photography, food, tobacco, and retailing, among others. Notably absent are the cyclic industries, namely, automobiles, steel, transportation, capital goods, and oil.

Many of the original nifty fifty stocks are still giants today. In 2001, 14 appear in the top 40 U.S. stocks in terms of market capitalization, and 5 (General Electric, Pfizer, Citigroup, IBM, and Johnson & Johnson) are still among the top 10. Corporate changes that have taken place in the original nifty fifty stocks are described in the Appendix at the end of the chapter.

The nifty fifty did sell at hefty multiples. The average P-E ratio of these stocks in 1972 was 41.9, more than double that of the Standard & Poor's (S&P) 500 Stock Index, and their 1.1 percent dividend yield was less than half that of other large stocks that yielded close to 2.7 percent. Over one-fifth of these firms sported P-E ratios in excess of 50, and Polaroid was priced at over 90 times earnings. These ratios, however, were far below the tech firms listed in Table 9-1.

Table 9-2 ranks these stocks according to their annual compound returns from December 1972 through November 2001.[4] December 1972 was chosen because an equally weighted portfolio of each of these stocks peaked in that month, which was considered the height of the nifty fifty mania.

Consumer brand-name stocks, such as PepsiCo, Heublein, Gillette, Anheuser-Busch, Coca-Cola, and others, did extremely well, besting the S&P 500 Index. Also beating the popular benchmark were the pharmaceuticals, such as Pfizer, Bristol-Myers (which absorbed Squibb), Merck, Eli Lilly, and Schering-Plough. The biggest winner, however, was Philip

---

[2]"The Nifty Fifty Revisited," *Forbes*, December 15, 1977, p. 52.
[3]Noted by M. S. Forbes, Jr., in "When Wall Street Becomes Enamored," *Forbes*, December 15, 1977, p. 72.
[4]I used the following procedure to compute total returns to the nifty fifty stocks over the entire period. If a stock merged with or was acquired by another firm, I combined the returns on the two stocks at the appropriate date of change. If the company went private, I spliced the return on the S&P 500 Index from that date forward.

TABLE 9-2

Nifty Fifty Returns from Market Peak (December 1972–November 2001)

	Symbol	Annualized Returns	1972 Actual P-E Ratio	Warranted P-E Ratio	EPS Growth
Philip Morris Cos. Inc.	MO	17.80%	24.0	68.1	13.33%
Pfizer Inc.	PFE	17.39%	28.4	79.5	12.90%
Bristol-Myers	BMY	15.60%	24.9	46.9	12.08%
Pepsico Inc.	PEP	15.58%	27.6	55.3	12.45%
General Electric Co.	GE	15.44%	23.4	43.3	11.58%
Merck & Co. Inc.	MRK	14.85%	43.0	70.1	15.10%
Heublein Inc.	HBL/RJR	14.75%	29.4	49.1	12.37%
Squibb Corp.	SQB/BMY	14.46%	30.1	45.3	13.29%
Gillette Co.	GS/G	14.07%	24.3	33.6	11.58%
Anheuser-Busch Inc.	BUD	13.41%	31.5	41.1	11.77%
Lilly Eli & Co.	LLY	13.38%	40.6	54.3	12.56%
Johnson and Johnson	JNJ	13.34%	57.1	74.8	13.83%
Schering Plough Corp.	SGP	13.22%	48.1	57.1	13.90%
First National City Corp.	FNC/CCI/C	13.20%	20.5	24.4	10.42%
Coca-Cola Co.	KO	13.18%	46.4	56.3	11.11%
American Home Products Corp.	AHP	13.09%	36.7	42.3	10.77%
American Hospital Supply Corp.	AHS/BAX	12.24%	48.1	50.2	11.24%
Procter & Gamble Co.	PG	11.89%	29.8	28.9	9.47%
Texas Instruments Inc.	TXN	11.83%	39.5	36.1	11.45%
AMP Inc.	AMP/TYC	11.19%	42.9	37.5	13.80%
Dow Chemical Co.	DOW	11.19%	24.1	21.2	5.12%
Chesebrough Ponds Inc.	CBM/UN	10.95%	39.1	31.8	4.47%
McDonald's Corp.	MCD	10.58%	71.0	52.1	16.08%
Upjohn Co.	UPJ/PNU/PHA	10.08%	38.8	27.8	9.72%
American Express Co.	AEXP/AXP	10.02%	37.7	26.8	9.17%
Baxter Labs	BAX	9.97%	71.4	45.2	10.52%
Schlumberger Ltd.	SLB	9.87%	45.6	27.9	6.39%
Minnesota Mining & Manufacturing Co.	MMM	9.69%	39.0	26.2	7.45%
International Business Machines	IBM	9.54%	35.5	22.1	8.15%
Disney Walt Co.	DIS	8.92%	71.2	37.6	5.81%
Int'l Telephone & Telegraph Corp.	ITT/HOT	8.74%	15.4	10.4	loss in '01
Lubrizol Corp.	LZ	7.29%	32.6	16.0	6.84%
Sears Roebuck & Co.	S	6.79%	29.2	13.6	0.53%
Schlitz Joe Brewing Co.	SLZ	6.78%	39.6	16.9	loss in '01
Avon Products Inc.	AVP	6.15%	61.2	28.4	5.24%
Int'l Flavors & Fragrances	IFF	5.77%	25.0	8.5	6.51%
Halliburton Co.	HAL	4.97%	35.5	10.3	2.52%
Revlon Inc.	REV	4.77%	69.1	21.9	loss in '01
Louisiana Land & Exploration Co.	LLX/BR	4.68%	26.6	9.1	2.28%
Penney J.C. Inc.	JCP	4.62%	31.5	10.4	loss in '01
Black and Decker Corp.	BDK	2.38%	50.0	10.0	4.92%
Simplicity Patterns	SYP/MXM	2.31%	43.5	9.6	9.00%
Eastman Kodak Co.	EK	1.82%	47.8	11.3	2.87%
Digital Equipment Corp.	DEC/CPQ	1.06%	56.2	2.6	10.16%
Xerox Corp.	XRX	0.15%	45.8	8.9	-2.72%
Kresge (S. S.) Co.	KM	-0.69%	49.5	7.0	loss in '01
Burroughs Co.	BGH/UIS	-1.82%	46.0	5.2	-0.55%
Emery Air Freight Corp.	EAF/CNF	-2.31%	55.3	7.2	loss in '01
M. G. I. C. Investment Corp.	MGI/LUK	-6.07%	68.5	3.6	1.49%
Polaroid Corp.	PRD/PRDCQ	-18.51%	94.8	2.3	loss in '01
Rebalanced Portfolio	rebalanced	**11.76%**	**41.9**	**39.7**	**10.14%**
Equally Weighted	non-rebalanced	**11.62%**	**41.9**	**38.7**	**10.14%**
S&P 500	SPX	**12.14%**	**18.9**	**18.9**	**6.98%**

Morris, which, despite crushing tobacco legislation in the 1990s, had an outstanding 17.8 percent annual return from December 1972 through November 2001.

Of course, there also were some big losers. Technology issues did badly in that not one of them managed to beat the S&P 500 Index. Who would have thought in the 1970s that PepsiCo, Anheuser-Busch, and Coca-Cola would trounce technology giants such as IBM, Digital Equipment, Texas Instruments, Xerox, and Burroughs over the next several decades?

EVALUATION OF DATA

Did the nifty fifty stocks become overvalued during the buying spree of 1972? Yes—but only by a very small margin. An equally weighted portfolio of nifty fifty stocks formed at the market peak in December 1972 and rebalanced monthly would have realized an 11.76 percent annual return through November 2001, just slightly below the 12.14 percent return on the S&P 500 Index.[5] The same portfolio would have returned 11.62 percent if it were never rebalanced over time.

Since the average dividend yield on the nifty fifty was more than 1½ percentage points below the yield on the S&P 500 Index, most of their return came from lightly taxed capital gains. The after-tax yield on a portfolio of nifty fifty stocks purchased at the market peak would have equaled or surpassed the after-tax yield on the S&P 500 Index for an upper-middle-income investor.

WHAT WAS THE RIGHT P-E RATIO TO PAY FOR THE NIFTY FIFTY?

If you could have presented long-term investors with a crystal ball in 1972 that revealed the 29 subsequent years of dividends, earnings, and 2001 prices of the nifty fifty stocks, what price would investors have paid for these stocks in December 1972? The answer is a price high or low enough so that given their subsequent dividends and November 2001 price, their total returns over the past 29 years would match the overall market.[6] Table 9-2 reports these prices relative to their 1972 earn-

---

[5]The average annualized return of a portfolio of stocks is larger than the average annualized return of the individual stocks because of the mathematics of compound returns.
[6]Finance theory states that the required return on an individual stock is also related to its beta with the market. Making this correction does not change the estimates given in Table 9-1 materially. See Jeremy Siegel, "The Nifty Fifty Revisited: Do Growth Stocks Ultimately Justify Their Price?" *Journal of Portfolio Management* 21(4)(Summer 1995):8–20.

ings. Since these prices are warranted by their future returns, these P-E ratios are called the *warranted P-E ratios*.

What is so surprising is that many of these stocks were worth far more than even the lofty heights that investors bid them. Investors should have paid 68.1 times the 1972 earnings for Philip Morris instead of the 24 they did pay, undervaluing the stock by almost 3 to 1. Pfizer was worth 79.5 times earnings, Merck 70.1 times, and Johnson & Johnson should have sported a 74.8 multiple.

In contrast to consumer brand-name stocks and pharmaceuticals, the technology stocks failed badly. IBM, which commanded a P-E ratio of 35 in the early 1970s, actually was worth only 22.1 times earnings despite its stellar comeback in the 1990s. In addition, while investors paid 45.8 times earnings for Xerox, it was worth only 8.9 times earnings on the basis of its future growth. It is ironic that Polaroid, the firm that sported the absolute highest P-E ratio among the original nifty fifty stocks and sold for a fantastic 94.8 times earnings in December 1972, declared bankruptcy in October 2001, and its stock price fell to 5 cents per share.

Despite its mix of winners and losers, the nifty fifty stocks as a portfolio were worth almost as much as investors paid at the market peak in December 1972. An equally weighted portfolio of nifty fifty stocks was worth 39.7 times its 1972 earnings, marginally less than the 41.9 ratio that investors paid for them. Forty times earnings clearly was not too much to pay for a good growth stock despite the conventional wisdom on Wall Street subsequent to the nifty fifty crash.

EARNINGS GROWTH AND VALUATION

Table 9-2 also reports the annual rate of growth of per-share earnings of each nifty fifty firm over the subsequent 29 years. The average annual rate of growth of earnings was about 10 percent per year, 3 percentage points higher than the 7 percent per-share earnings growth of the S&P 500 Index. This finding contrasts sharply with the conclusion of some researchers who maintained that growth stocks had no better subsequent earnings growth than other stocks.[7]

The relation between the P-E ratios and the earnings growth of the nifty fifty showed that investors were not irrational to pay the premium

---

[7]See I. M. D. Little, "Higgledy-Piggledy Growth," *Oxford Bulletin of Economics and Statistics* 24(4)(1962):387–412.

they did for these stocks. In December 1972, the average P-E ratio of the S&P 500 Index was 18.9, which corresponds to an earnings yield of 5.3 percent (the reciprocal of the P-E ratio). The nifty fifty, with a P-E ratio of 41.9, had an earnings yield of 2.4 percent, about 3 percentage points lower than the S&P 500 Index. However, the deficit in the earnings yield was almost exactly made up by the higher earnings growth rate, 10 percent for nifty fifty stocks compared with 7 percent for the S&P 500, so their total return closely matched that of the S&P 500 Index. Nifty fifty investors therefore properly accepted a lower earnings yield (and higher P-E ratio) to pay for higher subsequent earnings growth.

A rule of thumb for stock valuation that is popular on Wall Street is to calculate the sum of the expected growth rate of a stock's earnings plus its dividend yield and divide this by its P-E ratio. The higher the ratio, the better, and the famed money manager Peter Lynch recommends that investors select stocks with a ratio of 2 or higher and to avoid stocks with a ratio less than 1.

Yet this procedure would have eliminated all the best nifty fifty stocks. The top stocks had average annual earnings growths of between 10 and 15 percent per year from December 1972 to 2001, yet their warranted P-E ratios often exceeded 50. Stocks with persistent earnings growth often are worth far more than the multiple that Wall Street considers reasonable.

RETURNS OF HIGH AND LOW P-E NIFTY FIFTY STOCKS

One should not interpret the preceding results to mean that high P-E ratio stocks should not serve as a warning to investors. Table 9-3 shows that the 25 nifty fifty stocks with the highest P-E ratios in 1972 (averaging 54.1) returned more than 3 percentage points *less* than the 25 stocks with the lowest P-E ratios (averaging 29.6). Furthermore, only 6 stocks in the highest-valued group beat the S&P 500 Index, whereas almost half of the 25 stocks with the lowest P-E ratios accomplished this feat. It is of interest that the warranted P-E ratio of each group was an identical 34.4, proving that investors, on average, could not predict the winners from the losers of this popular group of stocks.

The fact that most of the stocks that sported a P-E ratio over 50 in 1972 did not perform well should have served as a red flag for investors when the Internet and technology sectors soared to unprecedented heights. Johnson & Johnson was the *only* stock with a P-E ratio above 50 in the original nifty fifty that subsequently outperformed the S&P 500

T A B L E   9–3

Returns of the High and Low P-E Nifty Fifty Firms (December 1972–November 2001)

High P-E			Low P-E		
Company Name	P-E Ratio	Returns	Company Name	P-E Ratio	Returns
Polaroid Corp.	94.8	-18.51%	Chesebrough Ponds Inc.	39.1	10.95%
Baxter Labs	71.4	9.97%	Minnesota Mining & Manufacturing Co.	39.0	9.69%
Disney Walt Co.	71.2	8.92%	Upjohn Co.	38.8	10.08%
McDonald's Corp.	71.0	10.58%	American Express Co.	37.7	10.02%
Int'l Flavors & Fragrances	69.1	5.77%	American Home Products Corp.	36.7	13.09%
M. G. I. C. Investment Corp.	68.5	-6.07%	International Business Machines	35.5	9.54%
Avon Products Inc.	61.2	6.15%	Halliburton Co.	35.5	4.97%
Johnson and Johnson	57.1	13.34%	Lubrizol Corp.	32.6	7.29%
Digital Equipment Corp.	56.2	1.06%	Anheuser-Busch Inc.	31.5	13.41%
Emery Air Freight Corp.	55.3	-2.31%	Penney J.C. Inc.	31.5	4.62%
Simplicity Patterns	50.0	2.31%	Squibb Corp.	30.1	14.46%
Kresge (S. S.) Co.	49.5	-0.69%	Procter & Gamble Co.	29.8	11.89%
Schering Corp.	48.1	13.22%	Heublein Inc.	29.4	14.75%
American Hospital Supply Corp.	48.1	12.24%	Sears Roebuck & Co.	29.2	6.79%
Black and Decker Corp.	47.8	2.38%	Pfizer Inc.	28.4	17.39%
Coca-Cola Co.	46.4	13.18%	Pepsico Inc.	27.6	15.58%
Burroughs Co.	46.0	-1.82%	Louisiana Land & Exploration Co.	26.6	4.68%
Xerox Corp.	45.8	0.15%	Revlon Inc.	25.0	4.77%
Schlumberger Ltd.	45.6	9.87%	Bristol-Myers	24.9	15.60%
Eastman Kodak Co.	43.5	1.82%	Gillette Co.	24.3	14.07%
Merck & Co. Inc.	43.0	14.85%	Dow Chemical Co.	24.1	11.19%
AMP Inc.	42.9	11.19%	Philip Morris Cos. Inc.	24.0	17.80%
Lilly Eli & Co.	40.6	13.38%	General Electric Co.	23.4	15.44%
Schlitz Joe Brewing Co.	39.6	6.78%	First National City Corp.	20.5	13.20%
Texas Instruments Inc.	39.5	11.83%	Int'l Telephone & Telegraph Corp.	15.4	8.74%
Average P-E Ratio	**54.1**		**Average P-E Ratio**	**29.6**	
Warranted P-E Ratio	**34.4**		**Warranted P-E Ratio**	**34.4**	
Annual Return*	**9.72%**		**Annual Return***	**12.90%**	

*Based on Non-Rebalanced Portfolio.

Index. Moreover, *no* stock in the original group deserved a P-E ratio above 80, no matter how good its subsequent returns proved to be. This implies that large growth stocks, no matter how boundless their prospects seem, should never be considered "buys at any price."

JUSTIFIED P-E RATIOS FOR INDIVIDUAL STOCKS

How much should investors be willing to pay for large growth stocks? There are five major variables that determine a *justified* P-E ratio. They are (1) investors' required rates of return, (2) the rate of earnings growth, (3) the number of years that the earnings growth can be maintained, (4) the P-E ratio at *maturity* (when the period of accelerated growth has ended and the stock returns to a long-term P-E ratio), and (5) the dividend yield.

Table 9-4 calculates these justified P-E ratios under two scenarios: one in which investors require a 10 percent rate of return (a 7 percent real

TABLE 9–4

Justified P-E Ratios for Technology and Nontechnology Firms

Nontech Firms				Tech Firms		
Assume a 10% Required Return and a Dividend Yield of 2%				Assume a 15% Required Return and No Dividend Yield		
EPS Growth Rates	5 Years	10 Years	29 Years	EPS Growth Rates	5 Years	10 Years
0%	17	12	3	0%	12	6
5%	22	19	11			
6%	23	21	15	5%	16	10
7%	24	23	19			
8%	25	25	25	10%	20	16
9%	26	27	33	15%	25	25
10%	27	30	43			
11%	29	33	55	20%	31	38
12%	30	36	72	25%	38	58
13%	31	39	93			
14%	33	43	120	30%	46	85
15%	34	47	154	35%	56	124
20%	42	72	531			
25%	52	108	N.A	40%	67	179
30%	63	160	N.A	45%	80	254
35%	76	233	N.A			
40%	92	335	N.A	50%	94	356
45%	109	476	N.A	55%	111	495
50%	129	668	N.A			
55%	152	927	N.A	60%	130	679

N.A = Not Applicable

return plus a 3 percent expected rate of inflation) and another in which a 15 percent rate of return is assumed, closer to the rate of return required by investors in the more volatile technology stocks. In both cases it is assumed that the P-E ratio at maturity is 25. The dividend yield is assumed to be 2 percent for stocks requiring a 10 percent return and zero for the technology stocks requiring a 15 percent return.

Table 9-1 shows that the average estimated earnings growth rate of the technology stocks in March of 2000 was less than 30 percent per year. One can see from Table 9-4 that if this 30 percent growth lasted 5 years (what analysts call *long-term growth*), the technology stocks listed would have justified a P-E ratio of 46. If this growth could have been maintained for 10 years, a P-E ratio of 85 would have been warranted. It is also apparent that based on the future 5-year growth estimates shown in Table 9-1, not one firm, save Yahoo!, would have justified a P-E ratio of 100. If Yahoo! had achieved the astounding 55.9 percent earnings growth rate that analysts had anticipated for the next 5 years, this premier Internet portal company would have deserved a P-E of 113. In March 2000, however, Yahoo! was selling over 600 times earnings, and its earnings fell precipitously in the very next quarter. Yahoo! declined more than 97 percent from its peak of $250 a share in January 2000 (a month after it was admitted into the S&P 500 Index) to a trough of $8 in September 2001.

Is it realistic to assume that once a firm has attained big capitalization status it can grow its earnings over 20 percent per year over the next 10 years? The answer is decidedly no. Table 9-5 shows the largest 20 stocks ranked by market value in 1955, 1965, 1975, and 1990 and their *subsequent* 10-year earnings growth. No firm on this list had attained a 20 percent per year earnings growth in the next 10 years, and very few were able to generate 10-year earnings growth rates in excess of 15 percent per year.

Table 9-4 also shows how nontech firms should be priced with a required rate of return of 10 percent per year and a 2 percent dividend yield under various assumptions about earnings growth. Table 9-2 shows that the average 29-year earnings growth of the nifty fifty was 10 percent, which warranted a P-E ratio of 43 from Table 9-4. Every 1 percentage point a firm adds to its 29-year earnings growth rate warrants an increase of approximately 10 points in its P-E ratio. This analysis shows that if a firm is able to increase its earnings growth in the very long run, this can have a dramatic effect on the price that investors should be willing to pay for the stock. However, extremely few stocks have managed to become these long-term winners.

TABLE 9–5

Subsequent 10-Year Earnings Growth of Largest Market Value Stocks

1955		1965	
AT&T Corp.	4.56%	AT&T Corp.	4.09%
Amoco Corp.	2.57%	Amoco Corp.	13.20%
Bethlehem Steel Corp.	-2.94%	Chevron Corp.	6.89%
Chevron Corp.	5.01%	Creole Petroleum Corp.	N/A
Dow Chemical	4.60%	du Pont (E I) de Nemours	-4.51%
du Pont (E I) de Nemours	-0.70%	Eastman Kodak Co.	9.49%
Eastman Kodak Co.	11.25%	Ford Motor Co.	-9.10%
General Electric Co.	4.93%	GTE Corp.	4.42%
General Motors Corp.	5.59%	General Electric Co.	4.88%
Gulf Corp.	6.47%	General Motors Corp.	-5.26%
Intl Business Machines	18.88%	Gulf Corp.	5.74%
International Paper Co.	-0.40%	Intl Business Machines	14.25%
Kennecott Corp.	-2.26%	Minnesota Mining and Mfg.	7.81%
USX-Marathon Group	3.27%	Mobil Corp.	9.70%
Mobil Corp.	5.18%	Procter & Gamble Co.	10.32%
Phillips Petroleum Co.	3.27%	Sears Roebuck & Co.	2.27%
Sears Roebuck & Co.	7.13%	Shell Oil Co.	7.03%
Shell Oil Co.	6.29%	Texaco. Inc.	2.65%
Texaco. Inc.	8.17%	Union Carbide Corp.	5.18%
Union Carbide Corp.	4.53%	Xerox Corp.	16.59%
Inflation	1.71%	Inflation	5.73%
1975		**1990**	
American Home Products	11.54%	AT&T Corp.	-5.77%
AT&T Corp.	2.10%	Amoco Corp.	9.92%
Amoco Corp.	10.72%	Atlantic Richfield Co.	5.71%
Chevron Corp.	7.11%	BellSouth Corp.	10.29%
Coca-Cola Corp.	9.99%	Bristol-Myers Squibb	9.58%
Dow Chemical	-21.31%	Chevron Corp.	10.10%
du Pont (E I) de Nemours	9.78%	Coca-Cola Corp.	5.61%
Eastman Kodak Co.	-5.36%	du Pont (E I) de Nemours	2.66%
General Electric Co.	12.48%	GTE Corp.	8.16%
General Motors Corp.	11.02%	General Electric Co.	12.31%
Gulf Corp.	4.94%	General Motors Corp.	0.72%
Intl Business Machines	12.33%	Intl Business Machines	5.72%
Johnson & Johnson	12.27%	Johnson & Johnson	14.93%
Merck & Co.	9.65%	Eli Lilly & Co.	11.21%
Minnesota Mining and Mfg.	9.59%	Merck & Co.	14.56%
Mobil Corp.	2.51%	Mobil Corp.	5.44%
Procter & Gamble Co.	6.81%	PEPSICo. Inc.	8.23%
Sears Roebuck & Co.	10.76%	Philip Morris Cos. Inc.	11.43%
Texaco. Inc.	5.26%	Procter & Gamble Co.	8.26%
Weyerhaeuser Co.	-1.14%	Wal-Mart Stores	17.76%
Inflation	7.01%	Inflation	2.66%

CONCLUSION

As so often happens in financial markets, investors learn their lessons too well.[8] After the wreckage of the nifty fifty in 1974, many investors vowed never to pay more than 30 times earnings for any stock, no matter how promising its growth prospects. But Wall Street drew the wrong lesson from the nifty fifty episode of the 1970s. The prevailing cautious attitude toward growth sent the nifty fifty stocks to dramatically undervalued levels throughout the 1980s and the early 1990s. It was not until the mid-1990s that investors recognized the true value of growth and began again to accumulate these shares.[9] But with the technology boom of 1999–2000, the pendulum swung to the other extreme, and many investors believed there was never a price too high to pay for a true growth stock.

By the year 2000, technology stocks, which have never been good long-term performers, reached P-E ratios that more than doubled those reached by the nifty fifty three decades earlier. The euphoria associated with the technology boom sent those stocks to prices that were impossible to justify even if the most optimistic predictions of earnings growth came true. The bear market that followed in these issues was inevitable. Most nontech growth stocks never became snagged in the technology bubble and remained reasonably priced relative to their long-term prospects. They suffered far less in the bear market that followed.

Did the 2000–2001 bear market bring large-capitalization growth stocks back to the undervalued position they found themselves in the late 1970s and 1980s? No one knows for sure, but buyers of growth stocks should be forewarned. No one stock or single industry is guaranteed to succeed. Diversification is a key to cutting risks and maintaining returns. Good growth stocks can be worth 40, 50, and even 60 times earnings, but no big-capitalization stock has even been worth more than 100 times earnings.

---

[8]See Chapter 13 for the reaction of the market to the onset of World War II as it wrongly thought it had "learned" a lesson from the market's reaction to World War I. Chapter 19 discusses the "representative bias," where investors believe a situation is similar when in fact it is not.

[9]In the early 1970s, some nifty fifty lists included Wal-Mart, which had a 26.97 percent annual return from December 1972 through November 2001, far eclipsing every stock on the Morgan Guaranty Trust list. If Wal-Mart had been included, the nifty fifty as a group would likely have been *undervalued* at the market peak. See Jeff Fesenmaier and Gary Smith, "The Nifty-Fifty Re-Revisited," Pomona College, 2002.

APPENDIX: CORPORATE CHANGES IN THE NIFTY FIFTY STOCKS

There have been 15 corporate changes to the nifty fifty over the past several decades:

- AMP, Inc., was purchased by Tyco, Inc., in April 1999.
- American Hospital Supply merged with Baxter Travenol (later Baxter International) in November 1985.
- Burroughs changed its name to Unisys (UIS) in 1987.
- Chesebrough Ponds was merged in Unilever NV in February 1987.
- Digital Equipment was purchased by Compaq in June 1998.
- Emery Air Freight merged with Consolidated Freightways in April 1989 (name changed to CNF Transportation in April 1997 and CNF, Inc., in December 2000).
- Heublein was merged into RJR Nabisco in October 1982, which became RJR Industries and was taken private on April 28, 1989.
- Louisiana Land Exploration was purchased by Burlington Resources in October 1997.
- MGIC Investment merged with Baldwin United in March of 1982, which went bankrupt and emerged from bankruptcy in November 1986 under the name PHL Corp. PHL was later absorbed by Leucadia National Corp. in January 1993.
- ITT was acquired by Starwood Hotels and Resorts in 1998.
- Revlon was subject to a leveraged buyout in July 1987 and went public again in 1996.
- Schlitz merged in June 1982 with Stroh Brewing, a privately held firm.
- Simplicity Pattern became Maxxam in May 1984 and then Maxxam Group in May 1988.
- Squibb was purchased on October 4, 1989, by Bristol-Myers (which became Bristol-Myers Squibb).
- Upjohn merged with Pharmacia AB (Sweden) in November 1995 and became Pharmacia & Upjohn, Inc. In 1997 the company merged with Pharmacia Corporation.

CHAPTER 10

GLOBAL INVESTING

Today let's talk about a growth industry. Because investing world-wide is a growth industry. The great growth industry is international portfolio investing.   JOHN TEMPLETON[1]

Chapter 1 showed that the superior long-term returns of stocks were not unique to the United States. Investors in Great Britain, Germany, and even Japan have accumulated substantial wealth through investing in stocks. For many years, however, foreign markets were almost exclusively the domains of native investors, considered too remote and risky to be entered by outsiders.

But this is the case no longer. *Globalization* has been the financial buzzword of the past decade. The United States, once the unchallenged giant of capital markets, has become only one of many countries in which investors can accumulate wealth. At the end of World War II, U.S. stocks comprised almost 90 percent of the world's equity capitalization; by 1970, they still comprised two-thirds. Today, however, the U.S. market constitutes less than half the world's stock values. To invest only in the United States is to ignore the majority of the world's capital.

---

[1]Transcript of address delivered to Annual Conference of the Financial Analysts Federation, May 2, 1984.

163

Yet foreign investing was not very profitable in the late 1990s, especially for dollar-based investors. The crash of the emerging markets in 1997–1998, the long bear market in Japan, and the fall of the European market have caused many people to question the need to invest abroad. This chapter analyzes the motivation for international diversification and determines whether the changing investment environment can still support the case for foreign investment.

CYCLES IN FOREIGN MARKETS

One of the greatest mistakes investors make is planning strategy based on short-term trends. Even data from periods as long as 10 or 20 years are insufficient to draw any definitive conclusions about what may happen in the future. This fact is illustrated in Table 10-1.

T A B L E   10–1

Compound Annual Dollar Returns in World Stock Markets, 1970–2001 (Standard Deviations in Parentheses)

Country or Region	1970 - 2001	1970 - 1979	1980 - 1989	1990 - 2001
World*	10.86%	6.96%	19.92%	19.92%
	(16.99)	(18.09)	(14.59)	(15.33)
EAFE**	10.96%	10.09%	22.77%	2.66%
	(22.42)	(22.77)	(23.28)	(17.45)
USA	11.59%	4.61%	17.13%	13.11%
	(16.99)	(19.01)	(12.52)	(16.78)
Europe	11.78%	8.57%	18.49%	9.10%
	(21.01)	(20.97)	(25.89)	(13.95)
Japan	11.12%	17.37%	28.66%	-6.03%
	(36.83)	(45.41)	(28.57)	(28.95)

*World = Value-Weighted World Index; **EAFE = Europe, Australasia, and the Far East

U.S. stock returns lagged behind those in both Europe and Japan in both the 1970s and 1980s. If investors interpreted this to mean that they should invest most of their wealth abroad, they would have missed the greatest bull market in U.S. history during the 1990s.

Japanese returns were even more misleading. In the 1970s and 1980s, Japanese dollar stock returns were more than 10 percent per year above the return in the U.S. market and dominated those from every other industrialized country. The Japanese market performed so well that by the end of 1989, for the first time since the early part of the twentieth century, the American equity market was no longer the world's largest. Japan, a country whose economic base was totally destroyed by U.S. military action 44 years earlier and who possesses only half the population and 4 percent of the land mass of the United States, became the home to a stock market that exceeded the valuation of both U.S. and European markets.

The superior returns on the Japanese market attracted billions of dollars of foreign investment. Valuations on many Japanese stocks reached stratospheric levels. Nippon Telephone and Telegraph (NTT), the Japanese version of America's AT&T, was priced at a price-earnings (P-E) ratio above 300. This stock had a market valuation of hundreds of billions of dollars, dwarfing the aggregate stock values of all but a handful of countries around the world.

Leo Melamed, president of the Chicago Mercantile Exchange, traveled to Japan in 1987 and questioned his hosts as to how such remarkably high valuations could be warranted. "You don't understand," they responded. "We've moved to an entirely new way of valuing stocks here in Japan." And this is when Melamed knew that Japanese stocks were doomed, for it is when investors cast aside the lessons of history that those lessons come back to haunt them.[2]

The Nikkei Dow Jones, which had surpassed 39,000 in December 1989, fell to nearly 14,000 by August of 1992—a fall worse than any experienced by the U.S. markets since the great 1929–1932 crash. The value of NTT shares fell from 3.2 million yen to under 500,000 yen. The mystique of the Japanese market was broken.

The collapse of the Japanese market shifted the emphasis of global enthusiasts to *emerging markets*—markets in developing or newly developed countries. Investors had already witnessed the stock booms of Taiwan, Korea, and Thailand. Now India, Indonesia, and even China were set to join the club.

---

[2]Martin Mayer, *Markets* (New York: W. W. Norton, 1988), p. 60.

Moreover, Asian countries were not the only markets put into play. Latin America, long a backwater of authoritarian, anti-free-market regimes (of both the right and left), had turned full circle and aggressively sought foreign investment. Equity gains were impressive in such countries as Argentina, Brazil, and Mexico.

Even China, the last major country ruled by communist leaders, developed stock markets. The opening of the first Chinese stock market in Shenzhen in 1998 was met with a riot as thousands of people stood for days in lines waiting to be allocated shares in firms in the world's most populated country. And who would have imagined that investors in Hong Kong would beat those in the United States during the last decade, despite the fact that the country was absorbed by communist China, once the sworn enemy of capitalism?

The term *emerging markets* evokes the image of a beautiful butterfly rising from its chrysalis, ready to soar to the heavens. However, the enthusiasm that greeted these markets' potential often far exceeded their ability to perform. Just as birds eat most butterflies soon after they take their first flight, bears devoured many of these newly emerging markets soon after investor enthusiasm had peaked.

One of the worst collapses in the history of emerging markets began in 1997. The emerging Asian economies, idolized by many investors who had sent their shares skyward, saw their currencies and equity prices plummet. In 1998, the contagion spread beyond the Pacific Basin to Latin America, eastern Europe, and Russia.

In that 2-year period, virtually no emerging market was safe. Most, if not all, of the countries' stock markets fell by at least 50 percent in dollar terms, and many fell much more. Measured in U.S. dollars, the Indonesian, Thai, and Russian markets fell more than 90 percent, and those in the Philippines and Korea fell more than 80 percent. Even stocks in the strongest and most advanced of these developing countries, Singapore and Hong Kong, fell 70 percent.

The collapse of these economies dimmed investors' enthusiasm for foreign investing. However, more troubles were brewing for U.S. investors seeking gains abroad. As the U.S. stock market soared and foreign currencies sank relative to the dollar, Europe's and Japan's dollar returns also fell behind those of U.S. stocks. The superior long-term gains that U.S. investors realized through many years of patient investing soon vanished.

Figure 10-1 shows the growth of $100 invested in Japan, the United States, the United Kingdom, and Germany since January 1970. What is

FIGURE 10–1

Total Dollar Returns in Major Markets, 1970–2001

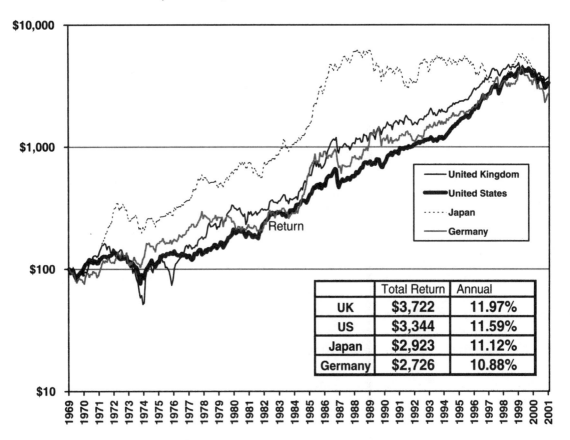

	Total Return	Annual
UK	$3,722	11.97%
US	$3,344	11.59%
Japan	$2,923	11.12%
Germany	$2,726	10.88%

astounding is that over this 32-year period, the returns of all the major markets of the world are nearly identical.[3] Certainly these returns show little better long-term performance than staying in the United States, and many other countries' returns, especially those from emerging markets, have significantly lagged those in the United States. Given the poor foreign returns of late, investors are right to ask: Can the case for international investing, put forth so enthusiastically in the 1980s and 1990s, still be made today?

---

[3]These returns are measured in dollars, but identical conclusions can be drawn measuring returns in *any* common currency.

DIVERSIFICATION IN WORLD MARKETS

Principles of Diversification

It might surprise investors that the principal motivation for investing in foreign stocks is not that the expected return is better investing abroad. Rather, the reason is that international investing allows you to diversify your portfolio more completely, and it therefore reduces total portfolio risk. In principle, foreign investing provides diversification in the same way investing in different sectors of the domestic economy provides diversification.

It is a statistical fact that dividing a portfolio among different sectors results in lower risk than investing in only one sector. This is so because the returns of one sector can rise at the same time those of another sector fall, and this asynchronous movement of returns dampens the volatility of the portfolio.

The degree of asynchronous movements of returns between sectors is measured by the *correlation coefficient*. The lower the correlation coefficient, the better is the diversification. For example, if there is no correlation between the returns of two sectors and the correlation coefficient is equal to zero, investors can divide their portfolio between each and reduce risk by almost one-third over what they would experience if they just invested in a single sector. As the correlation coefficient between the returns in each sector increases, the gains from diversification dwindle, and if there is perfect correlation in returns and the correlation coefficient equals 1, there is absolutely no gain from diversification.

Efficient Portfolios

How does one determine how much should be invested at home or abroad? The amount invested in each country depends not only on one's assessment of the risk and expected return in each country but, as noted above, also on the correlation of returns between countries.

An investor can vary the risk and return on his or her portfolio by varying the proportion invested in U.S. and international stocks. Figure 10-2 shows the risk-return trade-offs (called the *efficient frontier*) for investing in U.S. and foreign equities for dollar-based investors.[4] The curves in the figure are based on the historical data from U.S. and inter-

---

[4]Foreign equities here are the Europe, Australasia, and Far East (EAFE) index and the index of European, Australian, and Far East stocks compiled by Morgan Stanley.

FIGURE   10–2

Efficient Frontier between U.S. and EAFE Returns

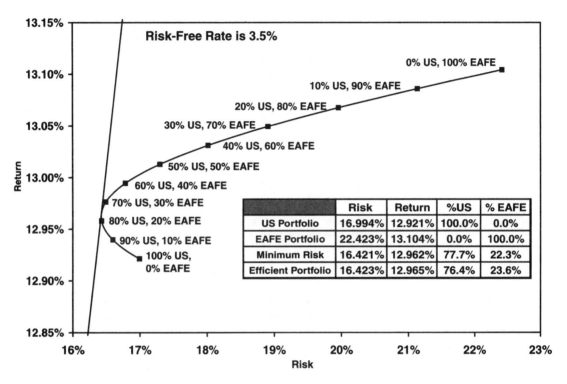

	Risk	Return	%US	% EAFE
US Portfolio	16.994%	12.921%	100.0%	0.0%
EAFE Portfolio	22.423%	13.104%	0.0%	100.0%
Minimum Risk	16.421%	12.962%	77.7%	22.3%
Efficient Portfolio	16.423%	12.965%	76.4%	23.6%

national stocks over the past 32 years, as summarized in Table 10-2.[5] The minimum risk of this diversified portfolio occurs with 22.3 percent allocated to foreign stocks, and the best risk-return portfolio (called the *efficient portfolio*) is at a slightly higher 23.6 percent foreign.[6]

Increase in Correlation between World Returns

The percentage of foreign stocks recommended by this formal portfolio analysis is higher than the percentage that most investors allocate to

---

[5]Risk-return analysis is done with *arithmetic* returns and not the geometric returns reported in Table 10-2. Over the period analyzed, foreign arithmetic returns outpaced U.S. arithmetic returns, although their geometric returns lagged.

[6]Readers who wish to understand risk-return analysis can go to Richard Brealey and Stewart Myers, *Principles of Corporate Finance*, 6th ed. (New York: McGraw Hill, 2000).

TABLE 10–2

Dollar Returns and Risks in Stocks, January 1970–December 2001

Country or Region	US $ Returns		Domestic Risk	Exchange Risk	Total Risk	Correlation Coefficient*
	Compound	Arithmetic				
World	10.86%	12.19%	16.47%	5.13%	16.99%	82.16%
EAFE	10.96%	13.10%	19.33%	10.16%	22.42%	53.24%
USA	11.59%	12.92%	16.99%	- - -	16.99%	100.00%
Europe	11.78%	13.59%	20.18%	11.04%	21.01%	67.75%
Japan	11.12%	17.71%	29.37%	13.22%	36.83%	26.92%

*Correlation between US dollar returns and foreign market US dollar returns.

non-U.S. stocks. As noted earlier, however, this recommended percentage is strongly influenced by the expected correlation between the returns on U.S. and foreign-based stocks. Figure 10-3a shows a 2-year moving average and Figure 10-3b shows a 9-year moving average of the correlation between U.S. and foreign stock returns. One can see that the correlation has increased dramatically to record levels in recent years.

This increased correlation has serious implications for the allocation of one's portfolio. Figure 10-4 shows, using the same historical data on return and risk used in Figure 10-3, how the recommended percentage in foreign stocks changes as the expected correlation between U.S. and foreign returns varies. At an expected correlation between U.S. and international returns of 66.5 percent, which has been the average over the last 9 years, the percentage recommended in foreign portfolio would drop to 15 percent. Based on a 2-year correlation of 83.5 percent, no funds should be put in foreign stocks![7]

What has caused the recent increase in the correlation between U.S. and foreign returns? Clearly, the globalization of both product and financial markets is one factor. As companies expand across the globe, it is becoming less and less important in which country a firm is headquartered.

---

[7]In fact, the analysis suggests that investors should hold 114 percent in U.S. stocks and short 14 percent of the value of their portfolio in foreign stocks.

FIGURE 10–3

Correlation between U.S. and EAFE Stock Returns

Figure A

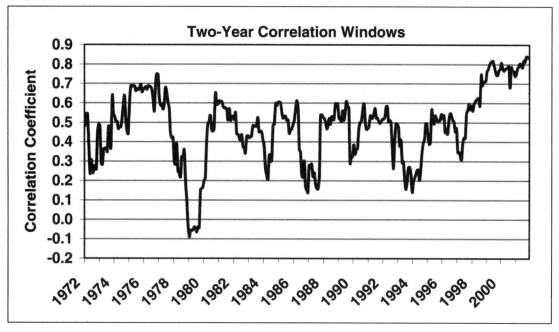

Figure B

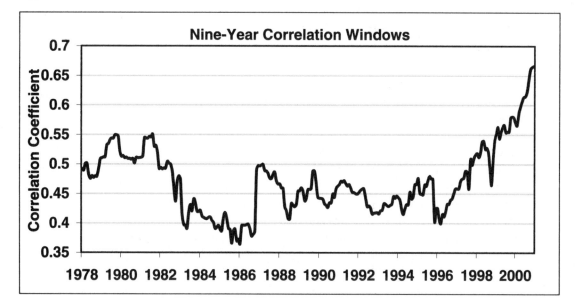

FIGURE 10–4

Percent of Optimal Portfolio Invested in U.S. Stocks

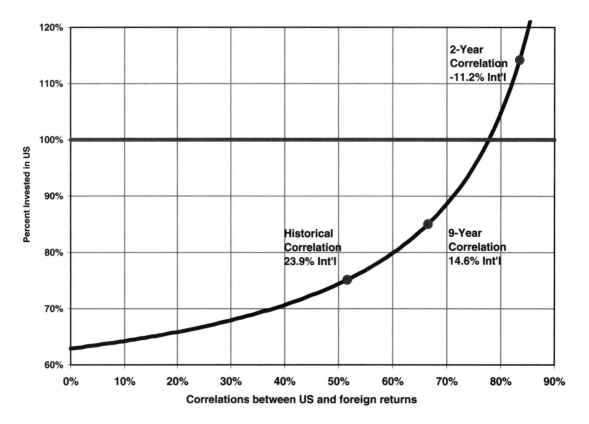

The increased communication between investors also causes higher correlations between returns. Information flows rapidly, and investors are more in touch with each other than ever before. It is difficult for traders to shield themselves from shifts in investor sentiment that envelope the investment community.

Another reason for the increase in correlation is the very high correlation of the returns of technology, media, and telecom stocks (often called *TMT*) between countries. The wild ride that these stocks experienced from 1999 to 2001 was similar in exchanges around the world.

One should not dismiss the increased correlation between world returns as just a one-time phenomenon related to these sectors, however. The returns of nontechnology stocks also showed an increased correlation, and it is quite likely that the globalization of trading will cause world markets to move more synchronously than they have in the past.

Sector Diversification

If countries' returns are becoming more correlated, where can an investor turn to obtain diversification? A better approach may be not only to examine the returns of different economic sectors, such as consumer stocks, financials, energy, and health care, but also to expand the set to include international as well as domestic firms. Figure 10-5 shows the trends in correlations between the major world industry sectors as classified by the Morgan Stanley Capital Market Indexes. In contrast to the correlation of country returns, which are rising, the correlation between sectors has been falling sharply since the mid-1990s. If this trend continues, a sector approach may supplant a country approach to investing and diversification.

FIGURE 10-5

Average Correlation of Global Industry Sectors with World Stock Index (2-Year Correlation Windows, January 1975–July 2001)

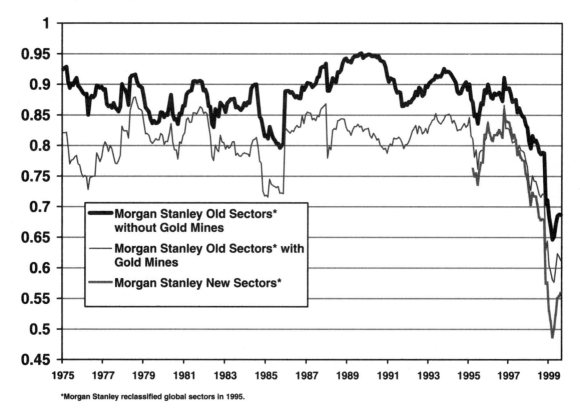

*Morgan Stanley reclassified global sectors in 1995.

The decreased correlation between sectors may be caused by the reduction in business cycle fluctuations. Investors can now focus more of their attention on the investment prospects of individual firms and industries rather than on the health of the entire economy.

Does this all mean that we should ignore the notion of country altogether when investing in stocks? Those supporting the country approach indicate that the country in which a multinational corporation is headquartered still substantially influences that firm's returns, even when most of the firm's sales and earnings come from abroad. This may be due to the fact that the home country importantly influences firms' legal obligations and liabilities and that governmental regulations also differ widely among countries.[8] Furthermore, despite globalization, most of the trading in each firm takes place on exchanges of the home country.

However, these home country influences likely will diminish in future years as globalization advances. In fact, one can envision a future where the headquartered country is a decidedly secondary consideration, and investment allocations are made on the basis of global economic sector diversification. Whatever criteria are used, foreign stocks will still play a role in a well-balanced portfolio.

HEDGING FOREIGN EXCHANGE RISKS

If foreign firms are going to be part of a well-diversified portfolio, dollar-based investors must realize that foreign risks cannot be ignored. The summary data on U.S. and foreign returns shown in Table 10-2 indicate that foreign stocks are more risky than U.S. stocks for dollar-based investors. There are two reasons for this. One is that foreign markets themselves have higher volatility (called *local risk*), and the second is that exchange-rate risk—unexpected changes in foreign currencies prices against the U.S. dollar—adds a second level of risk to owning foreign-based stocks.

It is very important to note that the total risk of holding foreign equities is substantially less than the sum of the local and exchange-rate risks. This is so because these risks are not perfectly correlated, so movements in the exchange rate and the local stock market frequently offset each other. In fact, for some countries, such as the United Kingdom, the exchange-rate risk offsets the local risk so much that a U.S. holder of

---

[8]Although most firms also must submit to the regulations of where they sell as well as where they produce.

British equities since 1970 has experienced less volatility in dollar returns than a British investor has in pounds sterling!

Nevertheless, since foreign exchange risk does add to the dollar risk of holding foreign securities, it could pay for an investor in foreign markets to hedge against currency movements. *Currency hedging* means taking a position in a currency market that offsets unexpected changes in the foreign currency relative to the dollar. Stock market fluctuations can cause enough anxiety without worrying about whether an adverse change in foreign exchange rates also will reduce the value of your foreign portfolio.

Although hedging seems like an attractive way to offset exchange-rate risk, in the long run it is often unnecessary and even detrimental. For example, in the United Kingdom from 1910 onward, the pound depreciated from $4.80 to about $1.50. It might seem obvious that an investor who hedged the fall of the pound would be better off than one who had not. However, this is not the case. Since the British interest rate was, on average, substantially higher than the rate in the United States, the cost of hedging for a dollar-based investor, which depends on the relative interest rates between the two countries, was high. The unhedged returns for British stocks in U.S. dollars actually exceeded the hedged accumulation despite the fall of the British pound.

For investors with long-term horizons, hedging currency risk in foreign stock markets is not important. In fact, there is some evidence that in the long run, currency hedges actually may increase the volatility of dollar returns.[9] In the long run, exchange-rate movements are determined primarily by changes in local prices. Equities are claims on real assets that compensate the stockholder for changes in the price level. To hedge such a long-run investment would be self-defeating because by buying a real asset you automatically hedge a depreciating currency.

HEDGING IN THE SHORT RUN

Nevertheless, if one is concerned about reducing short-term risk and if hedging can be done cheaply, it may be effective. There are circumstances, however, especially when there is a change in monetary policy, where exchange-rate hedging would be counterproductive and actually would increase the volatility of dollar returns. For example, if the European cen-

---

[9]See Kenneth A. Froot, "Currency Hedging over Long Horizons," NBER working paper no. 4355, Cambridge, Mass., May 1993.

tral bank tightens credit and raises interest rates, this may cause the Euro to rise. However, European stock prices may fall as rising interest rates increase the attractiveness of bonds relative to stocks.

If investors do not hedge, the upward movement of the Euro will offset the downward movement in the stock market, thereby reducing fluctuations in the dollar returns on European stocks. On the other hand, if investors hedge, they forgo the appreciation of the Euro that offsets the decline in the value of European stocks.

Although changes in exchange rates and stock prices often move in the opposite direction, this is not always so. Swings in optimism and pessimism about the growth prospects in a country often cause stock prices and currency values to move in the same direction. As I shall describe in more detail below, when investors became pessimistic about prospects in the emerging Asian markets, both currency and stock prices plummeted. Hedging, especially if in place before the crisis began, would have shielded investors from the worst of the downturn.

THE EMERGING MARKET CRISIS OF 1998

As noted at the beginning of this chapter, the problems in the emerging markets were the first sign that the unrestrained optimism about foreign investing was unfounded. Like all crises, however, this one snuck up on shareholders. Few U.S. investors noted the troubles in Thailand that developed in July 1997. Ranked just behind the four Asian "tigers" (Hong Kong, Singapore, Taiwan, and South Korea), Thailand had enjoyed a long boom fed by billions of dollars of foreign investment. However, sagging profits and adverse economic developments caused investor enthusiasm to wane. On July 7, 1997, Thailand was forced to relinquish its fixed exchange rate to the dollar and let its currency float on the international market.

Often relinquishing fixed exchange rates is good for the stock market. When Great Britain left the European monetary system in September 1992 and devalued the pound, stock prices jumped. Maintaining an overvalued currency involves tight credit and high interest rates—not a friendly environment for stocks.

For a developing economy, however, relinquishing fixed exchange rates is often a sign of deeper problems: a chronic and worsening deficit in its trade and current accounts, government deficit spending, and rising inflationary pressures. These developments lead to a loss of investor confidence and a rush to exit the country's financial markets.

Investors reasoned that if there were problems in Thailand, other Asian countries also must be in trouble. One by one the currencies of the Asian countries fell like dominoes. The Indonesian rupiah plunged in value, as did the Philippine peso and the Korean won. With the Asian currencies in trouble, many traders thought it was only a matter of time before Hong Kong would be forced to devalue its own dollar.

However, Hong Kong's exchange-rate system was different from those of the other Asian countries. After experiencing high inflation in the 1970s and early 1980s, Hong Kong fixed its value to the U.S. dollar in 1983 and simultaneously created a *currency board*, a monetary institution that backs each and every Hong Kong dollar with an equivalent value of U.S. government securities or U.S. dollar deposits. In other words, if everyone in Hong Kong decided to turn their Hong Kong dollars into U.S. dollars, the Hong Kong monetary authority would have the U.S. dollars to exchange for them.

Despite this protection, traders believed that the deep devaluations of other Asian countries would undermine any competitive advantage Hong Kong had, forcing Hong Kong to devalue. As a result, traders began to sell Hong Kong dollars, sending local interest rates soaring. With Hong Kong under attack, investors felt that a worldwide currency crisis was at hand. Invoking painful memories of the competitive devaluations between countries that took place in the early 1930s, investors sold stocks worldwide.

On October 27, 1997, selling on the New York Stock Exchange sent the Dow Jones Industrials down 350 points, a level that triggered a 1-hour halt in trading. When trading resumed, a crush of sell orders quickly sent the market down 200 more points to a daily limit of 550 points, at which point the market closed. This was the greatest point drop ever experienced by the Dow Jones Industrials up to that time, although, in terms of percentage changes, it was nowhere near the top.[10]

The attack on Hong Kong failed, and market anxiety eased. But not for long. The next spring, markets in South America came under pressure, and in August 1998, Russia defaulted on its bonds, the first such governmental bond default in many years. Visions of international financial crisis sent investors flocking to U.S. government bonds as a safe haven, and the differences between the yields on government and nongovernment bonds skyrocketed. Anxiety ran so high that many credit

---

[10]Chapter 13 lists the largest 1-day moves in the history of the market. Chapter 16 discusses market volatility and the policies on trading halts currently in place in U.S. markets.

markets "seized up" and stopped functioning, to use the words of Federal Reserve Chairman Alan Greenspan. The Dow Jones Industrials plummeted from nearly 9,400 to 7,400, their largest percentage decline since the 1990–1991 recession.

The dysfunction in the bond markets prompted the Federal Reserve (Fed) to facilitate the bailout of Long Term Capital Management, a hedge fund that bet heavily (and wrongly) that the risk spreads that widened in the spring would soon return to normal.[11] When the Fed reduced the fed funds rate three times in quick succession, markets recovered, and the crisis eased. Surprising many economists and forecasters, the U.S. economy maneuvered its way through the crisis with nary a scratch and posted a solid nearly 5 percent growth over the next 2 years.

AFTERMATH OF CRISIS

Despite the healthy U.S. economic performance, the Asian and emerging market crises had lasting effects on financial markets. The first was the recognition that developing economies could grow nowhere near as fast as many investors had hoped. Much of the rapid gross domestic product (GDP) growth of the early and middle 1990s was fueled by the indiscriminate inflow of investment dollars. Overinvestment and wasteful spending in many industries were the inevitable results of investor overenthusiasm.

The second important fallout was the demise of fixed exchange rates as a system of international monetary exchange. Floating exchange rates became the ruling system between virtually all countries in the world.[12] In fact, fixed exchange rates contributed to the boom and bust cycle in many of these economies. When foreign money flowed into their markets, the monetary authorities expanded credit in order to keep the currencies from appreciating against the U.S. dollar and to maintain the fixed exchange rate. Expanding credit poured fuel on the already hot markets and contributed to a consumption boom. Many of the dollars were recycled into imports, leading to large trade deficits. The growth of exports was not sufficient to cover the gap that developed on the current account and led to the eventual loss of confidence of foreign investors.

Another effect of the crisis was a significant reduction in U.S. inflation and the increasing view that U.S. government bonds should be

---

[11]For a description of the bailout, see Roger Lowenstein, *When Genius Failed* (New York: Random House, 2001).

[12]Hong Kong maintained a currency board system, and a number of very small countries maintain fixed exchange rates with the U.S. dollar or the Euro. Argentina disbanded its currency board and floated the peso in January 2002.

viewed as a hedge against market turmoil. As noted in Chapter 2, the year 1997 marked a shift in the short-run correlation between stock and government bond returns. Prior to the Asian crisis, stock and bond prices often moved in the same direction because inflation was the primary worry of investors. Subsequently, concern shifted to deflation and possible global crises, and U.S. government bonds became a safe haven. The correlation between stock and bond prices turned negative.

Finally, the action of the Fed greatly increased market confidence in the ability of the central bank to steer the economy through tough times. As the economy expanded subsequent to the summer of 1998, an increasing number of investors believed that perhaps the time finally had come when central bank action could put an end to the business cycle.

A similar confidence pervaded the stock market in the late 1920s. The fledgling Federal Reserve was seen as a guarantor of economic expansion. Accordingly, the economy expanded, and stock prices rose. Yet the 1929 stock market crash and the subsequent banking crisis overwhelmed the Fed's abilities to manage the crisis. Central banks today are clearly better equipped to prevent financial turmoil from turning into a deep economic downturn. Notwithstanding, the 2001 recession taught investors that market economies are still subject to cycles despite the best efforts of central banks to tame them.

CONCLUSION

The events of the late 1990s were not kind to international investors. The emerging market crises, the long bear market in Japan, and the strong dollar made it hard for dollar-based investors to match U.S. returns. Furthermore, the increased correlation between U.S. and foreign stock markets sharply lowered the diversifying properties of foreign stocks.

However, one has to be careful not to make the case against foreign investing too strongly. First, we do not know for sure if the high correlation between country returns will persist. Second, even if increased correlation is a by-product of the globalization of markets, there also has been an increase in liquidity and, to some degree, transparency in these foreign markets. The surge of securities that are cross-listed in the major markets has been accompanied by more uniform and improved accounting standards.

The most important change influencing international investing, however, is that one can no longer judge the desirability of stocks by noting the country in which the company is headquartered. The globalization of the world economy means that the strength of management, product line, and marketing are far more important factors than where a firm is domiciled. Correlations between the returns to major industry sectors are falling, indicating that investors should seek to diversify among the top worldwide firms rather than target specific country allocations.

The inexorable trend toward integration of the world's economies and markets most certainly will continue into the new millennium. No country will be able to dominate every market, and industry leaders are apt to emerge from anyplace on the globe. Sticking only to U.S. equities is a risky strategy for the long-term investor. Just as investors incorrectly extrapolated the spectacular gains in the emerging markets in the mid-1990s, it would be wrong to expect the recent subpar returns in many developed countries to persist.

ECONOMIC ENVIRONMENT
OF INVESTING

CHAPTER

11

GOLD, THE FEDERAL RESERVE, AND INFLATION

In the stock market, as with horse racing, money makes the mare go. Monetary conditions exert an enormous influence on stock prices.
MARTIN ZWEIG[1]

If Fed Chairman Alan Greenspan were to whisper to me what his monetary policy was going to be over the next two years, it wouldn't change one thing I do.
WARREN BUFFETT[2]

On September 20, 1931, the British government announced that England was going off the gold standard. It would no longer exchange gold for balances at the Bank of England or for British currency, the pound sterling. The government insisted that this action was only "temporary," that it had no intention of forever abolishing its commitment to exchange its money for gold. Nevertheless, it was to mark the beginning of the end of both Great Britain's and the world's gold standard—a standard that had existed for over 200 years.

---

[1] *Winning on Wall Street* (New York: Warner Books, 1990), p. 43.
[2] Linda Grant, "Striking Out at Wall Street," *U.S. News & World Report*, June 30, 1994, p. 59.

Fearing chaos in the currency market, the British government ordered the London Stock Exchange closed. New York Stock Exchange officials decided to keep the U.S. exchange open but also braced for panic selling. The suspension of gold payments by Great Britain, the second-greatest industrial power, raised fears that other industrial countries might be forced to abandon gold. For the first time ever, the New York Stock Exchange banned short selling to moderate the expected collapse in share prices. Central bankers called the suspension "a world financial crisis of unprecedented dimensions."[3]

Much to New York's surprise, however, stocks rallied sharply after an early sinking spell, and many issues ended the day higher. Clearly, British suspension was not seen as negative for American equities.

Nor was this "unprecedented financial crisis" a problem for the British stock market. When England reopened the exchange on September 23, prices soared. The Associated Press (AP) wire gave the following colorful description of the reopening of the exchange:

> Swarms of stock brokers, laughing and cheering like schoolboys, invaded the Stock Exchange today for the resumption of trading after the two-day compulsory close-down—and their buoyancy was reflected in the prices of many securities.[4]

Despite the dire predictions of government officials, shareholders viewed casting off the gold standard as good for the economy and even better for stocks. As a result of the gold suspension, the British government could expand credit, and the fall in the value of the British pound would increase the demand for British exports. The stock market gave a ringing endorsement to the actions that shocked conservative world financiers. In fact, September 1931 marked the low point of the British stock market, whereas the United States and other countries that stayed on the gold standard continued to sink into depression. The lesson from history: Money feeds the stock market, and the ability of the central banks to provide liquidity is a critical plus for stock values.

MONEY AND PRICES

In 1950, President Truman startled the nation in his State of the Union Address with a prediction that the typical American family income would reach $12,000 by the year 2000. Considering that median family

---

[3]"World Crisis Seen by Vienna Bankers," *New York Times*, September 21, 1931, p. 2.
[4]"British Stocks Rise, Pound Goes Lower," *New York Times*, September 24, 1931, p. 2.

income was about $3,300 at the time, $12,000 seemed like a kingly sum and implied that America was going to make unprecedented economic progress in the next half century. In fact, President Truman's prediction has proved quite modest. The median family income in 2000 was $41,349. However, that sum buys less than $6,000 in 1950 prices, a testament to the persistent inflation of the last half century.

Rising and falling prices have characterized economic history as far back as economists have gathered data. However, steady inflation is unique to the second half of the twentieth century. What has changed over the past 50 years that makes steady inflation the norm rather than the exception? The answer is simple: The control of money has shifted from gold to the government, and with it a whole new system relating money, government deficits, and inflation has come into being.

In Chapter 1, Figure 1-3 displayed the overall price level in the United States and Great Britain over the last 200 years. It is striking how similar the general trends are in these two countries: no overall inflation until World War II and then protracted inflation after. Until the last 50 years, inflation occurred only because of war, crop failures, or other crises. However, the behavior of prices in the postwar period has been entirely different. The price level has almost never declined; the only question is the rate at which prices have risen.

Economists have long known that one variable is paramount in determining the price level: the amount of money in circulation. The robust relation between money and inflation is strongly supported by the evidence. Take a look at Figure 11-1, which displays money and prices per unit output in the United States since 1830. The overall trend of the price level has closely tracked that of the money supply.

The strong relation between money and prices is a worldwide phenomenon. No sustained inflation is possible without continuous money creation, and every hyperinflation in history has been associated with an explosion of the money supply. The evidence is overwhelming that countries with high monetary growth experience high inflation and countries with restrained money growth have low inflation.

Why is the quantity of money so closely connected to the price level? Because the price of money, like any good, is determined by supply and demand. The supply of dollars is printed by the central bank. The demand for dollars is derived from households and firms transacting millions of goods and services in a complex economy. If the supply of dollars increases when there is not an equal increase in the quantity of goods transacted, this leads to inflation. The classic description of the in-

FIGURE 11–1

Money and Price Indexes in the United States, 1830–2001

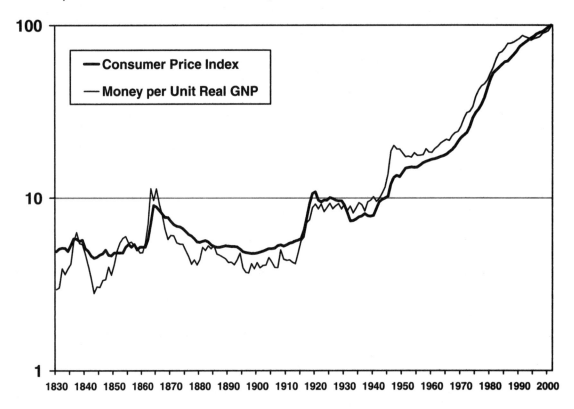

flationary process—too many dollars chasing too few goods—is as apt today as ever.

THE GOLD STANDARD

For the nearly 200 years prior to the Great Depression, most of the industrialized world was on a gold standard, meaning that governments obligated themselves to exchange their own money for a fixed amount of gold. To do this, governments had to keep gold reserves in sufficient quantity to assure money holders that they would always be able to make this exchange. Since the total quantity of gold in the world was fixed (except for new gold discoveries, which were a small fraction of the total outstanding), prices of goods in terms of either gold or government money held relatively constant or even declined.

The only times when the gold standard was suspended were during crises such as wars. Great Britain suspended the gold standard during both the Napoleonic War and World War I but in both cases returned to original parity with gold after the war. The United States also had suspended the gold standard temporarily but, like Great Britain, returned to the standard after the war.[5]

Adherence to the gold standard is the reason why the world experienced no overall inflation during the nineteenth and early twentieth centuries. However, overall price stability was not achieved without a cost. By setting the amount of money equal to the quantity of gold, the government essentially relinquished discretionary monetary control. This meant that the government was unable to provide extra money during times of depression or financial crisis or to expand the money supply to stabilize falling prices or accommodate rising output. Adherence to gold turned from being a symbol of government restraint and responsibility to a straitjacket from which the government sought to escape.

ESTABLISHMENT OF THE FEDERAL RESERVE

The problems of liquidity crises caused by strict adherence to the gold standard prompted Congress in 1913 to create the Federal Reserve System (Fed). One of the responsibilities of the Fed was to provide an "elastic" currency, which meant that in times of banking crises the Fed would become the lender of last resort. The central bank would provide currency to enable depositors to withdraw their deposits without forcing banks to liquidate loans and other assets.

In the long run, money creation by the Fed was constrained by the gold standard because Federal Reserve Notes promised to pay a fixed amount of gold, but in the short run, the Fed was free to create money as long as it did not threaten the convertibility. In fact, the Fed was never given any guidance or criteria by which to determine the right quantity of money.

FALL OF THE GOLD STANDARD

This lack of guidance on monetary policy had disastrous consequences just two decades later. In the wake of the stock market crash of 1929, the

---

[5]When the government issued non-gold-backed money during the Civil War, this money was called *greenbacks* because the only backing was the green ink printed on the note. Yet, just 20 years later, the government redeemed each and every one of those notes in gold, completely reversing the inflation of the Civil War period.

world economies entered a severe recession. Falling asset prices and failing businesses made banks subject to increased suspicion. Depositors withdrew billions of dollars of deposits and placed the banks at peril. In an astounding display of institutional ineptitude, the Fed failed to provide extra reserves needed to stem the currency drainage of the banks. Investors then sought even greater safety, turning their government notes into gold, a process that put extreme pressure on the gold reserves of the gold standard countries.

The first step toward the abandonment of the gold standard occurred on September 20, 1931, when Great Britain suspended all payments of gold for sterling. Eighteen months later, on April 19, 1933, the United States also suspended the gold standard as the depression worsened.

The reaction of the U.S. stock market to suspension was even more enthusiastic than that of the British market. Stocks soared over 9 percent on that day and almost 6 percent the next. This was the greatest 2-day rally in stock market history. Stockholders felt that the government could now provide extra liquidity to raise prices and stimulate the economy, which they regarded as a boon for stocks. Bonds, however, fell as investors feared the inflationary consequences of leaving the gold standard. *BusinessWeek,* in a positive editorial on the suspension, asserted:

> With one decisive gesture, . . . [President Roosevelt] throws out of the window all the elaborate hocus-pocus of "defending the dollar." He defies an ancient superstition and takes his stand with the advocates of managed money. . . . The job now is to manage our money effectively, wisely, with self-restraint. It can be done.[6]

POSTDEVALUATION POLICY

Ironically, while the right to redeem dollars for gold was denied U.S. citizens, it was soon reinstated for foreign central banks at the devalued rate of $35 per ounce. As part of the Bretton Woods agreement, which set up the rules of international exchange rates after World War II, the U.S. government promised to redeem for gold all dollars held by foreign central banks at a rate of $35 per ounce as long as they fixed their currency to the dollar.

However, postwar inflation made gold seem more and more attractive to foreigners at that price. The U.S. gold reserves began to dwindle

---

[6]"We Start," *BusinessWeek,* April 26, 1933, p. 32.

despite official claims that the United States had no plans to change its gold exchange policy. As late as 1965, President Johnson stated unequivocally in the *Economic Report of the President:*

> There can be no question of our capacity and determination to maintain the gold value of the dollar at $35.00 per ounce. The full resources of the Nation are pledged to that end.[7]

Yet 4 years later, in the 1969 *Economic Report of the President*, President Johnson declared:

> Myths about gold die slowly. But progress can be made—as we have demonstrated. In 1968, the Congress ended the obsolete gold-backing requirement for our currency.[8]

Myths about gold? Obsolete gold-backing requirement? The government finally admitted that monetary policy would not be subject to the discipline of gold, and the guiding principle of international finance and monetary policy for almost two centuries was summarily dismissed as a relic of incorrect thinking.

The United States continued to redeem gold at $35 an ounce, although private investors were paying over $40 in the private markets. Foreign central banks rushed to turn in their dollars for gold. The United States, which held almost $30 billion of gold at the end of World War II, was left with $11 billion by the summer of 1971, and hundreds of millions of dollars of gold were being withdrawn each month.

Something dramatic had to happen. On August 15, 1971, President Nixon, in one of the most extraordinary economic acts since Roosevelt's 1933 Bank Holiday, startled the world financial community by freezing wages and prices and forever closing the "gold window," the method by which foreigners turned in their Federal Reserve Notes for gold. The link of gold to money was permanently—and irrevocably—broken.

However, few shed a tear for the gold standard. The stock market responded enthusiastically to Nixon's announcement (which also was coupled with wage and price controls and higher tariffs), jumping almost 4 percent on record volume. This was not surprising. As mentioned earlier, suspensions of the gold standard or devaluations of currencies have witnessed some of the most dramatic stock market rallies in history.

---

[7]*Economic Report of the President* (Washington, DC: U.S. Government Printing Office, 1965), p. 7.
[8]*Economic Report of the President* (Washington, DC: U.S. Government Printing Office, 1969), p. 16.

POSTGOLD MONETARY POLICY

With complete dismantling of the gold standard, there was no longer any constraint on monetary expansion either in the United States or in foreign countries. The first inflationary oil shock during 1973–1974 caught most of the industrialized countries off guard, and all suffered significantly higher inflation as governments vainly attempted to offset falling output by expanding the money supply.

Because of the inflationary tendencies of monetary policy, Congress tried to control monetary expansion by the Fed. In 1975, a congressional resolution obliged the Federal Reserve to announce monetary growth targets. Three years later, Congress passed the Humphrey-Hawkins Act, which forced the Fed to testify on monetary policy and state monetary targets before Congress twice annually. It was the first time in over 60 years that Congress gave the Fed some guidance as to control of the stock of money in the economy. The financial markets closely watch this Humphrey-Hawkins testimony, which is delivered by the Chairman of the Federal Reserve System and takes place in February and July.[9]

Unfortunately, the Fed largely ignored the money targets it set in the 1970s. The surge of inflation in 1979 brought increased pressure on the Fed to change its policy and seriously control inflation. On October 6, 1979, Paul Volcker, who had been appointed in April to succeed G. William Miller as chairman of the board of the Federal Reserve System, announced a radical change in the implementation of monetary policy. No longer would the Fed set interest rates to guide policy. Instead, the Fed would exercise control over the supply of money without regard to interest-rate movements.

The prospect of sharply restricted liquidity was a shock to the financial markets. Although the Saturday night announcement (later referred to as the "Saturday night massacre" by traders in the bond and stock markets) did not immediately capture the popular headlines like Nixon's new economic policy, which had frozen prices and closed the gold window, the announcement roiled the financial markets. Stocks went into a tailspin, falling almost 8 percent on record volume in the 2½ days following the announcement. Stockholders shuddered at the prospect that the Fed was suddenly going to take away the money and credit that had sustained inflation during the past decade.

---

[9]In 2000, the Humphrey-Hawkins Act was allowed to lapse, but Fed Chairman Greenspan agreed to continue the semiannual testimony before Congress.

The tight monetary policy of the Volcker years eventually broke the inflationary cycle. The experience of the United States, as well as that of Japan and Germany, who also used monetary policy to stop inflation, proved that restricting money was the only real answer to controlling prices.

THE FEDERAL RESERVE AND MONEY CREATION

The process by which the Fed changes the money supply and controls credit conditions is straightforward. When the Fed wants to increase the money supply, it buys a government bond in the open market—a market where billions of dollars are transacted in bonds every day. What is unique about the Fed is that when it buys government bonds, it pays for them by crediting the reserve account of the bank of the customer from whom the Fed bought the bond—thereby creating money. A reserve account is a deposit a bank maintains at the Federal Reserve to satisfy reserve requirements and facilitate check clearing.

If the Fed wants to reduce the money supply, it sells government bonds from its portfolio. The buyer of these bonds instructs his or her bank to pay the Fed from his or her account. The Fed then debits the reserve account of the bank, and that money disappears from circulation.

The buying and selling of government bonds is called *open-market operations*. An open-market purchase increases reserves of the banking system, whereas an open-market sale reduces reserves.

HOW THE FED AFFECTS INTEREST RATES

When the Federal Reserve buys and sells government securities, it influences the amount of reserves of the banking system. There is an active market for these reserves among banks, where billions of dollars are bought and sold each day. This market is called the *federal funds market*, and the interest rate at which these funds are borrowed and lent is called the *federal funds rate*.

Although this market is called the *federal funds market*, the market is not run by the government, nor does it trade government securities. The federal, or fed, funds market is a private lending market among banks where rates are dictated by supply and demand. However, the Federal Reserve has powerful influence over the fed funds market. If the Fed buys securities, then the supply of reserves is increased, and the interest rate on fed funds goes down because banks have ample reserves to lend. Conversely, if the Fed sells securities, the supply of reserves is reduced, and the fed funds rate goes up as banks scramble for the remaining supply.

Although fed funds are borrowed for only 1 day, the interest rate on fed funds forms the anchor for all other short-term interest rates. These include the *prime rate*, which is currently the benchmark for most consumer borrowing, Treasury-bill rates, and Eurodollar lending rates. In total, the fed funds rate is the basis of literally trillions of dollars of loans and securities.

FED POLICY ACTIONS AND INTEREST RATES

In the short and intermediate run, interest rates are the single most important influence on stock prices. This is so because bonds compete with stocks in investment portfolios. Bonds become more attractive when interest rates rise, so investors sell stocks until their return again becomes attractive relative to bonds. The opposite occurs when interest rates fall.

Over the past 40 years, changes in the fed funds rates have been a very good predictor of future stock prices. Table 11-1 displays the return on the Standard & Poor's (S&P) 500 Stock Index from the beginning of the month after the fed funds rate has been changed to a date 3, 6, 9, and 12 months later.

The effects of Fed actions are dramatic: Following increases in the fed funds rate, the subsequent returns on stocks are significantly less than average; when the fed funds rate is decreased, stock returns are significantly higher than average. Since 1955, the total return on stocks has been 7.4 percent in the 12 months following the 99 increases in the fed funds rate, whereas it has been 16.6 percent following the 99 decreases in the fed funds rate. This compares with an average 12-month return over the period of 12.2 percent. If these results persist in the future, investors could significantly beat a buy-and-hold strategy by increasing their stock holdings when the Fed is easing credit conditions and reducing their stock holdings when the Fed is tightening credit.

Although this strategy has worked quite well in the 1950s, 1960s, 1970s, and 1980s, it has not worked well in the 1990s or early 2000s. One of the reasons for this is that the financial community has become so geared to watching and anticipating Fed policy that the effect of its tightening and easing is already discounted in the market. However, another reason is the rise and fall of technology stocks. Many investors thought these firms immune to rising interest rates since they borrowed little in the debt markets and technology spending would be the last to be cut from capital budget.

TABLE 11-1

Federal Funds Rate and Subsequent Stock Returns (Number of Changes in Parentheses)

1955-2001	3-month	6-month	9-month	12-month
Increases (99)	1.2%	2.9%	5.9%	7.4%
Decreases (99)	5.3%	9.7%	12.4%	16.6%
Benchmark*	3.0%	6.1%	9.1%	12.2%
1955-1959				
Increases (18)	5.0%	7.0%	10.1%	11.8%
Decreases (8)	6.4%	17.4%	27.8%	36.0%
Benchmark*	3.3%	6.4%	8.9%	11.4%
1960-1969				
Increases (22)	-1.2%	1.2%	1.4%	2.6%
Decreases (17)	3.5%	6.1%	7.4%	8.6%
Benchmark*	2.2%	4.1%	6.2%	8.4%
1970-1979				
Increases (29)	-1.9%	-1.2%	3.7%	4.8%
Decreases (26)	6.5%	11.1%	13.8%	17.7%
Benchmark*	1.9%	4.3%	6.7%	9.3%
1980-1989				
Increases (16)	3.9%	4.2%	9.1%	8.6%
Decreases (23)	6.5%	12.9%	14.9%	21.1%
Benchmark*	4.3%	8.8%	13.0%	16.9%
1990-2001**				
Increases (14)	3.2%	7.1%	8.8%	13.1%
Decreases (25)	4.0%	5.4%	7.4%	10.5%
Benchmark*	3.4%	6.8%	10.4%	14.4%

* Average of all time periods in selected sample.
** Assumes S&P 500 remains flat for 2002.

This incorrect thinking led to a continued rise in technology stocks in 1999 and 2000 as the Fed tightened. Although the S&P 500 Index peaked in March 2000, many technology stocks continued to rise through August. By that time they had become so overvalued that subsequent Fed easing did little to stop their plunge. Despite 11 rate reductions by the Fed in 2001, stock prices in general and technology stocks in particular ended significantly lower on the year.

So the best strategy for stock investors is not to count on the Federal Reserve having as predictable an effect on the market in the future as it has had in the past. The central bank policies, to be sure, remain crucial to the financial markets. Low interest rates and liquidity feed the stock market. But monetary policy actions, at least since 1990, have not evoked a consistent response in the equity market.

STOCKS AS INFLATIONARY HEDGES

Although the central bank has the power to moderate (but not eliminate) the business cycle, its policy has the greatest influence on inflation. As noted earlier, the inflationary decade of the 1970s was due to overexpansion of the money supply in the vain hope that the central bank could offset the contractionary effect of the OPEC oil supply restrictions. This expansionary monetary policy brought inflation to double-digit levels in most industrialized economies, peaking at 13 percent per year in the United States and over 24 percent in the United Kingdom.

In contrast to the inflation risk of fixed-income assets, historical evidence is convincing that the returns on stocks over long periods of time have kept pace with inflation. Since stocks are claims on the earnings of real assets—assets whose value is intrinsically related to labor and capital—it is reasonable to expect that their long-term returns would not be influenced by inflation. For example, the period since World War II has been the most inflationary half century in our history, yet the real return on stocks has exceeded that of the previous 150 years. The ability of an asset such as stocks to maintain its purchasing power during periods of inflation makes equities an *inflation hedge*.

Indeed, stocks were widely praised in the 1950s as hedges against rising consumer prices. As noted in Chapter 6, many investors stayed with stocks despite seeing the dividend yield on equities fall below the interest rate on long-term bonds for the first time. In the 1970s, however, stocks were ravaged by inflation, and it became unfashionable to view equity as an effective hedge against inflation.

What does the evidence say about the effectiveness of stocks as an inflation hedge? Figure 11-2 plots the annual compound returns on stocks, bonds, and Treasury bills against various rates of inflation over 1- and 30-year holding periods from 1871 to 2001.

These figures indicate that neither stocks, bonds, nor Treasury bills are good short-term hedges against inflation. Short-term real returns on these financial assets are highest when the inflation rates are low, and their returns fall as inflation increases. However, the returns on stocks are virtually immune to the inflation rate over longer horizons. Fixed-income assets, on the other hand, have not matched the returns on stocks over any holding period.

This was the principal conclusion of Edgar Smith in his book entitled *Common Stocks as Long-Term Investments*. Smith showed that stocks outperform bonds in times of falling as well as rising prices, taking the period after the Civil War and before the turn of the twentieth century as his test case. Smith's results are quite robust and have held since his study more than 70 years ago.

WHY STOCKS FAIL AS A SHORT-TERM INFLATION HEDGE

Higher Interest Rates

It is not at all apparent why stocks fail as a short-term inflation hedge. A popular explanation is that inflation increases interest rates on bonds, and higher interest rates on bonds depress stock prices. In other words, inflation must send stock prices down sufficiently to increase their dividend or earning yield to match the higher rate available on bonds. Indeed, this is the rationale of the Fed model described in Chapter 6.

However, this explanation is incomplete. It has long been known that expectations of rising prices do increase interest rates. Irving Fisher, a famous early-twentieth-century American economist, noted that lenders seek to protect themselves against inflation by adding a premium to the interest rate that they demand from borrowers. Fisher indicated that the market interest rate is composed of two parts: the real rate of interest—the rate prevailing in an economy with no inflation—plus the expected rate of inflation—a premium compensating lenders for the

Holding-Period Returns and Inflation, 1871–2001

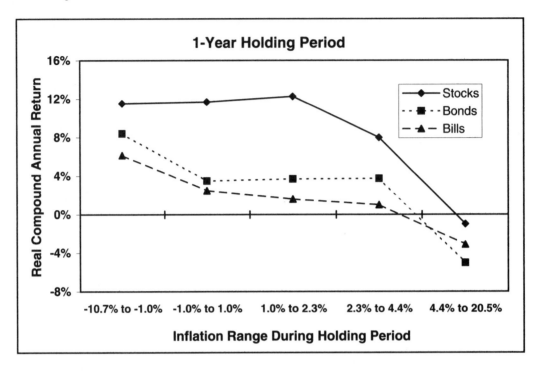

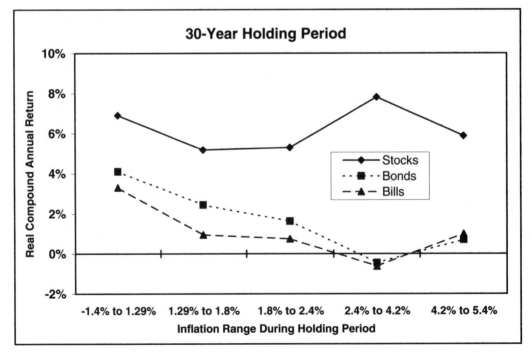

depreciation of the value of money.[10] This relation has been called the *Fisher equation* after its discoverer.[11]

Although higher expected inflation raises interest rates, inflation also raises the expected future cash flows available to stockholders. Stocks are claims on the earnings of real assets, whether these assets are the product of machines, labor, land, or ideas. While inflation raises the cost of inputs, output prices (which are in fact the measure of inflation) also must rise. Therefore, future cash flows also will rise with the price level.

It can be shown that when inflation has an equal impact on input and output prices, the present value of the future cash flows from stocks is not adversely affected by inflation even though interest rates rise. Higher future earnings will offset higher interest rates so that, over time, the price of stocks—as well as the level of earnings and dividends—will rise at the rate of inflation. The returns from stocks will keep up with rising prices, and stocks will act as a complete inflation hedge.

Supply-Induced Inflation

The preceding description is likely to hold when inflation is purely monetary in nature, influencing costs and profits equally. However, there are many circumstances when earnings cannot keep up with inflation. Stocks declined during the 1970s because the restriction in OPEC oil supplies dramatically influenced energy costs. Firms were not able to raise the prices of their output by as much as the soaring cost of their energy inputs.

Earlier in the chapter it was noted that the inflation of the 1970s was the result of bad monetary policy trying to offset the contractionary effect of OPEC's oil price hikes. Yet one should not minimize the harm done by OPEC's policies to U.S. corporate profits. U.S. manufacturers, who for years had thrived on low energy prices, were totally unprepared to deal with surging energy costs. The recession that followed the

---

[10]Since corporations can deduct interest expense from taxes, interest rates should rise by the expected rate of inflation divided by 1 minus the corporate tax rate (called the *Darby effect* after Professor Michael Darby) in order to keep the after-tax real cost of capital constant to corporations. Historically, interest rates do not appear to rise this much during inflation, giving firms a net benefit from debt financing during inflation.

[11]See Irving Fisher, *The Rate of Interest* (New York: Macmillan, 1907). The exact Fisher equation for the nominal rate of interest is the sum of the real rate plus the expected rate of inflation plus the cross product of the real rate and the expected rate of inflation. If inflation is not too high, this last term often can be ignored.

first OPEC oil squeeze pummeled the stock market. Productivity plum- meted, and by the end of 1974, real stock prices, measured by the Dow Jones Industrial Average, had fallen 65 percent from the January 1966 high—the largest decline since the crash of 1929. Pessimism ran so deep that nearly half of all Americans in August 1974 believed that the econ- omy was heading toward a depression such as the one the nation had experienced in the 1930s.[12]

FED POLICY, THE BUSINESS CYCLE, AND GOVERNMENT SPENDING

Inappropriate monetary policy in the face of restrictions on the supply of natural resources or declining productivity is not the only reason why stock prices might react poorly to inflation. Another is investor fear that the central bank will take restrictive action to curb rising prices, which invariably raises short-term real interest rates. Furthermore, inflation often appears late in the business cycle, which is taken as a sign by in- vestors that a recession, with lower profits, may be near. Under these cir- cumstances, it is perfectly rational for investors to take stock prices down when inflation heats up.

Inflation, especially in less-developed countries, is also closely linked with large government budget deficits and excessive government spending. Inflation therefore often signals that the government is taking too large a role in the economy, which leads to lower growth, lower cor- porate profits, and lower stock prices.

INFLATION AND THE U.S. TAX CODE

Another very important reason why stocks are poor short-term hedges against inflation is the U.S. tax code. There are two significant areas in which the tax code works to the detriment of shareholders during infla- tionary times: corporate profits and capital gains.

Inflation Distortions to Corporate Earnings

When analyzing stocks, analysts often point to the *quality* of earnings re- ported, which refers to the degree that earnings accurately reflect the earning power of firms. However, poor quality earnings are not always the fault of the firm. Reported earnings may be distorted by standard

---

[12]Gallup poll taken August 2–5, 1974.

and accepted accounting practices that do not properly take into account the effects of inflation on corporate profits. This distortion shows up primarily in the treatment of depreciation, inventory valuation, and interest costs.

Depreciation of plant, equipment, and other capital investments is based on *historical* costs. These depreciation schedules are not adjusted for any change in the price of capital that might occur during the life of the asset. During inflation, the cost of replacing capital rises, but depreciation in the earnings reports does not make any adjustment for this. Therefore, depreciation allowances are understated because adequate allowances for the rising cost of replacing capital are not taken into account. As a result, reported depreciation is understated, and reported earnings are overstated.

However, depreciation is not the only source of bias in reported earnings. In calculating the cost of goods sold, firms must use the historical cost with either "first in, first out" or "last in, first out" methods of inventory accounting. In an inflationary environment, the gap between historical costs and selling prices widens, producing inflationary profits for the firm. These "profits" do not represent an increase in the real earning power of the firm but record just that part of the firm's capital—namely, the inventory—that turns over and is realized as a monetary profit. This treatment of inventories differs from the firm's other capital, such as plant and equipment, which is not revalued on an ongoing basis for the purpose of calculating earnings.

The Department of Commerce, the government agency responsible for gathering economic statistics, is well aware of these distortions and has computed both a depreciation adjustment and an inventory-valuation adjustment in the national income and product accounts going back to 1929. The Internal Revenue Service, however, does not recognize any of these adjustments for tax purposes. Firms are required to pay taxes on reported profits, even when the profits are biased upward by inflation. These biases reduce the quality of the earnings that firms report to stockholders.

These inflationary biases are often significant. In the inflationary 1970s, reported corporate profits were overstated by up to 50 percent, meaning that the quality of reported earnings during that period was very low. On the other hand, in the low-inflation period of the late 1980s and 1990s, the quality of reported earnings measured by inflation biases increased dramatically.[13]

---

[13]Since 1990, firms have taken other liberties that have distorted earnings. See Chapter 6.

Inflation Biases in Interest Costs

There is another inflationary distortion to corporate profits that is not reported in government statistics. This is based on the inflationary component of interest costs and, in contrast to depreciation and inventory profits, often leads to a *downward* bias in reported corporate earnings during periods of inflation.

Most firms raise some of their capital by floating fixed-income assets such as bonds and bank loans. This borrowing leverages the firm's assets, since any profits above and beyond the debt service go to the stockholders. In an inflationary environment, nominal interest costs rise, even if real interest costs remain unchanged. However, corporate profits are calculated by deducting *nominal* interest costs, which overstates the real interest costs to the firm. Hence reported corporate profits are depressed compared with true economic conditions. Since the firm is paying back debt with depreciated dollars, the higher nominal interest expense is offset by the reduction in the real value of the bonds and loans owed by the firm. However, the reduction in real indebtedness is not reported in any of the earnings reports released by the firm.

Unfortunately, it is not easy to quantify this earnings bias because it is not easy to identify the share of interest due to inflation and that due to the real interest costs. The extent of the bias depends on the leverage of the firm and may in some cases offset the depreciation and inventory bias that raises reported corporate profits.

Inflation and the Capital Gains Tax

In the United States, capital gains taxes are paid on the difference between the cost of an asset and the sale price, with no adjustment made for inflation. If asset values rise with inflation, the investor accrues a tax liability that must be paid at the time the asset is sold, whether or not the investor has realized a real gain. This means that an asset that appreciates by less than the rate of inflation—meaning the investor is worse off in real terms—will be taxed on sale.

Chapter 4 showed that the tax code has a dramatic impact on investors' realized after-tax real return. For even a moderate inflation of 3 percent, an investor with a 5-year average holding period suffers a 50-basis-point (hundredths of a percentage point) reduction in average after-tax real return compared with the after-tax return if the rate of inflation were zero. If the inflation rises to 6 percent, the loss of return is more than 94 basis points.

The inflation tax has a far more severe effect on realized after-tax real returns when the holding period is short than when it is long. This is so because the more frequently an investor buys and sells assets, the more frequently the government can capture the nominal capital gains tax. However, even for very long-term investors, inflation cuts into real returns. And the tax effect is more serious if stocks have been sheltered in a tax-deferred account; in such a case, funds taken out are taxed at the ordinary income tax rate.

CONCLUSION

This chapter documents the role of money in the economy and financial markets. Before World War II, inflation in the United States and most industrialized countries was nonexistent. However, when the Great Depression dethroned the gold standard as the linchpin of the world's monetary system, the control of money and inflation was passed directly to the central banks. And with the dollar or other major currencies no longer being pegged to the quantity of gold, inflation, and not deflation, proved to be the evil that central banks sought to control.

Despite the fall in the rate of inflation at the turn of the millennium, U.S. investors need not worry that deflation will return. The Federal Reserve is very sensitive to the destructive forces of deflation—the increasing burden of debt, the rise in bankruptcies, and the destruction of profits. By freeing itself from the gold standard, the central bank can reflate the economy through the creation of money. Mild inflation on the order of 2 to 3 percent per year is what U.S. investors can expect over the next decade.

The message of this chapter is that stocks are not good hedges against increased inflation in the short run—but then again, no financial asset is. In the long run, stocks are extremely good hedges against inflation, whereas bonds are not. Stocks are also the best financial asset if you fear rapid inflation because many countries with high inflation can still have quite viable, if not booming, stock markets. Fixed-income assets, on the other hand, cannot protect investors from excessive monetary issuance.

Inflation, although kinder to stocks than to bonds, does have some downsides for equity holders. Fear that the Fed will tighten credit if inflation threatens causes traders to avoid stocks, at least in the short run.

Inflation also overstates corporate profits and increases the taxes firms have to pay. Furthermore, because the U.S. capital gains tax is not indexed, inflation causes investors to pay higher taxes than would exist in a noninflationary environment. The distortions of our tax system, which cause both firms and investors to pay higher taxes in an inflationary environment, can be remedied in part by indexing the capital gains and corporate income taxes.

CHAPTER

12

STOCKS AND THE BUSINESS CYCLE[1]

The stock market has predicted nine out of the last five recessions!
PAUL SAMUELSON[2]

I'd love to be able to predict markets and anticipate recessions, but since that's impossible, I'm as satisfied to search out profitable companies as Buffett is. PETER LYNCH[3]

A well-respected economist is about to address a large group of financial analysts, investment advisors, and stockbrokers. There is obvious concern in the audience. The stock market has been surging to new all-time highs almost daily, driving down dividend yields to record lows and price-earnings (P-E) ratios skyward. Is this bullishness justified? The audience wants to know if the economy is really going to do well enough to support these high stock prices.

The economist's address is highly optimistic. She predicts that the real gross domestic product (GDP) of the United States will increase

---

[1]This chapter is an adaptation of my paper, "Does It Pay Stock Investors to Forecast the Business Cycle?" *Journal of Portfolio Management* 18(Fall 1991):27–34. The material benefited significantly from discussions with Professor Paul Samuelson.
[2]"Science and Stocks," *Newsweek*, September 19, 1966, p. 92.
[3]Peter Lynch, *One Up on Wall Street* (New York: Penguin Books, 1989), p. 14.

over 4 percent during the next four quarters, a very healthy growth rate. There will be no recession for at least 3 years, and even if a recession occurs after that, it will be very brief. Corporate profits, one of the major factors driving stock prices, will increase at double-digit annual rates for at least the next 3 years. To boot, she predicts that a Republican will easily win the White House in next year's presidential elections, a situation obviously comforting to the overwhelmingly conservative audience. The crowd obviously likes what it hears. Their anxiety is quieted, and many are ready to recommend that their clients increase their stake in stocks.

The time of this address is the summer of 1987, with the stock market poised to take one of its sharpest falls in history, including the record-breaking 23 percent decline on October 19, 1987. In just a few weeks, most stocks can be bought for about half the price paid at the time of the address. The biggest irony of all, however, is that the economist is dead right in each and every one of her bullish economic predictions.

The lesson here is that the markets and the economy are often out of sync. It is not surprising that many investors dismiss economic forecasts when planning their market strategy. The substance of Paul Samuelson's famous words, cited at the beginning of this chapter, still remains true more than 30 years after they were first uttered.

However, do not dismiss the business cycle too quickly when examining your portfolio. The stock market still responds quite powerfully to changes in economic activity. Figure 12-1 shows the reaction of the Standard & Poor's (S&P) 500 Stock Index to the business cycle. Although there are many "false alarms" like 1987 when the market collapse was not followed by a recession, stocks almost always fall prior to a recession and rally rigorously at signs of an impending recovery. If you can predict the business cycle, you can beat the buy-and-hold strategy that has been advocated throughout this book.

This is no easy task, however. To make money by predicting the business cycle, one must be able to identify peaks and troughs of economic activity *before* they actually occur, a skill very few, if any, economists possess. Yet business cycle forecasting is a popular Wall Street endeavor not because it is successful—most of the time it is not—but because the potential gains are so large.

WHO CALLS THE BUSINESS CYCLE?

It is surprising to many that the dating of business cycles is not determined by any of the myriad government agencies that collect data on

FIGURE 12–1

S&P 500 Stock Index, Earnings, and Dividends during the Business Cycle, 1940–2001

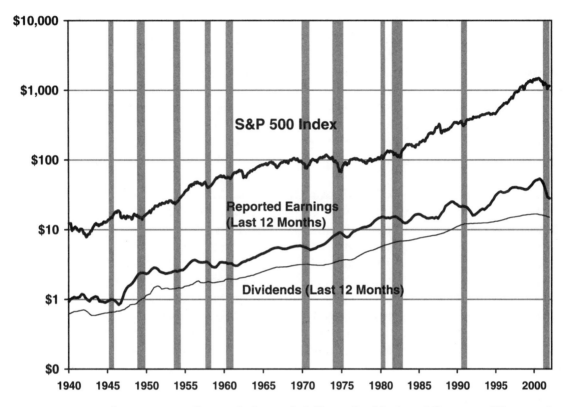

the economy. Instead, the task falls to the National Bureau of Economic Research (NBER), a private research organization founded in 1920 for the purpose of documenting business cycles and developing a series of national income accounts. In the early years of its existence, NBER's staff compiled comprehensive chronological records of the changes in economic conditions in many of the industrialized economies. In particular, the NBER developed monthly series on business activity for the United States and Great Britain back to 1854.

In a 1946 paper entitled "Measuring Business Cycles," Wesley C. Mitchell, one of the founders of the NBER, and Arthur Burns, a renowned business cycle expert who later headed the Federal Reserve Board, gave the following definition of a business cycle:

> Business cycles are a type of fluctuation found in the aggregate economic activity of nations that organize their work mainly in business enterprises: a cycle consists of expansion occurring at about the same time in many

economic activities, followed by similarly general recessions, or contractions, and revivals that merge into the expansion phase of the next cycle;
this sequence of changes is recurrent but not periodic; in duration business cycles vary from more than one year to ten or twelve years and they
are not divisible into shorter cycles of similar character.[4]

It is commonly assumed that a recession occurs when GDP, the
most inclusive measure of economic output, declines for two consecutive quarters. This is not necessarily so, however. Although this criterion
is a reasonable rule of thumb for indicating a recession, there is no single
rule or measure used by the NBER. Rather, the NBER focuses on four
different series to determine the turning points in the economy: employment, industrial production, real personal income, and real manufacturing and trade sales.

The Business Cycle Dating Committee of the NBER confirms the
business cycle dates. This committee consists of academic economists
who are associated with the NBER and who meet to examine economic
data whenever conditions warrant. Over the entire period from 1802 to
1997, the United States has experienced 41 recessions, averaging nearly
18 months in length, whereas the expansions have averaged almost 38
months. This means that over these 195 years, almost exactly one-third
of the time the economy has been in a recession. However, since World
War II, there have been 10 recessions, averaging 10 months in length,
whereas the expansions have averaged 50 months. Thus, in the postwar period, the economy has been in a recession only one-sixth of the
time.

The dating of the business cycle is of great importance. The desig-
nation that the economy is in a recession or an expansion has political as
well as economic implications. For example, when the NBER called the
onset of the 1990 recession in July rather than August, it raised quite a
few eyebrows in Washington. This is so because the Bush administration
had told the public that the Iraqi invasion of Kuwait and the surge in oil
prices were responsible for the economic recession. This explanation
was undermined when the NBER actually dated the onset of the recession a month earlier.

The Business Cycle Dating Committee is in no rush to call the turning points in the cycle. Never has a call been reversed because of new or
revised data that have become available—and the NBER wants to keep

---

[4]Wesley C. Mitchell and Arthur Burns, "Measuring Business Cycles," *NBER Reporter* (1946):3.

it that way. As Robert E. Hall, current head of the seven-member Business Cycle Dating Committee indicated, "The NBER has not made an announcement on a business cycle peak or trough until there was almost no doubt that the data would not be revised in light of subsequent availability of data."[5]

Recent examples of the NBER's dating make the point: The July 1981 peak was not called until early January 1982, whereas the November trough was not dated until July 1983. The July 1990 peak of the expansion was not officially called until 9 months later. The March 1991 trough was not designated until December 1992, 21 months later, and the March 2001 peak was not called until late in November. Clearly, waiting for the NBER to designate business cycles is far too late to be of any use in timing the market.

STOCK RETURNS AROUND BUSINESS CYCLE TURNING POINTS

Almost without exception the stock market turns down prior to recessions and rises before economic recoveries. In fact, of the 42 recessions from 1802 to the present, 39 of them, or 93 percent, have been preceded (or accompanied) by declines of 8 percent or more in the total stock returns index. The three exceptions were the 1829–1830 recession, the recession that followed the economic adjustment immediately following World War II, and the 1953 recession, when stock declines fell just shy of the 8 percent criterion.

Table 12-1 summarizes stock returns before the 10 post–World War II recessions. You can see that the stock return index peaked anywhere from 0 to 13 months before the beginning of a recession. The recessions that began in January 1980 and July 1990 are among the very few in U.S. history where the stock market gave no advance warning of the economic downturn.

As the Samuelson quote at the beginning of this chapter indicates, the stock market is also prone to false alarms, and these have increased in the postwar period. Excluding the war years, when declining stock markets coincided with expanding war economies, there have been 12 episodes since 1802 when the cumulative returns index for stocks fell by 8 percent or more, but the drop was not then followed by a recession within the next 12 months. This happened five times in the nineteenth

---

[5]Robert Hall, "Economic Fluctuations," *NBER Reporter* (Summer 1991):1.

T A B L E   12-1

Recessions and Stock Returns

Recession	Peak of Stock Index (1)	Peak of Business Cycle (2)	Lead Time Between Peaks (3)	Decline in Stock Index From (1) to (2) (4)	Maximum 12 Month Decline in Stock Index (6)
1948 - 49	May 1948	Nov 1948	6	-8.91%	-9.76%
1953 - 54	Dec 1952	Jul 1953	7	-4.26%	-9.04%
1957 - 58	Jul 1957	Aug 1957	1	-4.86%	-15.32%
1960 - 61	Dec 1959	Apr 1960	4	-8.65%	-8.65%
1970	Nov 1968	Dec 1969	13	-12.08%	-29.16%
1973 - 75	Dec 1972	Nov 1973	11	-16.29%	-38.80%
1980	Jan 1980	Jan 1980	0	0.00%	-9.55%
1981 - 82	Nov 1980	Jul 1981	8	-4.08%	-13.99%
1990 - 91	Jul 1990	Jul 1990	0	0.00%	-13.84%
2001	Aug 2000	Mar 2001	7	-22.94%	-26.55%
		Average	5.7	-8.21%	-17.47%

century and seven times in the twentieth century. All the occasions in this century have occurred since World War II.

Table 12-2 lists declines greater than 10 percent in the Dow Jones Industrial Average during the postwar period that were not followed by recessions. The 1987 decline of –35.1 percent, from August through November, is the largest decline in the nearly two-century history of stock returns data after which the economy did not fall into a recession. Chapter 16 will discuss the 1987 stock crash and explain why it did not lead to an economic downturn.

Table 12-3 compares the trough in the stock return index and the trough in the NBER business cycle. The average lead time between a market upturn and an economic recovery has been 5.1 months, and in eight of the nine recessions, the lead time has been in an extremely narrow range of 4 to 6 months. This compares with an average of 5.7 months that the peak in the market precedes the peak in the business cycle; this peak-to-peak lead time also has shown much greater variability and less predictability than the trough-to-trough lead time. It is very important to note that from the bottom of the stock market to the end of the recession, the stock market has risen almost 24 percent on average. If an investor

T A B L E   12–2

False Alarms by Stock Market (Postwar Declines of 10 Percent or More in the Dow Jones Industrial Average When No Recession Followed within 12 Months)

Peak of Stock Index	Trough of Stock Index	% Decline
May 29, 1946	May 17, 1947	-23.2%
Dec 13, 1961	Jun 26, 1962	-27.1%
Jan 18, 1966	Sept 29, 1966	-22.3%
Sept 25, 1967	Mar 21, 1968	-12.5%
Apr 28, 1971	Nov 23, 1971	-16.1%
Aug 17,1978	Oct 27, 1978	-12.8%
Nov 29, 1983	Jul 24, 1984	-15.6%
Aug 25, 1987	Dec 4, 1987	-35.1%
Aug 6, 1997	Oct 27, 1997	-13.3%
Jul 17, 1998	Aug 31, 1998	-19.3%

T A B L E   12–3

Expansions and Stock Returns, 1948–1991*

Recession	Trough of Stock Index (1)	Trough of Business Cycle (2)	Lead Time Between Troughs (3)	Rise in Stock Index From (1) to (2) (4)	Months Between 8% Stock Index Rise and (2) (5)
1948 - 49	May 1949	Oct 1949	5	15.59%	3
1953 - 54	Aug 1953	May 1954	9	29.13%	5
1957 - 58	Dec 1957	April 1958	4	10.27%	1
1960 - 61	Oct 1960	Feb 1961	4	21.25%	2
1970	Jun 1970	Nov 1970	5	21.86%	3
1973 - 75	Sep 1974	Mar 1975	6	35.60%	5
1980	Mar 1980	Jul 1980	4	22.60%	2
1981 - 82	Jul 1982	Nov 1982	4	33.13%	3
1990 - 91	Oct 1990	Mar 1991	5	25.28%	3
		Average	5.1	23.86%	3.0
		Std. Dev.	1.73	8.59%	1.41

*Data for 2001-2002 recession not available

waits for tangible evidence that the business cycle has hit bottom, he or she has missed a very substantial rise in the market.

GAINS THROUGH TIMING THE BUSINESS CYCLE

Table 12-4 displays the excess returns of investors who can time their investment strategies in relation to the peaks and troughs in economic activity. Since stocks fall prior to a recession, investors want to switch out of stocks and into Treasury bills before the business downturn begins (if they can identify the turning point) and return to stocks when prospects for economic recovery look good. *Switching returns* are defined as the returns of an investor who switches from stocks to bills a given number of months before (or after, if his or her predictions are not accurate) a business cycle peak and switches back to stocks a given number of months before (or after) a business cycle trough. *Buy-and-hold returns* are defined as the returns from holding the market through the entire business cycle. *Excess returns* are defined as switching returns minus the returns from the buy-and-hold strategy.[6]

---

[6]The returns of the buy-and-hold strategy are adjusted to reflect the same level of market risk as the buy-and-hold strategy.

T A B L E   12–4

Excess Returns around Business Cycle Turning Points, 1802–1991*

		Switching from Stocks to Bills Before Peaks				At Peak	Switching from Stocks to Bills After Peaks			
		4 month	3 month	2 month	1 month	Peak	1 month	2 month	3 month	4 month
Switching from Bills to Stocks Before Trough	4 month	**4.8**	4.0	4.2	4.1	3.3	2.7	2.1	2.2	1.9
	3 month	4.0	**3.3**	3.5	3.3	2.6	1.9	1.4	1.5	1.3
	2 month	3.3	2.6	**2.8**	2.6	1.9	1.2	0.7	0.8	0.7
	1 month	2.5	1.8	2.0	**1.8**	1.1	0.5	0.0	0.1	0.0
At Trough		1.9	1.2	1.4	1.2	**0.5**	-0.2	-0.7	-0.6	-0.7
Switching from Bills to Stocks After Trough	1 month	1.5	0.8	1.0	0.8	0.1	**-0.6**	-1.1	-1.0	-1.1
	2 month	0.9	0.2	0.4	0.2	-0.5	-1.1	**-1.7**	-1.6	-1.7
	3 month	0.5	-0.2	0.0	-0.2	-0.9	-1.5	-2.1	**-2.0**	-2.1
	4 month	0.3	-0.4	-0.2	-0.3	-1.1	-1.7	-2.2	-2.1	**-2.2**

*Data for 2001-2002 recession not available

In the postwar period, the switching return is slightly better than a buy-and-hold strategy if investors switch into Treasury bills exactly at the peak and into stocks exactly at the trough of the business cycle. In fact, investors switching into Treasury bills just 1 month after the business cycle peak and back into stocks just 1 month after the business cycle trough would have lost 0.6 percent per year compared with the benchmark buy-and-hold strategy.

Interestingly, it is more important to be able to forecast troughs of the business cycle than it is peaks. An investor who buys stocks before the trough of the business cycle gains more than an investor who sells stocks an equal number of months before the business cycle peak.

The maximum excess return of 4.8 percent per year is obtained by investing in Treasury bills 4 months before the business cycle peak and in stocks 4 months before the business cycle trough. The strategy of switching between Treasury bills and stocks gains almost 30 basis points (30/100 of a percentage point) in average annual return for each week during the 4-month period in which investors can predict the business cycle turning point.

The extra returns from forecasting the business cycle successfully are impressive. An increase of 1.8 percent per year in returns, achieved by predicting the business cycle peak and trough only 1 month before it occurs, will increase your wealth by over 60 percent over any buy-and-hold strategy over 30 years. If you can predict 4 months in advance, the annual increase of 4.8 percent in your returns will more than triple your wealth over the same time period compared with a buy-and-hold strategy.

HOW HARD IS IT TO PREDICT THE BUSINESS CYCLE?

Billions of dollars of resources are spent trying to forecast the business cycle. The preceding section showed that it is not surprising that Wall Street employs so many economists desperately trying to predict the next recession or upturn, since doing so dramatically increases returns. However, the record of predicting exact business cycle turning points is extremely poor.

Stephen McNees, vice president of the Federal Reserve Bank of Boston, has done extensive research into the accuracy of economic forecasters' predictions. He claims that a major factor in forecast accuracy is the time period over which the forecast was made. He concludes, "Errors were enormous in the severe 1973–1975 and 1981–1982 recessions, much smaller in the 1980 and 1990 recessions, and generally quite minimal apart from business cycle turning points."[7] However, it is precisely these business cycle turning points that turn a forecaster into a successful market timer.

The 1974–1975 recession was particularly tough for economists. Almost every one of the nearly two dozen of the nation's top economists invited to President Ford's anti-inflation conference in Washington in September 1974 was unaware that the U.S. economy was in the midst of its most severe postwar recession to date. McNees, studying the forecasts issued by five prominent forecasters in 1974, found that the median forecast overestimated gross national product (GNP) growth by 6 percentage points and underestimated inflation by 4 percentage points. Early recognition of the 1974 recession was so poor that many economists "jumped the gun" on the next recession, which did not strike until 1980, but most economists thought it had begun early in 1979.

For over 20 years, Robert J. Eggert has been documenting and summarizing the economic forecasts of a noted panel of economic and business experts. These forecasts are compiled and published in a monthly publication entitled "Blue Chip Economic Indicators."

In July 1979, the "Blue Chip Economic Indicators" noted that a strong majority of forecasters believed that a recession had already started—forecasting negative GNP growth in the second, third, and fourth quarters of 1979. However, the NBER declared that the peak of the business cycle did not occur until January 1980 and that the economy expanded throughout 1979.

By the middle of the next year, forecasters were convinced that a recession had begun. However, as late as June 1980, the forecasters believed that the recession had started in February or March and would last about a year, or about 1 month longer than the average recession. This prediction was reaffirmed in August when the forecasters indicated that the U.S. economy was about halfway through the recession. In fact, the recession had ended the month before, in July, and the 1980 recession turned out to be the shortest in the postwar period.

Forecasters' ability to predict the severe 1981–1982 recession, when unemployment reached a postwar high of 10.8 percent, was no better. The headline of the July 1981 "Blue Chip Economic Indicators" read, "Economic Exuberance Envisioned for 1982." Instead, 1982 was a disaster. By November 1981, the forecasters realized that the economy had faltered, and optimism turned to pessimism. Most thought that the

---

[7]Stephen K. McNees, "How Large Are Economic Forecast Errors?" *New England Economic Review* (July–August 1992):33.

economy had entered a recession (which it had done 4 months earlier), nearly 70 percent thought that it would end by the first quarter of 1982 (which it would not, instead tying the record for the longest postwar recession, ending in November), and 90 percent thought that it would be mild, like the 1971 recession, rather than severe (wrong again!).

In April 1985, with the expansion well underway, forecasters were queried as to how long the economy would be in an expansion. The average response was for another 20 months, which would put the peak at December 1986, more than 3.5 years before the cycle actually ended. Even the most optimistic forecasters picked spring 1988 as the latest date for the next recession to begin. This question was asked repeatedly throughout 1985 and 1986, and no forecaster imagined that the expansion of the 1980s would last as long as it did.

Following the stock market crash of October 1987, forecasters reduced their GNP growth estimates of 1988 over 1987 from 2.8 to 1.9 percent, the largest drop in the 11-year history of the survey. Instead, economic growth in 1988 was nearly 4 percent because the economy failed to falter following the stock market collapse.

As the expansion continued, belief that a recession was imminent turned into the belief that prosperity was here to stay. The continuing expansion fostered a growing conviction that perhaps the business cycle had been conquered—by either government policy or the "recession-proof nature" of our service-oriented economy. Ed Yardeni, senior economist at Prudential-Bache Securities, wrote a "New Wave Manifesto" in late 1988, concluding that self-repairing, growing economies were likely through the rest of the decade.[8] On the eve of one of the worst worldwide recessions in the postwar era, Leonard Silk, senior economics editor of the *New York Times*, stated in May of 1990:

> Most economists foresee no recession in 1990 or 1991, and 1992 will be another presidential year, when the odds tip strongly against recession. Japan, West Germany, and most of the other capitalist countries of Europe and Asia are also on a long upward roll, with no end in sight.[9]

By November 1990, "Blue Chip Economic Indicators" reported that the majority of the panel believed that the U.S. economy had already or was about to slip into a recession. By then, however, not only had the economy been in recession for 4 months, but the stock market also had already hit its bottom and was headed upward! Had investors given in

---

[8]"New Wave Economist," *Los Angeles Times*, March 18, 1990, Business Section, p. 22.
[9]Leonard Silk, "Is There Really a Business Cycle?" *New York Times*, May 22, 1990, p. D2.

to the prevailing pessimism at the time when the recession seemed con-firmed, they would have sold after the low was reached and stocks were headed for a strong 3-year rally.

The record 10-year expansion of the U.S. economy from March 1991 through March 2001 again spawned talk of "new era" economics and economies without recession.[10] Even in early 2001, the vast majority of forecasters did not see a recession. In fact, in September 2001, just before the terrorist attacks, only 13 percent of the economists surveyed by "Blue Chip Economic Indicators" believed that the United States was in a re-cession, even though the NBER subsequently had indicated that the U.S. recession began 6 months earlier in March.[11]

The business cycle has been a feature of every market-oriented economy since the industrial revolution. Although advances in mone-tary policy can prevent the type of banking collapse that occurred in the 1930s, it is quite premature to assume that fluctuations in business activ-ity will cease to be a problem. Consumer and business spending are sub-ject to the same psychological swings that influence the financial markets. And stock and bond markets do not show any signs of moder-ating fluctuations.

CONCLUSION

Stock values are based on corporate earnings, and the business cycle is a prime determinant of those earnings. The gains that can be made by being able to predict the turning points of the economic cycle are enor-mous, yet doing so with any precision has eluded economists of all per-suasions. Despite the growing body of economic statistics, predictions are not getting much better over time.

The worst course an investor can take is to follow the prevailing sentiment about economic activity. This will lead to buying at high prices when times are good and everyone is optimistic and selling at the low when the recession nears its trough and pessimism prevails.

The lesson to investors is clear: Beating the stock market by analyz-ing real economic activity requires a degree of prescience that forecasters do not yet have. Turning points are rarely identified until several months after the peak or trough has been reached. By then, it is far too late to act in the market.

---

[10]See Steven Weber, "The End of the Business Cycle?" *Foreign Affairs* (July–August 1997).
[11]"Blue Chip Economic Indicators," September 10, 2001, p. 14.

13

WORLD EVENTS THAT IMPACT FINANCIAL MARKETS

I can predict the motion of heavenly bodies, but not the madness of crowds.
ISAAC NEWTON

SEPTEMBER 11, 2001

As the sun rose over New York City on a beautiful Tuesday morning, September 11, 2001, traders expected a dull day on Wall Street. There were no economic data coming out of Washington nor any earnings releases scheduled. The preceding Friday the markets had fallen because of a horrible employment report, but on Monday the markets had bounced back slightly.

The U.S. equity markets were yet to open, but contracts on the Standard & Poor's (S&P) 500 Index futures, the best indicator of the current status of the stock market, had been trading all night on the electronic Globex exchange. The futures markets were up, indicating that Wall Street was expecting a firm opening. Then a report came at 8:48 a.m.: An airplane had crashed into one of the World Trade Center towers. The pattern of trading over these fateful minutes is shown in Figure 13-1.

The news spread quickly, but there were many questions. Was it a large plane or a small plane? Was it an accident? Or was it something

F I G U R E   13–1

S&P 500 Futures Market on Tuesday Morning, September 11, 2001

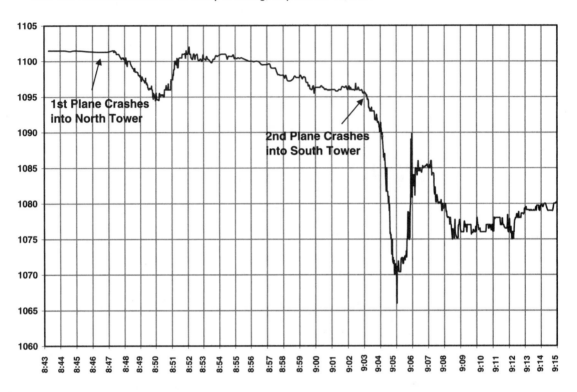

more sinister? Nobody knew. Immediately, the futures traded down a few points as they usually do when there is an increase in uncertainty. Within a few minutes, however, buyers reappeared, and the index returned to its previous level, signifying a belief that nothing significant had happened. As the minutes passed, traders learned that it was a large commercial airplane that had hit the tower. The futures traded down a few points, but at this juncture investors could not believe that this horrendous crash could be anything but an accident.

Fifteen minutes later, at 9:03 a.m., with news cameras focused on the World Trade Center and millions of people around the world watching, a second plane crashed into the towers. The entire world changed in that moment. Americans' worst fears had been realized. For the first time in 60 years, America was under direct attack.

Within 2 minutes S&P 500 Index futures traded down 30 points, which signified a nearly $300 billion decline in total U.S. stock market values. Miraculously, however, buyers did appear. Despite the enormity of the events unfolding, some traders bet that the market overreacted to these singular incidents, as it often does, and decided that this was a good time to buy stocks. The futures firmed and ended the session at 9:15 a.m. down only about 15 points, erasing half the loss.

However, the gravity of this attack quickly sunk in. All the exchanges delayed opening and soon canceled trading for the day. In fact, stock exchanges in the United States would remain closed for the remainder of the week. The worst terrorist attack in history forced the longest closing of the exchange since President Roosevelt called for a "Bank Holiday" in March 1933 to try to restore America's collapsing banking system.

Foreign stock exchanges remained open, however. It was 2 p.m. in London and 3 p.m. in central Europe. The German DAX Index immediately fell over 9 percent and ended the session at around that level. London suffered, but not as much. There was a feeling that with the United States, the world's financial center, vulnerable to attack, some business may cycle to the United Kingdom. The British pound rallied, as did the Euro, against the dollar. Normally, it is the United States that gains in international crises, but this time, with the attack centering on New York, foreign traders were unsure of which direction to go.

When the New York Stock Exchange reopened the following Monday, the Dow Jones Industrial Average fell 685 points, or 7.13 percent, the fourteenth largest percentage drop in its history. The Dow continued down during the week and closed Friday, September 21, at 8,236, down more than 14 percent from its September 10 close and nearly 30 percent from its all-time high of 11,723, reached on January 14, 2000.

WHAT MOVES THE MARKET?

Clearly, we knew *why* the markets fell on September 17 when trading resumed, but it might surprise investors that most of the time, major market movements are not accompanied by *any* news that explains why prices change. Since 1885, when Dow Jones averages were first formulated, there have been 126 days when the Dow Jones Industrial Average has changed by 5 percent or more. Of these, only 30 (or less than 1 in 4) can be identified with a specific world political or economic event, such as war, political change, or governmental policy shift. Table 13-1*a* ranks the 51 largest changes, and Table 13-1*b* identifies changes greater than

T A B L E   13–1A

Daily Changes over 5 Percent in the Dow Jones Industrial Average (Negative Changes Are Boldface and Asterisks Denote Changes Associated with News Items; Excludes 15.34 Percent Change from March 3–15, 1933, for U.S. Bank Holiday)

Rank	Date	Change	Rank	Date	Change	Rank	Date	Change
1	**Oct 19, 1987**	**-22.61%**	18	**Aug 12, 1932**	**-8.40%**	35	**Jan 8, 1988**	**-6.85%**
2*	Oct 6, 1931	14.87%	19	**Mar 14, 1907**	**-8.29%**	36	Oct 14, 1932	6.83%
3	**Oct 28, 1929**	**-12.82%**	20	**Oct 26, 1987**	**-8.04%**	37	**Nov 11, 1929**	**-6.82%**
4	Oct 30, 1929	12.34%	21	Jun 10, 1932	7.99%	38*	**May 14, 1940**	**-6.80%**
5	**Oct 29, 1929**	**-11.73%**	22	**Jul 21, 1933**	**-7.84%**	39	**Oct 5, 1931**	**-6.78%**
6	Sep 21, 1932	11.36%	23	**Oct 18, 1937**	**-7.75%**	40*	**May 21, 1940**	**-6.78%**
7	Oct 21, 1987	10.15%	24*	Sep 5, 1939	7.26%	41	Mar 15, 1907	6.70%
8	**Nov 6, 1929**	**-9.92%**	25*	**Feb 1, 1917**	**-7.24%**	42*	Jun 20, 1931	6.64%
9	Aug 3, 1932	9.52%	26*	**Oct 27, 1997**	**-7.18%**	43	Jul 24, 1933	6.63%
10*	Feb 11, 1932	9.47%	27	**Oct 5, 1932**	**-7.15%**	44*	**Jul 26, 1934**	**-6.62%**
11*	Nov 14, 1929	9.36%	28*	**Sep 17, 2001**	**-7.13%**	45	**Dec 20, 1895**	**-6.61%**
12	Dec 18, 1931	9.35%	29	Jun 3, 1931	7.12%	46*	**Sep 26, 1955**	**-6.54%**
13	Feb 13, 1932	9.19%	30	Jan 6, 1932	7.12%	47	Jun 19, 1933	6.38%
14*	May 6, 1932	9.08%	31	**Sep 24, 1931**	**-7.07%**	48	May 10, 1901	6.36%
15*	Apr 19, 1933	9.03%	32	**Jul 20, 1933**	**-7.07%**	49	**Oct 23, 1929**	**-6.33%**
16	**Dec 18, 1899**	**-8.72%**	33*	**Oct 13, 1989**	**-6.91%**	50	Aug 6, 1932	6.33%
17	Oct 8, 1931	8.70%	34*	**Jul 30, 1914**	**-6.90%**	51*	**Jul 26, 1893**	**-6.31%**

5 percent that were associated with specific events.[1] Also note that 4 of the 5 largest moves in the stock market over the past century for which there is a clearly identifiable cause have been directly associated with changes in monetary policy.

Of the 10 largest daily market moves, only 2 can be attributed to news. The record 22.6 percent 1-day fall in the stock market on October 19, 1987, is not associated with any readily identifiable news event. Since 1940, there have been only 4 days of big moves where the cause has been identified: the 7.13 percent drop on September 17, 2001, when the markets reopened after the terrorist attacks; the 7.18 percent drop on October 27, 1997, when there was an attack on the Hong Kong dollar; the 6.91 percent drop on Friday, October 13, 1989; and the 6.54 percent drop on September 26, 1955, when President Eisenhower suffered a heart attack. The decline in October 1989 has often been attributed to the collapse of the leveraged buyout of United Airlines, although the

---

[1]This expands the research originally published in David M. Cutler, James M. Poterba, and Lawrence H. Summers, "What Moves Stock Prices," *Journal of Portfolio Management* (Spring 1989):4–12.

T A B L E   13–1B

Largest News-Related Movements in the Dow Jones Industrial Average (Negative Changes Are Boldface)

Rank	Date	Change	News Headline
2	Oct 6, 1931	14.87%	Hoover Urges $500M Pool to Help Banks
10	Feb 11, 1932	9.47%	Liberalization of Fed discount policy
11	Nov 14, 1929	9.36%	Fed Lowers Discount Rate/Tax Cut Proposed
14	May 6, 1932	9.08%	U.S. Steel Negotiates 15% Wage Cut
15	Apr 19, 1933	9.03%	U.S. Drops Gold Standard
24	Sep 5, 1939	7.26%	World War II Begins in Europe
25	**Feb 1, 1917**	**-7.24%**	**Germany announces unrestricted submarine warfare**
26	**Oct 27, 1997**	**-7.18%**	**Attack on Hong Kong Dollar**
28	**Sep 17, 2001**	**-7.13%**	**World Trade Center and Pentagon Terrorist Attacks**
33	**Oct 13, 1989**	**-6.91%**	**United Airline Buy-out Collapses**
34	**Jul 30, 1914**	**-6.90%**	**Outbreak of World War I**
38	**May 14, 1940**	**-6.80%**	**Germans Invade Holland**
40	**May 21, 1940**	**-6.78%**	**Allied Reverses in France**
42	Jun 20, 1931	6.64%	Hoover Advocates Foreign Debt Moratorium
44	**Jul 26, 1934**	**-6.62%**	**Fighting in Austria; Italy mobilizes**
46	**Sep 26, 1955**	**-6.54%**	**Eisenhower Suffers Heart Attack**
51	**Jul 26, 1893**	**-6.31%**	**Erie Railroad Bankrupt**
65	Oct 31, 1929	5.82%	Fed Lowers Discount Rate
66	**Jun 16, 1930**	**-5.81%**	**Hoover to Sign Tariff Bill**
67	Apr 20, 1933	5.80%	Continued Rally on Dropping of Gold Standard
73	May 2, 1898	5.64%	Dewey Defeats Spanish
76	Mar 28, 1898	5.56%	Dispatches of Armistice with Spain
85	Dec 22, 1916	5.47%	Lansing Denies U.S. Near War
88	**Dec 18, 1896**	**-5.42%**	**Senate votes for Free Cuba**
89	**Feb 25, 1933**	**-5.40%**	**Maryland Bank Holiday**
93	Oct 23, 1933	5.37%	Roosevelt Devalues Dollar
95	**Dec 21, 1916**	**-5.35%**	**Sec. of State Lansing implies U.S. Near War**
104	Apr 9, 1938	5.25%	Congress Passes Bill Taxing U.S. Government Bond Interest
125	Oct 20, 1931	5.03%	ICC Raises Rail Rates
126	**Mar 31, 1932**	**-5.02%**	**House Proposes Stock Sales Tax**

market was already down substantially before this news was announced late in the day. It is interesting that September 17, 2001, was the first time the market dropped 5 percent or more during a U.S. involvement in any war during this century and more than doubled the 3.5 percent drop that occurred on the day following the attack on Pearl Harbor.

Even when the market moves substantially, there can be sharp disagreement over the cause. On November 15, 1991, when the Dow fell over 120 points, or nearly 4 percent, *Investor's Business Daily* entitled an article about the market "Dow Plunges 120 in a Scary Stock Sell-Off: Biotechs, Programs, Expiration and Congress Get the Blame."[2] In contrast, a New York writer for the London *Financial Times* entitled a front-page article "Wall Street Drops 120 Points on Concern at Russian Moves." What is interesting is that such news, specifically that the Russian government had suspended oil licenses and taken over the gold supplies, was not mentioned even once in the U.S. article. That one major newspaper can highlight "reasons" that another does not even report illustrates the difficulty in finding fundamental explanations for the movements of markets.

UNCERTAINTY AND THE MARKET

The market fears uncertainty and events that jar investors from their customary framework for analyzing the world. September 11 serves as the perfect example. Americans were not sure what these terrorist attacks meant for their daily lives. How severe would the drop in air travel be? How big a hit would the approximately $600 billion tourist industry take? These unanswered questions instill anxiety in investors and the market.

As noted earlier, President Eisenhower's heart attack on September 26, 1955, caused a 6.54 percent decline in the Dow, the seventh largest in the postwar period. The drop was a clear sign of Eisenhower's popularity with the market. President Kennedy's assassination on November 22, 1963, caused the Dow to drop 2.9 percent and persuaded the New York Stock Exchange to close 2 hours early to prevent panic selling. Yet, when the market reopened the following Tuesday and Lyndon Johnson took over the reins of government, the market soared 4.5 percent, representing one of the best days in the postwar period.

The market almost always declines in reaction to sudden, unexpected changes related to the presidency. When William McKinley was shot on September 14, 1901, the market dropped by more than 4 percent. However, stocks regained all their losses on the following trading day. The death of Warren Harding caused a milder setback, which was soon erased. Sell-offs such as these provide good opportunities for investors

---

[2]Virginia Munger Kahn, *Investor's Business Daily*, November 16, 1991, p. 1.

to step up and buy stocks because the market usually reverses itself quickly following the change in leadership.[3]

DEMOCRATS AND REPUBLICANS

It is well known that the stock market prefers Republicans to Democrats. Most corporate executives and stock traders are Republicans, and many Republican policies are perceived to be favorable to stock prices and capital formation. Democrats are perceived to be less amenable to favorable tax treatment of capital gains and more in favor of regulation and income redistribution. Yet the stock market actually does better under Democrats than under Republicans.

Figure 13-2 shows the performance of the Dow Jones Industrials during every administration since Grover Cleveland was elected in 1888. The greatest bear market in history occurred during the Hoover administration, and stocks did quite well under Franklin Roosevelt, despite the fact that he was frequently reviled in boardrooms and brokerage houses around the country.

Table 13-2 records the performance of the Dow during each presidential term since 1888. The immediate reaction of the market—the day before the election to the day after—does indeed conform to the fact that investors like Republicans better than Democrats. Since 1888, the market fell an average of 0.5 percent on the day following a Democratic victory but rose by 0.7 percent on the day following a Republican victory. However, the market's reaction to the success of Republicans in presidential elections has been muted since World War II. There have been occasions, such as Clinton's second-term election victory, when the market soared because the Republicans kept control of Congress, not because a Democrat was reelected.

It is also instructive to examine the returns in the first, second, third, and fourth years of a presidential term, also displayed in Table 13-2. The returns in the third year of a presidential term are clearly the best, especially since 1948. It is striking that this is true over the past 113 years because this period includes the disastrous 43.3 percent drop that occurred in 1931 during the third year of Hoover's ill-fated administration.

Why the third year stands out is not clear. One would think that the fourth year of a presidential term, when the administration might put pressure on the Federal Reserve (Fed) to stimulate the economy for the

---

[3]However, there are some whom the market never forgives. Stocks rallied over 4 percent in the week following the news of the death of Franklin Roosevelt, who was never a favorite on Wall Street.

FIGURE 13-2

The Dow Jones Industrial Average and Presidential Terms (Lines Represent a
Change of Administration, Dark Lines Represent a Change of Party, and Shaded
Areas Represent a Democratic President in Office)

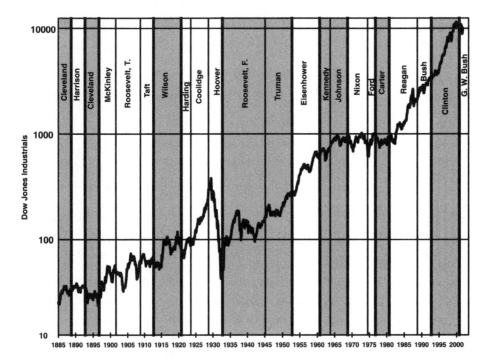

upcoming election, should be the best year for stocks. However, the
fourth year, although good, is clearly not the best. Perhaps the market
anticipates favorable economic policies in the election year, causing
stock prices to rise the year before.

The superior performance under the Democrats in recent years is
documented in Table 13-3. This table records the total real and nominal
returns in the stock market, as well as the rate of inflation, under Democratic and Republican administrations. Since 1888, the market has fared
better in nominal terms under Democrats than under Republicans, but
since inflation has been lower when the Republicans have held office,
real stock returns have been slightly higher under Republicans than
under Democrats. This has not been true over the past 50 years, when
the market performed far better under the Democrats whether or not
inflation is factored in. Perhaps this is why the market's reaction to a
Democratic presidential victory has not been as negative in recent years
as it was in the past.

TABLE 13–2

Stock Returns during Presidential Administrations (Measured in Percent by S&P Total Return Index; Italics Represent Democratic Administrations)

President's Name	Party	Election Date	From: 1 day before / To: 1 day after	First Year of Term	Second Year of Term	Third Year of Term	Fourth Year of Term
Harrison	R	11/6/1888	0.4	6.9	-6.2	18.7	6.2
Cleveland	D	11/8/1892	*-0.5*	*-19.1*	*3.2*	*5.0*	*3.0*
McKinley	R	11/3/1896	2.7	20.2	29.1	3.8	21.2
McKinley	R	11/6/1900	3.3	19.7	8.3	-17.4	31.4
Roosevelt T.	R	11/8/1904	1.3	21.3	0.8	-24.5	38.9
Taft	R	11/3/1908	2.4	16.4	-3.6	3.4	7.3
Wilson	D	11/5/1912	*1.8*	*-5.1*	*-5.9*	*31.1*	*8.7*
Wilson	D	11/7/1916	*-0.4*	*-18.5*	*17.1*	*19.6*	*-14.3*
Harding	R	11/2/1920	-0.6	9.2	29.6	5.1	26.6
Coolidge	R	11/4/1924	1.2	25.7	11.6	37.5	43.6
Hoover	R	11/6/1928	1.2	-8.4	-24.9	-43.3	-8.2
Roosevelt F.	D	11/8/1932	*-4.5*	*54.0*	*-1.4*	*47.7*	*33.9*
Roosevelt F.	D	11/3/1936	*2.3*	*-35.0*	*31.1*	*-0.4*	*-9.8*
Roosevelt F.	D	11/5/1940	*-2.4*	*-11.6*	*20.3*	*25.9*	*19.8*
Roosevelt F.	D	11/7/1944	*-0.3*	*36.4*	*-8.1*	*5.7*	*5.5*
Truman	D	11/2/1948	*-3.8*	*18.8*	*31.7*	*24.0*	*18.4*
Eisenhower	R	11/4/1952	0.4	-1.0	52.6	31.6	6.6
Eisenhower	R	11/6/1956	-0.9	-10.8	43.4	12.0	0.5
Kennedy	D	11/8/1960	*0.8*	*26.9*	*-8.7*	*22.8*	*16.5*
Johnson	D	11/3/1964	*-0.2*	*12.5*	*-10.1*	*24.0*	*11.1*
Nixon	R	11/5/1968	0.3	-8.5	4.0	14.3	19.0
Nixon	R	11/7/1972	-0.1	-14.7	-26.5	37.2	23.8
Carter	D	11/2/1976	*-1.0*	*-7.2*	*6.6*	*18.4*	*32.4*
Reagan	R	11/4/1980	1.7	-4.9	21.4	22.5	6.3
Reagan	R	11/6/1984	-0.9	32.2	18.5	5.2	16.8
Bush	R	11/8/1988	-0.4	31.5	-3.2	30.5	7.7
Clinton	D	11/3/1992	*-0.9*	*10.0*	*1.3*	*37.6*	*23.0*
Clinton	D	11/5/1996	*2.6*	*33.4*	*28.6*	*21.0*	*-9.1*
Bush, G.W.	R	11/7/2001*	-1.6	-19.1			

*Outcome of race was officially undetermined until December 13, 2001

Average from 1888 to 2001	Democratic	-0.5	7.3	8.1	21.7	10.7
	Republican	0.7	7.2	10.3	9.1	16.5
	Overall	0.1	7.3	9.3	15.0	13.8
Average from 1948 to 2001	Democratic	-0.4	15.7	8.2	24.6	15.4
	Republican	-0.2	0.6	15.7	21.9	11.5
	Overall	-0.3	7.1	12.3	23.2	13.3

TABLE 13–3

Presidential Administrations and Stock Returns (Stock Returns Taken from Election Date
or Date of Taking Office, Whichever Is Earlier; Italics Represent Democratic Administrations)

President's Name	Party	Date	Months in Office	Annualized Nominal Stock Return	Annualized Inflation	Annualized Real Return
Harrison	R	11/88 - 10/92	48	5.74	0.04	5.70
Cleveland	*D*	*11/92 - 10/96*	*48*	*-3.31*	*-1.91*	*-1.43*
McKinley	R	11/96 - 8/01	58	20.66	0.00	20.66
Roosevelt T.	R	9/01 - 10/08	86	4.81	1.39	3.38
Taft	R	11/08 - 10/12	48	7.54	0.82	6.67
Wilson	*D*	*11/12 - 10/20*	*96*	*4.68*	*9.42*	*-4.33*
Harding	R	11/20 - 7/23	33	5.48	-4.05	9.93
Coolidge	R	8/23 - 10/28	63	28.04	0.12	27.88
Hoover	R	11/28 - 10/32	48	-20.42	-6.29	-15.08
Roosevelt F.	*D*	*11/32 - 3/45*	*149*	*11.52*	*2.36*	*8.94*
Truman	*D*	*4/45 - 10/52*	*91*	*14.66*	*5.54*	*8.64*
Eisenhower	R	11/52 - 10/60	96	14.96	1.35	13.42
Kennedy	*D*	*11/60 - 10/63*	*36*	*15.15*	*1.11*	*13.88*
Johnson	*D*	*11/63 - 10/68*	*60*	*10.39*	*2.77*	*7.42*
Nixon	R	11/68 - 7/74	69	-1.32	6.03	-6.93
Ford	R	8/74 - 10/76	27	17.21	7.27	9.27
Carter	*D*	*11/76 - 10/80*	*48*	*11.04*	*10.02*	*0.93*
Reagan	R	11/80 - 10/88	96	15.18	4.46	10.26
Bush	R	11/88 - 10/92	48	14.44	4.22	9.81
Clinton	*D*	*11/92 - 10/00*	*96*	*19.01*	*2.58*	*16.01*
Bush, G.W.	*R*	*11/00- 12/01*	*13*	*-16.01*	*1.66*	*-17.38*
Average from 1888 to October 2001	Democrat	45.9%	10.84	4.12	6.48
	Republican	54.1%	8.79	1.48	7.20
	Overall	100%	9.72	2.68	6.86
Average from 1948 to October 2001	Democrat	46.0%	15.23	3.64	11.25
	Republican	54.0%	10.31	3.96	6.11
	Overall	100%	12.55	3.81	8.41

STOCKS AND WAR

Since 1885, the U.S. economy has been at war or on the sidelines of a
world war about one-fifth of the time. The stock market does equally
well in nominal returns whether there is war or peace. Inflation, however, has averaged nearly 6 percent during wartime and less than 2 per-

cent during peacetime, so the real returns on stocks during peacetime greatly outstrip those during wars.

It is of interest that the volatility of the market, measured as the monthly standard deviation of the Dow Jones Industrial Average, actually has been greater, on average, during peacetime than during war. The greatest volatility in U.S. markets occurred in the late 1920s and early 1930s, well before the United States was engaged in a worldwide conflict. Only during World War I and the short Gulf War did stocks have higher volatility than average.

In theory, war should have a profound influence on stock prices. Governments commandeer tremendous resources, while high taxes and huge government borrowings compete with investors' demand for stock. Whole industries are nationalized to further the war effort. Moreover, if losing the war is deemed a possibility, stocks could well decline as the victors impose sanctions on the vanquished. However, as demonstrated in Chapter 1, the economies of Germany and Japan were restored to health quickly following World War II, and stocks subsequently boomed.

The World Wars

The volatility of the market during World War I greatly exceeded that during World War II. The market rose nearly 100 percent during the early stages of World War I, fell 40 percent when the United States became involved in the hostilities, and finally rallied when the "Great War" ended. In contrast, during the 6 years of World War II, the market never deviated more than 32 percent from its prewar level.

The outbreak of World War I precipitated a panic as European investors scrambled to get out of stocks and into gold and cash. After the declaration of war by Austria-Hungary on Serbia on July 28, 1914, all the major European stock exchanges closed. The European panic spread to New York, and the Dow Jones Industrial Average closed down nearly 7 percent on Thursday, July 30, the most since the 8.3 percent drop during the so-called Panic of 1907. Minutes before the opening of the New York Stock Exchange on Friday, the exchange voted to close for an indefinite period.

The market did not reopen until December. Never before had the New York Stock Exchange been closed for such an extended period. Emergency trades were permitted, but only by approval of a special committee and only at prices at or above the last trade before the exchange closed. Even then, trading prohibition was observed in the breach as illegal trades were made outside the exchange (on the curb) at prices that continued to decline through October. Unofficially, by autumn, prices were said to be 15 to 20 percent below the July closing.

It is ironic that the only extended period during which the New York Stock Exchange was closed occurred when the United States was not at war or in any degree of financial or economic distress. In fact, when the exchange was closed, traders realized that the United States would be a strong economic beneficiary of the European conflict. Once investors realized that America was going to make the munitions and provide raw materials to the belligerents, public interest in stocks soared.

By the time the exchange reopened on December 12, prices were rising rapidly. The Dow Jones Industrials finished that historic Saturday session about 5 percent higher than the closing prices in July. The rally continued, and 1915 records the best single-year increase in the history of the Dow as stocks rose a record 82 percent.

The message of the great boom of 1915 was not lost on traders a generation later. When World War II erupted, investors took their cue from what happened at the beginning of the preceding world war. When Great Britain declared war on Germany on September 3, 1939, the rise was so explosive that the Tokyo Exchange was forced to close early. When the market opened in New York, a buying panic erupted. The Dow gained over 7 percent, and even the European stock exchanges were firm when trading reopened.

The enthusiasm that followed the onset of World War II quickly faded. President Roosevelt was determined not to let corporations earn easy profits, as they had in World War I. These profits had been a source of public criticism because Americans felt that the war costs were not being borne equally. Its young men had died overseas, while its corporations earned record income. An excess profits tax enacted by Congress during World War II removed the wartime premium that investors had expected from the conflict.

The day before the Japanese attacked Pearl Harbor, the Dow was down 25 percent from its 1939 high and still less than one-third its 1929 peak. Stocks fell 3.5 percent on the day following Pearl Harbor and continued to fall until they hit a low on April 28, 1942, when the United States suffered losses in the early months of the war in the Pacific.

However, when the tide turned toward the Allies, the market began to climb. By the time Germany signed its unconditional surrender on May 7, 1945, the Dow was 20 percent above its prewar level. The detonation of the atomic bomb over Hiroshima, a pivotal event in the history of warfare, caused stocks to surge 1.7 percent as investors recognized that the end of the war was near. However, World War II did not prove as profitable for investors as World War I, since the Dow was up only 30 percent during the 6 years from the German invasion of Poland to V-J Day.

Post-1945 Conflicts

The Korean War took investors by surprise. When North Korea invaded its southern neighbor on June 25, 1950, the Dow fell 4.65 percent, greater than the day following Pearl Harbor. However, the market reaction to the growing conflict was contained, and stocks never fell more than 12 percent below their prewar level.

The war in Vietnam was the longest and least popular of all U.S. wars. The starting point for U.S. involvement in the conflict can be placed at August 2, 1964, when two American destroyers were reportedly attacked in the Gulf of Tonkin.

One and a half years after the Gulf of Tonkin incident, the Dow reached an all-time high of 995, more than 18 percent above its prewar level. However, it fell nearly 30 percent in the following months after the Fed tightened credit to curb inflation. By the time American troop strength reached its peak in early 1968, the market had recovered. Two years later, the market fell again when Nixon sent troops into Cambodia, and soaring interest rates coupled with a looming recession sent the market down nearly 25 percent from its prewar point.

The Peace Pact between the North Vietnamese and the Americans was signed in Paris on January 27, 1973. However, the gains made by investors over the 8 years of war were quite small because the market was held back by rising inflation, rising interest rates, and other problems not directly related to the Vietnamese conflict.

If the war in Vietnam was the longest American war, the Gulf War against Iraq was the shortest. Hostilities began on August 2, 1990, when Iraq invaded Kuwait, sending oil prices skyward and sparking a U.S. military buildup in Saudi Arabia. The rise in oil prices combined with an already slowing U.S. economy to drive the United States deeper into a recession. The stock market fell precipitously, and by October 11, the Dow had slumped over 18 percent from its prewar level.

U.S. offensive action began on January 17, 1991. It was the first major war fought in a world where markets for oil, gold, and U.S. government bonds were traded around the clock in Tokyo, Singapore, London, and New York. The markets judged Americans victorious in a matter of hours. Bonds sold off in Tokyo for a few minutes following the news of the U.S. bombing of Baghdad, but the stunning reports of the Allied successes sent bonds and Japanese stocks straight upward in the next few minutes. Oil prices, which were being traded in the Far East, collapsed, as Brent crude fell from $29 a barrel before hostilities to $20 a barrel the next day.

On the following day, stock prices soared around the world. The Dow jumped 115 points, or 4.4 percent, and there were large gains throughout Europe and Asia. By the time the United States deployed ground troops to invade Kuwait, the market had known for 2 months that victory was at hand. The war ended on February 28, and by the first week in March, the Dow was more than 18 percent higher than when the war started.

As noted at the onset of this chapter, the war against terrorism began with the terrorist attacks on New York and the Pentagon on September 11, 2001. The Dow Jones Industrials were down 16 percent from their close of 9,606 on September 10 to an intraday low of 8,062 reached on Friday, September 21. However, the market rebounded sharply by the next week and had recovered to 9,120 by the time the United States began offensive action against the Taliban in Afghanistan on October 7.

Because of aggressive easing policies by the Federal Reserve and successful execution of the war, the Dow surpassed its September 10 level on November 13 and continued rising to year-end. From its intraday low on September 21 to its intraday high of 10,184 on December 28, the Dow had risen an astounding 26.3 percent in 3 months.

Perhaps the buyers who had miraculously appeared in the S&P futures market minutes after the second plane hit the World Trade Center towers were right. Despite the announcement by the National Bureau of Economic Research (NBER) in November that a recession had officially begun in March, the market expected a successful war against terrorism and a vigorous economic recovery.

CONCLUSION

When investigating the causes of major market movements, it is sobering to realize that less than one in four can be associated with a news event of major political or economic import. This confirms the unpredictability of the market and difficulty in predicting market moves. Those who sold in panic at the outbreak of World War I missed out on the greatest year in the market. Yet the surge in buying that occurred at the onset of World War II also was misplaced because the government was determined to cap wartime profits. Wars, political campaigns, and even recessions, which seem so all-consuming when they occur, prove to be minor factors against a backdrop of economic growth and political stability that has proved to be the major theme of the past century.

CHAPTER 14

REACTIONS OF FINANCIAL MARKETS TO ECONOMIC DATA

The thing that most affects the stock market is everything.
JAMES PALYSTED WOOD, 1966

It is 8:28 a.m. Eastern Daylight Time, Friday, July 5, 1996. Normally, a trading day wedged between a major U.S. holiday and a weekend is slow, with little volume or price movement. But not today. Traders around the world have anxiously gathered around their terminals, eyes riveted on the scrolling news that displays thousands of headlines every day. It is just 2 minutes before the most important announcement each month—the U.S. employment statistics.

All week, stock, bond, and currency traders have anticipated this day. The Dow Jones Industrial Average has been trading within a few points of its all-time high, reached at the end of May. However, interest rates have been rising, giving traders cause for concern. The seconds tick down. At 8:30 a.m. sharp, the words come across the screen:

PAYROLL UP 239,000, UNEMPLOYMENT AT SIX-YEAR LOW OF 5.3 PERCENT, WAGES UP 9 CENTS AN HOUR, BIGGEST INCREASE IN 30 YEARS.

President Clinton hailed the economic news, claiming, "We have the most solid American economy in a generation; wages for American workers are finally on the rise again."

However, the financial markets were stunned. Figure 14-1 tells the story. Long-term bond prices immediately collapsed on both domestic and foreign exchanges because traders expected higher interest rates. Rates on long- and short-term bonds climbed nearly a quarter point. Although the stock market would not open for an hour, the Standard & Poor's (S&P) 500 Index futures, which represent claims on this benchmark index and are described in detail in Chapter 15, fell from 676 to 656, about 2 percent. European stock markets, which had been open for hours, sold off immediately. The benchmark DAX Index in Germany, the CAC in France, and the FT-SE in Great Britain instantly fell almost 2 percent. Within seconds, world equity markets lost $200 billion, and world bond markets fell at least as much.

This episode demonstrates that what most of the population interprets as "good" news often causes security prices to fall. There is a strong

FIGURE   14–1

Market Reactions to a Strong Employment Report, July 5, 1996

(A) US Bonds

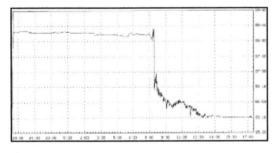

(B) US Stocks

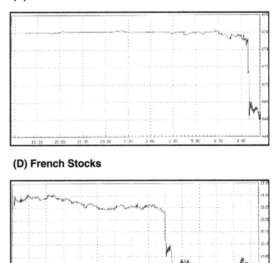

(C) German Stocks

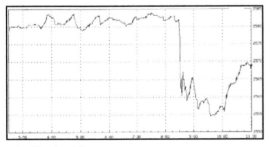

(D) French Stocks

SOURCE: Bloomberg L.P.

market reaction to the employment report because it contains the most comprehensive and timely data on the U.S. economy and provides the best clue to the future direction of the Federal Reserve's monetary policy.

ECONOMIC DATA AND THE MARKET

News moves markets. The timing of much news is unpredictable—such as war, political developments, and natural disasters. But most news, especially data about the economy, comes at preannounced times that have been set a year in advance. There are over 300 scheduled releases of economic data each year—mostly by government agencies but increasingly by private firms. Virtually all the announcements deal with economic growth and inflation, and all have the potential to move the market significantly.

Economic data not only frame the way traders view the economy but also have an impact on traders' expectations of how the central bank will implement its monetary policy. Stronger economic growth or higher inflation increases the probability that the central bank will either tighten monetary policy or stop easing credit. Economic releases influence the expectations of traders about the future course of interest rates, the economy, and ultimately, stock prices.

PRINCIPLES OF MARKET REACTION

Markets do not respond directly to the size of the number being announced; rather, they respond to the *difference* between what the participants in the financial markets expect to be announced and what is actually announced. Whether the news by itself is good or bad is of no importance. If the market expects that 200,000 jobs were lost last month, but the report shows that only 100,000 jobs were lost, this will be considered "strong economic news" by the financial markets—having about the same effect as a gain of 200,000 jobs when the market expected a gain of only 100,000.

The reason why markets react only to differences between expectations and actual announcements is that the prices of securities in actively traded markets already include expected information. If a firm is expected to report bad earnings, the market has already priced the stock to reflect this gloomy information. If the earnings report is not as bad as anticipated, the price will rise on the announcement. The same principle applies to the reaction of bonds, stocks, and foreign exchange to economic data.

To understand why the market moves the way it does, you must identify the *market expectation* for the data released. The market expectation, often referred to as the *consensus estimate*, is gathered by news and re-search organizations. They poll economists, professional forecasters, traders, and other market participants for their estimates of an upcoming government or private release. The results of their survey are sent to the financial press and reported widely in many major newspapers and online.[1]

INFORMATION CONTENT OF DATA RELEASES

The economic data are analyzed for their implications for future economic growth, inflation, and central bank policy. The following principle summarizes the reaction of the bond markets to the release of data relating to economic growth:

> Stronger-than-expected economic growth increases both long- and short-term interest rates. Weaker-than-expected economic growth causes interest rates to fall. The effect of unanticipated economic growth on stock prices is ambiguous.

Faster economic growth raises interest rates for several reasons. First, a stronger economy increases private loan demands. Consumers feel more confident and are more willing to borrow against future income. Faster economic growth also motivates firms to expand production to meet increased consumer demand. As a result, both firms and consumers increase their demand for credit. The increase in credit demand pushes interest rates higher in the bond market.

A second reason why interest rates rise with a stronger-than-expected economic report is that such growth may be inflationary, especially if it is near the end of an economic cycle. Growth associated with increases in productivity, which often occurs in the early and middle stages of a business expansion, is rarely inflationary.

Inflationary fears were the principal reason why interest rates soared when the Labor Department released its report on July 5. Traders feared that the large increase in wages caused by the tight labor markets and falling unemployment rate would cause inflation, a nemesis to both the bond and stock markets.

These reports also have significant implications for the actions of central banks around the world. A rise in inflation will make it likely that the central bank will tighten credit. If aggregate demand is expanding too rapidly relative to the supply of output, the monetary authority can use its open-market operations to drain reserves from the

---

[1]Usually both the median and range of estimates are reported. The consensus estimate does vary a bit from service to service, but the estimates usually are quite close.

banking system in order to raise interest rates and prevent the economy from overheating.

Of course, in the case of a weaker-than-expected employment report, the bond market will respond favorably, especially if it is associated with lower inflationary fears and comes late in the economic cycle. Such a report increases the probability that the central bank will add reserves to the system, lowering interest rates and increasing the demand for stocks and bonds.

ECONOMIC GROWTH AND STOCK PRICES

It surprises the general public (and often the financial press) when a strong economic report actually sends the stock market lower. However, rapid economic growth has two important implications for the stock market, and each tugs in the opposite direction. A strong economy increases future corporate earnings, which is bullish for stocks, but it also raises interest rates, which pulls investors toward bonds. Similarly, a weak economic report lowers expected earnings, but since interest rates decline, stock prices possibly could move up.

Which effect is stronger—the interest-rate or corporate-earnings effect—depends on where the economy is in the business cycle. Recent analysis shows that in a recession, a stronger-than-expected economic report increases stock prices (and a weaker-than-expected report depresses stock prices) because the state of the economy is more important to investors than the direction of interest rates.[2] During economic expansions, and particularly toward the end of an expansion, the interest-rate effect is usually stronger.

Sometimes the opposing forces of interest rates and earning prospects will fight each other to a standstill through the day. The impact of interest-rate changes often dominates stock trading right at the time of the announcement, whereas the impact of a strong report for corporate earnings often, but certainly not always, is seen later. In a down economy, the implications for corporate earnings often dominate from the start.

At the exact time of economic announcements, many stock traders, especially those trading in the stock index futures market, look at the movements in the bond market to guide their trading. This is particu-

---

[2]See John Boyd, Jian Hu, and Ravi Jagannathan, "The Stock Market's Reaction to Unemployment News: Why Bad News Is Usually Good for Stocks," NBER working paper W8092, Cambridge, MA, 2001.

larly true of portfolio managers who actively apportion their portfolio between stocks and bonds on the basis of interest rates and expected returns. When bond prices rise after a weak economic report, these investors are ready to buy stocks. Later, as more stock investors recognize that the weak employment report means lower earnings, they may become more bearish about equity prospects. The stock market often gyrates through such a day as investors digest the implications of the data for stock earnings and interest rates.

THE EMPLOYMENT REPORT

The employment report, compiled by the Bureau of Labor Statistics (BLS), is the key release each month. Of great importance to traders is the change in the nonfarm payroll (the number of farm workers is excluded because it is very volatile and not associated with cyclic economic trends). The payroll survey, sometimes called the *establishment survey*, collects payroll data from nearly 400,000 business establishments, covering nearly 50 million workers, about 40 percent of the total. It is this survey that most forecasters use to judge the future course of the economy.

The unemployment rate, however, which is released with the nonfarm payroll, usually gets the top billing in the evening news and the financial press. The unemployment rate is determined from an entirely different survey than the payroll data. The unemployment rate is calculated from a *household survey*, which includes data from about 60,000 households and asks, among other questions, whether anyone in the household has actively sought work over the past 4 weeks. Those who answer in the affirmative are classified as unemployed. The unemployed divided by the total labor force yields the unemployment rate. The labor force in the United States, defined as those employed plus unemployed, comprises about two-thirds of the adult population, a ratio that has risen steadily as more women have successfully sought work.

Because the payroll and household data are based on totally different surveys, it is not unusual for payroll employment to go up at the same time that the unemployment rate rises, and vice versa. This is so because the payroll survey counts jobs, but the household survey counts people, so workers with two jobs are counted once in the household survey but twice in the payroll survey.[3] Furthermore, increases in the num-

---

[3] Early in 1994, the household survey was improved to include this question.

ber seeking work from the labor market pool will increase the unemployment rate. In fact, it is well known that the unemployment rate often rises in the early stages of an economic recovery due to the influx of job seekers into an improved labor market.

For these reasons, economists and forecasters have long dismissed the unemployment rate as unimportant in forecasting the business cycle. However, this does not diminish the political importance of the unemployment rate. It is an easily understood number that represents the fraction of the workforce looking for but not finding work. The public looks more to this rate than to any other to judge the health of the economy. As a result, pressure can mount on the president and Congress, as well as the Federal Reserve, whenever the unemployment rate rises.

THE CYCLE OF ANNOUNCEMENTS

The employment report is just one of several dozen economic announcements that come out every month. Table 14-1 displays a typical

TABLE 14–1

Monthly Economic Calendar

Monthly Economic Calendar

Monday	Tuesday	Wednesday	Thursday	Friday
1 10:00 PMI**	2 8:30 Leading Economic Indicator* (2 months lag)	3	4 8:30 Jobless Claims** 4:30 Money Supply*	5 8:30 Employment Report****
8 10:00 Service PMI**	9	10	11 8:30 Jobless Claims** 4:30 Money Supply*	12 8:30 Retail Sales** 8:30 Producer Prices****
15	16 8:30 Consumer Prices****	17 8:30 Housing Starts*** 9:15 Industrial Production*	18 8:30 Merchandise Trade* 8:30 Jobless Claims** 4:30 Money Supply*	19 10:00 Philadelphia Fed Rep* 10:00 Consumer Expect.** (Univ. of Mich., Prelim.)
22	23 8:30 Durable Goods Orders**	24	25 8:30 Jobless Claims** 4:30 Money Supply*	26 8:30 Gross Dom. Prod.***†
29	30 10:00 Consumer Expect. (Conference Board)***	31 10:00 Chicago Purchasing Managers**		

Stars Rank Importance to Market (** = most important)**
†First (Preliminary) report of quarter (January, April, July, and October) is of moderate importance.
Other months' GDP reports of minor importance.

month and the usual release dates for the data. The number of asterisks represents the importance of the report to the financial market.

The employment statistics are the culmination of important data on economic growth that come out around the turn of the month. On the first business day of each month, a survey by the Institute for Supply Management (formerly the National Association of Purchasing Managers) is released. This survey has become increasingly important at providing information to help forecast the all-important employment report.

The institute's report surveys 250 purchasing agents of manufacturing companies and inquires as to whether orders, production, employment, etc. are rising or falling and forms a purchasing managers' index (PMI) from these data. A reading of 50 means that half the managers report rising activity and half report falling activity. A reading of 52 or 53 is the sign of a normally expanding economy. A reading of 60 represents a strong economy where three-fifths of the managers report growth. A reading below 50 represents a contracting manufacturing sector, and a reading below 40 is almost always a sign of recession.

Because of the huge importance of the monthly employment report, there is much pressure on traders to obtain earlier data that might give some hint as to the state of the economy, thereby improving the estimate of the monthly payroll change. The purchasing managers' survey fulfills this function. Of particular importance in the PMI is the employment category, for this is the first comprehensive picture of the labor market, and it provides a clue as to what might be revealed in the important manufacturing category of the employment report.

However, traders do have access to even earlier data: The Chicago Purchasing Managers' Report comes out on the last business day of the previous month, the day before the PMI report. The Chicago area is well diversified in manufacturing, so about two-thirds of the time the Chicago index will move in the same direction as the national index.

In addition, if you want an even earlier reading on the economy, there are the consumer sentiment indicators: one from the University of Michigan and another from the Conference Board, a business trade association. These surveys query consumers about their current financial situation and their expectations of the future. The Conference Board survey, released on the last Tuesday of the month, is considered a good early indicator of consumer spending. The University of Michigan index was for many years not released until the month following the survey, but pressure for early data has persuaded the university to release a preliminary report to compete with the report from the Conference Board.

INFLATION REPORTS

Although the employment report forms the capstone of the news about economic growth, the market knows that the Federal Reserve (Fed) is also preoccupied with inflation. The Fed does not normally ease credit unless it is assured that inflationary pressures are under control. The central bank recognizes that it is the guardian of the currency and cannot ignore inflation. Some of the earliest signals of these pressures arrive with the midmonth inflation statistics.

The first monthly inflation release is the producer price index (PPI), formerly the *wholesale price index.* The PPI measures the prices received by producers at the first commercial sale, usually to retailers. The prices of consumer goods represent about three-quarters of the PPI, whereas the prices of capital goods comprise the rest. About 15 percent of the PPI is energy-related.

The second monthly announcement, which follows the PPI by a day or so, is the all-important consumer price index (CPI). In contrast to the PPI, the CPI does not include the prices of capital goods, but it covers the prices of services as well as goods. Services, which include rent, housing costs, transportation, and medical services, now comprise over half the weight of the CPI.

The CPI is considered the benchmark measure of inflation. When price-level comparisons are made, both on an historical and an international basis, the CPI is almost always the chosen index. The CPI is also the price index to which so many private and public contracts, as well as Social Security, are linked.

The financial market probably gives a bit more weight to the CPI than to the PPI because of the CPI's widespread use and political importance. The CPI does have the advantage of including the prices of services, which the PPI does not. However, many economists regard the PPI as more sensitive to early price trends because increased prices often show up at the wholesale level before they are passed on to the consumer. Furthermore, at the same time that the PPI is announced, indexes for the prices of intermediate and crude goods are released, both of which track inflation at earlier stages of production.

Core Inflation

Of interest to investors are not only the month-to-month changes of the PPI and CPI but also the changes excluding the volatile food and energy sectors. Since weather has such an undue influence on food prices, a rise or fall in the price of food over a month does not have much meaning for the overall inflationary trend. Similarly, oil and natural gas prices fluctuate due to weather conditions and supply disruptions that are not usually repeated in coming months. Hence the BLS, which gathers inflation data, also releases the core price index, which excludes food and energy.

Most traders regard changes in the core rate of inflation as more important than changes in the overall index, since core inflation is apt to be persistent and have an impact on long-term inflation trends. Forecasters usually are able to predict the core rate of inflation better than the overall rate because the latter is influenced by the volatile food and energy sectors. A three-tenths of a percent error in the consensus forecast for the month-to-month rate of inflation might not be that serious, but such an error would be considered quite large for the core rate of inflation and would affect the financial markets significantly.

Employment Costs

Other important releases bearing on inflation relate to employment costs. The monthly employment report issued by the BLS contains a report on the hourly wage rate. This report indicates wage pressures arising from the labor market. Since labor costs are nearly two-thirds of a firm's production costs, increases in the hourly wage not matched by increases in productivity increase costs and threaten to result in inflation.

Every calendar quarter the government also releases the employment cost index (ECI). This index includes benefit costs as well as wages and is considered the most comprehensive report of labor costs. Since the Fed chairman has indicated that this is an important indicator of inflation, the financial markets closely scrutinize these data.

IMPACT ON FINANCIAL MARKETS

The following summarizes the impact of inflation on the financial markets:

> A lower-than-expected inflation report lowers interest rates and boosts stock prices. Inflation worse than expected raises interest rates and depresses stock prices.

That inflation is bad for bonds should come as no surprise. Bonds are fixed-income investments whose cash flow is not adjusted for inflation. Bondholders demand higher interest rates in response to worsening news of inflation not only to protect their purchasing power but also because of the increased concern that the Fed will tighten credit.

However, worse-than-expected inflation is also bad for the stock market. As I noted in Chapter 11, stocks have proven to be poor hedges against inflation in the short run. Stock investors fear that worsening inflation will increase the taxes on corporate earnings, raise the effective tax on capital gains, and induce the central bank to tighten credit.

CENTRAL BANK POLICY

Monetary policy is of primary importance to financial markets. There are few fundamental or technical analysts who do not rely heavily on monetary policy indicators, such as the federal funds rate, the discount rate, or money supplies, in their forecast of future stock returns.

Martin Zweig, one of the foremost money managers, shares the opinion of others when he states:

> In the stock market, as with horse racing, money makes the mare go. Monetary conditions exert an enormous influence on stock prices. Indeed, the monetary climate—primarily the trend in interest rates and Federal Reserve policy—is the dominant factor in determining the stock market's major direction.[4]

Easing monetary policy, by definition, involves lowering short-term interest rates. This is almost always extremely positive for stock prices. As demonstrated in Chapter 11, stocks thrive on liquidity provided by the central bank. When the central bank eases credit, it lowers the rate at which stocks' future cash flows are discounted and provides a monetary stimulus to future earnings. Only if the central bank eases excessively, so that the market fears it might spark inflation, will stocks react poorly. If this happens, however, an investor should prefer to be in stocks than bonds because fixed-income assets are clearly hurt the most by unanticipated inflation.

CONCLUSION

The reaction of financial markets to the release of economic data is not random but based on sound economic analysis. Strong economic growth invariably raises interest rates, but it has an ambiguous effect on stock prices, depending on the state of the business cycle and whether inflationary fears are increased. Higher inflation is bad for both the stock and bond markets. Central bank easing is very positive for

---

[4]Martin Zweig, *Winning on Wall Street* (New York: Warner Books, 1986), p. 43.

stocks—historically, it has sparked some of the strongest rallies the market has experienced.

Although employment data usually comprises the most important monthly report for the market, the focus of traders constantly shifts. In the 1970s, inflation announcements took center stage, but after Fed Chairman Paul Volcker shifted the focus to monetary aggregates, the Thursday afternoon money supply announcements captured the attention of traders. Later, in the 1980s when the dollar was soaring, trade statistics were given top billing. The 1990–1991 recession and subsequent slow economic recovery put employment data back on top with traders. In 1996 and early 1997, traders were looking for every hint of inflation as business activity expanded. Late in 1997, traders turned their attention to the turmoil in the Asian markets and the value of foreign currencies. And in 2001, the crash of the tech sector and the first recession in over 10 years concentrated traders' interests on employment data and business cycle indicators.

This chapter has focused on the very short-run reaction of financial markets to economic data. Many people claim that it would be best for investors to ignore such information because the data are often conflicting and revised at a later date. Such advice would be appropriate if you plan to stay invested for the long run, a strategy strongly advocated in this book. Traders put these bits of information together and try to form a picture of where the economy is headed. It is fascinating to observe the market's reaction to economic data, but most investors will do much better watching from the sidelines and sticking to a long-run investment strategy.

PART 4

STOCK FLUCTUATIONS IN THE SHORT RUN

CHAPTER 15

SPIDERS, CUBES, FUTURES, AND OPTIONS

When I was a kid—a runner for Merrill Lynch at 25 dollars a week, I'd heard an old timer say, "The greatest thing to trade would be stock futures—but you can't do that, it's gambling."

LEO MELAMED[1]

Warren Buffett thinks that stock futures and options ought to be outlawed, and I agree with him.

PETER LYNCH[2]

If someone were to ask you what stock traded the largest dollar volume in the United States in 2001, what would you guess? Cisco Systems? Microsoft? One of the Internet stocks, like Yahoo! or AOL? Or General Electric (GE), the stock with the world's largest market value? The surprising answer is a stock that was not in existence before 1999 and does not even

---

[1]Leo Melamed is founder of the International Money Market, the home of the world's most successful stock index futures market. Quoted in Martin Mayer, *Markets* (New York: W. W. Norton, 1988), p. 111.
[2]Peter Lynch, *One Up on Wall Street* (New York: Penguin Books, 1989), p. 280.

represent a company. The security with the highest dollar volume is "cubes," the nickname given to the Nasdaq 100 Index Tracking Stock, an exchange-traded fund that represents the top 100 firms, ranked by market value, that are traded on the Nasdaq.[3] If you want to buy or sell a diversified portfolio of technology stocks, there is no cheaper way to do this than to trade the cubes on either the American or New York Stock Exchanges.[4] By the fall of 2001, cubes had an average daily volume in excess of $3 billion.

EXCHANGE-TRADED FUNDS

What do the cute names—*spiders, cubes,* and *diamonds*—have in common? All of them are the nicknames for the most innovative and successful new financial instruments in nearly two decades, exchange-traded funds (ETFs). ETFs are portfolios of securities, usually of well-known stock indexes but increasingly of industry-sector and country indexes, that trade like individual stocks.

The first successful ETF was introduced by the American Stock Exchange in 1993 and was called *Standard & Poor's (S&P) Depository Receipts (SPDRs),* nicknamed "spiders." SPDRs represent ownership in a trust designed to match the performance of the S&P 500 Index by owning all 500 stocks in the same proportion as the index. SPDRs trade like a stock, are listed on the American Stock Exchange, and have a value of one-tenth the value of the S&P 500 Index. Shortly after their launch, SPDRs became the most actively traded security on the American Stock Exchange. This exchange followed up on its success with another ETF, nicknamed "diamonds" (ticker symbol DIA), that tracks the Dow Jones Industrial Average.

These ETFs track their respective indexes extremely closely because institutions and large investors can turn in shares of the index for ETFs or exchange ETFs for their representative shares. For the spiders, the minimum size for such an exchange, called a *creation unit,* is 50,000 shares, which, at current prices, costs over $5 million. Exchanging these creation units for shares and vice versa is a very active trade and keeps the price of the ETF extremely close to that of the index. Trading is so active that the bid-ask spread for actively traded ETFs is just a few pennies.

---

[3]"Cubes" gets its name from a corruption of the ticker symbol of the security, QQQ.
[4]It should be noted that there are many large technology stocks that trade on the New York Stock Exchange and not on Nasdaq, such as Lucent Technologies, Hewlett-Packard, Nortel Networks, AOL, EMC Corporation, and Texas Instruments, among others.

There are several advantages of ETFs over mutual funds that track similar indexes. First, unlike mutual funds, ETFs can be bought or sold at any time during the day. Second, an investor can easily sell ETFs short, hoping to make a profit by buying them back at a lower price.[5] This proves to be a very convenient way of hedging one's overall portfolio if an investor fears the market may fall. And finally, ETFs are extremely tax efficient because, unlike mutual funds, they generate almost no capital gains while held by investors. Yet these new exchange-traded securities do have some drawbacks. Later in this chapter I will list the advantages and disadvantages of ETFs as compared with alternative forms of index investing.

STOCK INDEX FUTURES

ETFs are really the outgrowth of the single most important innovation in the postwar period—the development of stock index futures. Despite the enormous popularity of these new ETFs, the total dollar volume in ETFs is still dwarfed by the dollar volume represented by trading in index futures, most of which are traded in Chicago. Shifts in overall market sentiment first affect the index futures market in Chicago and then are transmitted to stocks traded in New York.

To understand how important index futures are, one need only look at what happened on April 13, 1992, which began as an ordinary trading day. At about 11:45 a.m., however, the two big Chicago futures exchanges, the Chicago Board of Trade and the Chicago Mercantile Exchange, were closed when a massive leak caused runoff from the Chicago River to course through the tunnels under the financial district, triggering extensive power outages. Figure 15-1 shows the intraday movement of the Dow Jones Industrial Average and the S&P 500 Index futures. As soon as Chicago futures trading was halted, the volatility of the stock market declined significantly.

It almost looks as if the New York Stock Exchange went brain dead when there was no lead from Chicago. The volume in New York dropped by more than 25 percent on the day the Chicago futures market was closed; and some dealers claimed that if the futures exchange remained inoperative, it would cause liquidity problems and difficulty in executing some trades in New York.[6] Michael Metz, however, a market

---

[5]ETFs are exempt from the uptick rule that restricts shorting stock when the price is falling.
[6]Robert Steiner, "Industrials Gain 14.53 in Trading Muted by Futures Halt in Chicago," *Wall Street Journal*, April 14, 1992, p. C2.

F I G U R E   15–1

When Stock Index Futures Closed Down, April 13, 1992

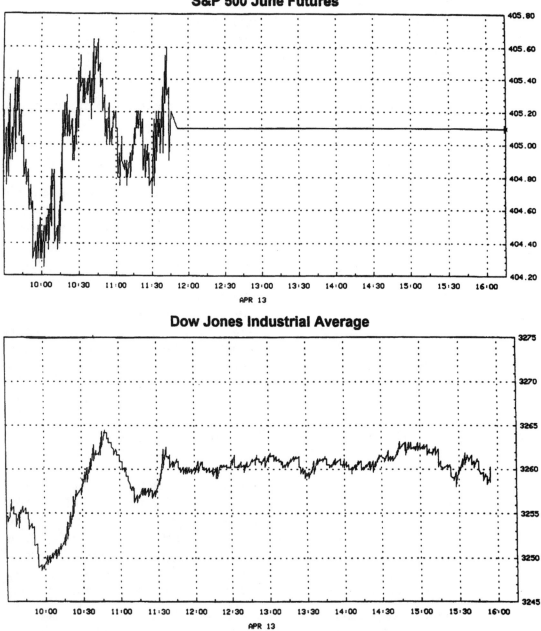

SOURCE: Bloomberg L.P.

strategist at Oppenheimer & Co., declared of April 13, "It's been absolutely delightful; it seems so sedate. It reminds me of the halcyon days on Wall Street before the program traders took hold."[7]

Who are these program traders that investors hear so much about, and what do they do? In the mid-1980s, just a few years after index futures were introduced, the floor of the New York Stock Exchange was alive with a constant din of people scurrying about delivering orders and making deals. Every so often, however, the background noise was punctuated by the rat-tat-tat of dozens of automated machines printing hundreds of buy or sell tickets. These orders were almost always from stock index future arbitrageurs, a type of program trader who relies on the difference between the prices of stock index futures traded in Chicago and the prices of the component stocks traded in New York. The tickets signaled that the futures market was moving quickly and that stock prices would soon change accordingly in New York. It was an eerie warning, something akin to the buzz of locusts in biblical times, portending decimated crops and famine. And famine it might be, for during the 1980s and early 1990s some of the most vicious declines in stock prices have been preceded by computers tapping out orders emanating from the futures markets.

It surprises many that in the short run, changes in the overall level of stocks do not originate on Wall Street but on Wacker Drive at the Chicago Mercantile Exchange. Specialists on the New York Stock Exchange, dealers assigned to make and supervise markets in specific stocks, keep their eyes glued on the futures markets to find out where stocks are heading. These dealers have learned from experience not to stand in the way of index futures. If you do, you might get caught in an avalanche of trading such as the one that buried several specialists on October 19, 1987, that fateful day when the Dow crashed nearly 23 percent.

THE IMPACT OF INDEX FUTURES

Most investors regard index futures and options as esoteric securities that have little to do with the market in which stocks are bought and sold. Many investors do very well trading stocks without any knowledge of these new instruments. But no one can comprehend short-run market movements without an understanding of stock index futures.

Pick up a newspaper and read of the day's trading in stocks. Chances are good that you will see references to program trading, espe-

---

[7]"Flood in Chicago Waters Down Trading on Wall Street," *Wall Street Journal*, April 14, 1992, p. C1.

cially if the market was volatile. Program trading is the way by which large movements that originate in the Chicago futures pit are transmitted to the New York markets.

The following descriptions of volatile markets appeared in the *New York Times* of July 19, 1997:

> Stock prices plunged yesterday in a broad sell-off, just two days after the Dow Jones Industrial Average breached the 8,000-point level. . . . Some of the losses—and part of the volatility that helped the Dow plunge 145 points early in the day—were attributed to heavy program trading and "double witching," the expiration of some options on stocks and stock indexes.[8]

Figure 15-2 shows the behavior of the stock and futures markets on that day, which will be described later in this chapter. Most large stock movements are dominated by events that are first felt in the stock index futures markets.

BASICS OF FUTURES MARKETS

The stock index futures market is the greatest single innovation to come to stock trading since invention of the ticker tape. Index futures now trade in virtually every major stock market in the world and have become the instrument of choice for institutional investors who want to change their international stock allocations.

Futures trading goes back hundreds of years. The term *futures* was derived from the promise to buy or deliver a commodity at some future date at some specified price. Futures trading first flourished in agricultural crops, where farmers wanted to have a guaranteed price for the crops they would not harvest until later. Markets developed where buyers and sellers who wanted to avoid uncertainty could come to an agreement on the price for future delivery. The commitments to honor these agreements, called *futures contracts*, were freely transferable, and markets developed where they were actively traded.

Stock index futures were launched in February 1982 by the Kansas City Board of Trade using the Value Line Index of about 1,700 stocks. Two months later in Chicago, however, at the Chicago Mercantile Exchange, the world's most successful stock index future, based on the S&P 500 Index, was introduced. Only 2 years after its introduction, the value of the contracts traded on this index future surpassed the dollar

---

[8]David Barboza, "Stocks Tumble, Wiping Out Week's Gain," *New York Times*, July 19, 1997, p. 31. See later in this chapter for a description of double witching.

FIGURE 15–2

Trading Bands and Futures Trading, July 18, 1997

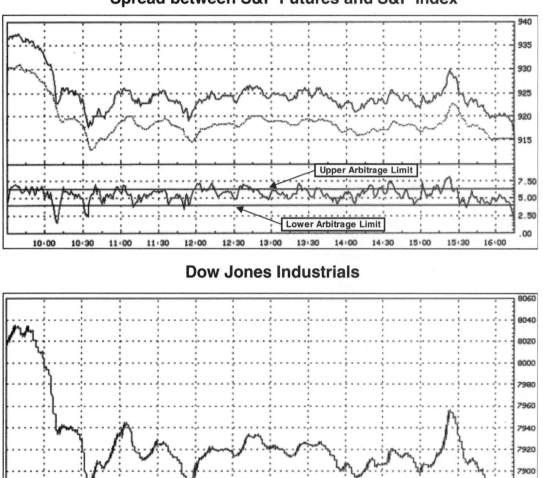

SOURCE: Bloomberg L.P.

volume on the New York Stock Exchange for all stocks. Today the S&P 500 Index futures trade about 180,000 contracts a day, worth about $50 billion. Although there are stock index futures for the Nasdaq and the Dow, as well as others, the S&P 500 Index dominates in the United States, comprising well over half the value of such trading.

All stock index futures are constructed similarly. The S&P 500 Index future is a promise to deliver (in the case of the seller) or receive (in the case of the buyer) a fixed multiple of the value of the S&P 500 Index at some date in the future, called a *settlement date*. The multiple for the S&P 500 Index future is 250, so if the S&P 500 Index is 1,000, the value of one contract is $250,000.

There are four evenly spaced settlement dates each year. They fall on the third Friday of March, June, September, and December. Each settlement date corresponds to a contract. If you buy a futures contract, you are entitled to receive (if positive) or obligated to pay (if negative) 250 times the difference between the value of the S&P 500 Index on the settlement date and the price at which you purchased the contract.

For example, if you buy one September S&P 500 Index futures contract at 1,000 and on that third Friday in September the S&P 500 Index is at 1,010, you have made 10 points, which translates into $2,500 profit ($250 × 10 points). Of course, if the index falls to 990 on the settlement date, you would lose $2,500. For every point the S&P 500 Index goes up or down, you make or lose $250 per contract.

On the other hand, the returns to the seller of an S&P 500 Index futures contract are the mirror image of the returns to the buyer. The seller makes money when the index falls. In the preceding example, the seller of the S&P 500 Index futures contract at 1,000 will lose $2,500 if the index on the settlement date rises to 1,010, whereas he or she would make the same amount if the index fell to 990.

One source of the popularity of stock index futures is their unique settlement procedure. With standard futures contracts, you are obligated at settlement to receive (if purchased) or deliver (if sold) a specified quantity of the good for which you have contracted. Many apocryphal stories abound about how traders, forgetting to close out their contract, find bushels of wheat, corn, or frozen pork bellies dumped on their lawn on settlement day.

If commodity delivery rules applied to the S&P 500 Index futures contract, delivery would require a specified number of shares for each of the 500 firms in the index. Surely this would be extraordinarily cumbersome and costly. To avoid this problem, the designers of the stock index futures contract specified that settlement be made in *cash*, computed simply by taking the difference between the contract price at the time of the trade and the value of the index on the settlement date. No delivery of stock takes place. If a trader fails to close a contract before settlement, his or her account would just be debited or credited on the settlement date.

The creation of cash-settled futures contracts was no easy matter. In most states, particularly Illinois, where large futures exchanges are located, settling a futures contract in cash was considered a wager—and wagering, except in some special circumstances, was illegal. In 1974, however, the Commodity Futures Trading Commission, a federal agency, was established by Congress to regulate all futures trading. And since there was no federal prohibition against wagering, the state laws were superseded.

INDEX ARBITRAGE

The prices of commodities (or financial assets) in the futures market do not stand apart from the prices of the underlying commodity. If the value of a futures contract rises sufficiently above the price of the commodity that can be purchased for immediate delivery in the open market (often called the *cash* or *spot market*), traders can buy the commodity, store it, and then deliver it at a profit against the higher-priced futures contract on the settlement date. If the price of a futures contract falls too far below its current spot price, owners of the commodity can sell it today, buy the futures contract, and take delivery of the commodity later at a lower price—in essence, earning a return on goods that would be in storage anyway.

Such a process of buying and selling commodities against their futures contracts is one type of arbitrage. *Arbitrage* involves traders who take advantage of temporary discrepancies in the prices of identical or nearly identical goods or assets. Those who reap profits from such trades are called *arbitrageurs*.

Arbitrage is very active in the stock index futures market. If the price of futures contracts sufficiently exceeds that of the underlying S&P 500 Index, it pays for arbitrageurs to buy the underlying stocks and sell the futures contracts. If the futures price falls sufficiently below that of the index, arbitrageurs will sell the underlying stocks and buy the futures. On the settlement date, the futures price must equal the underlying index by the terms of the contract, so the difference between the futures price and the index—called a *premium* if it is positive and a *discount* if it is negative—is an opportunity for profit.

In recent years, index arbitrage has become a finely tuned art. The price of stock index futures usually stays within very narrow bands of the index value based on the price of the underlying shares. When the buying or selling of stock index futures drives the futures price outside this band, arbitrageurs step in, and hundreds of orders to buy or sell are transmitted immediately to the exchanges that trade the underlying stocks in the index. These simultaneously placed orders are called *buy programs* to buy stock and *sell programs* to sell stock. When market commentators talk about sell programs hitting the market, they mean that index arbitrageurs are selling stock in New York and buying futures that have fallen to a discount (or a small enough premium) in Chicago.

As with any arbitrage, speed is of the essence. Both ends of the transaction must be completed quickly to lock in a profit. Access to the stocks in the S&P 500 Index, which almost all trade on the New York Stock Exchange, is usually made through an automated order system called the *Designated Order Turnaround (DOT) System.* This system used to punch out the buy and sell orders that could be heard on the exchange floor whenever index arbitrage occurred.

Let's take a look at the market on July 18, 1997. As noted earlier, futures trading was a significant factor forcing stock prices down on that day. Figure 15-2 shows the value of the index, the futures prices, and the difference between the two from the 9:30 a.m. opening to the 4:15 p.m. close of the futures market.

Index arbitrageurs do not engage in arbitrage whenever the index and futures prices differ by small amounts. Because of transaction costs, there must be a sufficient spread between the index and the future prices before traders will undertake the arbitrage. Figure 15-2 displays the upper and lower limits under which index arbitrage occurs for reasonable levels of transactions costs, although some engage in index arbitrage before these limits are reached.

Shortly after 10:00 a.m. on July 18, the S&P 500 Index futures price for September delivery began to break downward in Chicago as traders became pessimistic about the prospects for the market. As a result, the futures price fell well below the price at which arbitrage becomes profitable. Index arbitrageurs then bought the depressed index futures and sold the stocks comprising the index.

Look at the chart of the Dow Jones Industrial Average in Figure 15-2. The character of the intraday movements in the stock average changed markedly when the sell programs kicked in. The sharp downward movements occurred when the arbitrageurs sold stock in response to the falling futures prices. Instead of moving a few points at a time, the Dow experienced sudden drops of 10 to 15 points in a matter of seconds. This occurred when a number of the Dow stocks, which are weighted heavily in the S&P 500 Index, simultaneously traded lower. The specialists assigned to the big stocks, noting that the futures had fallen to a discount, marked down the price of their stocks in anticipation of imminent sell orders. These adjustments by the specialists speed up the process by which index arbitrage keeps prices in New York aligned with prices of futures in Chicago. It also can been seen that after the New York Stock Exchange closed, the futures contract again sold at a discount from its fair market range.

PREDICTING THE NEW YORK OPEN WITH GLOBEX TRADING

Although trading the index futures at the Chicago Mercantile Exchange closes at 4:15 p.m. Eastern Standard Time, trading reopens in these futures 30 minutes later in an electronic market called *Globex*. Globex has no centralized floor; traders post their bids and offers on computer screens where all interested parties have instant access. Trading in Globex proceeds all night until 9:15 a.m. the next day, 15 minutes before the start of trading at both the New York Stock Exchange and in the futures pits in Chicago. In Chapter 13 we saw the reaction of S&P 500 Index futures to the terrorist attacks on the morning of September 11, 2001.

Index futures trading can be active just after the close of regular trading on the New York Stock Exchange and Nasdaq because this is the time when many firms release their earnings reports and give their guidance about the accuracy of Wall Street's projections. Unless there is important breaking news, trading is usually slow during the night hours, although activity can pick up if there is dramatic movement on the Tokyo exchange. Trading again becomes very active around 8:30 a.m., when many of the government economic calculations, such as the employment report and the consumer and producer price indexes, are announced. In the preceding chapter we saw the dramatic fall in the S&P 500 Index futures traded on Globex in response to the strong July 5, 1996, employment report.

Market watchers can use the Globex futures in the S&P 500, Nasdaq, and Dow indexes to predict how the market will open in New York. The fair market value of the S&P 500 Index futures is calculated based on the arbitrage conditions between the futures and the cash market using the closing of the appropriate index on the preceding day. If Globex is trading above the fair market value of the index futures based on yesterday's close, the stock market likely will open strong; if it is trading below the fair market value, the market likely will open weak.

The difference between the close on Globex at 9:15 a.m. (EST) and the fair market value predicts how much the S&P 500 Index will open up or down, assuming that no significant news is reported in the 15-minute period before 9:30 a.m., when neither Globex nor the Chicago market is open. Many financial news channels post the Globex trading in the early hours to keep viewers informed of the state of the market.

DOUBLE AND TRIPLE WITCHING

Index futures play some strange games with stock prices on the days when contracts expire. Recall that index arbitrage works through the simultaneous buying and selling of stocks against futures contracts. On the day that a contract expires, arbitrageurs unwind their stock positions at precisely the same time that their futures contracts expire.

Index futures contracts expire on the third Friday of the last month of each quarter: in March, June, September, and December. Index options and options on individuals stocks, which are described later in this chapter, settle on the third Friday of every month. Hence four times a year all three types of contracts expire at once. This expiration has produced violent price movements in the market and is termed *triple witching*. The third Friday of a month when there is no futures contract settlement is called *double witching*, which displays less volatility than triple witching.

There is no mystery why the market is volatile during double or triple witching. On these days, the specialists on the New York Stock Exchange are instructed to buy or sell large blocks of stock on the close, whatever the price. If there is a huge imbalance of buy orders, prices will soar; if sell orders predominate, prices will plunge. These swings, however, do not matter to arbitrageurs because the profit on the future position will offset losses on the stock position and vice versa.

In 1988, the New York Stock Exchange urged the Chicago Mercantile Exchange to change its procedures, ending futures trading at the close of Thursday's trading and settling the contracts at Friday opening prices rather than Friday closing prices. This change gave specialists more time to seek out balancing bids and offers and has greatly moderated the movements in stock prices on triple-witching dates.

MARGIN AND LEVERAGE

One of the reasons for the popularity of futures contracts is that the cash needed to enter into the trade is a very small part of the value of the contract. Unlike stocks, there is no money that transfers between the buyer and seller when a futures contract is entered. A small amount of good-faith collateral, or *margin*, is required by the broker from both the buyer and the seller to ensure that both parties will honor the contract at settlement. For the S&P 500 Index, the current initial margin is $20,000, or about 8 percent of the value of the contract. This margin can be kept in Treasury bills with interest accruing to the investor, so trading a futures contract involves neither a transfer of cash nor a loss of interest income.

The *leverage*, or the amount of stock that you control relative to the amount of margin you have to put down with a futures contract, is enormous. For every dollar of cash (or Treasury bills) that you put in margin against an S&P 500 Index futures contract, you command about $12 of stock. And for *day trading*, when you close your positions by the end of the day, the margin requirements are cut in half, so you can leverage about 25 to 1. These low margins contrast with the 50 percent margin requirement for the purchase of individual stocks that has prevailed since 1974.

This ability to control $12 or even $25 of stock with $1 of cash is reminiscent of the rampant speculation that existed in the 1920s before the establishment of minimum stock margin requirements. In the 1920s, individual stocks frequently were purchased with a 10 percent margin. It was popular to speculate with such borrowed money, for as long as the market was rising, few lost money. However, if the market dropped precipitously, margin buyers could find that not only was their equity wiped out, but also they were indebted to the brokerage firm. The tendency of this low margin to fuel market volatility is discussed in Chapter 16.

USING ETFs OR FUTURES

The use of ETFs or index futures greatly increases your flexibility in managing portfolios. Suppose that an investor has built up some good gains in individual stocks but is now getting nervous about the market. Selling one's individual stocks is unsatisfactory because that would trigger a large tax liability. Furthermore, the investor may believe that his or her stocks will outperform the market during a decline, so selling now and buying them back later would entail large transactions costs.

With ETFs (or futures), however, all this worry becomes unnecessary. The investor sells a number of ETF shares or contracts corresponding to the value of his or her portfolio that he or she seeks to hedge and continues to hold his or her individual stocks. If the market declines, the investor profits on the ETF position, offsetting the losses of the stock portfolio. If the market instead goes up, contrary to expectation, the loss on ETF will be offset by the gains on the individual stock holdings. This is called *hedging stock market risk*. Since the investor never sells his or her individual stocks, he or she triggers no tax liability.

Another advantage of ETFs is the ability to profit from a decline in the market even if one does not own any stock. Selling ETFs substitutes for shorting stock, or selling stock you do not own in anticipation that the price will fall and you can buy it back at a lower price. Using ETFs to bet on a falling market is much more convenient than shorting a portfolio of stocks because individuals stocks cannot be shorted if the price is declining, but ETFs are exempt from this rule.

COMPARING ETFs, FUTURES, AND INDEX MUTUAL FUNDS

With the development of index futures and ETFs, investors have three major choices if they wish to invest by matching the performance of either the overall market or one of the popular indexes: ETFs, index futures, and index mutual funds, which are open-ended mutual funds designed to match the indexes (discussed in Chapter 20). Table 15-1 compares important characteristics of each investment.

As far as trading flexibility is concerned, ETFs and index futures far outshine mutual funds. ETFs can be bought and sold at any time during the trading day, and index futures also can be traded all night through Globex. In contrast, mutual funds can only be bought and sold at the market close, and the investor's order often must be put in several hours earlier. ETFs and index futures also can be shorted to hedge one's portfolio or speculate on a market decline, which mutual funds cannot. Moreover, ETFs can be margined like any stock (with current Federal Reserve regulations at 50 percent), whereas index futures possess the

TABLE 15–1

Comparison of Indexed Investments

	ETFs	Index Futures	Indexed Mutual Funds
Continuous Trading	Yes	Yes	No
Can Be Sold Short	Yes	Yes	No
Leverage	Can borrow 50%	Can borrow over 90%	None
Expense Ratio	Extremely Low	None	Very Low
Trading Costs	Stock Commission	Futures Commission	None
Dividend Reinvestment	No	No	Yes
Tax Efficiency	Extremely Good	Poor	Very Good

highest degree of leverage because investors can control stocks worth 20 or more times the value of cash raised.

The flexibility of ETFs or futures can be either a bane or a boon to investors. It is easy to overreact to the continuous stream of optimistic and pessimistic news, causing an investor to sell near the low or buy near the high for the day. Furthermore, the ability to short stocks (except for hedging) or use leverage might tempt investors to play their short-term hunches on the market. This is a very dangerous game. For most investors, restricting the frequency of trades and reducing leverage are beneficial to their total returns.

On the cost side, all these vehicles are very efficient. Index mutual funds are available at an annual cost of less than 20 basis points per year,[9] and some ETFs cost even less. However, both ETFs and futures must be bought through a broker, and this involves paying commissions and a bid-ask spread (which is quite low for these active instruments). On the other hand, most index funds are *no-load funds,* meaning that there is no commission when they are bought or sold. Furthermore, although index futures involve no annual costs, these contracts must be rolled over into new contracts at least once a year, entailing additional commissions.

It is on the tax side that ETFs really shine. Because of the structure of ETFs, over time these funds generate very few capital gains, and in some years they generate none at all. Index mutual funds are also very tax efficient, but they do throw off capital gains when funds must sell individual shares from their portfolio as investors redeem their shares in the mutual fund. Although this has been small for most index funds, it is larger than for ETFs.[10] Futures are not tax efficient because any gains or losses must be realized at the end of the year whether the contracts are sold or not.

These tax differences between ETFs and index mutual funds do not matter if an investor holds these funds in a tax-sheltered account, such as an Individual Retirement Account (IRA) or Keogh plan (futures are not allowed in these accounts). However, if held in taxable accounts, the after-tax return on ETFs is apt to be slightly higher than those of even the most efficient index funds.

The bottom line is that unless you are a speculator or like to use a lot of leverage and are willing to accept margin calls from your broker,

---

[9]The Vanguard 500 Index Fund actually has managed to marginally beat the index. See Chapter 20.
[10]From 1993 through 2001, the average capital gains distribution of spiders as a percentage of net asset value was 3 basis points per year as opposed to 35 basis points for the Vanguard 500 Index Fund, a very tax-efficient mutual fund.

you will want to avoid index futures. If you want to speculate on the direction of the market and use leverage at the same time, I recommend index options, which are described below and which limit one's loss to the cash invested.

Whether to hold ETFs or low-cost indexed mutual funds is a very close decision. If you like to move in and out of the market frequently (which I do not recommend), ETFs are for you. If you like to invest in the market on a monthly basis or automatically reinvest your dividends, then no-load index funds are the better instrument. It might be best to own both, using mutual funds for your long-term accumulations, dividend reinvestment, and periodic savings and using ETFs for short-run adjustments and hedging.

INDEX OPTIONS

Although index futures influence the overall stock market far more than options, the options market has caught the fancy of many investors. And this is not surprising. The beauty of an option is embedded in its very name: You have the option, but not the obligation, to buy or sell at the terms specified. This automatically limits your liability if you made the wrong decision.

There are two major types of options: *puts* and *calls*. Calls give you the right to buy a stock (or stocks) at a fixed price within a given period of time. Puts give you the right to sell. Puts and calls have existed on individuals stocks for decades, but organized trading did not exist on them until establishment of the Chicago Board of Options Exchange (CBOE) in 1974.

What attracts investors to puts and calls is that liability is strictly limited. If the market moves against options buyers, they can forfeit the purchase price, forgoing the option to buy or sell. This contrasts sharply with a futures contract, where, if the market goes against buyers, losses can mount quickly. In a volatile market, futures can be extremely risky, and it could be impossible for investors to exit a contract without substantial losses.

In 1978, the CBOE began trading options on the popular stock indexes, such as the S&P 500 Index.[11] Options trade in multiples of $100

---

[11]In fact, the largest 100 stocks of the S&P 500 Index, called the *S&P 100*, comprise the most popularly traded index options. Options based on the S&P 500 Index are used more widely by institutional investors.

per point of index value—cheaper than the $250-per-point multiple on the popular S&P 500 Index futures.

An index allows investors to buy the stock index at a set price within a given period of time. Assume that the S&P 500 Index is now selling for 1,000, but you believe that the market is going to rise. Let us assume that you can purchase a call option at 1,020 for 3 months for 30 points, or $3,000. The purchase price of the option is called the *premium*, and the price at which the option begins to pay off—in this case 1,020— is called the *strike price*. At any time within the next 3 months you can, if you choose, exercise your option and receive $100 for every point that the S&P 500 Index is above 1,020.

You need not exercise your option to make a profit. There is an extremely active market for options, and you can always sell them before expiration to other investors. In this example, the S&P 500 Index will have to rise above 1,050 for you to show a profit because you paid $3,000 for the option. However, the beauty of options is that if you guessed wrong and the market falls, the most you can lose is the $3,000 premium you paid.

An index put works exactly the same way as a call, but in this case the buyer makes money if the market goes down. Assume that you buy a put on the S&P 500 Index at 980, paying a $3,000 premium. Every point the S&P 500 Index moves below 980 will recoup $100 of your initial premium. If the index falls to 950 by expiration of the option, you will have broken even. Every point below 950 gives you a profit on your option.

The price that you pay for an index option is determined by the market and depends on many factors, including interest rates and dividend yields. The most important factor, however, is the expected volatility of the market itself. Clearly, the more volatile the market, the more expensive it is to buy either puts or calls. In a dull market, it is unlikely that the market will move sufficiently high (in the case of a call) or low (in the case of a put) to give option buyers a profit. If this low volatility is expected to continue, the prices of options are low. In contrast, in volatile markets, the premiums on puts and calls are bid up as traders consider it more likely that the option will have value by the time of its expiration.[12]

The price of options depends on the judgments of traders as to the likelihood that the market will move sufficiently to make the rights to

---

[12]Chapter 16 will discuss a valuable index of option volatility called *VIX*.

buy or sell stock at a fixed price valuable. However, the theory of option pricing was given a big boost in the 1970s when two academic economists, Fischer Black and Myron Scholes, developed the first mathematical formula to price options. The Black-Scholes formula was an instant success. It gave traders a benchmark for valuation where previously only intuition was used. The Black-Scholes formula was programmed on traders' handheld calculators and personal computers (PCs) around the world. Although there are conditions under which the formula must be modified, empirical research has shown that the Black-Scholes formula closely approximates the price of traded options.

Options have opened a new market for investors. Now investors can trade the volatility of the market as well as the level. Those who expect that the market will be more volatile than normal will buy puts and calls, whereas those who feel that the market will be less volatile than usual will tend to sell options. If investors buy volatility, they are buying either puts or calls (or both), expecting large market movements over the life of the option. If investors sell volatility, they expect a relatively quiet market and expect the options to expire worthless or at prices far below what they paid for them. It is fascinating that even if the market is unchanged day after day, investors can make large profits by selling options.

BUYING INDEX OPTIONS

Options are actually more basic instruments than futures or ETFs. You can replicate any future or ETF with options, but the reverse is not true. Options offer the investor far more strategies than futures. Such strategies can range from the very speculative to the extremely conservative.

Suppose that an investor wants to be protected against a decline in the market. He or she can buy an index put, which increases in value as the market declines. Of course, he or she has to pay a premium for this option, very much like an insurance premium. If the market does not decline, the investor has forfeited his or her premium. However, if the market does decline, the increase in the value of the put has cushioned (if not completely offset) the decline in the investor's stock portfolio.

Another advantage of puts is that you can buy just the amount of protection that you like. If you want to protect yourself against only a total collapse in the market, you can buy a put that is way *out of the money,* in other words, a put whose strike price is far below that of the current level of the index. This option pays off only if the market declines precipitously. In addition, you also can buy puts with a strike price above the current market so that the option retains some value even if the market does not decline. Of course, these *in-the-money* puts are far more expensive.

There are many recorded examples of fantastic gains in puts and calls. However, for every option that gains so spectacularly in value, there are thousands that expire worthless. Some market professionals estimate that 85 percent of individual investors who play the options market lose money. Not only do option buyers have to be right about the direction of the market, but also their timing must be nearly perfect and their selection of the strike price must be appropriate.

SELLING INDEX OPTIONS

Of course, for anyone who buys an option, someone must sell (or write) an option. The sellers, or writers, of call options believe that the market will not rise sufficiently to make a profit for option buyers. Sellers of call options make money most of the time they sell options because the vast majority of options expire worthless. However, should the market move sharply against the option sellers, their losses could be enormous.

For this reason, most sellers of call options are investors who already own stock. This strategy, called *buy and write*, is popular with many investors because it is seen as a win-win proposition. If stocks go down, sellers collect a premium from buyers of the call and so are better off than if they had not written the option. If stocks do nothing, they also collect the premium on the call and are still better off. If stocks go up, call writers still gain more on the stocks they own than they lose on the calls they wrote, so they are still ahead. Of course, if stocks go up strongly, they miss a large part of the rally because they have promised to deliver stock at a fixed price. In this case, call writers certainly would have been better off if they had not sold the call. But they still make more money than if they had not owned the stock at all.

The buyers of put options are insuring their stock against price declines. But who are the sellers of these options? They are primarily those who are willing to buy the stock, but only if the price declines. A seller of a put collects a premium but receives the stock only if it falls sufficiently to go below the strike price. Since put sellers are not as common as call sellers, premiums on puts that are out of the money are frequently quite high.

LONG-TERM TRENDS AND STOCK INDEX FUTURES

The development of stock index futures and options in the 1980s was a major development for stock investors and money managers. Heavily capitalized firms, such as those represented in the Dow Jones Industrial Average, have always attracted money because of their outstanding liquidity. With stock index futures, however, investors now can buy the whole market as represented by the S&P 500 Index. Index futures have higher liquidity than any highly capitalized blue-chip stock. Therefore, when money managers want to take a position in the market, it is most easily done with stock index futures.

International investors and those involved in global asset allocation want index futures and options so that they can easily alter the fraction of assets they have invested in each country. For many of these money managers, the first portfolio decision is the percentage of funds invested in each country. Buying or selling stock index futures is clearly the way to alter that percentage. In fact, some money managers shun countries that do not trade index futures because their absence deprives them of the liquidity they so strongly need.

ETFs are also an excellent way to buy a basket of stocks and for many investors are superior to index futures. These index instruments are much more familiar to individuals who feel uncomfortable dealing with the high volatility and leverage in the futures market. ETFs make ideal hedges for investors who wish to lock in profits without taking the tax consequences of selling individual stocks.

CHAPTER **16**

MARKET VOLATILITY

The word crisis *in Chinese is composed of two characters: the first, the symbol of danger, . . . the second, of opportunity.*

A comparison of the Dow Jones Industrial Average from 1922–1929 and 1980–1987 is shown in Figure 16-1. There is an uncanny similarity between these two bull markets. The editors of the *Wall Street Journal* felt that the similarity was so portentous that they printed a similar comparison in the edition that hit the streets on the morning of October 19, 1987. Little did they know that that day would witness the greatest 1-day drop in stock market history, exceeding the great crash of October 29, 1929. In fact, the market in 1987 continued to trade like 1929 for the remainder of the year. Many forecasters, citing the similarities between the two periods, were certain that disaster loomed and advised their clients to sell everything.

However, the similarity between 1929 and 1987 ended at year's end. The stock market recovered from its October 1987 crash and, by August of 1989, hit new high ground. In contrast, 2 years after the October 1929 crash, the Dow, in the throes of the greatest bear market in U.S. history, had lost more than two-thirds of its value and was about to lose two-thirds more.

What was different? Why did the eerie similarities between these two events finally diverge so dramatically? The simple answer is that in

F I G U R E   16–1

1929 and 1987 Stock Crashes

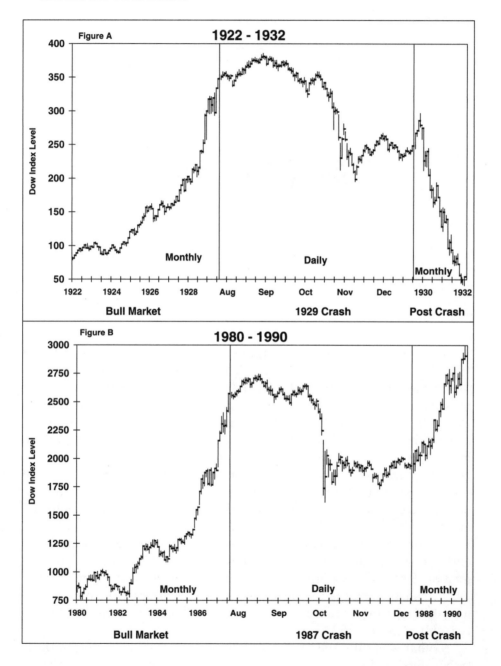

1987 the central bank had the power to control the ultimate source of liquidity in the economy—the supply of money—and, in contrast to 1929, did not hesitate to use it. Heeding the painful lessons of the early 1930s, the Federal Reserve temporarily flooded the economy with money and pledged to stand by all bank deposits to ensure that all aspects of the financial system would function properly.

The public was reassured. There were no runs on banks, no contraction of the money supply, and no deflation in commodity and asset values. Indeed, the economy itself moved upward despite the market collapse. The October 1987 stock market crash taught investors an important lesson—that a crisis can be an opportunity for profit, not a time to panic.

THE STOCK MARKET CRASH OF OCTOBER 1987

The stock market crash of Monday, October 19, 1987, was one of the most dramatic financial events of the postwar era. The 508-point, or 22.6 percent, decline in the Dow Jones Industrial Average from 2,247 to 1,739 was by far the largest point drop up to that time and the largest percentage drop in history. Volume on the New York Stock Exchange soared to an all-time record, exceeding 600 million shares on Monday and Tuesday, and for that fateful week, the number of shares traded exceeded the volume for the entire year of 1966.

The crash on Wall Street reverberated around the world. Tokyo, which 2 years later was going to enter its own massive bear market, fell the least but still experienced a record 1-day drop of 15.6 percent. Stocks in New Zealand fell nearly 40 percent, and the Hong Kong market closed because collapsing prices brought massive defaults in their stock index futures market. In the United States alone, stock values dropped about $500 billion on that infamous day, and the total worldwide decline in stock values exceeded $1 trillion. This sum is more than the entire gross national product (GNP) of the continent of Africa.

The fall in the stock market began in earnest the week prior to "Black Monday," as October 19 came to be called. At 8:30 a.m. on the preceding Wednesday, the Department of Commerce reported that the United States suffered a $15.7 billion merchandise trade deficit, one of the largest in U.S. history and far in excess of market expectations. The reaction to the announcement in the financial markets was immediate. Yields on long government bonds rose to over 10 percent for the first time since November 1985, and the dollar declined sharply in the foreign exchange market. The Dow fell 95 points on Wednesday, a record point drop at that time.

The situation continued to worsen on Thursday and Friday as the Dow fell 166 more points. Late Friday afternoon, about 15 minutes prior to close, heavy selling hit the stock index futures markets in Chicago. The indexes had fallen below crucial support levels, which led to the barrage of selling in Chicago by those wanting to get out of stocks at almost any price.

The December Standard & Poor's (S&P) 500 Index futures fell to an unprecedented 6 points (or almost 3 percent) below the spot index. The development of such a wide discount meant that money managers were willing to sell large orders at a significant concession in order to execute with speed rather than risk sell orders for individual stocks that might sit unexecuted in New York. At the close of trading on Friday, the stock market had experienced its worst week in nearly five decades.

Before the opening on Monday, ominous events hung over the market. Overnight in Tokyo, the Nikkei average fell 2½ percent, and there were sharp declines in stock markets in Sydney and Hong Kong. In London, prices had fallen by 10 percent because many money managers were trying to sell U.S. stocks before the anticipated decline hit New York.

Trading on the New York Stock Exchange on Black Monday was chaotic. No Dow Jones stock opened at the 9:30 a.m. bell. Only 7 Dow stocks traded before 9:45 a.m., and 11 still had not opened by 10:30 a.m. Portfolio *insurers,* described later in this chapter, were selling heavily, trying to insulate their customers' exposure to the plunging market. By late afternoon, the S&P 500 Index futures were selling at a 25-point, or 12 percent, discount to the spot market, a spread that previously was considered inconceivable. By the late afternoon, huge sell orders transmitted by program sellers cascaded onto the New York Stock Exchange through the computerized system. The Dow collapsed almost 300 points in the final hour of trading, bringing the toll to 508 points for the day.

Although October 19 is remembered in history as the day of the great stock crash, it was actually on the next day—"Terrible Tuesday," as it has become known—that the market almost failed. After opening up over 10 percent from Monday's low, the market began to plunge by mid-morning and shortly after noon fell below its Monday close. The S&P 500 Index futures market collapsed to 181—an incredible 40 points, or 22 percent, below the reported index value. If index arbitrage had been working, the futures prices would have dictated a Dow at 1,450. Stock prices in the world's largest market, on the basis of this measure, were off nearly 50 percent from their high of 2,722 set just 7 weeks earlier.

It was at this point that near meltdown hit the market. The New York Stock Exchange did not close, but trading was halted in almost 200 stocks. For the first time, trading also was halted in S&P 500 Index futures in Chicago. The only futures market of any size that remained open was the Major Market Index, representing blue-chip stocks and traded on the Chicago Board of Trade.

After the crash, an investigative report by the *Wall Street Journal* suggested that this futures market was a key to reversing the market collapse.[1] The Major Market Index, a stock index future patterned after the Dow Jones Industrials, was selling at such deep discounts to the prices in New York that the values seemed irresistible. And since it was the only market that remained open, buyers stepped in, and the futures market shot up an equivalent of 120 Dow points, or almost 10 percent, in a matter of minutes. When traders and the exchange specialists saw the buying come back into the blue chips, prices rallied in New York, and the worst of the market panic passed.

CAUSES OF THE STOCK MARKET CRASH

There was no single precipitating event—such as a declaration of war, terrorist acts, assassination, or bankruptcy—that caused Black Monday. However, worrying trends had threatened the buoyant stock market for some time: sharply higher interest rates caused by a falling dollar in international currency markets, program trading, and portfolio insurance. The latter was born from the explosive growth of stock index futures markets, markets that did not even exist 6 years earlier.

EXCHANGE-RATE POLICIES

The roots of the surge in interest rates that preceded the October 1987 stock market crash are found in the futile attempts by the United States and other G7 countries (Japan, the United Kingdom, Germany, France, Italy, and Canada) to prevent the dollar from falling in the international exchange markets. The dollar had bounded to unprecedented levels in the middle of the 1980s on the heels of huge Japanese and European investment in the United States and a strong economic recovery. Foreign investment was based on the optimism about the U.S. economy and the high dollar interest rates, in part driven by record U.S. budget deficits.

---

[1]James Stewart and Daniel Hertzberg, "How the Stock Market Almost Disintegrated a Day After the Crash," *Wall Street Journal*, November 20, 1987, p. 1.

By February 1985, the dollar became massively overvalued, and U.S. exports became very uncompetitive in world markets, severely worsening the trade deficit.

Central bankers initially cheered the fall of the overpriced dollar, but they grew concerned when the dollar continued to decline and the U.S. trade deficit worsened. Finance ministers met in February 1987 in Paris with the goal of supporting the price of the dollar. Foreign central bankers were worried that if the dollar became too cheap, their own exports to the United States, which had grown substantially when the dollar was high, would suffer.

The Federal Reserve reluctantly participated in the dollar stabilization program, which depended either on an improvement in the deteriorating U.S. trade position or, absent such an improvement, a commitment by the Fed to raise interest rates to support the dollar. However, the trade deficit did not improve; in fact, it worsened after initiation of the exchange stabilization policies. Traders, nervous about the deteriorating U.S. trade balance, demanded higher and higher interest rates to hold U.S. assets. Leo Melamed, chairman of the Chicago Mercantile Exchange, was blunt when asked about the origins of Black Monday: "What caused the crash was all that f—— around with the currencies of the world."[2]

The stock market initially ignored rising interest rates. The U.S. market, like most equity markets around the world, was booming. The Dow Jones Industrials, which started 1987 at 1,933, reached an all-time high of 2,725 on August 22, 250 percent above the August 1982 low reached 5 years earlier. Over the same 5-year period, the British stock market was up 164 percent; the Swiss, 209 percent; the German, 217 percent; the Japanese, 288 percent; and the Italian, 421 percent.

However, rising bond rates and higher valuations spelled trouble for the equity markets. The long-term government bond rate, which began the year at 7 percent, topped 9 percent in September and continued to rise. As stocks rose, the dividend yield fell, and in August it reached a postwar low of 2.69 percent. The gap between the real yield on bonds and the earnings yield on stocks reached a postwar high. By the morning of October 19, the long-term bond yield had reached 10.47 percent despite the fact that inflation was well under control. The record gap between earnings and dividend yields on stocks and real returns on bonds set the stage for the stock market crash.

---

[2]Martin Mayer, *Markets* (New York: W. W. Norton, 1988), p. 62.

THE STOCK MARKET CRASH AND THE FUTURES MARKET

One cannot overemphasize the importance of the S&P 500 Index futures market in contributing to the market crash. Since introduction of the stock index futures market, a new trading technique, called *portfolio insurance*, had been introduced into portfolio management.

Portfolio insurance was, in concept, not much different from an often-used technique called a *stop-loss order*. If an investor buys a stock and wants to protect himself or herself from a loss (or if it has gone up, protect his or her profit), it is possible to place a sell order below the current price that will be triggered when and if the price falls to or below this specified level.

However, stop-loss orders are not guarantees that you can get out of the market. If the stock falls below your specified price, your stop-loss order becomes a market order to be executed at the *next best price*. If the stock *gaps* downward, your order could be executed far below your hoped-for price. This means that a panic might develop if many investors place stop-loss orders around the same price. A price decline could trigger a flood of sell orders, overwhelming the market.

Portfolio insurers, who sold the stock index futures against large portfolios to insure them against market decline, felt they were immune to such problems. It seemed extremely unlikely that S&P 500 Index futures would ever gap in price and that the whole U.S. capital market, the world's largest, could fail to find buyers.

However, the entire market did gap on October 19, 1987. During the week of October 12, the market declined by 10 percent, and a large number of sell orders flooded the markets. Traders and managers using portfolio insurance strategies began to sell index futures to protect their clients' profits. The stock index futures market collapsed. There were absolutely no buyers, and liquidity vanished.

How could the world's largest corporations fail to attract any buyers? What was once inconceivable became a reality. Portfolio insurers were shell-shocked, and since the prices of index futures were so far below the prices of the stocks selling in New York, investors halted their buying of shares in New York altogether.

Portfolio insurance withered rapidly after the crash. It was shown not to be an insurance scheme at all because the continuity and liquidity of the market could not be ensured. There was, however, an alternative form of portfolio protection: index options. With the introduction of these options markets in the 1980s, you could explicitly purchase insurance against market declines by buying puts on a market index. With puts, you never needed to worry about price gaps or being able to get out of your position because the price of the insurance is specified in advance.

Certainly there were factors other than portfolio insurance that contributed to the stock market crash. Nevertheless, portfolio insurance and its ancestor, the stop-loss order, abetted the fall. All these schemes are rooted in the basic trading philosophy of letting profits ride and cutting losses short. Whether implemented with stop-loss orders, index futures, or just a mental note to get out of a stock once it declines by a certain amount, this philosophy can set the stage for dramatic market moves.

CIRCUIT BREAKERS

As a result of the crash, the Chicago Mercantile Exchange, where S&P 500 Index futures are traded, and the New York Stock Exchange implemented rules that restrict or halt trading when certain price limits have been triggered. To prevent destabilizing speculation when the Dow Jones Industrial Average changes by at least 2 percent, the New York Stock Exchange's Rule 80a placed "trading curbs" on index arbitrage between the futures market and the New York Stock Exchange.

Of greater importance, however, are measures that sharply restrict or stop trading in both the futures market and the New York Stock Exchange when market moves are very large. When the S&P 500 Index futures fall by 5 percent, trading is halted for 10 minutes. If the Dow declines by 10 percent before 2 p.m., the New York Stock Exchange will declare a 1-hour trading halt.[3] If the decline is 20 percent, a 2-hour halt will be declared, and if the Dow declines by 30 percent, the New York Stock Exchange will close for the day.[4] Futures trading will halt when the New York Stock Exchange is closed.[5]

The rationale behind these measures is that halting trading gives investors time to reassess the situation and formulate their strategy

---

[3]If the decline occurs between 2:00 and 2:30 p.m., the halt is ½ hour. After 2:30 p.m., there is no trading halt.

[4]These percentage changes are converted into points in the Dow Jones Industrials and adjusted once each quarter.

[5]These limits were established in 1998. Previously, the New York Stock Exchange suspended trading for ½ hour when the Dow fell by 350 points and closed for the day when the Dow fell by 550 points. Both these halts were triggered on October 27, 1997, when the Dow fell by 554 points. Because of intense criticism of these closings, the exchange sharply widened the limits to keep trading open. The new trading limits for closing the exchange have never yet been breached.

based on rapidly changing prices. This timeout could bring buyers into the market and help market makers maintain a liquid market.

The argument against halts is that they increase volatility by discouraging short-term traders from buying because they might be prevented from selling during a trading halt in the near future. This sometimes leads to an acceleration of price declines toward the price limits, thereby increasing short-term volatility.[6]

However, restrictions on liquidity also might have a more insidious effect. Many investors will enter only liquid markets that enable them to move quickly in and out. Any restrictions on the liquidity of markets lower the desirability of these markets and therefore lower prices. The effect of liquidity on price can be seen easily in the U.S. government bond market, where the latest bond issued (the "on the run" bond) sells at a higher price than virtually identical bonds that do not have such liquidity.

THE NATURE OF MARKET VOLATILITY

Although most investors express a strong distaste for market fluctuations, volatility must be accepted to reap the superior returns offered by stocks. Risk and volatility are the essence of above-average returns: Investors cannot make any more than the risk-free rate of return unless there is some possibility that they can make less.

While the volatility of the stock market deters many investors, it fascinates others. The ability to monitor a position on a minute-by-minute basis fulfills the need of many people to know quickly whether their judgment, which affects not only money but also ego, has been validated. For many people, the stock market is truly the world's largest gambling casino.

Yet this ability to know exactly how much one is worth at any given moment also can provoke anxiety. Many investors do not like the instantaneous verdict of the financial market. Some retreat into investments such as real estate, for which daily quotations are not available. They believe that not knowing the current price makes an investment somehow less risky. As Keynes stated over 50 years ago about the investing attitudes of the endowment committee at Cambridge University:

---

[6]This was a major criticism of what happened October 27, 1997. When the markets reopened after the 350-point limit was reached, traders were so anxious to exit that the 550-point limit was reached in a matter of minutes.

Some Bursars will buy without a tremor unquoted and unmarketable investment in real estate which, if they had a selling quotation for immediate cash available at each audit, would turn their hair grey. The fact that you do not know how much its ready money quotation fluctuates does not, as is commonly supposed, make an investment a safe one.[7]

HISTORICAL TRENDS OF STOCK VOLATILITY

Figure 16-2 plots the variability (measured by the standard deviation) of the monthly returns on stocks calculated yearly from 1834 to the present. It is striking that there is so little overall trend in the volatility of the market. One can see that the period of greatest volatility was during the Great Depression, and the year of highest volatility was 1932. The annualized volatility of 1932 was over 65 percent, 17 times higher than 1964, which is the least volatile year on record. The volatility of 1987 was the highest since the Great Depression, but the volatility in the mid-1990s fell to near record lows. Excluding the 1929–1939 period, the average volatility of the market has remained remarkably stable at about 14 percent over the past 165 years.

Nevertheless, there was an increase of volatility in 2000 and 2001. This occurred mostly because of the volatility of the technology sector, which became a large part of the market in 2000, as well as the recession and terrorist shocks that hit the economy in 2001. Given the exceptional nature of these events, it is quite likely that volatility will decline to average levels in subsequent years.

These trends are confirmed by examining Figure 16-3a, which displays the average daily percentage change on the Dow Jones Industrial Average during each year since 1896. The downward trend in Dow volatility in the early twentieth century is partially due to the increase in the number of stocks in the Dow from 12 to 20 and then to 30 in 1928. The average daily change in the Dow over the past 100 years is 0.73 percent, slightly less than three-quarters of 1 percent. Since the 1930s, there have been only 3 years, 1974, 1987, and 2000, where the average daily change has exceeded 1 percent.[8]

Figure 16-3b shows the percentage of trading days when the Dow changed by more than 1 percent. This has averaged 23 percent over the period, or about one per week. However, it has ranged from as low as 1.2

---

[7]"Memo for the Estates Committee, King's College, Cambridge, May 8, 1938," in Charles D. Ellis (ed.), *Classics* (Homewood, IL: Dow Jones-Irwin, 1989), p. 79.
[8]The average percentage change in the Dow in 2001 was 0.9934 percent.

Annual Volatility of Stock Returns (Annualized Standard Deviation of Monthly Returns), 1834–2001

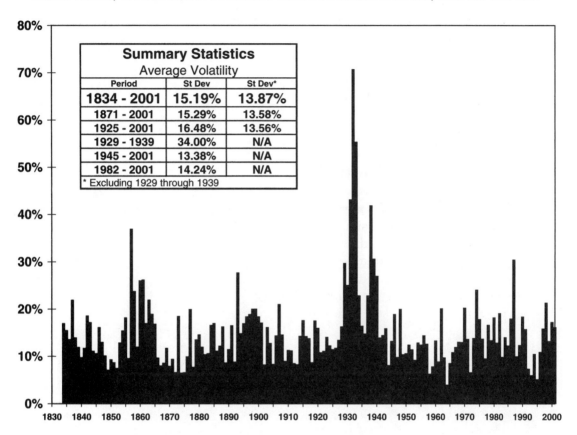

Summary Statistics		
Average Volatility		
Period	St Dev	St Dev*
1834 - 2001	**15.19%**	**13.87%**
1871 - 2001	15.29%	13.58%
1925 - 2001	16.48%	13.56%
1929 - 1939	34.00%	N/A
1945 - 2001	13.38%	N/A
1982 - 2001	14.24%	N/A
* Excluding 1929 through 1939		

percent in 1964 to a high of 67.6 percent in 1932. In that volatile year, the Dow changed by more than 1 percent on 2 of every 3 trading days.

Most of the periods of high volatility occur when the market has declined. In recessions, the standard deviation of daily returns is about 25 percent more than during expansions. There are two reasons why volatility increases in a recession. First, as noted in Chapter 12, a decline in the market frequently portends an economic slowdown and therefore generates uncertainty for investors. Second, if the market declines because of lower earnings forecasts, investors become much more concerned about the debt and other fixed-income obligations of firms. Since bondholders have first claim on the assets of firms, the probability of severe financial stress and bankruptcy increases when earnings decline. This leads to increased volatility in the equity value of firms.

FIGURE 16–3

Daily Risk on the Dow Jones Industrial Average

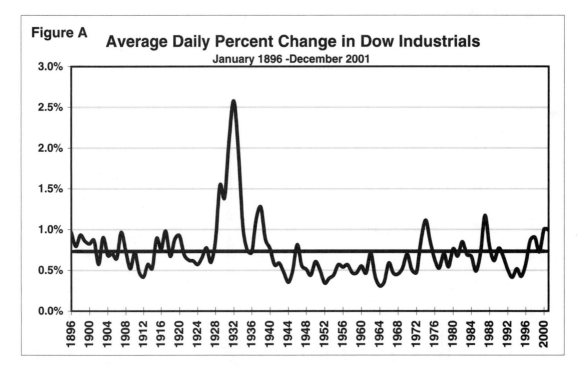

Figure A

Average Daily Percent Change in Dow Industrials
January 1896 -December 2001

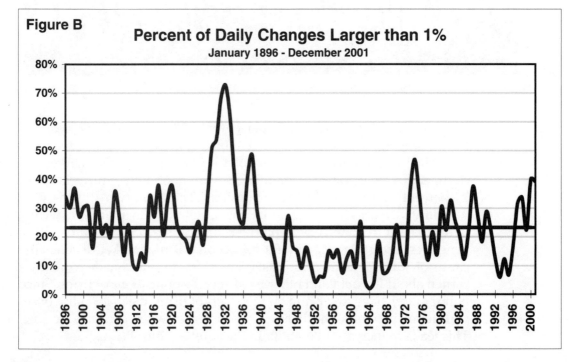

Figure B

Percent of Daily Changes Larger than 1%
January 1896 - December 2001

If the market believes that the value of a firm is at or below that of the indebtedness to bondholders or banks, the stock market can become extremely volatile. Since stockholders lay claim to only the value of a firm above debt obligations, the valuation of the stock of a firm that is in trouble becomes much like that of an out-of-the-money option that pays off only if the firm does well and otherwise is worthless. Such options are extremely volatile.

VIX: THE VOLATILITY INDEX

Measuring *historical* volatility is a simple matter, but it is far more important to measure the volatility investors *expect* in the market. This is so because expected volatility is a signal of the level of anxiety in the market, and periods of high anxiety often have marked turning points for stocks.

By examining the prices of put and call options on the major stock market indexes, one can determine the volatility that is built into the market, which is called the *implied volatility*.[9] In 1993, the Chicago Board Options Exchange (CBOE) introduced a volatility index, called *VIX*, based on actual index option prices and calculated this index back to the mid-1980s.[10] A weekly plot of the VIX from 1986 appears in Figure 16-4.

In the short run, there is a strong negative correlation between the VIX and the *level* of the market. When the market is falling, the VIX rises because investors are willing to pay more for downside protection. When the market is rising, the VIX typically goes down because investors become less willing to insure their portfolios against a loss.

This correlation may seem puzzling because one might expect investors to seek more protection when the market is high rather than low. One explanation of the behavior of the VIX is that historical volatility is higher in bear markets than in bull markets, so falling markets should cause the VIX to rise. However, a more persuasive argument is that changes in investor anxiety that are reflected in the VIX cause changes in stock prices, not vice versa. As uncertainty increases, investors increase the risk premium that they demand in stock returns, sending the price of

---

[9]This is done by solving for the volatility using the Black-Scholes option-pricing formula. See Chapter 15.

[10]VIX is the average of the implied volatility on eight put and call index options adjusted to a 30-day maturity and evaluated at the money, or at a strike price that is at the current level of the market. The options are based on the OEX Index, which is the S&P 100 (the largest 100 stocks in the S&P 500 Index). OEX options are very active and liquid and have an extremely high correlation with the S&P 500 Index.

FIGURE 16-4

VIX: Volatility Index, 1986–2002

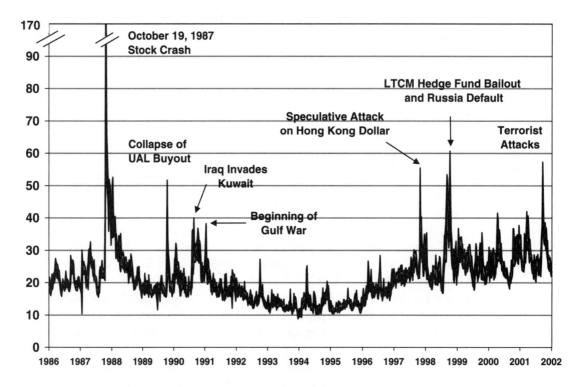

stocks downward. The reverse occurs when investors feel more confident of stock returns.

When anxiety in the market is high, the VIX is high, and when complacency rules, the VIX is low. It is easy to see in Figure 16-4 that the peaks in the VIX corresponded to periods of extreme uncertainty and sharply lower stock prices. The VIX peaked at 172 on the Tuesday following the October 19, 1987, stock market crash, far eclipsing any other high.

In the early and middle 1990s, the VIX sank to between 10 and 20. With the onset of the Asian crises in 1997, however, the VIX moved up to a range of 20 to 30. Spikes between 50 and 60 in the VIX occurred on three occasions: when the Dow fell 550 points during the attack on the Hong Kong dollar in October 1987, in August of 1998 when Long-Term Capital Management needed to be bailed out, and in the week following the terrorist attacks of September 11, 2001.

All these spikes in the VIX were excellent buying opportunities for investors. On the other hand, low levels of the VIX often reflect too much investor complacency. In recent years, the VIX has fallen in the summer months, a period that often has been followed by stormy markets. Volatility was especially low in August 2000 just before the bear market of 2000–2001 got underway in earnest. As will be shown in Chapter 19, peaks in the VIX also correspond to periods of extreme pessimism on the part of investors.

Buying when the VIX is high and selling when it is low have proved profitable in recent years. However, so has buying during market spills and selling during market peaks. The real question is how high is high and how low is low. For instance, an investor may have been tempted to buy into the market on Friday, October 16, 1987, when the VIX reached 40. Yet such a purchase would have proved disastrous given the record 1-day collapse that followed on Monday.

DISTRIBUTION OF LARGE DAILY CHANGES

Chapter 13 noted that there were 126 days from 1885 through the present when the Dow Jones Industrial Average changed by 5 percent or more: 59 days up and 67 days down. Seventy-nine of these days, or nearly two-thirds of the total, were in the period 1929–1933. The most volatile year by far in terms of daily changes was 1932, which contained 35 days when the Dow moved by at least 5 percent. The longest period of time between two successive changes of at least 5 percent was the 17-year period that preceded the October 19, 1987, stock crash.

Figure 16-5 records some of the properties of large daily changes. Monday has seen only slightly more large changes than the rest of the week, and Tuesday has seen significantly fewer. Monday has the largest number of down days, but Wednesday has by far the highest number of up days.

Thirty of the large changes occurred in October, which is notorious for being a month of great volatility in the stock market. This reputation is fully justified. Not only has October witnessed 30 of the 126 largest changes, but it also has seen the two greatest stock market crashes in history. It is interesting to note that nearly two-thirds of the total days with large declines have occurred in the last 4 months of the year. I shall present the seasonal aspects of stock price changes in Chapter 18.

One of the most surprising bits of information about large market moves relates to the period of the greatest stock market collapse. From September 3, 1929, through July 8, 1932, the Dow Jones Industrials col-

FIGURE 16–5

Distribution of Dow Changes over 5 Percent, 1885–2001

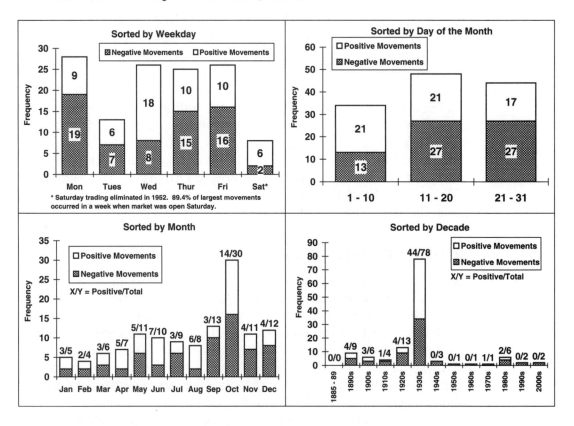

lapsed nearly 89 percent. During that period, there were 37 episodes when the Dow changed by 5 percent or more. Surprisingly, 21 of these episodes were increases!

Many of these sharp rallies were the result of *short covering* as those speculators who thought the market was on a one-way street downward rushed to sell stock they did not own. They were forced to buy back, or cover their positions, once the market rallied. It is not uncommon for markets that appear to be trending in one direction to experience occasional sharp moves in the other direction. In a bull market, the expression "up the staircase, down the elevator" is an apt description of price performance. Professional traders who play the trend are quick to bail out when they see a correction coming, making it hazardous for ordinary investors who believe they can profit from major trends in financial markets.

THE ECONOMICS OF MARKET VOLATILITY

Many of the complaints about market volatility are grounded in the belief that the market reacts excessively to changes in news. How news should affect the market, though, is so difficult to determine that few can quantify the proper impact of an event on the price of a stock. As a result, traders often "follow the crowd" and try to predict how other traders will react when news strikes.

Over half a century ago, Keynes illustrated the problem of investors who try to value stock by economic fundamentals as opposed to following the crowd:

> Investment based on genuine long-term expectation is so difficult today as to be scarcely practicable. He who attempts it must surely lead much more laborious days and run greater risk than he who tries to guess better than the crowd how the crowd will behave; and, given equal intelligence, he may make more disastrous mistakes.[11]

In 1981, Robert Shiller of Yale University devised a method of determining whether stock investors tended to overreact to changes in dividends and interest rates, the fundamental building blocks of stock values.[12] From an examination of historical data, he calculated what the value of the S&P 500 Index should have been given the subsequent realization of dividends and interest rates. We know what this value is because, as shown in Chapter 6, stock prices are the present discounted value of future cash flows.

What he found was that stock prices were far too variable to be explained merely by the subsequent behavior of dividends and interest rates. Stock prices appeared to overreact to changes in dividends, failing to take into account that most of the deviations from the growth trend in dividends were only temporary. In other words, investors priced stocks in a recession as if they expected dividends to go much lower, completely contrary to historical experience.

The word *cycle* in business cycle implies that ups in economic activity will be followed by downs, and vice versa. Since earnings and profits tend to follow the business cycle, they too should behave in a cyclic manner, returning to some average value over time. Under these circumstances, a temporary drop in dividends (or earnings) during a re-

---

[11]John Maynard Keynes, *The General Theory of Employment, Interest, and Money* (New York: Harcourt, Brace, & World, 1965, First Harbinger Edition), p. 157.

[12]Robert Shiller, *Market Volatility* (Cambridge, MA: MIT Press, 1989). The seminal article that spawned the excess volatility literature was "Do Stock Prices Move Too Much to Be Justified by Subsequent Changes in Dividends?" *American Economic Review* 71(1981):421–435.

cession should have a very minor effect on the price of a stock, which discounts dividends into the infinite future.

When stocks are collapsing, worst-case scenarios loom large in investors' minds. On May 6, 1932, after stocks had plummeted 85 percent from their 1929 high, Dean Witter issued the following memo to its clients:

> There are only two premises which are tenable as to the future. Either we are going to have chaos or else recovery. The former theory is foolish. If chaos ensues, nothing will maintain value; neither bonds nor stocks nor bank deposits nor gold will remain valuable. Real estate will be a worthless asset because titles will be insecure. No policy can be based upon this impossible contingency. Policy must therefore be predicated upon the theory of recovery. The present is not the first depression; it may be the worst, but just as surely as conditions have righted themselves in the past and have gradually readjusted to normal, so this will again occur. The only uncertainty is when it will occur. . . . I wish to say emphatically that in a few years present prices will appear as ridiculously low as 1929 values appear fantastically high.[13]

Two months later the stock market hit its all-time low and rallied strongly. In retrospect, these words reflected great wisdom and sound judgment about the temporary dislocations of stock prices. Yet, at the time they were uttered, investors were so disenchanted with stocks and so filled with doom and gloom that the message fell on deaf ears. Chapter 19 discusses why investors often overreact to short-term events and fail to take the long view of the market.

EPILOGUE TO THE CRASH

Despite the drama of the October 1987 market collapse, which often has been compared with 1929, there was amazingly little lasting effect on the world economy or even the financial markets. Because this stock market crash did not augur either a further collapse in stock prices or a decline in economic activity, it probably will never attain the notoriety of the crash of 1929. Yet its lesson is perhaps more important: Economic safeguards, such as prompt Federal Reserve action to provide liquidity to the economy and ensure the financial markets, can prevent an economic debacle of the kind that beset our economy during the Great Depression.

---

[13]Memorandum from Dean Witter, May 6, 1932.

This does not mean that the markets are exempt from violent fluctuations. Since the future will always be uncertain, psychology and sentiment often dominate economic fundamentals. As Keynes perceptively stated 60 years ago in *The General Theory,* "The outstanding fact is the extreme precariousness of the basis of knowledge on which our estimates of prospective yield have to be made."[14] Precarious estimates are subject to sudden change, and prices in free markets will always be volatile. But history has shown that investors who are willing to step into the market when others are panicking to leave reap the benefits of market volatility.

---

[14]Keynes (1965), p. 149.

TECHNICAL ANALYSIS AND INVESTING WITH THE TREND

Many skeptics, it is true, are inclined to dismiss the whole procedure [chart reading] as akin to astrology or necromancy; but the sheer weight of its importance in Wall Street requires that its pretensions be examined with some degree of care.

BENJAMIN GRAHAM, 1934[1]

THE NATURE OF TECHNICAL ANALYSIS

Flags, pennants, saucers, and head-and-shoulders formations. Stochastics, moving average convergence-divergence indicators, and candlesticks. Such is the arcane language of the technical analyst, an investor who forecasts future returns based on past price trends. Few areas of investment analysis have attracted more critics, yet no other area has a core of such dedicated supporters. Technical analysis, often dismissed by academic economists as being no more useful than astrology, is being given a new look, and some of the recent evidence is surprisingly positive.

Technical analysts, or *chartists* as they are sometimes called, stand in sharp contrast to fundamental analysts, who use such variables as

---

[1]Benjamin Graham and David Dodd, *Security Analysis* (New York: McGraw-Hill, 1934), p. 618.

dividends, earnings, and book values to forecast stock returns. Chartists ignore these fundamental variables, maintaining that virtually all useful information is summarized by past price patterns. These patterns may be the result of market psychology or informed traders who accumulate and distribute stock. If these patterns are read properly, chartists maintain, investors can use them to share in the gains of those who are more knowledgeable about a stock's prospects.

CHARLES DOW, TECHNICAL ANALYST

The first well-publicized technical analyst was Charles Dow, the creator of the Dow Jones Averages. However, Charles Dow did not analyze only charts. In conjunction with his interest in market movements, Dow founded the *Wall Street Journal* and published his strategy in editorials in the early part of the twentieth century. Dow's successor, William Hamilton, extended Dow's technical approach and published *The Stock Market Barometer* in 1922. Ten years later, Charles Rhea formalized Dow's concepts in a book entitled *Dow Theory*.

Charles Dow likened the ebb and flow of stock prices to waves in an ocean. He claimed that there was a primary wave, which, like the tide, determined the overall trend. On this trend were superimposed secondary waves and minor ripples. He also claimed that you could identify which trend the market was in by analyzing a chart of the Dow Jones Industrial Average, the volume in the market, and the Dow Jones Rail (now called the Transportation) Average.

It is widely acknowledged that the use of Dow theory would have gotten an investor out of the stock market before the October 1929 crash but not before the crash of October 1987. Martin J. Pring, a noted technical analyst, argues that starting in 1897, investors who purchased stock in the Dow Jones Industrial Average and followed each Dow theory buy and sell signal would have seen an original investment of $100 reach $116,508 by January 1990 as opposed to $5,682 with a buy-and-hold strategy (these calculations exclude reinvested dividends).[2] However, confirming profits that come from trading based on the Dow theory is difficult because the buy and sell signals are purely subjective and cannot be determined by precise numerical rules.

---

[2]Martin Pring, *Technical Analysis Explained*, 3d ed. (New York: McGraw-Hill, 1991), p. 31. Also see David Glickstein and Rolf Wubbels, "Dow Theory Is Alive and Well!" *Journal of Portfolio Management* (April 1983):28–32.

RANDOMNESS OF STOCK PRICES

Although Dow theory may not be as popular as it once was, technical analysis is still alive and well. The idea that you can identify the major trends in the market, riding bull markets while avoiding bear markets, is still a fundamental pursuit of technical analysts.

Yet most economists still attack the fundamental tenet of the chartists—that stock prices follow predictable patterns. To these academic researchers, the movements of prices in the market more closely conform to a pattern called a *random walk* than to trends that forecast future returns.

The first to make this connection was Frederick MacCauley, an economist in the early part of the twentieth century. His comments at a 1925 dinner meeting of the American Statistical Association on the topic of forecasting security prices were reported in the association's official journal:

> MacCauley observed that there was a striking similarity between the fluctuations of the stock market and those of a chance curve which may be obtained by throwing dice. Everyone will admit that the course of such a purely chance curve cannot be predicted. If the stock market can be forecast from a graph of its movements, it must be because of its difference from the chance curve.[3]

More than 30 years later, Harry Roberts, a professor at the University of Chicago, simulated movements in the market by plotting price changes that resulted from completely random events, such as flips of a coin. These simulations looked like the charts of actual stock prices, forming shapes and following trends that are considered by chartists to be significant predictors of future returns. However, since the next period's price change was, by construction, a completely random event, such patterns could not logically have any predictive content. This early research supported the belief that the apparent patterns in past stock prices were the result of completely random movements.

However, does the randomness of stock prices make economic sense? Factors influencing supply and demand do not occur randomly and often are quite predictable from one period to the next. Should not these predictable factors make stock prices move in nonrandom patterns?

In 1965, Professor Paul Samuelson of the Massachusetts Institute of Technology showed that the randomness in security prices did not con-

---

[3]"Comments made at the Aldine Club in New York on April 17, 1925," *Journal of the American Statistical Association* 20(June 1925):248.

tradict the laws of supply and demand.[4] In fact, such randomness was a result of a free and efficient market in which investors had already incorporated all the known factors influencing the price of the stock. This is the crux of the *efficient market hypothesis*.

If the market is efficient, prices will change only when new, unanticipated information is released to the market. Since unanticipated information is as likely to be good or bad, the resulting movement in stock prices is random. Price charts will look like a random walk because the probability that stocks will go up or down is completely random and cannot be predicted.[5]

SIMULATIONS OF RANDOM STOCK PRICES

If stock prices are indeed random, their movements should not be distinguishable from counterfeits generated randomly by a computer. Figure 17-1 extends the experiment conceived by Professor Roberts 40 years ago. Instead of generating only closing prices, I programmed the computer to generate intraday prices, creating the popular high-low-close bar graphs that are found in most newspapers and chart publications.

Figure 17-1 contains eight charts. A computer, using a random-number generator, has simulated four of these charts. In these graphs, there is absolutely no way to predict the future from the past, since future movements are designed to be totally independent from the past. The other four charts were chosen from actual data of the Dow Jones Industrial Average over recent years. Before reading further, try to determine which are real historical prices and which are computer-generated prices.

Such a task is quite difficult. In fact, most of the top brokers at a leading Wall Street firm found it impossible to tell the difference between the real and counterfeit data. Only Figure 17-1*d*, which depicts the period around the October 19, 1987, stock crash, was correctly identified by two-thirds of the brokers. With the remaining seven graphs, the brokers showed no ability to distinguish actual from counterfeit data. The true historical prices are represented by the graphs in Figure 17-1*b*, *d*, *e*,

---

[4] Paul Samuelson, "Proof That Properly Anticipated Prices Fluctuate Randomly," *Industrial Management Review* 6(1965):49.

[5] More generally, the sum of the product of each possible price change and the probability of its occurrence is zero. This is called a *martingale*, of which a random walk (50 percent probability up and 50 percent probability down) is a special case.

FIGURE 17–1

Real and Simulated Stock Indexes

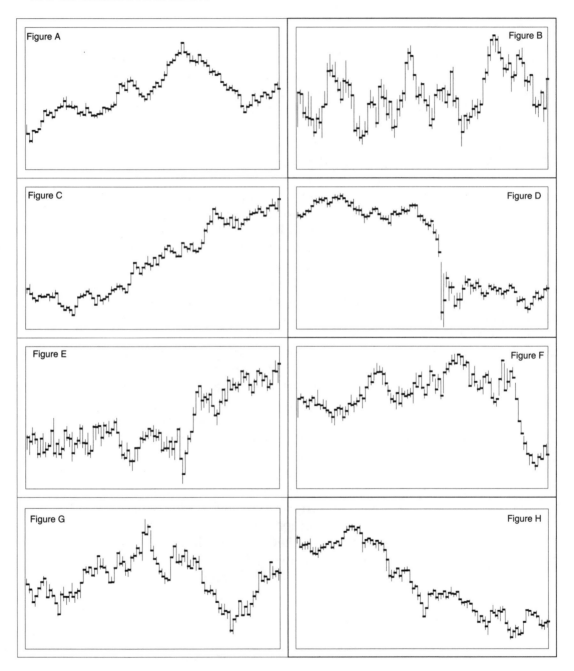

and *h*, whereas the computer-generated data are the graphs in Figure 17-1*a*, *c*, *f*, and *g*.[6]

TRENDING MARKETS AND PRICE REVERSALS

Despite the fact that many so-called trends are in fact the result of the totally random movement of stock prices, many traders will not invest against a trend they believe they have identified. Two of the best-known sayings of market timers are "Make the trend your friend" and "Trust the thrust."

Martin Zweig, a well-known market timer who uses fundamental and technical variables to forecast market trends, has forcefully stated, "I can't overemphasize the importance of staying with the trend of the market, being in gear with the tape, and not fighting the major movements. Fighting the tape is an open invitation to disaster."[7]

When a trend appears established, technical analysts draw channels that enclose the path of stock prices. A channel encloses the upper and lower bounds within which the market has traded. The lower bound of a channel frequently is called a *support level*, and the upper bound, a *resistance level*. When the market breaks the bounds of the channel, a large market move often follows.

The very fact that many traders believe in the importance of trends can induce behavior that makes trend following so popular. While the trend is intact, traders sell when prices reach the upper end of the channel and buy when they reach the lower end, attempting to take advantage of the apparent back-and-forth motion of stock prices. If the trend line is broken, many of these traders will reverse their positions, buying if the market penetrates the top of the trend line and selling if it falls through the bottom. This behavior often accelerates the movement of stock prices and reinforces the importance of the trend.

Option trading by trend followers reinforces the behavior of market timers. When the market is trading within a channel, traders will sell put and call options at strike prices that represent the lower and upper bounds of the channel. As long as the market remains within the channel, these speculators collect premiums as the options expire worthless.

If the market penetrates the trading range, option sellers are ex-

---

[6] Figure 17-1*b* covers February 15 to July 1, 1991, Figure 17-1*e* covers January 15 to June 1, 1992, and Figure 17-1*h* covers from June 15 to November 1, 1990.
[7] Martin Zweig, *Winning on Wall Street* (New York: Warner Books, 1990), p. 121.

posed to great risks. Recall that sellers of options (as long as they do not own the underlying stock) face a huge potential liability, a liability that can be many times the premium that they collected on sale of the option. When such unlimited losses loom, these option writers "run for cover," or buy back their options, accelerating the movement of prices.

MOVING AVERAGES

Successful technical trading requires not only identifying the trend but also, more important, identifying when the trend is about to reverse. A popular tool for determining when a trend might change examines the relationship between the current price and a moving average of past price movements, a technique that goes back to at least the 1930s.[8]

A *moving average* is simply the arithmetic average of a given number of past closing prices of a stock or index. For example, a 200-day moving average is the average of the past 200 days' closing prices. For each new trading day, the oldest price is dropped, and the most recent price is added to compute the average.

Moving averages fluctuate far less than daily prices. When prices are rising, the moving average trails the market and, technical analysts claim, forms a support level for stock prices. When prices are falling, the moving average is above current prices and forms a resistance level. Analysts claim that a moving average allows investors to identify the basic market trend without being distracted by the day-to-day volatility of the market. When prices penetrate the moving average, this indicates that powerful underlying forces are signaling a reversal of the basic trend.

The most popular moving average uses prices for the past 200 trading days and therefore is called the *200-day moving average*. It is frequently plotted in newspapers and investment letters as a key determinant of investment trends. One of the early supporters of this strategy was William Gordon, who indicated that over the period from 1897 to 1967, buying stocks when the Dow broke above the moving average produced nearly seven times the returns as buying when the Dow broke below the average.[9] Robert Colby and Thomas Meyers claim that for the

---

[8]See William Brock, Josef Lakonishok, and Blake LeBaron, "Simple Technical Trading Rules and the Stochastic Properties of Stock Returns," *Journal of Finance* 47(5)(December 1992):1731–1764. The first definitive analysis of moving averages comes from a book by H. M. Gartley, *Profits in the Stock Market* (New York: H. M. Gartley, 1930).
[9]William Gordon, *The Stock Market Indicators* (Palisades, NJ: Investors Press, 1968).

United States, the best time period for a moving average of weekly data is 45 weeks, just slightly longer than the 200-day moving average.[10]

TESTING THE DOW JONES MOVING-AVERAGE STRATEGY

In order to test the 200-day moving-average strategy, I examined the daily record of the Dow Jones Industrial Average from 1885 to the present. In contrast to previous studies on moving-average strategies, the holding-period returns include the reinvestment of dividends when the strategy suggests investing in the market and interest when one is not invested in the stock market.[11] Annualized returns are examined over the entire period as well as the subperiods.

I adopted the following criteria to determine the buy-sell strategy: Whenever the Dow closed *at least 1 percent above* its 200-day moving average, stocks were purchased at these closing prices. Whenever the Dow closed by *at least 1 percent below* its 200-day moving average, stocks were sold. The portfolio was then invested in Treasury bills and earned interest income.

There are two noteworthy aspects of this strategy. The 1 percent band around the 200-day moving average is used in order to reduce the number of times an investor would have to move in and out of the market. Without this band, investors using the 200-day moving-average strategy often would be *whipsawed,* a term used to describe the frequent buying and then selling and then buying again of stocks in an attempt to beat the market. Such trades dramatically lower investor returns because of the large transaction costs incurred.

The second aspect of this strategy assumes that an investor buys or sells stocks at the closing price rather than at any price reached during the day. Only in recent years has the exact intraday level of the averages been computed. Using historical data, it is impossible to determine times when the market average penetrated the 200-day moving average during the day but closed at levels that did not trigger a signal. By specifying that the average must close above or below the signal, I present a theory that could have been implemented in practice.[12]

---

[10]Robert W. Colby and Thomas A. Meyers, *The Encyclopedia of Technical Market Indicators* (Homewood, IL: Dow Jones-Irwin, 1988).

[11]The dividend yield was estimated from yearly data of dividend yields, as described in Chapter 1.

[12]Historically, the daily high and low levels of stock averages were calculated on the basis of the highest or lowest price of each stock reached at any time during the day. This is called the *theoretical high or low.* The *actual high* is the highest level reached at any given time by the stocks in the average.

Figure 17-2 shows the daily and 200-day moving average of the Dow Jones Industrial Average during two selected periods: 1924–1936 and 1982–2001. The time periods when investors are out of the stock market are shaded; otherwise, investors are fully invested in stocks.

Over the entire 117-year history of the Dow, the 200-day moving-average strategy had its greatest triumph during the boom and crash of the 1920s and early 1930s. Using the criteria outlined earlier, investors would have bought stocks on June 27, 1924, when the Dow was 95.33 and, with only two minor interruptions, ridden the bull market to the top at 381.17 on September 3, 1929. Investors would have exited the market on October 19, 1927, at 323.87, ten days before the great crash. Except for a brief period in 1930, the strategy would have kept investors out of stocks through the worst bear market in history. They finally would have reentered the market on August 6, 1932, when the Dow was 66.56, just 25 points higher than its postcrash low.

Investors following the 200-day moving-average strategy also would have avoided the October 19, 1987, crash, selling out on the preceding Friday, October 16. However, in contrast with the 1929 crash, in 1987 stocks did not continue downward. Although the market fell 23 percent on October 19, investors would not have reentered the market until the following June when the Dow was only about 5 percent below the exit level of October 16. Nonetheless, following the 200-day moving-average strategy would have avoided October 19 and 20, traumatic days for many investors who held stocks.

Table 17-1 summarizes the returns from the 200-day moving-average strategy and a buy-and-hold strategy of not timing the market. From 1885 through December 2001, the 10.43 percent annual return from the timing strategy beat the annual return on the holding strategy of 9.76 percent. As noted earlier, however, the timing strategy has its biggest success from avoiding the 1929–1932 crash. If that period is excluded, the returns of the timing strategy are about ½ percent behind those of the holding strategy, although the timing strategy has lower risk.

Moreover, if the transaction costs of implementing the timing strategy are included in the calculations, the excess returns over the whole period, including the 1929–1932 great crash, more than vanish. Transaction costs include brokerage costs and bid-ask spreads, as well as the capital gains tax incurred when stocks are sold, and are assumed to be, on average, ½ percent when buying or selling the market. This number probably underestimates such costs, especially in the earlier years. Each

FIGURE 17–2

Dow Jones Industrials and the 200-Day Moving Average (Shaded Areas Are Out of Market)

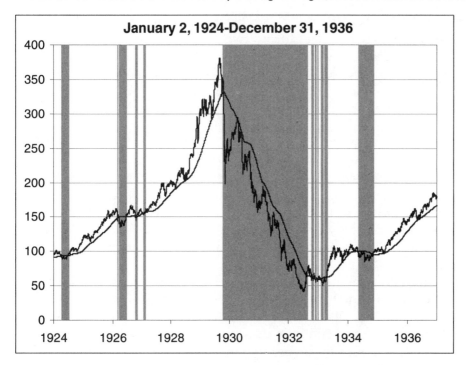

January 2, 1924–December 31, 1936

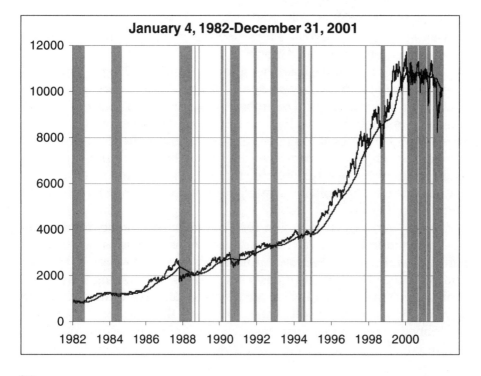

January 4, 1982–December 31, 2001

TABLE 17–1

Timing and Holding Strategy Annualized Returns, January 1886–December 2001

Period	Holding Strategy		Timing Strategy					
	Return	Risk	No Trans Costs		Net Trans Costs		% in Market	# of Switches
			Return	Risk	Return	Risk		
1886 - 2001	**9.76%**	21.8%	**10.43%**	16.8%	**8.89%**	17.4%	**62.8%**	325
Subperiods								
1886 - 1925	9.08%	23.7%	9.77%	17.7%	8.11%	18.0%	57.1%	122
1926 - 1945	6.25%	31.0%	11.10%	21.8%	9.44%	22.7%	62.7%	60
1946 - 2001	11.53%	16.2%	10.66%	14.2%	9.25%	15.1%	67.7%	143
1990 - 2001	14.09%	14.3%	7.39%	18.4%	5.21%	19.9%	77.4%	49
Excl. 1929 - 1932 Crash								
1886 - 2001	**11.51%**	20.7%	**11.05%**	16.6%	**9.54%**	17.3%	**64.1%**	309
1926 - 1945	**17.72%**	25.9%	**15.75%**	21.3%	**14.24%**	22.1%	**71.2%**	44

0.1 percentage point increase of transaction costs lowers the compound annual returns by 29 basis points.

Although the excess returns from the timing strategy disappear when transactions costs are considered, the major gain from the timing strategy is a reduction in risk. Since the market timer is in the market less than two-thirds of the time, the standard deviation of returns is reduced by about one-quarter. This means that on a risk-adjusted basis, the return on the 200-day moving-average strategy is quite impressive, even when transactions costs are included.

Unfortunately, the timing strategy has broken down in the last 14 years. Since the crash in 1987, the buy-and-hold strategy has beaten the timing strategy *every* year except 1995 and 1996, when the two strategies yielded equal returns. 2000 was a particularly disastrous year for the timing strategy. With the Dow meandering most of the year above and below the 200-day moving average, the investor pursuing the timing strategy was whipsawed in and out of the market, executing a record 16 switches into and out of stocks.

Each switch incurs transactions costs and must overcome the 1 percent pricing band. As a result, even ignoring transactions costs, the timing strategist lost over 28 percent in 2000, whereas the buy-and-hold strategist lost less than 5 percent. Since 1990, the buy-and-hold strategy has returned 14.09 percent annually, whereas the timing strategy has returned only 7.39 percent, even before transactions costs.

Note that during the 1990–2001 period the risk, measured in *annual returns*, is surprisingly higher for the timing strategy than for the holding strategy. This unusual reversal of risks is due to the extremely poor returns for the timing strategy in 2000. If *monthly* returns are considered, the timing strategy had lower risk than the holding strategy over the same period.

Even over the last decade, use of the timing strategy did avoid some nasty bear markets. A timing strategist would have exited the market on June 25, 2001, and avoided the entire drop associated with the terrorist attacks. However, what looked like a big gain for the market timer was mostly eliminated by the sharp stock rally to close the year. The timing strategist would have reentered the market on January 3, 2002, at a price only 2.3 percent below the exit price 6 months earlier. Had the market remained at its lower levels following the terrorist attacks, the market timer would have avoided a more than 20 percent decline.

THE NASDAQ MOVING-AVERAGE STRATEGY

It is remarkable that during the 1990–2001 period when the moving-average strategy on the Dow Jones Industrials failed to generate good returns, the exact same strategy proved very successful on the Nasdaq. Table 17-2 shows that the timing strategy outperformed the holding strategy by nearly 5 percent per year since 1972 and by nearly 4 percent per year since 1990. Again, the market timer achieved these superior returns with much lower risk.

What is most important about the moving-average strategy is that it keeps investors in major bull markets and out of major bear markets. The strategy worked beautifully during the technology bubble of 1999–2001. Using the timing strategy, an investor would have entered the Nasdaq market at 1,801 on November 2, 1998, and ridden the market to the peak of 5,049 on March 10, 2000. After moving in and out of the market several times, the market timer would have exited the Nasdaq market at 3,896 on September 11, 2000, and stayed out until December 5, 2001, when the Nasdaq was at 2,046, almost 50 percent lower. For those 15 months, the timing strategist in Nasdaq would have avoided the most crushing bear market since the 1929–1932 stock market crash.

T A B L E   17–2

Nasdaq Timing and Holding Strategy Annualized Returns, January 1972–December 2001

Period	Holding Strategy		Timing Strategy					
	Return	Risk	No Trans Costs		Net Trans Costs		% in Market	# of Switches
			Return	Risk	Return	Risk		
1972-2001	11.92%	27.2%	16.67%	20.1%	15.20%	20.5%	68.4%	77
1990 - 2001	13.73%	35.4%	17.52%	29.1%	15.81%	29.9%	72.4%	34

DISTRIBUTION OF GAINS AND LOSSES

There is no question that the 200-day moving-average strategy, even with transactions costs, avoids large losses, but it suffers many small defeats. Figure 17-3 shows the distribution of yearly gains and losses in the timing strategy after transactions costs and the holding strategy for the Dow from 1886 to 2001. As noted earlier, the timing strategist participates in most of the winning markets and avoids most of the losing markets but suffers many small losses. These losses occur when the market does not follow a definite trend. Despite use of the 1 percent band to reduce whipsawing, investors in a trendless market often find themselves moving in and out of the market frequently, sometimes incurring heavy transactions costs and trading losses as occurred in 2000.

The distribution in Figure 17-3 is quite similar to a buy-and-hold investor purchasing index puts on the market. As noted in Chapter 15, purchasing index puts is equivalent to buying an insurance policy on the market, but the buyer must continually pay the premium. Similarly, the timing strategy involves a large number of small losses that come from moving into and out of the market while avoiding most severe declines.

CONCLUSION

Proponents of technical analysis claim that it helps investors identify the major trends of the market and when those trends might reverse. Yet there is considerable debate about whether such trends exist or whether they are just runs of good and bad returns that are the result of random price movements.

FIGURE 17–3

Distribution of Yearly Gains and Losses: Dow Industrials Timing Strategy versus Holding Strategy

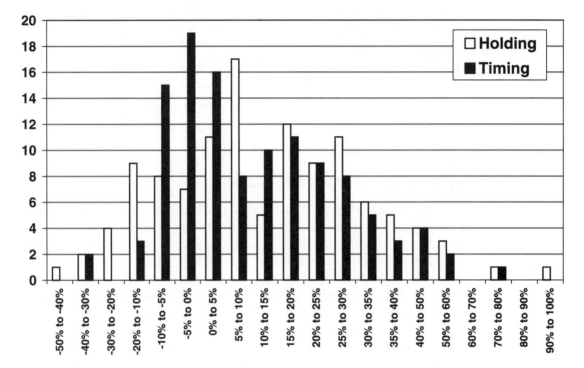

Burton Malkiel has been quite clear in his denunciation of technical analysis. In his best-selling work, *A Random Walk Down Wall Street*, he proclaims:

> Technical rules have been tested exhaustively by using stock price data on both major exchanges, going back as far as the beginning of the 20th century. The results reveal conclusively that past movements in stock prices cannot be used to foretell future movements. The stock market has no memory. The central proposition of charting is absolutely false, and investors who follow its precepts will accomplish nothing but increasing substantially the brokerage charges they pay.[13]

---

[13]Burton Malkiel, *A Random Walk Down Wall Street* (New York: W. W. Norton, 1990), p. 133.

Yet this contention, once supported nearly unanimously by academic economists, is cracking. Recent econometric research has shown that such simple trading rules as 200-day moving averages can be used to improve returns.[14]

Despite the ongoing academic debate, technical analysis and trend following draw huge followings on Wall Street and many savvy investors. The analysis in this chapter gives a cautious nod to the strategy based on moving averages, as long as transactions costs are not high. However, this strategy must be monitored closely. In October 1987, the Dow fell below its 200-day moving average on the Friday before the crash and gave a sell signal, but if you failed to get through to your broker that Friday afternoon, you would have been swept downward by the 22 percent nightmare decline of Black Monday.

Furthermore, as I have noted repeatedly throughout this book, actions by investors to take advantage of the past will change returns in the future. As Benjamin Graham stated so well more than 60 years ago:

> A moment's thought will show that there can be no such thing as a scientific prediction of economic events under human control. The very "dependability" of such a prediction will cause human actions which will invalidate it. Hence thoughtful chartists admit that continued success is dependent upon keeping the successful method known to only a few people.[15]

---

[14]See William Brock, Josef Lakonishok, and Blake LeBaron "Simple Technical Trading Rules and the Stochastic Properties of Stock Returns," *Journal of Finance* 47(5)(December 1992):1731–1764; and Andrew Lo, Harry Mamaysky, and Jiang Wang, "Foundations of Technical Analysis: Computational Algorithms, Statistical Inference, and Empirical Implementation, *Journal of Finance* 55(2000): 1705–1765.

[15]Graham and Dodd (1934), p. 619.

CHAPTER 18

CALENDAR ANOMALIES

October. This is one of the peculiarly dangerous months to speculate in stocks. The others are July, September, April, November, May, March, June, December, August, and February.

MARK TWAIN

The dictionary defines *anomaly* as something inconsistent with what is naturally expected. And what is more unnatural than to expect to beat the market by predicting stock prices based solely on the day or week or month of the year? Yet it appears that you can. Recent research has revealed that there are predictable times during which stocks as a whole and certain classes of stocks in particular excel in the market.

The most important calendar anomaly is that small stocks have far outperformed larger stocks in one specific month of the year: January. In fact, January is the only reason that small stocks have greater total returns than large stocks over the past 70 years! This phenomenon has been dubbed the *January effect*. Its discovery in the early 1980s by Don Keim,[1] based on research he did as a graduate student at the University of Chicago, was the first and in some ways the most significant finding

[1]Don Keim, "Size-Related Anomalies and Stock Return Seasonality: Further Empirical Evidence," *Journal of Financial Economics* 12(1983):13–32.

in a market where researchers had failed previously to detect any predictable pattern to stock prices.

The January effect may be the granddaddy of all calendar anomalies, but it is not the only one. For inexplicable reasons, stocks generally do much better in the first few days of a month, and they also fare much better on Fridays than on Mondays. Furthermore, they do exceptionally well on the day before a major holiday, particularly on December 31, which is actually the day that launches the January effect.

Why these anomalies occur is not well understood, and whether they will continue to be significant in the future is an open question. However, their discovery has put economists on the spot. No longer can researchers be so certain that the stock market is thoroughly unpredictable and impossible to beat.

THE JANUARY EFFECT

Of all the calendar-related anomalies, the January effect has been the most publicized. From 1925 through 2001, the average arithmetic return on the Standard and Poor's (S&P) 500 Index in January was 1.7 percent, whereas the average returns on the small stocks came to 6.5 percent. The 4.8 percent average excess return of small stocks in January exceeds the entire 4.6 percent yearly difference in arithmetic returns between large and small stocks. In other words, from February through December, the returns on small stocks are lower than those on large stocks. On the basis of history, the only profitable time to hold small stocks is the month of January.

To see how important the January effect is, look at Figure 18-1. It shows the total return index on large and small stocks and on small stocks if the January return on small stocks is replaced with that of the S&P 500 Index in January. As shown in Chapter 6, a single dollar invested in small stocks in 1926 would grow to $6,609 by the end of 2001, whereas the same dollar would grow to only $2,021 in large stocks. Yet, if the small stocks' return in January is eliminated, the total return to small stocks accumulates to only $230, merely 11 percent of the return on large stocks.

Figure 18-1 also shows that if these January small-stock returns continue in the future, it could lead to some astounding investment results. By buying small stocks at the end of December and transferring them back to the S&P 500 Index at the end of January, your accumulation would grow to $58,173, or a 15.5 percent annual rate of return. In fact,

Small and Large Stocks, with and without the January Effect, 1926–2001

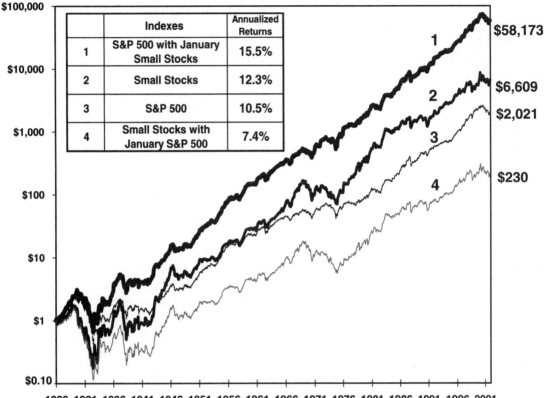

	Indexes	Annualized Returns
1	S&P 500 with January Small Stocks	15.5%
2	Small Stocks	12.3%
3	S&P 500	10.5%
4	Small Stocks with January S&P 500	7.4%

history dictates that you should borrow and leverage as much as you can to take advantage of this January anomaly.

There have been only 14 years since 1925 when large stocks have outperformed small stocks in January. Furthermore, when small stocks underperform large stocks, it is usually not by much: The worst under-performance was 5.1 percent in January 1929. In contrast, since 1925, small-stock returns have exceeded large-stock returns in January by at least 5 percent for 28 years, by at least 10 percent for 13 years, and by over 20 percent for 2 years.

The January effect also prevailed during the most powerful bear market in our history. From August 1929 through the summer of 1932, when small stocks lost over 90 percent of their value, small stocks posted consecutive January monthly returns of plus 13, 21, and 10 percent in 1930, 1931, and 1932. It is testimony to the power of the January effect that investors could have increased their wealth by 50 percent during the greatest stock crash in history by buying small stocks at the end of December of those 3 years and selling them at the end of the month, putting their money in cash for the rest of the year.

A fascinating feature of the January effect is that you have not had to wait the entire month to see the big returns from small stocks roll in. Most of the buying in small stocks begins on the last trading day of December (often in the late afternoon) as some investors pick up the bargains that are dumped by others on New Year's Eve. Strong gains in small stocks continue on the first trading day of January and with declining force through the first week of trading. On the first trading day of January alone, small stocks earn nearly 4 percentage points more than large stocks.[2] By the middle of the month, the January effect is largely exhausted.

When any anomaly such as the January effect is found, it is important to examine its international reach. When researchers turned to foreign markets, they found that the January effect was not just a U.S. phenomenon. In Japan, the world's second-largest capital market, the excess returns on small stocks in January come to 7.2 percent per year, more than in the United States.[3] As you shall see later in this chapter, January is the best month for both large and small stocks in many other countries of the world.[4]

How could such a phenomenon go unnoticed for so long by investors, portfolio managers, and financial economists? Because in the United States January is nothing special for large stocks, and these stocks form the base of the popular indexes, such as the Dow Jones Industrials and the S&P 500. This is not to say that January is not a good month for those stocks too. As explained later, large stocks do quite well in January, particularly in foreign markets. In the United States, however, January is by no means the best month for stocks of large firms.

It should be noted that these superior January returns do not always materialize. There are many years when small stocks have under-

---

[2]Robert Haugen and Josef Lakonishok, *The Incredible January Effect* (Homewood, IL: Dow Jones-Irwin, 1989), p. 47.

[3]See Gabriel Hawawini and Donald Keim, "On the Predictability of Common Stock Returns: World-Wide Evidence," in Jarrow et al. (eds.), *Handbooks in Operations Research and Management Science*, Vol. 9 (1995), Chapter 17, pp. 497–544.

[4]For an excellent summary of all this evidence, see Gabriel Hawawini and Don Keim, "The Cross Section of Common Stock Returns: A Review of the Evidence and Some New Findings," working paper, May 1997, Wharton School, University of Pennsylvania.

performed larger stocks in January, and this has happened with greater frequency recently. The widespread publicity of the January effect actually may be leading to its demise.

CAUSES OF THE JANUARY EFFECT

Why do investors tend to favor small stocks in January? No one knows for sure, but there are several hypotheses. Individual investors, in contrast to institutions, hold a disproportionate amount of small stocks, and they are more sensitive to the tax consequences of their trading. Small stocks, especially those that have declined in the preceding 11 months, are subject to tax-motivated selling in December. This selling depresses the price of individual issues.

There is some evidence to support this explanation. Stocks that have fallen throughout the year fall even more in December and then often rise dramatically in January. Furthermore, there is some evidence that before introduction of the U.S. income tax in 1913, there was no January effect. Moreover, in Australia, where the tax year runs from July 1 through June 30, there are abnormally large returns in July.

If taxes are a factor, however, they cannot be the only one, for the January effect holds in countries that do not have a capital gains tax. Japan did not tax capital gains for individual investors until 1989, but the January effect was still present. Furthermore, capital gains were not taxed in Canada before 1972, and yet there was a January effect in that country as well. Finally, stocks that have risen throughout the previous year and should not be subject to tax-loss selling still rise in January, although not by as much as stocks that have fallen the previous year.

There are other potential explanations for the January effect. Individuals often receive an influx of funds, such as bonuses and money that becomes available from tax-loss selling, at year-end. These individuals often wait several days to invest their cash and then buy in the first week of January. Data show that there is a sharp increase in the ratio of public buy orders to public sell orders around the turn of the year. Since the public holds a large fraction of small stocks, this could be an important clue to understanding the January effect.[5]

Another possible explanation is that portfolio managers often buy small stocks at the beginning of the year but then sell them by the time their balance sheets are inspected at year-end. They do this because if

---

[5]Jay Ritter, "The Buying and Selling Behavior of Individual Investors at the End of the Year," *Journal of Finance* 43(1988):701–717.

these small stocks have done well, the managers can lock in their superior performance, in other words beat the S&P, by indexing on the S&P 500 stocks for the rest of the year. And if these small, often risky stocks have not done well, they also will sell them because they do not want their clients to see them on their year-end balance sheets.

Another factor contributing to the January effect is that returns are calculated on the basis of the last price recorded during the day. If a buyer motivates the last sale, no matter how small, the final price will be recorded at the ask or offer price. For small, illiquid stocks, this could be 5 percent or more above the price at which the last sale was made. A buying flurry at the end of the day, centered especially in small stocks, could cause a substantial rise in small-stock indexes. This appears to be important at the end of calendar quarters, especially on December 31. However, researchers have concluded that it can explain just a small part of the January effect.[6]

Although all these explanations appear quite reasonable, none jibes with what is called an *efficient capital market.* If money managers know that stocks (especially small ones) will surge in January, they should be bought well before New Year's Day to capture these spectacular returns. This would cause a boom in small stocks in December, which would prompt other managers to buy them in November, and so on. In the process of acting on the January effect, the price of stocks would be smoothed out over the year, and the phenomenon would disappear.

Of course, to eliminate the January effect, money managers and investors with significant capital must know of the effect and feel comfortable about acting on it. Those in a fiduciary position might feel uneasy justifying what appears to be a very unusual investment strategy to their clients, especially if it does not work out. Others might be reluctant to take advantage of a phenomenon that seems to have no economic rationale.

In fact, the January effect has been much weaker in recent years. Small stocks (measured as the bottom quintile of capitalization value) underperformed larger stocks in January of 1996, 1997, 1998, and 1999, the only consecutive 4-year period since 1926 when this has occurred.[7] In

[6]Marshall E. Blume and R. F. Stambaugh, "Biases in Computed Returns: An Application to the Size Effect," *Journal of Financial Economics* 12(1983):387–404.
[7]Depending on the index used, the streak of small-stock underperformance lasted for 5 years. The Ibbotson Small-Stock Index, which since 1982 has used the DFA 9/10 Stock Fund returns, very slightly outperformed the S&P 500 Index in 1995. However, the Russell 2000 Index significantly underperformed large stocks in January of that year.

the back of many investors' minds is a lingering suspicion that the January effect will not last when more investors catch on by reading this and other books that have been written about it.

THE JANUARY EFFECT IN VALUE STOCKS

In addition to the small-stock effect, there is another January effect in the stock market that has received virtually no publicity. As noted in Chapter 8, value stocks—large as well as small—have a substantially higher return than growth stocks in the month of January. Table 18-1 reports the return on various size-based portfolios for value and growth stocks over

T A B L E 18–1

Annual Compound Returns by Size and Book-to-Market Ratio, July 1963–December 2000

Entire Period		Size Quintiles				
		Small	2	3	4	Large
Book-to-Market Quintiles	Value	23.26%	15.94%	17.44%	16.18%	13.59%
	2	20.40%	15.23%	14.60%	15.18%	11.27%
	3	18.03%	13.96%	14.75%	11.39%	11.02%
	4	12.87%	11.99%	11.83%	10.37%	12.13%
	Growth	6.41%	5.15%	5.93%	10.71%	10.28%

Excluding January		Size Quintiles				
		Small	2	3	4	Large
Book-to-Market Quintiles	Value	12.11%	10.13%	11.92%	11.72%	10.57%
	2	10.70%	10.61%	11.13%	12.18%	9.30%
	3	8.79%	9.32%	11.07%	8.30%	9.08%
	4	3.51%	7.56%	9.20%	8.16%	10.52%
	Growth	-2.45%	2.05%	3.90%	9.42%	9.06%

the period from July 1963 through December 2000. Over the entire period, value stocks outperform growth stocks for all size firms. With January removed, however, the gap between the returns on large growth stocks and large value stocks shrinks by more than 50 percent.

Why value stocks do well in the month of January is not known. It might reflect a New Year's reassessment of fundamental value-based criteria. The week between Christmas and New Year historically has been the best week of the year. After such holiday exuberance, portfolio managers start the new year on a sober note, downplaying the earnings projections of high-growth firms and focusing instead on firms that have more conservative valuations. Perhaps this phenomenon is related to the beginning-of-the-year funding of tax-exempt accounts with value stocks to avoid the taxation of dividends. A clearer picture of the reasons for this January effect in value stocks must await further research.

MONTHLY RETURNS

There are other seasonal patterns to stock returns besides the January effect. Figure 18-2 displays the monthly returns on the Dow Jones Industrial Average and the S&P 500 Index. December has been the best month since World War II for both indexes but only the fifth best month since 1885. In striking contrast, August, which was the best month for the past 116 years, is actually the second-to-worst month since World War II for the Dow and third-worst month for the S&P 500 Index. Since the end of World War II, there is really no evidence of the "summer rally" that is much trumpeted by brokers and investment advisors.

These monthly patterns have a worldwide reach. Although January is a good month in the United States, it is a far better month for most countries abroad. Figure 18-3 shows the January returns for the 20 countries covered by the Morgan Stanley Capital Market Index. In every country but Austria, January returns are greater than average. Outside the United States, January returns constitute 25 percent of total stock returns on a value-weighted basis. Investor enthusiasm in January also seems to infect the neighboring months of December and February. Nearly two-thirds of all returns outside the United States occur in the 3 months of December through February.[8]

---

[8]The data presented in Figure 18-3 are from a value-weighted stock index calculated on large stocks. As noted previously, there is evidence that smaller stocks experience even higher January returns, so the January returns shown in Figure 18-3 probably are much lower than those that can be gained in the average stock.

Monthly Returns on the Dow Jones Industrial Average and the S&P 500 Index

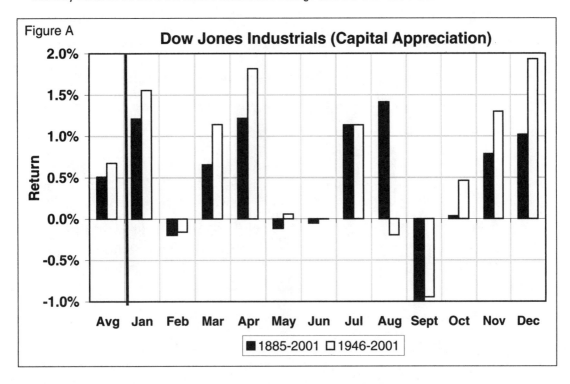

Figure A

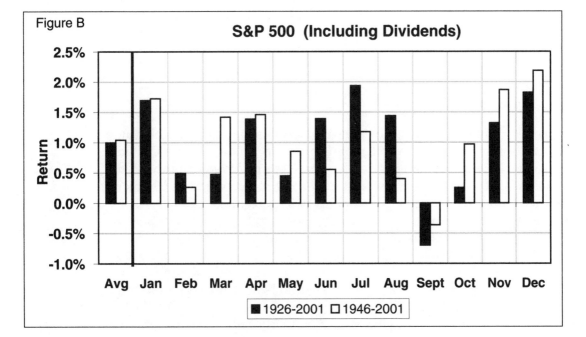

Figure B

FIGURE 18–3

International January and September Effects, 1970–2001

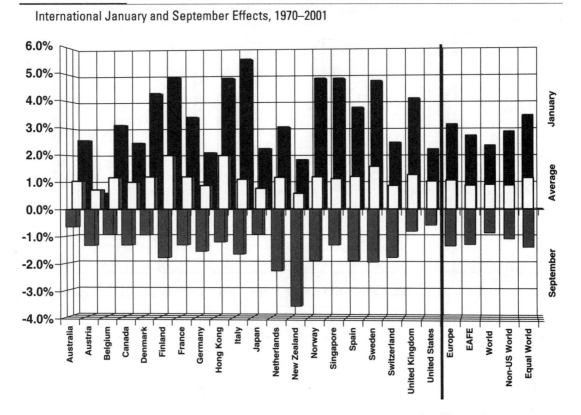

THE SEPTEMBER EFFECT

Summer months are good, but after the summer holidays, watch out! September is by far the worst month of the year and, in the United States, is the only month to have a negative return *including* reinvested dividends. September is followed closely by October, which, as Chapter 16 indicated already, has a disproportionate percentage of crashes. In contrast to the summer rally, the poor returns in September have persisted over the last century and since World War II.

Figure 18-4 shows the Dow Jones Industrial Average from 1885 through 2001, both including and excluding the month of September. One dollar invested in the Dow in 1885 would be worth $394 by the end of 2001 (dividends excluded). In contrast, one dollar invested in the Dow only in the month of September would be worth only 25 cents! On the

FIGURE 18–4

The September Effect: Dow Jones Industrial Average, 1885–2001

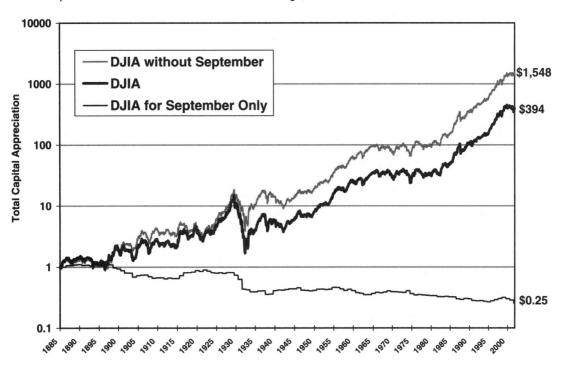

contrary, if you put your money in the stock market every month except September, it would have been worth $1,548 at the end of 2001.

The poor returns in September also prevail in the rest of the world. It is amazing that September is the only month of the year that has negative returns in the value-weighted index. September has been the worst month in 15 of the 20 countries analyzed, including the European Index, the Europe, Australasia, and Far East (EAFE) Index, and the equally weighted world index. It should be noted that these data include reinvested dividends, so, historically, stock investors would have been better off in hard cash that earns nothing rather than in stocks during the month of September. Yet this phenomenon has gone largely unnoticed, and there has been little research to date on this September effect.

Why the market experiences these monthly variations is unknown. Maybe the poor returns in late fall have nothing directly to do with economics but are related to the approach of winter and the depressing effect of rapidly shortening days. In fact, psychologists stress that sunlight is an essential ingredient to well-being. Recent research has confirmed that the New York Stock Exchange does significantly worse on cloudy days than it does on sunny days.[9] However, September is also a poor month in Australia and New Zealand, where it marks the beginning of spring and longer days.[10]

Perhaps the poor returns in September are the result of investors liquidating stocks (or holding off buying new stocks) to pay for their summer vacations. As shown below, historically, Monday has been the worst performance day of the week. For many, September is the monthly version of Monday: the time you face work after a period of leisure.

INTRAMONTH RETURNS

Although psychologists say that many silently suffer depression around the joyful season of Christmas and New Year's, stock investors believe that it is the season to be jolly. Daily price returns between Christmas and New Year's, as Table 18-2 indicates, average 10 times normal from 1885 to 2001.

Even more striking is the difference between the returns in the first half of the month compared with those in the second half.[11] Over the entire 117-year period studied, the percentage change in the Dow Jones Industrial Average during the first half of the month—which includes the last trading day of the preceding month up to and including the fourteenth day of the current month—is almost nine times the gain that occurs during the second half.[12]

Figure 18-5 shows the average percentage change in the Dow Jones Industrial Average over every calendar day of the month. It is striking that the average percentage gain on the last trading day of the month (and the thirtieth calendar day, when that is not the last trading day) and the first six calendar days is more than equal to the entire return for the month. The net change in the Dow is negative for all the other days.

---

[9]Edward M. Saunders, Jr., "Stock Prices and Wall Street Weather," *American Economic Review* 83(December 1993):1337–1345.

[10]Of course, many investors in the Australian and New Zealand market live north of the equator.

[11]R. A. Ariel, "A Monthly Effect in Stock Returns," *Journal of Financial Economics* 18(1987):161–174.

[12]The difference in the returns to the Dow stocks between the first and second halves of the month is accentuated by the inclusion of dividends. Currently, about two-thirds of the Dow stocks pay dividends in the first half of the month, which means that the difference between the first and second half returns is accentuated even more.

T A B L E   18–2

Dow Jones Industrial Average Daily Price Returns, February 1885–December 2001

	1885 - 2001	1885 - 1925	1926 - 1945	1946 - 2001
Overall Averages				
Whole Month	0.0238%	0.0192%	0.0147%	0.0316%
First Half of Month	0.0428%	0.0203%	0.0621%	0.0538%
Second Half of Month	0.0048%	0.0182%	-0.0316%	0.0088%
Last Day of Month	0.1040%	0.0875%	0.1633%	0.0903%
Days of the Week				
Monday	-0.0997%	-0.0874%	-0.2106%	-0.0689%
Tuesday	0.0403%	0.0375%	0.0473%	0.0397%
Wednesday	0.0594%	0.0280%	0.0814%	0.0742%
Thursday	0.0258%	0.0012%	0.0627%	0.0304%
Friday	0.0710%	0.0994%	0.0064%	0.0734%
With Sat	0.0699%	0.0994%	0.0064%	0.0864%
Without Sat	0.0724%			0.0724%
Saturday	0.0578%	0.0348%	0.0964%	0.0962%
Holiday Returns				
Day before Holiday				
July 4th	0.3271%	0.2118%	0.8168%	0.2366%
Christmas	0.3781%	0.4523%	0.3634%	0.3291%
New Year's	0.3292%	0.5964%	0.3931%	0.1107%
Holiday Avg	0.3448%	0.4201%	0.5244%	0.2255%
Christmas Week	0.2482%	0.3242%	0.2875%	0.1768%

The strong gains at the turn of the month are almost certainly related to the inflow of funds into the equity market that result from monthly flows of income to consumers. It is surprising, however, that these flows have been the dominant source of gains in the market over the past 117 years.

DAY-OF-THE-WEEK EFFECTS

Many people hate Mondays. After 2 days of relaxing and doing pretty much what you like, having to face work on Monday is not fun. And stock investors apparently feel the same way. Monday is by far the worst

F I G U R E   18–5

Daily Price Returns on the Dow Jones Industrial Average, 1885–2001

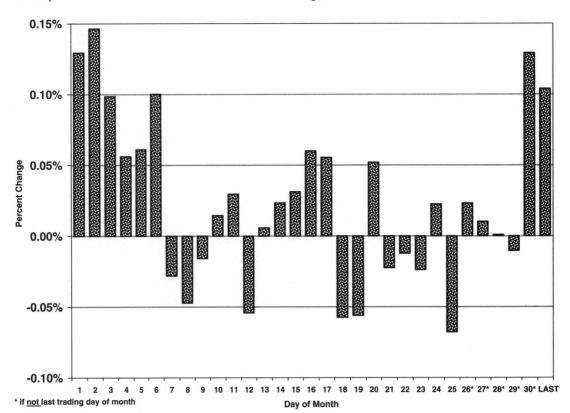

day of the week for the market and has been throughout all the time periods examined. Over the past 117 years, the returns on Monday have been decisively negative—so negative that if Monday returns were instead like Tuesday through Friday, the Dow Jones Industrial Average would have reached 40 million today.

Although investors hate Mondays, they relish Fridays. Friday is the best day of the week, yielding price returns about three times the daily average. Even when markets were open on Saturday (every month before 1946 and nonsummer months before 1953), Friday price returns were the best.

Once again, the Monday effect is not confined to U.S. equity markets. Throughout most of the world, Monday is a poor day, garnering negative returns not only in the United States but also in Canada, the United Kingdom, Germany, France, Japan, Korea, and Singapore. On the other hand, none of the major countries have negative returns on Wednesday, Thursday, or Friday. Tuesday is also a poor day for the markets, especially in Asia and Australia.[13] This might be due to the poor Monday just experienced in Western countries, since daily returns in the United States have been found to influence Asian markets the next day.

The daily patterns in returns, although conforming to the conventional popularity of the workweek, do not correspond to economic rationale. Since the return on Monday covers the 3-day period from Friday's close, you might think the return should be three times larger than that of other days, given that capital is committed for three times the length of time (and with more risk). But this is not the case.[14]

Fridays are not the only good days in the market. The market does well before virtually any holiday. Price returns before the three holidays of the Fourth of July, Christmas, and New Year's are shown in Table 18-2. They are, on average, 14 times the average daily price return. Research on behavior before other exchange holidays shows the same pattern. And, as indicated earlier, the last day of the month is a winner too.

Finally, there appears to be a diurnal pattern of stock returns. Evidence has shown that there is usually a sinking spell in the morning, especially on Monday. During lunch, the market firms, and then it pauses or declines in midafternoon before rising strongly in the last half hour of trading. This often leads the market to close at the highest level of the day.

WHAT'S AN INVESTOR TO DO?

These anomalies are an extremely tempting guide to formulating an investing strategy, but those who choose to play by them should be aware of two additional issues: risk and transactions costs. As noted earlier, these calendar-related returns do not always occur, and as investors become more aware of them, they may not occur as frequently or even at all in the future. In addition, investing in these anomalies requires the buying and selling of stock, which incurs transactions costs.

The advent of no-load mutual funds and online trading has made the cost of transacting extremely low. However, unless you are investing

---

[13]These results are taken from Hawawini and Keim, "On the Predictability of Common Stock Returns: World-Wide Evidence" in R. Jarrow et al. (1995), pp. 497–544.
[14]Dividends are fairly evenly spread during the week. They were slightly higher on Monday during the early period but higher on Friday more recently.

with tax-sheltered funds, realizing the gains from playing these anomalies can incur significant taxes. Chapter 4 demonstrated that realizing capital gains each year rather than deferring them to the future substantially lowers your total returns. Nevertheless, investors who have already decided to buy or sell but have some latitude in choosing the exact time of their transaction would be well advised to take these calendar anomalies into account.

CHAPTER 19

BEHAVIORAL FINANCE AND THE PSYCHOLOGY OF INVESTING

The rational man—like the Loch Ness monster—is sighted often, but photographed rarely.

DAVID DREMAN, 1998[1]

The market is most dangerous when it looks best; it is most inviting when it looks worst.

FRANK J. WILLIAMS, 1930[2]

This book is filled with data, figures, and charts that support a diversified, long-term outlook for stock investors. Yet advice is much easier to take in theory than to put in practice. The finance profession is increasingly aware that psychological factors can thwart rational analysis and prevent investors from achieving the best results for their portfolio. The study of these psychological factors has burgeoned into the field of *behavioral finance*.

---

[1]David Dreman, *Contrarian Investment Strategies: The Next Generation* (New York: Simon & Schuster, 1998).
[2]Frank J. Williams, *If You Must Speculate, Learn the Rules* (Burlington, VT: Freiser Press, 1930).

This chapter is written as a narrative to make it easier to understand the basic research and issues of behavioral finance. The chapter closes with an analysis of two strategies that have enhanced portfolio returns based on shifts in investor sentiment.

As you read through this narrative, connect with Dave, the individual investor in the story, who falls into psychological traps that prevent him from being an effective investor. You may notice similarities between his behavior and your own. If you do, the advice given in this chapter should relieve much of the anxiety you experience with stocks and ultimately should make investing both more enjoyable and more profitable.

THE TECHNOLOGY BOOM, 1999–2001

TIME: OCTOBER 1999

Dave: Jen, I've made some important investment decisions. Our portfolio contains nothing but these old fogy stocks like Philip Morris, Procter and Gamble, and Exxon. These stocks just aren't doing anything right now. My friends Bob and Paul at work have been making a fortune in Internet stocks. I talked with my broker, Allan, about the prospects of these stocks. He said the experts think it is the wave of the future. I'm selling a lot of our stocks that just aren't moving, and I am getting into the Internet stocks like Amazon, Yahoo!, Inktomi, and others.

Jennifer: I've heard that those stocks are very speculative. Are you sure you know what you're doing?

Dave: Allan says that we are entering a "New Economy," spurred by a communications revolution that is going to completely change the way we do business. Those stocks that we owned are "Old Economy" stocks. They had their time, but we should be investing for the future. I know these Internet stocks are volatile, and I'll watch them very carefully so we won't lose money. Trust me. I think we're finally on the right track.

TIME: MARCH 2000

Dave: Jen, have you seen our latest financial statements? We're up 60 percent since October. The Nasdaq crossed 5,000, and no one I heard believes it will stop there. The excitement about the market is spreading, and it has become *the* topic of conversation around the office.

Jen: You seem to be trading in and out of stocks a lot more than you did before. I can't follow what we own!

Dave: Information is hitting the market faster and faster. I have to continuously adjust our portfolio. Commissions are so cheap now that it pays to trade on any news affecting stocks. Trust me. We are up 60 percent in the last 6 months.

TIME: JULY 2000

Jen: Dave, look at our broker's statement. We don't hold those Internet stocks any more. Now we own Cisco, EMC, Oracle, Sun Microsystems, Nortel Networks, and JDS Uniphase. I don't know what any of these companies do. Do you?

Dave: When the Internet stocks crashed in April, I sold right before we lost all our gains. Unfortunately, we didn't make much on those stocks, but we didn't lose either.

I think we're on the right track now. Those Internet companies weren't making any money. All the new firms we now own form the backbone of the Internet, and all are profitable. Allan told me an important story: In the California gold rush of the 1850s, do you know who made the most money? Not the gold miners. Oh, a few of the first found gold, but afterwards, most found almost nothing. The real winners from the gold rush were those that sold supplies to the miners—pick axes, boots, pans, and hiking gear. The lesson is very clear: Most of the Internet companies are going to fail, but those supplying the backbone of the Internet—the routers, software, and fiber-optic cables—will be the big winners.

Jen: But I think I heard some economist say that they are way overpriced now; they're selling for hundreds of times earnings.

Dave: Yes, but look at their growth over the last 5 years—no one has ever seen this before. The economy is changing, and many of the traditional yardsticks of valuation don't apply. Trust me; I'll monitor these stocks. I got us out of those Internet stocks in time, didn't I? Don't worry.

TIME: NOVEMBER 2000

Dave (to himself): What should I do? The last few months have been dreadful. I'm down about 20 percent. Just over 2 months ago, Nortel was over 80. Now it is around 40. Sun Microsystems was 65, and now it is around 40. These prices are so cheap. I think I'll use some of my remaining cash to buy more at these lower prices. Then my stocks don't have to go up as much for me to get even.

TIME: AUGUST 2001

Jen: Dave. I've just looked at our broker's statement. We've been devastated! Almost three-quarters of our retirement money is gone. I thought you were going to monitor our investments closely. Our portfolio shows nothing but huge losses.

Dave: I know; I feel terrible. All the experts said these stocks would rebound, but they kept going down.

Jen: This has happened before. I don't understand why you do so badly. For years you watch the market closely, study all these financial reports, and seem to be very well informed, yet you seem to always make the wrong decisions. You buy near the highs and sell near the lows. You hold on to losers while selling your winners. You . . .

Dave: I know, I know. My stock investments always go wrong. I think I'm giving up on stocks and sticking with bonds.

Jen: Listen, Dave. I have talked to a few other people about your investing troubles, and I want you to go see an investment counselor. They use behavioral psychology to help troubled investors understand why they do poorly. The investment counselor even suggests ways to correct this behavior. Dave, I made you an appointment already. Please go see her.

BEHAVIORAL FINANCE

TIME: NEXT WEEK

Dave was skeptical. He thought that understanding stocks required knowledge of economics, accounting, and mathematics. Dave never heard the word *psychology* used in any of those subjects. Yet he knew that he needed help, and it couldn't hurt to check it out.

Investment counselor (IC): I have read your profile and talked to your wife extensively. You are very typical of the investors that we counsel here. I adhere to a new branch of economics called *behavioral finance*. Many of the ideas my profession explores are based on psychological concepts that have rarely before been applied to the stock market and portfolio management.

Let me give you some background. Until recently, finance was dominated by theories that assumed that investors maximized their expected *utility*, or well-being, and always acted rationally. This was an extension of the rational theory of consumer choice under certainty applied to uncertain outcomes.

In the 1970s, two psychologists, Amos Tversky and Daniel Kahneman, noted that many individuals did not behave as this theory predicted. They developed a new model—called *prospect theory*—of how individuals actually behave and make decisions when faced with uncertainty.[3] Their model established them as the pioneers of behavioral finance, and their research has been making much headway in the finance profession.

Fads, Social Dynamics, and Stock Bubbles

IC: Let us first discuss your decision to get into the Internet stocks. Think back to October 1999. Do you remember why you decided to buy those stocks?

Dave: Yes. My stocks were simply not going anywhere. My friends at work were investing in the Internet and making a lot of money. There was so much excitement about these stocks; everyone claimed that the Internet was a communications revolution that would change business forever.

IC: When everyone is excited about the market, you should be extremely cautious. Stock prices are based not just on economic values but also on psychological factors that influence the mood of the market. Yale economist Robert Shiller, one of the leaders of the behavioral finance movement, has emphasized that fads and social dynamics play a large role in the determination of asset prices.[4] Shiller showed that stock prices have been far too volatile to be explained by fluctuations in economic factors such as dividends or earnings.[5] He hypothesized that much of the extra volatility can be explained by fads and fashions that have a great impact on investor decisions.

Dave: I did have my doubts about these Internet stocks, but everyone else seemed so sure they were winners.

IC: Note how others influenced your decision, against your better judgment. Psychologists have long known how hard it is to remain separate from a crowd. This was confirmed by a social psychologist named Solomon Asch. He conducted a famous experiment where subjects were presented with four lines and asked to pick the two that were the same length. Even though the answer was obvious, when confederates of Dr. Asch presented conflicting views, the subjects often gave the incorrect answer.[6]

---

[3]Daniel Kahneman and Amos Tversky, "Prospect Theory: An Analysis of Decision Under Risk," *Econometrica* 47(2)(March 1979).
[4]Robert Shiller, "Stock Prices and Social Dynamics," *Brookings Papers on Economic Activity* (1984).
[5]Robert Shiller, "Do Stock Prices Move Too Much to Be Justified by Subsequent Movements in Dividends?" *American Economic Review* 71(3)(1981):421–436.
[6]Solomon Asch, *Social Psychology* (Englewood Cliffs, NJ: Prentice-Hall, 1952).

Follow-up experiments confirmed that it was not social pressure that led the subjects to act against their own best judgment but rather their disbelief that a large group of people could be wrong.[7]

Dave: Exactly. So many were hyping these stocks that I felt there had to be something there. If I didn't buy the Internet stocks, I thought that I was missing out.

IC: I know. The Internet and technology bubble is a perfect example of social pressures influencing stock prices. The conversations around the office, the newspaper headlines, the analysts' predictions—they all fed the craze to invest in these stocks. Psychologists call this penchant to follow the crowd the *herding instinct,* the tendency of individuals to adapt their thinking to the prevailing opinion.

The influence of social psychology in financial matters has long been recognized. In 1852, Charles Mackay's *Extraordinary Delusions and the Madness of Crowds* identified a number of financial bubbles where speculators were driven into a frenzy by the upward movement of prices: the South Sea bubble in England in 1720, the Mississippi bubble in France about the same time, and the tulip mania in Holland a century earlier.

Let me read you my favorite passage from the book. See if you can relate with this:

> We find that whole communities suddenly fix their minds upon one subject, and go mad in its pursuit; that millions of people become simultaneously impressed with one delusion and run after it. . . . Sober nations have all at once become desperate gamblers, and risked most their existence upon the turn of a piece of paper. . . . Men, it has been well said, think in herds . . . they go mad in herds, while they only recover their senses slowly and one by one.[8]

Dave (shaking his head): This happens again and again through history. Even though others were pointing to those very same excesses last year, I was convinced that "this time is different."

IC: As were many others. The propensity of investors to follow the crowd is a permanent fixture of financial history. And following the crowd is not always irrational, although it may lead to some very bad results.

---

[7]Morton Deutsch and Harold B. Gerard. "A Study of Normative and Informational Social Influences upon Individual Judgment," *Journal of Abnormal and Social Psychology* 51(1955):629–636.
[8]Charles Mackay, *Memoirs of Extraordinary Popular Delusions and the Madness of Crowd* (London: Bentley, 1841).

Dave, have you ever been in a new town and found yourself choosing between two restaurants that are close to one another? One perfectly rational way of deciding where to eat is to see which restaurant is busier, since there's a good chance that at least some of those people have tried both restaurants and have chosen to eat at the better one. But when you eat at the busier restaurant, you are increasing the chance that the next diner, using the same reasoning, will also eat there, and so on. Eventually, everybody will be eating at that one restaurant even though the other one could be much better.

Economists call this decision-making process an *information cascade* and believe that it happens often in financial markets.[9] For example, when one company bids for another, often other suitors will join in. When an initial public offering (IPO) gets a strong following, other investors join in bidding. Individuals have a feeling that "someone knows something" and that they shouldn't miss out. Sometimes that's right, but very often that is wrong.

Excessive Trading, Overconfidence, and the Representative Bias

IC: Dave, let me shift the subject. From examining your trading records, I see that you were an extremely active trader.

Dave: I had to be. Information on the industry was changing so quickly, I felt I had to reposition myself constantly to reflect the new information.

IC: Let me tell you something. Trading does nothing for you but cause extra anxiety and losses. A couple of economists published an article entitled "Trading Is Hazardous to Your Wealth"—*and*, I may add, to your *health*.[10] Examining the records of tens of thousands of traders, they showed that the returns of the heaviest traders were 7.1 percent below those who traded infrequently.

Dave: You're right. I think trading has hurt my returns. I thought that I was one step ahead of the other guy, but I guess I wasn't.

IC: It is extraordinarily difficult to be a successful trader. Even bright people who devote their entire energies to trading stocks rarely make superior returns.

---

[9]Robert Shiller, "Conversation, Information, and Herd Behavior," *American Economic Review* 85(2) (1995):181–185; S. D. Bikhchandani, David Hirshleifer, and Ivo Welch, "A Theory of Fashion, Social Custom and Cultural Change," *Journal of Political Economy* 81(1992):637–654; and Abhijit V. Banjeree, "A Simple Model of Herd Behavior," *Quarterly Journal of Economics* 107(3)(1992):797–817.

[10]Brad Barber and Terrance Odean, "Trading Is Hazardous to Your Wealth: The Common Stock Investment Performance of Individual Investors," *The Journal of Finance* 55(2000):773–806.

The problem is that most people are simply *overconfident* in their own abilities. To put it another way, research has confirmed that the average individual—be he or she a student, a trader, a driver, or whatever—believes that he or she is better than average, which of course is statistically impossible.[11]

Dave: What causes this overconfidence?

IC: Overconfidence comes from several sources. First, there is what we call a *self-attribution bias* that causes one to take credit for a favorable turn of events when credit is not due.[12] Remember in March 2000 bragging to your wife about how smart you were to have bought those Internet stocks?

Dave: Yes. Boy, was I wrong!

IC: Your early success fed your overconfidence.[13] You and your friends attributed your stock gains to skillful investing, even though those outcomes were frequently the result of chance.

Another source of overconfidence comes from the tendency to see too many parallels between events that seem the same but are remarkably different.[14] This is called the *representative bias*. This bias actually arises because of the human learning process. When we see something that looks familiar, we form a representative heuristic to help us learn. However, the parallels we see are often not valid, and our conclusions are misguided.

Dave: The investment newsletters I get say that every time that such and such an event occurred in the past, the market has moved in a certain direction, implying that it is bound to do so again. But when I try to use that advice, it never works.

IC: Conventional finance economists have been warning for years about finding patterns in the data when in fact there are none. Searching past

---

[11]B. Fischhoff, P. Slovic, and S. Lichtenstein, "Knowing with Uncertainty: The Appropriateness of Extreme Confidence," *Journal of Experimental Psychology: Human Perception and Performance* 3(1977): 552–564.

[12]A. H. Hastorf, D. J. Schneider, and J. Polefka, *Person Perception* (Reading, MA: Addison-Wesley, 1970).

[13]For reference to a model that incorporates success as a source of overconfidence, see Simon Gervais and Terrance Odean, "Learning to Be Overconfident," *Review of Financial Studies* 14(1)(2001): 1–27.

[14]For references to models that incorporate the representative heuristic as a source of overconfidence, see either N. Barberis, A. Shleifer, and R. Vishny, "A Model of Investor Sentiment," NBER Working Paper 5926, Cambridge, MA, 1997; Kent Daniel, David Hirshleifer, and Avandihar Subrahmanyam, "Investor Psychology and Security Market Under- and Overreactions," *Journal of Finance* 53(6)(1998):1839–1886.

data for patterns is called *data mining,* and it is easier than ever to do with inexpensive computer programs.[15] Throw in a load of variables to explain stock price movements, and you are sure to find some spectacular fits—like over the past 100 years stocks have risen on every third Thursday of the month when the moon is full.

Representative bias has been responsible for some spectacularly wrong moves in the stock market, even when the situations seem remarkably similar. When World War I broke out in July 1914, the United States thought that it was such a financial calamity that the New York Stock Exchange closed the market for 5 months. Wrong! The United States became the arms merchant for Europe; business boomed, and 1915 was one of the single best years in stock market history.

When Germany invaded Poland in September 1939, investors looked at the behavior of the market in World War I. They bought stocks like mad and sent the market up by more than 7 percent on the next day's trading! However, this was wrong again. Franklin Roosevelt was determined not to let the corporations prosper from World War II as they did from World War I. After a few more up days, the stock market headed into a severe bear market, and it was not until nearly 6 years later that the market returned to its September 1939 level. Clearly, representative bias was the culprit for this error, and the two events were not as similar as people thought.

Psychologically, human beings are not designed to accept all the randomness that is out there. It is very discomforting for many to learn that most movements in the market are random and do not have any identifiable cause or reason. Individuals possess this deep psychological need to know *why* something happens. This is where the reporters and so-called experts come in. They are more than happy to fill the holes in our knowledge with explanations that are wrong more often than not.

Dave: I can relate personally to this representative bias. I remember that before I bought the technology stocks in July of 2000, my broker compared these companies to the suppliers providing the gear for the gold rushers of the 1850s. It seemed like an insightful comparison at the time, but in fact the situations were very different. It is interesting that my broker, who is supposed to be the expert, is subject to the same overconfidence that I am.

---

[15]For a reference to data mining, see Andrew Lo and Craig MacKinlay, "Data-Snooping Biases in Tests of Financial Asset Pricing Models," *Review of Financial Studies* 3(3)(Fall 1999):431–467.

IC: There is actually evidence that experts are even more subject to over-confidence than the layperson. These so-called experts have been trained to analyze the world in a particular way, and selling their advice depends on finding supporting, not contradictory evidence.[16]

Recall the failure of analysts to change their earnings forecasts of the technology sector despite being bombarded with bad news that suggested that something was seriously wrong with their view of the whole industry. After being fed great news by the corporations for years, supported by 20 to 30 percent earnings growth rates, they had no idea how to handle downbeat news, so most just ignored it.

The propensity to shut out bad news was even more pronounced among analysts in the Internet sector. Many were so convinced that these stocks were the wave of the future that despite the flood of ghastly news, many only downgraded these stocks *after* they had fallen 80 or 90 percent!

The predisposition to disregard news that does not correspond to your worldview arises from what psychologists call *cognitive dissonance.* Cognitive dissonance is the discomfort we encounter when we confront evidence that conflicts with our view or suggests that our abilities or actions are not as a good as we thought. We all display a natural tendency to minimize this discomfort, which makes it difficult for us to recognize our overconfidence.

Prospect Theory, Loss Aversion, and Holding onto Losing Trades

Dave: I see. Can we talk about individual stocks? Why do I end up holding so many losers in my portfolio?

IC: Remember I said before that Kahneman and Tversky kicked off behavioral finance with prospect theory? A key finding of theirs was that individuals form a *reference point* from which they judge their performance. They found that from that reference point individuals are much more upset about losing a given amount of money than they are from gaining the same amount. They called this behavior *loss aversion* and suggested that the decision to hold or sell an investment will be dramatically influenced by whether your stock has gone up or down, in other words, whether you have a gain or a loss.

Dave: One step at a time. What is this reference point you talk about?

IC: When you buy a stock, how do you track its performance?

---

[16]Dreman, *Contrarian Investment Strategies: The Next Generation* (1998).

Dave: I calculate how much the stock has gone up or down since I bought it.

IC: Exactly. Often the reference point is the purchase price that investors pay for the stock. Investors become fixated on this reference point to the exclusion of any other information. Richard Thaler from the University of Chicago, who has done seminal work on investor behavior, refers to this as *mental accounting.*[17]

When you buy a stock, you open a mental account with the purchase price as the reference point. Similarly, when you buy a group of stocks together, you will either think of the stocks individually or you may aggregate the accounts together.[18] Whether your stocks are showing a gain or a loss will influence your decision to hold or sell the stock. Moreover, in accounts with multiple losses, you are likely to aggregate individual losses together because thinking about one big loss is an easier pill for you to swallow than thinking of many smaller losses. Avoiding the realization of losses becomes the primary goal of many investors.

Dave: You're right. The thought of realizing the losses on my technology stocks petrified me.

IC: That is a completely natural reaction. Your pride is one of the main reasons why you avoided selling at a loss. Every investment involves an emotional as well as a financial commitment that makes it hard to evaluate objectively. You felt good that you sold out of your Internet stocks with a small gain, but the networking stocks you subsequently bought never showed a gain. Even as prospects dimmed, not only did you hang onto those stocks, but you also bought more, hoping against hope that they would recover.

Prospect theory predicts that many investors will do as you did—increase your position, and consequently your risk, in an attempt to get even.[19]

Dave: I thought that buying more stock would increase my chances of recouping my losses.

IC: You and millions of other investors. In 1982, Leroy Gross wrote a manual for stockbrokers and called this phenomenon the "get-even-itis"

---

[17]Richard H. Thaler, "Mental Accounting and Consumer Choice," *Marketing Science* 4(3)(Summer 1985):199–214.

[18]Richard H. Thaler, "Mental Accounting Matters," *Journal of Behavioral Decision Making* 12(1999): 183–206.

[19]Hersh Shefrin and Meir Statman, "The Disposition to Sell Winners Too Early and Ride Losers Too Long: Theory and Evidence," *Journal of Finance* 40(3)(1985):777–792.

disease.[20] He claimed "get-even-itis" probably has caused more destruction to portfolios than any other mistake.

It is hard for us to admit that we have made a bad investment, and it is even harder for us to admit that mistake to others. To be a successful investor, however, you have no choice but to do so. Decisions on your portfolio must be made on a *forward-looking* basis. What has happened in the past cannot be changed. It is a "sunk cost," as economists say. When prospects do not look good, sell the stock whether or not you have a loss.

Dave: I thought the stocks were cheap when I bought more shares. Many were down 50 percent or more from their highs.

IC: Cheap relative to what? Cheap relative to their past price or their future prospects? You thought that a price of 40 for a stock that had been 80 made the stock cheap, yet you never considered the fact that maybe 40 was still too high. This demonstrates another one of Kahneman and Tversky's behavioral findings: *anchoring,* or the tendency of people facing complex decisions to use an anchor, or a suggested number, to form their judgment.[21] Figuring out the correct stock price is such a complex task that it is natural to use the recently remembered stock price as an anchor and then judge the current price a bargain.

Dave: If I follow your advice and sell my losers whenever prospects are dim, I'm going to register a lot more losses on my trades.

IC: Good! Most investors do exactly the opposite and realize poor returns. Research has shown that investors sell stocks for a gain 50 percent more frequently than they sell stocks for a loss.[22] This means that stocks that are above their purchase price are 50 percent more likely to be sold than stocks that are in the red. Traders do this even though it is a horrible strategy from the point of view of paying taxes.

Let me tell you of one short-term trader I successfully counseled. He showed me that 80 percent of his trades made money, but he was down overall because he lost so much money on his losing trades that they drowned out his winners.

After I counseled him, he became a successful trader. Now he says that only one-third of his trades make money but that overall he is way ahead. When things do not work out as he planned, he gets rid of losing trades quickly while holding onto his winners. There is an old adage on

[20]Leroy Gross, *The Art of Selling Intangibles* (New York: New York Institute of Finance, 1982).

[21]Amos Tversky and Daniel Kahneman, "Judgment under Uncertainty: Heuristics and Biases," *Science* 185(1974):1124–1131.

[22]Terrance Odean, "Are Investors Reluctant to Realize Their Losses?" *Journal of Finance* 53(5)(October 1998):1786.

Wall Street that sums up successful trading: "Cut your losers short, and let your winners ride."

Rules to Avoid Behavioral Traps

Dave: I don't feel secure enough to trade again soon. I just want to master investing. How can one get over these behavioral traps and be a successful long-term investor?

IC: Dave, I'm glad you are not trading, since trading is right for only a very small fraction of my clients.

Researchers have found that you must set up rules and incentives to keep your investments on track—this is called *precommitment*.[23] Set an asset allocation rule and then stick to it. If you have enough knowledge, you can do this alone or else with an investment advisor. Do not try to second-guess your rule. Remember that the basic factors generating returns change far less than we think as we watch the day-to-day ups and downs of the market. A disciplined investment strategy is almost always a winning strategy.

Furthermore, you need to get rid of the temptations to trade stocks. One way to do this is by closing all your trading and online accounts. If you have to pay higher commissions, you are less likely to trade more frequently. Moreover, if you find a broker or advisor that charges a fee as a percentage of assets instead of a commission on stock trades, that broker will not have an incentive to suggest unnecessary transactions.

If you do buy stocks for a short-term trade, set a stop-loss order to minimize your losses. You do not want to let your losses mount, rationalizing that the stock will eventually come back. If you are tempted to sell a stock that has a gain, think of the taxes you will have to pay, and if you are reluctant to sell a stock that has a loss, think of the tax savings you will realize. Finally, do not tell your friends about your trades. Living up to their expectations will make you even more reluctant to take a loss and admit that you were wrong.

Dave: I'll have to admit that I sometimes enjoyed trading.

IC: If you really enjoy trading, establish a rule that every year you are going to establish a small trading account that is completely separate from the rest of your portfolio. All brokerage costs and all taxes must be paid from this account. Consider the money you put into the account

---

[23]Hersh Shefrin and Richard H. Thaler, "An Economic Theory of Self-Control," *Journal of Political Economy* 89(21)(1981):392–406.

lost, because most likely it will wither to nothing, being consumed by transactions costs and trading losses. And you should never consider exceeding the rigid limit you place on how much money you put into that account.

If that does not work, or if you feel nervous about the market and have a compulsion to trade, call me—I can help. And according to an article in *US News and World Report*, there are some reformed traders who are establishing Traders' Anonymous (TA) programs designed to help people who cannot resist the temptations of trading too frequently.[24] Maybe you should look into one of those.

Myopic Loss Aversion, Portfolio Monitoring, and the Equity Risk Premium

Dave: Because of how badly I was doing in the market, I even considered giving up on stocks and sticking with bonds, although I know that in the long run that is a very bad idea. How often do you suggest that I monitor my stock portfolio?

IC: Important question. If you buy stocks, it is very likely that at some time shortly after your purchase, the portfolio value will drop below the price you paid for it. And we already talked about how your loss aversion makes this decline very disturbing to you. However, since the long-term trend in stocks is upward, if you monitor stocks less frequently, the probability that your portfolio will show a loss decreases.

Two economists tested whether the monitoring interval affected the choice among assets.[25] They conducted a "learning experiment" in which they allowed individuals to see the returns on two unidentified assets. One group was shown the yearly returns on stocks and long-term bonds, and another group was given the returns on the same assets but over minimum periods of 5, 10, and 20 years. The subjects were then asked to pick an allocation between stocks and bonds.

The group that saw yearly returns invested a much smaller fraction in stocks than the group that saw returns grouped by longer intervals. This tendency to base decisions on the short-term fluctuations in the market has been referred to as *myopic loss aversion*. Since over longer pe-

---

[24]See Paul Sloan, "Can't Stop Checking Your Stock Quotes," *US News and World Report,* July 10, 2000.
[25]Shlomo Bernartzi and Richard H. Thaler, "Myopic Loss Aversion and the Equity Premium Puzzle," *Quarterly Journal of Economics* (1995):73–91.

riods the probability of stocks showing a loss is smaller, investors influenced by loss aversion would be more likely to hold stocks if they monitored them infrequently.

Dave: That's so true. When I look at stocks in the very short run, they seem so risky that I wonder why anyone holds them. Over the long run, however, the superior performance of equities is so overwhelming that I wonder why anyone doesn't hold only stocks!

IC: Exactly. Bernartzi and Thaler claim that myopic loss aversion is the key to solving the *equity premium puzzle*.[26] For years, economists have been trying to figure out why stocks have returned so much more than fixed-income investments. Studies show that over periods of 20 years or more, a diversified portfolio of equities not only offers higher after-inflation returns but is actually safer than government bonds. However, because investors concentrate on too short an investment horizon, stocks seem risky, and investors must be enticed to hold stocks with a fat premium. If investors evaluated their portfolios less frequently, the equity premium would fall dramatically.

Since 1926, the margin by which stocks have outperformed long-term bonds is 4.8 percent, and it is 6.2 percent against short-term bonds. Bernartzi and Thaler have shown that these premia are consistent with myopic loss aversion and yearly monitoring of returns. However, they also showed that if the evaluation interval rose to 10 years, the equity premium need only be 2 percent to entice investors into stocks. With an evaluation period of 20 years, the premium falls to only 1.4 percent, and it would be close to 1 percent if the evaluation period were 30 years.

Dave: Are you saying that perhaps I should not look at my stocks too frequently?

IC: You can look at them all you want, but do not alter your long-term strategy! Remember to set up rules and incentives. Commit to a long-run portfolio allocation, and do not alter it unless there is significant evidence that a certain sector becomes greatly overpriced relative to its fundamentals. A warning sign is when any sector achieves a 30 percent or greater weight in the Standard & Poor's (S&P) 500 Index. Oil did in 1980 and technology in 2000. Subsequent returns to both sectors were very poor.

---

[26]See Chapter 7 for a statement of the equity premium puzzle.

Contrarian Investing and Investor Sentiment: Two Strategies to Enhance Portfolio Returns

Dave: If all these behaviors are so destructive to people's portfolios and are widespread, is it possible for an investor to take advantage of them and earn superior returns?

IC: For longer-term investors, standing apart from the crowd might be quite profitable.

Such an investor is said to be a *contrarian*, or one who dissents from the prevailing opinion. Contrarian strategy was first put forth by Humphrey B. Neill in a pamphlet called "It Pays to Be Contrary," first circulated in 1951 and later turned into a book entitled *The Art of Contrary Thinking*. In it Neill declared, "When everyone thinks alike, everyone is likely to be wrong."[27]

Some contrarian approaches focus on fundamentals, such as earnings, prices, or dividends, and others are based on more psychologically driven indicators such as investor sentiment. The underlying idea is that most investors are unduly optimistic when stock prices are high and unduly pessimistic when they are low.

This is not a new concept either. The great investor Benjamin Graham stated nearly 65 years ago, ". . . the psychology of the speculator militates strongly against his success. For by relation of cause and effect, he is most optimistic when prices are high and most despondent when they are at bottom."[28]

Dave: But how do I know when the market is too pessimistic and too optimistic? Is that not subjective?

IC: Not entirely. Investors' Intelligence, a firm based in New Rochelle, New York, has published one of the long-standing indicators of investment sentiment. Over the past 40 years, President Michael Burke and his associates have evaluated scores of market newsletters, determining whether each letter is bullish, bearish, or neutral about the future direction of stocks.

From Investors' Intelligence data, I computed an index of investor sentiment by finding the ratio of bullish newsletters to bullish plus bearish newsletters (omitting the neutral category). I then measured the subsequent returns on stocks.

The results, shown in Table 19-1, indicate a strong predictive content to the sentiment index. Whenever the index of investor sentiment is

---

[27]Humphrey B. Neill, *The Art of Contrary Thinking* (Caldwell, ID: Caxton Printers, 1954), p. 1.
[28]Benjamin Graham and David Dodd, *Security Analysis* (New York: McGraw-Hill, 1934), p. 12.

Investor Confidence and Subsequent Dow Price Returns, Sentiment = BULL/(BULL + BEAR)
BULL and BEAR from Investors' Intelligence, Inc., New Rochelle, NY

1970-2001		Annualized Returns Subsequent to Sentiment Readings (January 2, 1970 - Jan 18, 2002)			
Sentiment	Frequency	Three Month	Six Month	Nine Month	Twelve Month
0.2 - 0.3	1.32%	18.52%	15.40%	22.79%	20.74%
0.3 - 0.4	9.56%	12.23%	13.87%	16.54%	15.81%
0.4 - 0.5	17.33%	19.74%	15.06%	13.25%	13.71%
0.5 - 0.6	28.57%	15.72%	13.63%	11.62%	10.70%
0.6 - 0.7	25.46%	11.78%	8.63%	8.07%	7.54%
0.7 - 0.8	12.49%	11.76%	7.30%	7.45%	7.21%
0.8 - 0.9	4.54%	-0.40%	0.31%	-2.85%	-1.51%
0.9 - 1.0	0.72%	-1.65%	-4.78%	-9.98%	-10.94%
Overall	100.00%	13.78%	11.42%	10.57%	10.19%

1970s		Annualized Returns Subsequent to Sentiment Readings			
Sentiment	Frequency	Three Month	Six Month	Nine Month	Twelve Month
0.2 - 0.3	2.30%	14.36%	3.49%	16.58%	12.96%
0.3 - 0.4	11.88%	2.12%	8.96%	15.14%	11.81%
0.4 - 0.5	16.28%	0.93%	0.92%	-0.35%	1.66%
0.5 - 0.6	20.50%	11.04%	7.25%	3.22%	3.55%
0.6 - 0.7	16.67%	8.97%	6.21%	3.12%	3.09%
0.7 - 0.8	20.31%	12.66%	4.00%	3.01%	2.36%
0.8 - 0.9	9.77%	-7.17%	-6.19%	-5.46%	-6.84%
0.9 - 1.0	2.30%	-1.65%	-4.78%	-9.98%	-10.94%
Overall	100.00%	6.32%	3.91%	3.15%	2.77%

1980s		Annualized Returns Subsequent to Sentiment Readings			
Sentiment	Frequency	Three Month	Six Month	Nine Month	Twelve Month
0.2 - 0.3	1.92%	23.51%	29.70%	30.24%	30.08%
0.3 - 0.4	11.49%	19.11%	16.35%	17.15%	16.72%
0.4 - 0.5	22.41%	23.06%	20.35%	18.52%	18.15%
0.5 - 0.6	20.69%	19.38%	17.67%	13.02%	9.94%
0.6 - 0.7	20.31%	19.73%	11.06%	11.80%	8.85%
0.7 - 0.8	18.39%	10.13%	11.16%	12.48%	12.42%
0.8 - 0.9	4.79%	13.41%	13.56%	2.49%	9.34%
0.9 - 1.0	0.00%	NO DATA	NO DATA	NO DATA	NO DATA
Overall	100.00%	18.34%	15.61%	14.21%	13.15%

1990-2001		Annualized Returns Subsequent to Sentiment Readings			
Sentiment	Frequency	Three Month	Six Month	Nine Month	Twelve Month
.30-.35	1.59%	20.59%	17.64%	17.64%	21.87%
.35-.40	4.44%	15.98%	17.80%	17.21%	20.42%
.40-.45	6.35%	27.50%	22.34%	21.81%	23.11%
.45-.50	7.62%	39.20%	21.55%	17.80%	16.89%
.5-.55	20.48%	21.55%	18.68%	16.82%	15.80%
.55.60	21.43%	11.84%	11.85%	12.70%	12.57%
.60-.65	24.76%	9.32%	8.67%	10.14%	9.40%
.65-.70	12.22%	6.88%	7.55%	4.54%	7.32%
.70-.75	0.95%	21.73%	4.34%	6.91%	10.56%
.75-.80	0.16%	11.84%	3.30%	-1.04%	0.74%
Overall	100.00%	15.61%	13.24%	13.15%	13.46%

high, subsequent returns on the market are poor, and when the index is low, subsequent returns are above average. The index is a particularly strong predictor of market return over the next 9 to 12 months.

Dave: Has this predictive power been consistent over the 40 years that Burke has been measuring these indicators?

IC: Yes, with a few qualifications. Since 1990, the index has not predicted well over 3-month periods, but it had done very well over longer periods, especially over 9 to 12 months.

Figure 19-1 plots the sentiment indicator since January 1986. The crash of October 1987 was accompanied by investor pessimism. For the next few years, whenever the market went down, as it did in May and December 1988 and February 1990, investors feared another crash and sentiment dropped sharply. The index also fell below 50 percent during the Iraqi invasion of Kuwait, the bond market collapse of 1994, the Asian crisis in October 1997, the Long-Term Capital Management bailout of the

FIGURE 19–1

Investors' Intelligence Sentiment Indicator

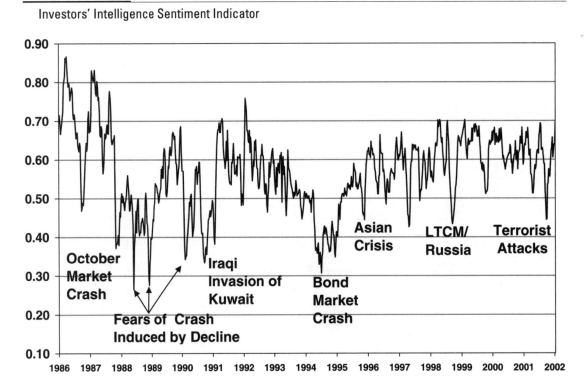

late summer of 1998, and the terrorist attacks in September 2001. These have all been excellent times to invest.

From October 1998 through September 2001, the sentiment index remained over 50 percent, the longest period of time in the 40-year history of the index. Interestingly, the sentiment index also remained above 50 percent in 2000 and the first half of 2001 despite the recession and the bear market. This was a warning that the bear market was not yet over. The index first fell below 50 percent after the terrorist attacks on New York and Washington, which proved to be another great short-term buying opportunity.

It is of note that the volatility index (VIX), the measure of implied market volatility computed from option prices, spikes upward at virtually the same time investor sentiment drops.[29] Anxiety in the market, which can be measured from the premiums on options prices, is strongly correlated with investor bearishness.

Dave: Are there other measures of investor sentiment?

IC: Richard Bernstein, director of quantitative and equity research at Merrill Lynch, developed a similar sentiment indicator based on the recommended portfolio allocations of portfolio managers. Whenever their recommended allocation to stocks falls below 50 percent, indicating a high level of pessimism about the market's prospects, subsequent returns have been high. Bernstein calls this his single most powerful quantitative market-timing barometer. Over the past 12 years, 1-year market returns have exceeded 20 percent whenever allocation percentages fall below 50 percent.

Out-of-Favor Stocks and the Dow 10 Strategy

Dave: Can you use contrarian strategy to pick individual stocks?

IC: Yes. Contrarians believe that the swings of optimism and pessimism infect individual stocks as well as the overall markets. Therefore, buying out-of-favor stocks can be a winning strategy.

Werner De Bondt and Richard Thaler examined portfolios of both past stock winners and losers to see if investors became overly optimistic or pessimistic about future returns from studying the returns of the recent past.[30] Portfolios of winning and losing stocks were analyzed

---

[29]A discussion of the VIX is found in Chapter 16. Compare Figure 19-1 with Figure 16-4.
[30]Werner De Bondt and Richard H. Thaler. "Does the Stock Market Overreact?" *Journal of Finance* 49 (3)(1985):793–805.

over 5-year intervals. Portfolios that had been winners in the past 5 years subsequently lagged the market by 10 percent, whereas the subsequent returns on the loser portfolio beat the market by 30 percent.

One of the explanations for why this strategy works relates to the representativeness heuristic we talked about before. People overly extrapolate recent trends in stock prices to predict how well a stock will perform in the future. In short, they become overly optimistic after stocks have done well and become unduly pessimistic when stocks have performed poorly.

One specific strategy that is based on out-of-favor stocks is called the "dogs of the Dow," or the *Dow 10 strategy.*

Dave: I have heard of the Dow 10. Tell me more about it.

IC: The Dow 10 system has been regarded as one of the most successful investment strategies of all time. James Glassman of the *Washington Post* claimed that John Slatter, a Cleveland investment advisor and writer, invented the Dow 10 system in the 1980s.[31] Harvey Knowles and Damon Petty popularized the strategy in their book, *The Dividend Investor,* written in 1992, as did Michael O'Higgins and John Downes in *Beating the Dow.*

The strategy calls for investors to buy the 10 highest-yielding stocks in the Dow Jones Industrial Average. Since firms reduce cash dividend payouts infrequently, stocks with a high dividend yield are often those that have fallen in price and are out of favor with investors. For this reason, the Dow 10 strategy is often called the "dogs of the Dow."

The compound annual returns from investing in the Dow 10, as compared with the Dow Jones Industrial Average and the S&P 500 Index, are shown in Table 19-2. From 1928 through 2001, the average compound return on the Dow 10 of 12.90 percent per year has exceeded the equally weighted Dow 30 (the return on all the Dow Industrial stocks) by 1.52 percent annually and the S&P 500 Index by 2.19 percent per year.

Dave: Has there been consistent performance of this strategy?

IC: Yes. The Dow 10 strategy has outperformed both the Dow 30 and the S&P 500 Index in every decade except the 1930s and the 1990s. And the only reason the Dow 10 failed to outperform the S&P 500 Index in the 1990s was because of 1999, the single worst year for the strategy, when it underperformed the S&P 500 Index by 18.34 percent.

---

[31]John R. Dorfman, "Study of Industrial Averages Finds Stocks with High Dividends Are Big Winners," *Wall Street Journal,* August 11, 1988, p. C2.

TABLE 19–2

The Dow 10 Strategy versus Standard Benchmarks: Compound Returns (Standard Deviations in Parentheses; Strategy: One Holds the 10 Highest-Yielding Dow Stocks on December 31 for the Following Year)

	Dow 10	Dow	S&P 500
1928-2001	12.90% (21.8%)	11.38% (22.4%)	10.71% (20.3%)
1940-2001	15.45% (18.1%)	12.71% (16.2%)	12.46% (16.8%)
1970-2001	16.31% (15.8%)	13.02% (16.0%)	12.39% (16.5%)
1930s	-1.04%	2.23%	-0.05%
1940s	12.62%	9.73%	9.17%
1950s	20.38%	19.24%	19.35%
1960s	9.18%	6.66%	7.81%
1970s	13.32%	6.79%	5.86%
1980s	21.78%	18.59%	17.55%
1990s	17.15%	17.45%	18.16%
2000-2001	-2.10%	-4.94%	-9.22%

Since the 1930s, the Dow 10 strategy has outperformed the Dow 30 in 43 of the 62 years. And in 11 of the 19 years the Dow 10 failed to match the Dow 30, it did so by less than 2 percentage points. In only 4 years did it underperform the Dow 30 by more than 5 percentage points, with its poorest performance by far being in 1999 when technology surged and value stocks fell out of favor. In contrast, the Dow 10 outperformed the Dow 30 by more than 10 percentage points in 9 of the 43 years.

You might think that these spectacular returns were achieved with higher risk, but that is not the case. The standard deviation of annual returns on the Dow 10 strategy actually was lower than that of the Dow 30 and only slightly more than the S&P 500 Index. And the Dow 10 was spectacular during the 1973–1974 bear market. During those 2 years when the Dow 30 was down by 26.5 percent and the S&P 500 Index was down by 37.3 percent, the Dow 10 strategy actually gained 2.9 percent!

Dave: Does picking stocks with high dividend yields work outside the Dow Industrials?

IC: Not necessarily. It works for the Dow Industrials because these stocks are a group of superior "survivor" firms. It can be shown mathematically that a contrarian strategy of choosing losers works much better with firms that are unlikely to enter financial distress. The editors at Dow Jones who select the firms that comprise the Dow Jones Industrial Average do seem to have superior stock-picking abilities.[32] The Dow Industrials have even better returns than the hard-to-beat S&P 500 Index.

Dave: How do I play the Dow 10?

IC: There are basically two ways to play the Dow 10 strategy. You can either purchase the highest-yielding Dow stocks individually or buy them through a unit investment trust, which is sold by brokerage firms. The latter is more convenient, but the fees, which sometimes amount to 2 percent or more of assets, can eat up most, if not all, of the historical advantage of the strategy.[33]

An important caveat: The Dow 10 strategy performs best in January. Therefore, it would be wise to make Dow 10 purchases before the end of the year.

Dave: Why is it that the Dow 10 performs better in January?

---

[32]The managing editor of the *Wall Street Journal* is primarily responsible for selecting the Dow stocks.
[33]There is no mutual fund for the Dow 10 because the Securities and Exchange Commission (SEC) requires more than 10 stocks in open-ended (redeemable) mutual funds. There are some mutual funds available containing the S&P 500 stocks plus the Dow 10.

IC: We talked before about how investors are averse to taking losses. That is, they have a disposition to sell their winners and hold onto their losers. December is the only month when investors realize more losses than gains from selling stocks.[34]

It is possible that investors set a rule for themselves that December is a time to evaluate their portfolios and weed out their losses for tax purposes. In other words, the investors are more willing to close their mental accounts at a loss in December, whereas the rest of the year getting even is a primary goal.

Dave: Do you think the Dow 10 strategy will do as well in the future as it has in the past?

IC: Maybe not. Whenever a strategy gets well publicized, it often does not work. The Dow 10 strategy reached its peak in 1996, after working 6 years in a row. But the strategy fell slightly behind in 1997 and 1998, before being crushed in 1999 when growth stocks soared. The strategy again beat the S&P 500 Index handily in 2000 and 2001, but that did not offset its 1999 losses.

There are billions of dollars already invested in the Dow 10 strategy, and professionals say that money is still flowing in. The flow of money could push the prices of these stocks up and significantly erode the advantage of the Dow 10 or similar strategies in the future. Remember that historical returns (as well as historical risks) can be altered as investors attempt to take advantage of them.

Dave: There has been so much to absorb from today's session. It seems like I fell into almost all these behavioral traps. The comforting news is that I am not alone and that your counseling has helped other investors.

IC: Not only have they been helped, but they also have prospered. For many people, investment success requires a much deeper knowledge of themselves than success at their jobs or even in personal relationships. There is much truth to the old Wall Street adage, "The stock market is a very expensive place to find out who you are."

---

[34]Odean, *Journal of Finance* (1998).

PART 5

BUILDING WEALTH
THROUGH STOCKS

CHAPTER 20

FUND PERFORMANCE, INDEXING, AND BEATING THE MARKET

I have little confidence even in the ability of analysts, let alone un-trained investors, to select common stocks that will give better than average results. Consequently, I feel that the standard portfolio should be to duplicate, more or less, the DJIA.

BENJAMIN GRAHAM[1]

How can institutional investors hope to outperform the market . . . when, in effect, they are the market? CHARLES D. ELLIS[2]

There is an old story on Wall Street. Two managers of large equity funds go camping in a national park. After setting up camp, the first manager mentions to the other that he overheard the park ranger warning that black bears had been seen around this campsite. The second manager smiles and says, "I'm not worried; I'm a pretty fast runner." The first manager shakes his head and says, "You can't outrun black bears;

---

[1]Benjamin Graham, *The Memoirs of the Dean of Wall Street* (New York: McGraw-Hill, 1996), p. 273.
[2]Charles D. Ellis, "The Loser's Game," *Financial Analysis Journal* (July–August 1975).

they've been known to sprint over 25 miles an hour to capture their prey!" The second manager responds, "Of course I know that I can't outrun the bear. The only thing that's important is that I can outrun you!"

In the competitive world of money management, performance is measured not by absolute return but by the return relative to some benchmark. These benchmarks include the Standard and Poor's (S&P) 500 Stock Index, the Wilshire 5000 Index, the Russell indexes, and the latest "style" indexes popular on Wall Street. However, there is a crucially important difference between investing and virtually any other activity. Most of us have no chance of being as good as the average in any pursuit that others practice for hours to hone their skills. Anyone, however, can be as good as the average investor in the stock market with no practice at all.

The basis for this surprising statement is a very simple fact: Since the sum of each investor's holdings must be equal to the market, the performance of the whole market must, by definition, be the *average* performance of each and every investor. Therefore, for each investor's dollar that outperforms the market, there must be another investor's dollar that underperforms the market. By just matching the performance of the market, you are guaranteed to do no worse than average.

How do you match the performance of the market? Until recently, this goal would have been very difficult for the average investor to achieve. No one holds shares in each of the nearly 10,000 firms listed on U.S. exchanges. Over the past decade, however, index mutual funds and exchange-traded funds (ETFs) have skyrocketed in popularity by matching the performance of a broad stock index. Now the average investor can match the performance of a wide variety of broad-based market indexes with very low costs and a very modest investment.

PERFORMANCE OF EQUITY MUTUAL FUNDS

Many people claim that striving for average market performance is not the best strategy. If there are enough poorly informed traders who consistently underperform the market, then it might be possible, by researching firms or finding professionals who actively manage funds, to outperform the market.

Unfortunately, the past record of the vast majority of such actively managed funds does not support this contention. Table 20-1 shows that from January 1971 through October 2001, the average equity mutual

T A B L E 20–1

Equity Mutual Funds and Benchmark Returns: Annual Compound Returns (Excluding Sales and Redemption Fees), January 1971–October 2001 (Standard Deviation in Parentheses)

	All Funds	"Survivor" Funds	Wilshire 5000	S&P 500	Small Stocks	All Funds Minus Wilshire 5000	"Survivor" Funds Minus Wilshire 5000
1971-2001	10.72% (16.9%)	11.80% (16.8%)	12.09% (17.6%)	12.36% (17.1%)	13.93% (22.8%)	-1.37%	-0.29%
1975-1983	18.83% (12.9%)	19.97% (13.1%)	17.94% (15.0%)	15.74% (15.5%)	35.32% (14.3%)	0.89%	2.03%
1984-2001	11.47% (15.3%)	12.13% (14.8%)	13.63% (16.2%)	14.82% (15.8%)	10.10% (18.2%)	-2.15%	-1.50%

fund returned 10.72 percent annually, 1.37 percentage points behind the Wilshire 5000 and 1.64 percentage points behind the S&P 500 Index.[3]

The long-term returns on mutual funds are difficult to measure because of the *survivorship bias* that is inherent in the data. This survivorship bias exists because poorly performing funds are often terminated, leaving only the most successful ones with long-term track records. This imparts an upward bias to the indexes of long-term fund returns. Table 20-1 shows that the survivor funds did return 1.08 percentage points more than all funds, yet even these underperformed the market averages.

The average mutual fund did outperform the Wilshire 5000 and the S&P 500 Index during the 1975–1983 period when small stocks returned a spectacular 35.32 percent per year. Equity mutual funds generally do well when small stocks outperform large stocks because many money managers seek to outperform the averages by buying middle- and small-sized firms. Since 1983, when small stocks have done poorly relative to large stocks, the performance of the average mutual fund has fallen more than 2 percentage points per year behind the Wilshire 5000 and 3 percentage points behind the S&P 500.

Figure 20-1 displays the percentage of general equity funds that have outperformed the Wilshire 5000 and the S&P 500 Index. During

---

[3]Fund data provided by the Vanguard Group and Lipper Analytical Services. See John C. Bogle, *Bogle on Mutual Funds* (Burr Ridge, IL: Irwin Professional Publishing, 1994), for a description of these data.

FIGURE 20–1

Yearly Percentage of General Equity Funds That Outperform the S&P 500 and the Wilshire 5000 (Excluding Sales and Redemption Fees)

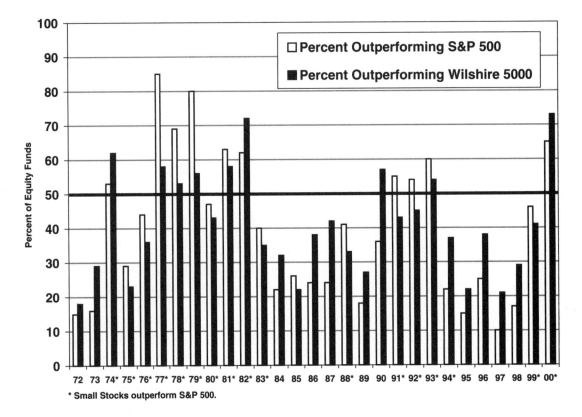

* Small Stocks outperform S&P 500.

this 29-year period, there were only 9 years when more mutual funds beat the Wilshire 5000 than fell short. All but one of these years occurred during a period when small stocks outperformed large stocks. Since 1982, there have been only 3 years—1990, 1993, and 2000—when the average equity mutual fund outperformed the market.[4]

The underperformance of mutual funds did not begin in the 1970s. In 1970, Becker Securities Corporation startled Wall Street by compiling the track record of managers of corporate pension funds. Becker showed that the median performance of these managers lagged behind the S&P

---

[4]As poor as the data make mutual funds look, they actually overstate the performance of the average equity fund. These mutual fund returns ignore the sales and redemption fees (front- and back-end loads) that many funds impose. Therefore, most mutual fund returns are even lower than these results indicate.

500 by 1 percentage point and that only one-quarter of them was able to outperform the market.[5] This study followed on the heels of academic articles, particularly by William Sharpe and Michael Jensen, that also confirmed the underperformance of equity mutual funds.[6]

Figure 20-2a displays the distribution of the difference between the returns of 171 mutual funds that have survived since January 1971 and the Wilshire 5000, whereas Figure 20-2b does the same for the period since January 1984, which excludes the period from 1975 to 1983 that is so favorable to small stocks.[7] Also included in Figure 20-2 is the theoretical distribution of fund returns assuming that the average return would be the same as the Wilshire 5000.[8]

Only 75, or less than 44 percent, of the 171 funds that have survived over the past 29 years have been able to outperform the Wilshire 5000. Only 19, or exactly 1 in 9 of these funds, have been able to outperform the market by more than 1 percent per year, whereas only 12 of the 171, or 7 percent, have bettered the market by at least 2 percent.[9] This contrasts with the 37 and 25 percent one would expect on the basis of random performance to outperform the benchmark by these magnitudes. In contrast, more than 63 percent of the funds lagged the market by 1 percent or more, and 75, or about 44 percent, lagged the market by more than 2 percent.

In the period from 1984 through October 2001, the performance of mutual funds is markedly worse. This is so because during this period the S&P 500 Index outperformed mid- and small-cap stocks. As shown in Figure 20-2b, only 39 of the 276 surviving mutual funds outperformed the Wilshire 5000 during this period, whereas almost half the funds lagged the market by at least 2 percent per year.

Despite the generally poor performance of equity mutual funds, there are some real winners. The most outstanding mutual fund performance over the entire period is that of Fidelity's Magellan Fund, whose 18.3 percent annual return from 1971 through October 2001 beat the market by over 6 percent per year. The probability that this perform-

[5] Burton Malkiel, *A Random Walk Down Wall Street* (New York: McGraw-Hill, 1990), p. 362.

[6] For an excellent review of the studies on mutual funds, see Richard A. Ippolito, "On Studies of Mutual Fund Performance, 1962–1991," *Financial Analysts Journal* (January–February 1993):42–50.

[7] Lipper Analytical Services provided the data on survivor funds.

[8] The expected returns are assumed to be identical to those of the Wilshire 5000 Index. The average annual standard deviation of the Wilshire 5000 Index during this period (measured with annual data) is 16.7 percent. The standard deviation of the average mutual fund is slightly higher, assumed to be 18.1 percent, with a correlation coefficient of 0.87.

[9] These performance ratings, as noted earlier, do not include the load, or front-end (and sometimes back-end) fees and commissions.

F I G U R E   20–2

Performance of Surviving Mutual Funds Relative to the Wilshire 5000

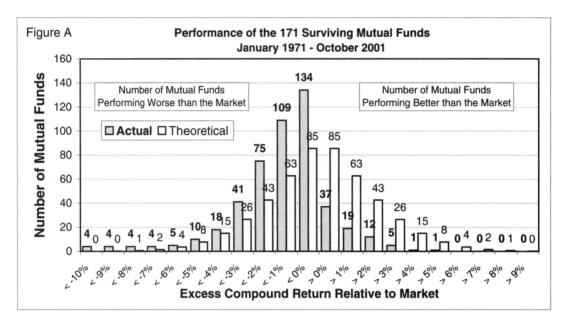

Figure A

Performance of the 171 Surviving Mutual Funds
January 1971 - October 2001

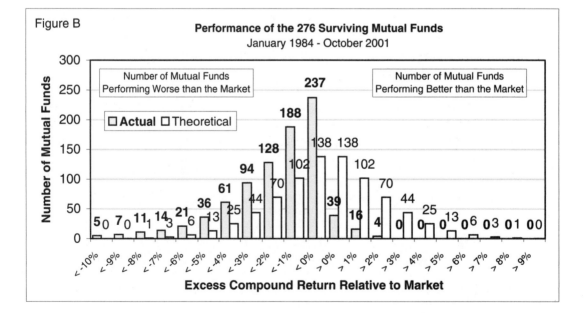

Figure B

Performance of the 276 Surviving Mutual Funds
January 1984 - October 2001

ance was based on luck alone is about 1 in 50. However, this means that out of the 171 mutual funds that survived the period, there is a very good chance that 3 would have performed as well as the Magellan Fund by chance alone.

Yet luck could not explain Magellan's performance from 1977 through 1990. During that period, the legendary stock picker, Peter Lynch, ran the Magellan Fund and outperformed the market by an incredible 13 percent per year. Magellan took somewhat greater risks in achieving this return,[10] but the probability that Magellan would outperform the Wilshire 5000 by this margin over that 14-year period by luck alone is only 1 in 500,000!

FINDING SKILLED MONEY MANAGERS

It is easy to determine that Magellan's performance during the Lynch years was due to his skill in picking stocks. For more mortal portfolio managers, however, it is extremely difficult to determine with any degree of confidence that the superior returns of money managers are due to skill or luck. Table 20-2 computes the probability that managers with better than average stock-picking ability will outperform the market.[11]

The results are surprising. Even if money managers choose stocks that have an expected return of 1 percent per year better than the market, there is less than a 55 percent probability that they will exceed the average market return after 10 years, and after 30 years, the probability rises to only 72 percent. If managers pick stocks that will outperform the market by 2 percent per year, there is still only a 75 percent chance that they will outperform the market after 10 years. This means that there is a 1 in 4 chance that they will still fall short of the average market performance. Table 20-2 shows that the length of time needed to be reasonably certain that superior managers will outperform the market most certainly will be longer than the trial period for determining their real worth.

Detecting a bad manager is an equally difficult task. In fact, a money manager would have to underperform the market by 4 percent

---

[10] The standard deviation of the Magellan Fund over Lynch's period is 21.38 percent, compared with 13.88 percent for the Wilshire 5000, whereas its correlation coefficient with the Wilshire was 0.86.

[11] Money managers are assumed to expose their clients to the same risk as the market and have a correlation coefficient of 0.88 with market returns, which has been typical of equity mutual funds since 1971.

Probability of Outperforming the Wilshire 5000 (Assumptions: Baseline Expected Return = 11.3 Percent; Standard Deviation = 16.7 Percent; Correlation Coefficient = 0.87; These Assumptions Are Based on Data Extending from 1971–2001)

Expected Excess Return	Holding Period (years)						
	1	2	3	5	10	20	30
1%	54.2%	55.9%	57.3%	59.3%	63.1%	68.2%	71.9%
2%	58.3%	61.7%	64.2%	68.1%	74.7%	82.6%	87.5%
3%	62.3%	67.2%	70.7%	75.9%	84.0%	92.0%	95.7%
4%	66.2%	72.2%	76.5%	82.4%	90.6%	96.9%	98.9%
5%	69.8%	76.8%	81.6%	87.7%	95.0%	99.0%	99.8%

per year for almost 15 years before you could be statistically certain (defined to mean being less than 1 chance in 20 of being wrong) that the manager is actually poor and not just having bad luck. By that time, your assets would have fallen to half of what you would have had by indexing to the market.

Even extreme cases are hard to identify. Surely you would think that a manager who picks stocks that are expected to outperform the market by an average of 5 percent per year, a feat achieved by no fund other than Magellan since 1970, would easily and quickly stand out. However, this is not necessarily so. After 1 year, there is only a 7 in 10 chance that such a manager will outperform the market. And the probability rises to only 76.8 percent that the manager will outperform the market after 2 years.

Assume that you gave a young, undiscovered Peter Lynch, someone who over the long run will outperform the market with a 5 percent per year edge, an ultimatum—that he will be fired if he does not at least match the market after 2 years. Table 20-2 shows that the probability that he will beat the market over 2 years is only 76.8 percent. This means that there is almost a 1 in 4 chance that he will still underperform the market and you will fire this superior manager after judging him incapable of picking winning stocks!

REASONS FOR UNDERPERFORMANCE OF MANAGED MONEY

The generally poor performance of funds relative to the market is not due to the fact that managers of these funds pick losing stocks. Their performance lags the benchmarks largely because funds impose fees and trading costs that average 2 percent per year. First, in seeking superior returns, a manager buys and sells stocks, which involves brokerage commissions and paying the bid-ask spread, or the difference between the buying and the selling price of shares. Second, investors pay management fees (and possibly sales or load fees) to the organizations and individuals who sell these funds. Finally, managers often are competing with other managers with equal or superior skills at choosing stocks. As noted earlier, it is a mathematical impossibility for everyone to do better than the market—for every dollar that outperforms the average, some other investor's dollar must underperform the average.

A LITTLE LEARNING IS A DANGEROUS THING

It is an interesting fact that an investor who has a little knowledge of the principles of equity valuations often performs worse than someone with no knowledge. For example, take the novice—an investor who is just learning about stock valuation. This is the investor to whom most of the books entitled *How to Beat the Market* are sold. A novice might note that the stock has just reported very good earnings, but its price does not rise as much as he believes is justified by this good news. The novice might think that the price should have gone up much more, and so he buys the stock.

Yet informed investors know that special circumstances caused the earnings to increase and that these circumstances likely will not be repeated in the future. Informed investors therefore are more than happy to sell the stock to novices, realizing that even the small rise in the price of the stock is not justified. Informed investors make a return on their special knowledge. They make their return from novices who believe they have found a bargain. Uninformed investors, who do not even know what the earnings of the company are, do better than the investor who is just beginning to learn what equities are worth.

The saying "A little learning is a dangerous thing" proves itself to be quite apt in financial markets. Many seeming anomalies or discrepancies in the prices of stocks (or most other financial assets, for that matter) are due to the trading of informed investors with special information that is not easily processed by others. When a stock looks too cheap or too dear, the easy explanation—that emotional or ignorant traders have incorrectly priced the stock—is often wrong. Most (but certainly not all) of the time there is a good reason why stocks are priced as they are. This is why beginners who buy individual stocks on the basis of their own research often do quite badly.

PROFITING FROM INFORMED TRADING

As novices become more informed, they will no doubt find some stocks that are genuinely under- or overvalued. Trading these stocks will begin to offset their transactions costs and poorly informed trades. At one point, a novice might become well enough informed to overcome the transactions costs and match or perhaps exceed the market return. The key word here is *might,* since the number of investors who have consistently been able to outperform the market is small indeed. And for individuals who do not devote much time to analyzing stocks, the possibility of consistently outperforming the averages is remote.

Yet the apparent simplicity of picking winners and avoiding losers lures many investors into active trading. You learned in Chapter 19 that there is an inherent tendency of individuals to view themselves and their performance as above average. The investment game draws some of the best minds in the world. Many investors are wrongly convinced that they are smarter than the next person who is playing the same investing game. However, even being just as smart as the next investor is not good enough, for being average at the game of finding market winners will result in underperforming the market as transactions costs diminish returns.

In 1975, Charles D. Ellis, a managing partner at Greenwood Associates, wrote an influential article entitled "The Loser's Game." In it he showed that with transactions costs taken into account, average money managers must outperform the market by margins that are not possible given that they themselves are the major market players. Ellis concludes: "Contrary to their oft articulated goal of outperforming the market averages, investment managers are not beating the market; the market is beating them."[12]

HOW COSTS AFFECT RETURNS

Trading and managerial costs of 2 or 3 percent per year may seem small compared with the year-to-year volatility of the market and to investors

---

[12]Charles D. Ellis, "The Loser's Game," *Financial Analysts Journal* (July–August 1975):19.

who are gunning for 20 or 30 percent annual returns. However, such costs are extremely detrimental to long-term wealth accumulation. One thousand dollars invested at a compound return of 11 percent per year, the average nominal return on stocks since World War II, will accumulate $23,000 over 30 years. A 1 percent annual fee will reduce the final accumulation by almost a third. With a 3 percent annual fee, the accumulation amounts to just over $10,000, less than half the market return. Every extra percentage point of annual costs requires investors aged 25 to retire 2 years later than they would have in the absence of such costs.

DEVELOPMENT OF INDEXING AND PASSIVE INVESTING

Many investors have realized that the poor performance of actively managed funds relative to benchmark indexes strongly implies that they would do very well to just *equal* the market return of one of the broad-based indexes. Thus the 1990s witnessed an enormous increase in *passive investing*, the placement of funds whose sole purpose was to match the performance of an index.

The oldest and most popular of the index funds is the Vanguard 500 Index Fund.[13] The fund, started by visionary John Bogle, raised only $11.4 million when it debuted in 1976, and few people thought the concept would survive. Slowly and surely, however, indexing gathered momentum, and the fund's assets reached $17 billion at the end of 1995.

In the latter stages of the 1990s' bull market, the popularity of indexing soared. By March 2000, when the S&P 500 Index reached its all-time high, Vanguard claimed the title of the world's largest equity fund, with assets of over $100 billion. Indexing became so popular that in the first 6 months of 1999, nearly 70 percent of the money that was invested went into index funds.[14]

One of the attractions of index funds is their extremely low cost. The total annual cost in the Vanguard 500 Index Fund is only 0.18 percent of market value (and even lower for larger investors). Even more remarkable is that over the last 5 years the average return on the fund has actually outperformed the index.[15] Since its creation in 1976, the Vanguard 500 Index has outperformed most *surviving* equity mutual funds

---

[13] Five years before the Vanguard Index funds, Wells Fargo created an equally weighted index fund called Samsonite, but its assets remained relatively small.

[14] Heather Bell, "Vanguard 500 Turns 25, Legacy in Passive Investing," *Journal of Index Issues* (fourth quarter 2001): 8–10.

[15] The fund can do so by earning interest on securities it loans from its portfolio as well as using a few proprietary trading techniques.

despite the tremendous returns on small stocks from 1975 to 1983 that hurt the relative performance of large stock funds.

The popularity of indexing was strengthened by the development of exchange-traded funds (ETFs). ETFs are baskets of stocks belonging to the S&P 500 Index and other indexes that can be traded like a single stock throughout the day.[16] At the end of 2001, the estimated value of ETFs surpassed $100 billion and exceeded the value of the Vanguard 500 Index Fund.

POTENTIAL PITFALLS OF INDEXING

The popularity of indexing, especially those funds linked to the S&P 500 Index, may cause problems for index investors in the future. The reason is simple. If a firm's mere entry into the S&P 500 causes the price of its stock to rise, index investors ultimately will hold overpriced stocks that will depress future returns.

An extreme example of overpricing occurred when Yahoo!, the well-known Internet firm, was added to the S&P 500 Index in December 1999. Figure 20-3 graphically depicts Yahoo!'s price during this period. S&P announced after the close of trading on November 30 that Yahoo! would be added to the index on December 8. The next morning, Yahoo! opened up almost $9 per share at $115 and continued upward to close at $174 per share on December 7, when index funds had to buy the shares in order to match the index. In just 5 trading days between the announcement of Yahoo!'s inclusion in the index until it formally became a member, the stock surged 64 percent. Volume during those 5 days averaged 37 million shares, more than 3 times the average on the previous 30 days. On December 7, when index funds had to own the stock, volume hit 132 million shares, representing $22 billion of Yahoo! stock traded.

This story is repeated with virtually every stock added to the index, although the average size of the gain is considerably less than Yahoo!'s. S&P published a study in September 2000 that determined how adding a stock to an S&P index influenced the price.[17] This study noted that from the announcement date to the effective date of admission in the S&P 500 Index, shares rose by an average of 8.49 percent. During the next 10 days following their entry, these stocks fell by an average of 3.23 percent, or about one-third of the preentry gain. Yet 1 year after the an-

---

[16] These ETFs are described in detail in Chapter 15.

[17] Roger J. Bos, "Event Study: Quantifying the Effect of Being Added to an S&P Index," Standard and Poor's, September 2000.

F I G U R E   20–3

Yahoo! Admission to S&P 500

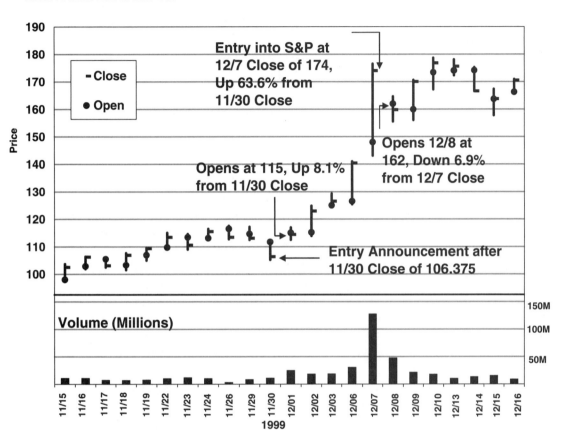

nouncement, these postentry losses were wiped out, and the average gain of new entrants was 8.98 percent. All these percentages were corrected for movements in the overall market.

EFFECT OF OVERPRICING ON RETURNS

The increase in the stock price between the date of announcement and the date of entry, which I term the *entry premium*, hurts investors in two ways. If the price of the new entry retreats after the admission date and fund buying ceases, then investors in index funds will take a capital loss on the fall in value of these shares.

However, even if the price does not settle back, index investors are harmed. The value of a stock, as I noted in Chapter 6, is the present value of all its cash flows. Certainly admittance to the S&P 500 Index does not increase these cash flows.[18] As a result, if the price of a stock is *permanently* higher as a result of its inclusion in an index, the return to investors purchasing this stock must decline. The long-term increase in share price resulting from membership in the S&P 500 Index is what I term the *permanent premium*. In general, the entry premium is higher than the permanent premium, but this may not be the case if indexing is a growing phenomenon and an increasing number of funds are required to buy shares that are already in the index.

Even though the permanent premium is generally smaller than the entry premium, it is far more detrimental to shareholders' returns. The entry premium is paid only on stocks added to the index each year. The percentage of the S&P 500 Index affected by the entry premium has averaged only about 5 percent per year over the last 5 years. In contrast, the permanent premium influences all stocks in the index all the time.

Although the average size of the entry premium has been 8.59 percent over the past 10 years, this premium appears to be increasing over time.[19] Furthermore, there is some evidence that traders speculate on which companies will be the new entrants into the index and bid them up to a premium before an actual announcement is made. Therefore, the 8.59 percent figure should be considered a lower bound on the size of the current entry premium.

The size of the permanent premium is harder to establish. In contrast to the entry premium, which is measured over the short period of time between announcement and entry, there is no natural time frame to measure the permanent premium. Some economists have measured the permanent premium by looking at differences in the valuation of similar stocks in and out of the S&P 500 Index and found it to be substantial—in excess of 40 percent.[20] However, the size of the permanent premium is

---

[18] There are some people who maintain that being chosen by S&P for inclusion is an endorsement of the financial strength of the firm and a signal for higher future earnings. See Upinder Dhillon and Herb Johnson, "Changes in the Standard and Poor's 500 List," *Journal of Business* (1991):75–85. Yet this contention has been challenged. See Aditya Kaul, Vikas Mehrotra, and Randall Morck, "Demand Curves for Stocks Do Slope Down: New Evidence from an Index Weights Adjustment," *Journal of Finance* (April 2000):893–913.

[19] David M. Blitzer, "The S&P 500," paper presented at the Indexing and ETF Summit, Broomfield, CO, March 26, 2001.

[20] Randall Morck and Fan Yang, "The Mysterious Growing Value of S&P 500 Membership," NBER Working Paper 8654, Cambridge, MA, December 2001. This work shows overvaluation of the S&P stock as 46.6 percent and positively tied to the level of overall indexing in the economy.

controversial, and some people have found no significant overvaluation of stocks in this popular index.[21] Nevertheless, there is a growing consensus that both an entry premium and a permanent premium exist for this popular benchmark.[22]

To many investors, it would seem quite natural for stock prices to rise when they are purchased by an index fund. Yet in an efficient market this should not happen. If a stock or a group of stocks is overpriced, they should attract short sellers that push the price down to the level that correctly reflects their true value. Yet the supply of arbitrage funds is limited. The risk that overpriced stocks will become more overpriced before they fall limits the amount of capital willing to sell these stocks. Arbitrage funds migrate primarily to investments where the short-term payoffs are more certain.

Some economists believe that the prices of stocks in the S&P 500 Index will permanently contain a premium because of their greater liquidity.[23] This liquidity is reflected by narrower bid-ask spreads and the ability of institutional investors to trade large blocks of stock at near-market prices. The premium can be thought of as the discounted value of the reduction in trading costs brought about by the enhanced liquidity. As I noted in Chapter 7, greater liquidity is one reason why the entire stock market should sell at a higher valuation than in the past. This liquidity may be highly valued by the frequent trader, but it may lower the return to the long-term investor.

EFFECTS OF OVERPRICING ON PORTFOLIO ALLOCATION

The effect of the premiums on S&P 500 Index stock returns can be readily calculated. Table 20-3 shows the impact of the entry premium and the permanent premium on the S&P 500 Index returns assuming that 5 percent of the S&P 500 Index is replaced annually and that stocks earn a 7 percent annual real return, in line with historical averages.

In the S&P study cited previously, the entry premium averaged about 8.5 percent and the permanent premium averaged about 5.25 per-

[21] See Burton Malkiel and Aleksander Radisich, "The Growth of Index Funds and the Pricing of Equity Securities," *Journal of Portfolio Management* (Winter 2001):9–21.
[22] Firms often lobby hard for inclusion in the S&P 500 Index because of the recent decision by S&P to include real estate investment trusts (REITs) in the index after much well-directed lobbying by the industry. It is hard to believe that higher prices for REIT stocks were not foremost in the minds of managers.
[23] See a number of papers by Yakov Amihud and Haim Mendelson, starting with "Asset Pricing and the Bid-Ask Spread," *Journal of Financial Economics* 17(1986):223–239.

TABLE 20-3

Reduction in Yearly Return on S&P 500 Index Due to Premium Prices

Permanent Premium	Entry Premium				
	0%	**5%**	**10%**	**15%**	**20%**
0%	0.00%	-0.25%	-0.49%	-0.70%	-0.42%
5%	-0.07%	-0.33%	-0.58%	-0.80%	-0.51%
10%	-0.10%	-0.38%	-0.64%	-0.87%	-0.56%
15%	-0.12%	-0.41%	-0.67%	-0.91%	-0.60%
20%	-0.11%	-0.41%	-0.69%	-0.94%	-0.61%

cent over the last 10 years. These premiums cause a 51 basis point per year reduction in the return on the S&P 500 Index portfolio compared with returns if there were no price premiums. Because of the growth of indexing, premiums have increased over time, and the potential drag on returns currently may be substantially larger.

What does this drag on S&P 500 Index stock returns mean for portfolio allocation? If one believes that the level of funds that are indexed is at or near the peak, the percentage allocation of S&P 500 Index stocks relative to the rest of the market (indicated by the Wilshire 4500) should be reduced.[24] However, if the popularity of indexing continues to grow, the price of S&P 500 Index stocks could rise relative to the rest of the market, further boosting the returns of index investors. In this case, the S&P 500 Index could continue to be a winning portfolio. These important questions imply that investors should closely monitor the net flows into or out of products indexed to the S&P 500 Index. Investors must be aware of the risks involved if indexing becomes less popular.[25]

---

[24] My own preliminary results suggest that with an 8.5 percent entry premium and a 5.25 percent permanent premium, the weight on the S&P 500 Index should be reduced from about 82 to 69 percent of the portfolio.

[25] The S&P study shows that there are also premiums in stocks added to the S&P Small Cap 600 Index and Mid Cap 400 Index, although they are smaller than the S&P 500 Index.

CONCLUSION

The past performance of actively managed funds is not encouraging. The fees that most funds charge do not provide investors with superior returns and can be a significant drag on wealth accumulation. Furthermore, a good money manager is extremely difficult to identify, for luck plays some role in all successful investment outcomes.

When costs are taken into account, most actively managed funds significantly lag the benchmark indexes. It is for this reason that the past decade has witnessed strong growth of index funds and more recent ETFs linked to indexes.

However, the enormous popularity of these index funds, particularly those tied to the S&P 500 Stock Index, may lower the future returns to investors. This is so because stocks that are added to the index rise to a premium before entry and most likely retain a premium while a member of the popular index. These premium prices will hurt long-term investors because they will lower the value of future cash flows per dollar invested.

For investors or money managers who trade large stocks hoping to beat the averages, the improvement in the liquidity of stocks in the popular indexes is a positive development that actually may outweigh the negatives of overvaluation. The reduction in bid-ask spreads for trading large blocks of stocks may boost their returns. For long-term investors, however, the liquidity benefit is of little importance. Consequently, investors should be sensitive to indexing trends and realize that the very popularity of passive investing may mean lower future returns for indexers.

CHAPTER 21

STRUCTURING A PORTFOLIO FOR LONG-TERM GROWTH

[The] long run is a misleading guide to current affairs. In the long run we are all dead. Economists set themselves too easy, too useless a task if in tempestuous seasons they can only tell us when the storm is long past, the ocean will be flat.

JOHN MAYNARD KEYNES[1]

My favorite holding period is forever.

WARREN BUFFETT[2]

No one can argue with Keynes' statement that in the long run we are all dead. However, vision for the long run must be used as a guide to current action. Those who keep their focus and perspective during trying times are far more likely to emerge successful. Knowing that the sea will be flat after the storm passes is not useless but enormously comforting.

It is particularly important that the principles of investment strategy be guided by long-run expectations. Keynes was right when he wrote,

---

[1]John Maynard Keynes, *A Tract on Monetary Reform,* (London: Macmillan, 1924), p. 80.
[2]Linda Grant, "Striking Out at Wall Street," *US News & World Report,* June 20, 1994, p. 58.

"Our knowledge of the factors which will govern the yield of an invest-ment some years hence is usually very slight and often negligible."[3] However, the fact that such expectations are tenuously held does not jus-tify their abandonment. The well-known saying that the most successful are those who keep their heads about them when everyone else is losing theirs is particularly applicable to investment decisions.

PRINCIPLES OF LONG-TERM INVESTING

To be a successful long-term investor is easy in principle but difficult in practice. It is easy in principle because buying and holding a diversified portfolio of stocks, foregoing any forecasting ability, is available to all in-vestors, no matter what their intelligence, judgment, or financial status. Yet it is difficult in practice because we are subject to many emotional forces. Tales of those who have quickly achieved great wealth in the market tempt us to play a game very different from that of the long-term investor.

Those who follow the market closely often exclaim, "I knew that stock (or the market) was going up! If I had only acted on my judgment, I would have made so much money!" However, hindsight plays tricks on our minds. We forget the doubts we had when we made the decision not to buy. Hindsight often distorts the past and encourages us to play hunches and outguess other investors, who in turn are playing the same game.

For most of us, trying to beat the market leads to disastrous results. We take far too many risks, our transactions costs are high, and we often find ourselves giving in to the emotions of the moment—pes-simism when the market is down and optimism when the market is high. We end up frustrated that our misguided actions only lead to sub-stantially lower returns than we could have achieved by just staying in the market.

Achieving good long-term returns in stocks is not difficult and is available to all who seek to gain through investing. The principles enu-merated below enable both new and seasoned investors to increase their returns while minimizing their risk.

1. **Reduce your expectations on the future returns on equity to realis-tic levels. There are many favorable factors that justify an increase in the long-term price-earnings (P-E) ratio of the market from its histori-**

---

[3]John Maynard Keynes, *The General Theory of Employment, Interest, and Money* (New York: Harcourt, Brace & World, 1965, First Harbinger Edition), p. 149.

cal level of 15 to the low 20s. But looking forward, returns on diversified portfolios of common stocks from these higher valuations should only average 5 to 7 percent after inflation, at or slightly below their long-term historical average.

The period 1982–1999 witnessed one of the greatest bull markets in history. The returns over that period were almost double the long-term average. If investors today expect these above-average returns to persist, they will be disappointed. Chapter 7 enumerates the favorable factors justifying a higher P-E ratio for the market. However, these higher valuations suggest a somewhat lower future return to equity.

With inflation likely to be in the 2 to 3 percent range, stock returns before inflation are expected to be between 7 and 10 percent per year, just one-half of what they averaged during the last bull market. The gap between stock and bond returns will be lower in the future than it has been historically, but stocks will still significantly outperform bonds over the long run.

2. Stocks should constitute the overwhelming proportion of all long-term financial portfolios. The new government inflation-indexed bonds should be the asset of choice for long-term investors who want to reduce their exposure to equities.

Chapter 2 demonstrated that portfolio composition is crucially dependent on the holding period of the investor, and holding periods are often far longer than most investors realize. Uncertain inflation makes standard nominal bonds risky in the long run. Based on historical evidence, even the most conservative investors should place most of their financial wealth in common stocks.

The new government inflation-indexed bonds offer after-inflation returns that are likely to surpass those of standard bonds and are much safer in terms of purchasing power. Although inflation-indexed bonds currently yield about one-half the long-term return on stocks, these bonds will outperform equities about one-quarter of the time over 10-year periods. Investors worried about equity exposure should consider these bonds as the safe alternative to stocks.

3. Invest the largest percentage—the core holdings of your stock portfolio—in either highly diversified mutual funds with low expense ratios, exchange-traded funds (ETFs), or indexed mutual funds.

To replicate the returns described in this book, it is necessary to hold a highly diversified portfolio of stocks. Unless you can consistently choose stocks with superior returns, a goal very few investors have accomplished, maximum diversification is achieved by holding each stock in proportion to its market capitalization.

The late 1990s witnessed the continued growth and proliferation of ETFs and indexed mutual funds. Both offer returns extremely close to those of the major market indexes, such as the Standard & Poor's (S&P) 500 Stock Index. An index fund does not attempt to beat the market, but by holding a large number of stocks in the proper proportion, it can match the market with an extremely low cost. For the largest of these funds, the annual expense ratio is 0.20 percent or lower. A further advantage of indexed funds is that their turnover is very low, and therefore, they are very tax efficient.

Chapter 20 showed that the Wilshire 5000 Index has outperformed about two of three mutual funds since 1976 and a far higher percentage over the past 15 years. By matching the market year after year, as you can with index funds, you are likely to be near the top of the pack when the final returns are tallied.

4. Slightly overweight non-S&P 500 stocks relative to the market in your domestic equity portfolio. Up to one-third of your portfolio should be in small and midsized stocks.

The tremendous growth of funds indexed to the S&P 500 Index may lower returns to this benchmark index going forward. As was shown in Chapter 20, when a stock enters this popular index, its price jumps, and it acquires an undeserved premium. Because index funds must buy these stocks at the higher prices, this may lead to lower S&P 500 returns in the long run. This said, one should not lower the weighting of the S&P 500 Index significantly because, if indexing becomes even more popular, the price of these stocks may rise to an even higher premium and further increase returns for S&P 500 Index investors.

The broadest indexed equity portfolio—to invest in every stock in proportion to its market value—requires an investment in thousands of stocks, a strategy that would be prohibitively expensive. To approximate returns of stocks not in the S&P 500, small-cap index funds choose a representative subset of stocks that they believe will track the indexes well. There are small-stock mutual funds and ETFs that attempt to match the Wilshire 4500 Index (essentially all stocks not in the S&P 500 Index) and the Russell 2000 Index (the smallest 2,000 stocks of the top 3,000) and the S&P 1000 (the 400 mid-cap stocks and 600 small-cap stocks in the S&P 1500). For those investors who do not want to combine large and small index funds, there are mutual funds and ETFs that replicate the Wilshire 5000 Total Market Index, the broadest index of all stocks.

It is debatable whether indexing small-cap stocks will be as successful as indexing large stocks has been in the past. There are clearly more inefficiencies in the small-cap markets because far fewer analysts can cover each stock. A good money manager in the small- and mid-cap markets is more likely to outperform the averages. Beware, however, because fees are usually higher for these funds and can easily wipe out the differential return you would achieve by searching out the best of the small-cap managers.

5. The rationale for international diversification, based on country-wide returns, is weakening. However, the rationale for investing in foreign firms on the basis of sector diversification is strengthening. For firms with global markets, investors should not allocate based on the country in which the firm is headquartered. Look for the emergence of world sector–based funds.

The primary motivation for international diversification comes from a desire to lower the overall risk of a portfolio. International stocks diversify risk for U.S.-based investors as long as they have a low correlation with stocks in the United States.

The analysis in Chapter 10 shows that one should invest about a quarter of one's assets in foreign equities based on historical world returns. However, there is convincing evidence that the correlations among countries' returns are increasing, thus lowering the benefits of diversification. If we set future returns at their historical level, and if one believes that this trend toward increased world correlations will persist, the percentage allocated to foreign equities falls drastically.

A better approach to international investing could come from diversification based on global sectors instead of country of origin. While correlations among countries are increasing, correlations between global economic sectors are decreasing.

There are three ways to invest in international stocks: open-ended mutual funds, which allow for buying and selling shares from investors at the net asset value of their portfolios; closed-end funds, which trade like shares of a portfolio and are run by an active manager; and the newest innovations, iShares, (issued by Barclay's Global Investors), which are pools of funds invested in a broad index of foreign stocks.

Barclay's Global Investors, in partnership with Standard & Poor's, has recently issued iShares for five major sectors: energy, financials, health care, technology, and telecommunications. These shares represent market-weighted allocations in the leading *international* firms in each sector, irrespective of the headquarters country. It is likely that iShares will soon be introduced for the remaining major S&P sectors: consumer discretionary, consumer staples, industrials, materials, and utilities. The expense ratio for these ETFs is 0.65 percent per year, not as low as the 0.35 percent charged by some broad-based international index funds but far lower than is typical of internationally based portfolios.[4]

As with small-cap stocks, the evidence in favor of indexing international stocks is not yet as persuasive as among domestic high-cap stocks. This is so because there are more inefficiencies in the pricing of international stocks that can be exploited by skillful money managers. Nevertheless, there is not sufficient evidence to determine whether these active managers can overcome their high fees and provide extra value for shareholders.

Since almost two-thirds of the world's capital is now located outside the United States, international equities must be included in any well-diversified portfolio. The world's economies and markets most certainly will continue to become more integrated in the future. No country will be able to dominate every market, and industry leaders are apt to emerge from anywhere on the globe. Sticking only to U.S. equities is thus a risky strategy for the long-term investor.

6. On the basis of historical returns, large value stocks have a small edge over large growth stocks. Large growth stocks with P-E ratios over 50 are particularly vulnerable to disappointment.

Chapter 8 shows that among the S&P 500 Index stocks, large value firms have outperformed large growth firms by 1.86 percent per year since 1975. However, since August 1982, when the great bull market began, cumulative returns for growth and value investors have been almost identical, even counting the dramatic collapse of growth stocks in 2000 and 2001.

Chapter 9 showed that the "nifty fifty" large growth stocks that sported an average P-E ratio in excess of 50 experienced significantly lower returns than growth stocks that were more reasonably priced.

Growth stocks are often rewarded with sky-high P-E ratios in hope of spectacular future earnings growth. However, the lesson of the nifty fifty stock bubble in 1972 and the tech bubble of 1999–2000 is that once a firm reaches large-capitalization status, its ability to generate double-

---

[4]Quite a number of index-tracking products are now traded in Europe. Barclay's has partnered with Bloomberg to produce European sector funds, and Merrill Lynch has developed a product called *leaders* (listed diversified return products, or LDRS) that trade 13 global sectors on the Euronext Amsterdam exchange. As of January 2002, these products are not available for purchase by U.S. investors.

digit earnings growth into the far future is sharply limited. There have been very few large stocks whose subsequent histories have justified P-E ratios in excess of 50. On the other hand, if very long-term earnings growth of just a few percentage points over the S&P 500 Index can be achieved, P-E ratios of 30 to 50 can be readily justified.

7. Small value stocks have significantly outperformed small growth stocks over long periods of time. As a result, small- and mid-cap holdings should have a much stronger value bias than large-cap holdings. Avoid initial public offerings (IPOs) unless you buy at the offering price.

In contrast to the large-capitalization stocks, value does appear to outperform growth significantly among the mid- and small-cap stocks. Dreams of buying a new Microsoft or Wal-Mart often compel investors to overpay for these issues. The very small growth stocks do the worst of any class of stocks examined. From July 1963 through December 2000, small value stocks beat small growth stocks by almost 17 percent *per year.*

If you can buy new issues at their offering price, it is usually wise to do so. But do not hold on. IPOs, which often include small growth stocks, are extremely poor performers for long-term investors.

8. Maximize your contribution to your tax-deferred account [IRA, 401(k), or Keogh]. Generally, fund your tax-deferred account with stocks. If your total stock portfolio exceeds your tax-deferred account, hold high-dividend (or value) stocks in the tax-deferred account and low-dividend (or growth) stocks in your taxable account. However, do not overweight your tax-deferred account with high-dividend stocks just to shelter dividends.

Chapter 4 showed how taxes can reduce the returns on your portfolio. You can minimize the tax bite by building a tax-deferred account that accumulates gains at before-tax rates of return. This is best accomplished through investing in the stock market. The deferral of taxes on capital gains and dividends is usually worth more than the advantage of the lower capital gains tax in the taxable account.

If your stock portfolio exceeds the size of your tax-deferred account, put the high-yielding stocks in that account in order to maximize the deferral of taxes. Stocks with low dividends should be placed in taxable accounts. Watch out for high turnover of stocks in taxable accounts, for they will generate taxable gains even if you do not sell your shares. Do not stretch to fill your tax-deferred account with high-dividend stocks such as REITs or utilities. This will unbalance your portfolio and expose you to too much risk.

9. **Finally, establish firm rules to keep your portfolio on track, especially if you find yourself giving into the emotion of the moment. If you find yourself becoming particularly anxious about the market, sit down and read the first two chapters of this book again. On the other hand, remember that money that you must have in the next 5 years should not be risked in the stock market.**

Swings in investor emotion almost always outrun changes in the long-run fundamentals that determine stock market values. The temptation is to buy when everyone is bullish and sell when they are bearish. Since it is so hard to stand apart from this market sentiment, most investors who trade frequently and stay close to the market often have poor returns. Chapter 19 shows how the field of behavioral finance helps investors understand and avoid common psychological pitfalls that cause poor market performance.

RETURN-ENHANCING STRATEGIES

The following return-enhancing strategies are not necessary to achieve good long-run returns. As this book indicates, you will do quite well with a buy-and-hold strategy pegged to a well-diversified low-cost mutual fund or ETF. However, if you like the hunt and get a thrill out of attempting to beat the market, these strategies have yielded superior returns in the past.

1. **There is some evidence that contrarian strategies of increasing stock exposure when most investors are bearish and decreasing exposure when they are bullish can improve long-term returns.**

Chapter 19 indicated that investor sentiment might be an important indicator of the future course of equity values. It has long been noted that investors often are most optimistic when the market is at a peak and most pessimistic when stocks are hitting a bottom. Stock returns, especially over periods of 9 and 12 months, may be enhanced by looking at the level of market sentiment, such as those derived from the bull and bear figures offered by Investors' Intelligence.

Contrarian strategies for individual stocks, such as buying out-of-favor firms that have fallen in value relative to their fundamentals, sometimes yields superior returns. The Dow 10 strategy of buying the 10 highest-yielding Dow Industrial stocks has outperformed the market over most long-term periods. Since most of the Dow Industrials have been superior companies in their respective industries, these stocks are very responsive to a contrarian strategy.

2. Investing when the Federal Reserve is easing short-term interest rates has, during most of the last 50 years, produced significantly higher returns than investing when the Fed is restricting credit and interest rates are rising.

Interest rates and earnings are the two most significant short-term influences on stock prices. Chapter 11 showed that investing in stocks during periods when the Fed is tightening credit has resulted in significantly lower returns than investing when the Fed is easing credit.

However, this has not been true during all periods. Because of the increased number of Fed watchers, this strategy has not worked particularly well since 1990. Any strategy widely followed and acted on will nullify its own past performance. However, during periods when inflation threatens, Fed actions can be very important to the market.

3. There is significant evidence that many calendar anomalies persist over time. Furthermore, some technical trading rules have been shown to reduce risk and enhance returns.

For investors who closely follow the market, the evidence presented in Chapter 17 suggests that pursuing certain trend-following strategies may reduce stock risks, and Chapter 18 describes regular calendar patterns in stock returns. Calendar anomalies include the excess returns to small stocks in the month of January, as well as the superior returns to stocks that occur at the very end of the month and the beginning of the next month.

The 200-day moving average has been investigated as a method of timing the market. Although the overall returns are not always superior to a buy-and-hold strategy, there is some evidence that risk is reduced. The strategy works very well for strongly trending markets and, if based on the Nasdaq Composite Index, would have allowed investors to ride the technology wave upward while avoiding most of the bear market that followed.

4. All these return-enhancing strategies should be pursued from your tax-deferred account using no-load mutual funds, ETFs, or, for those who want to maximize their leverage, index futures.

Return-enhancing strategies often require shifting in and out of equities, which incurs transactions costs, front-load fees in mutual funds, and taxes. For this reason, pursuing these strategies is best done using no-load mutual funds that do not restrict the number of switches you can make. ETFs and index futures are low-cost ways of taking a position in benchmark indexes and are discussed in Chapter 15.

Again, it is important to remember that with any system, a significant increase in the number of investors who use any strategy will cause price movements that will tend to nullify its effect. There is some evidence that the January effect and other calendar anomalies are becoming weaker over time.

IMPLEMENT THE PLAN AND THE ROLE OF AN INVESTMENT ADVISOR

I wrote *Stocks for the Long Run* to demonstrate what returns could be reasonably expected on stocks and fixed-income assets and to analyze the major factors influencing those returns. Many investors will consider this book a "do-it-yourself guide" to choosing stocks and structuring a portfolio. And for some, this will indeed be the case. However, knowing the right investments is not the same as implementing the right investment strategy. As Peter Bernstein so aptly indicates in his Foreword to this edition, there are many pitfalls on the path to successful investing that cause investors to fail to achieve their intended goals.

The first pitfall is the lack of diversification. Many investors are not satisfied earning a 10 percent average annual return on stocks when they know that there are always individual issues that will double or triple in price over the next 12 months. Finding such gems is extremely gratifying, and many people dream of buying the next corporate giant in its infancy.

However, as Chapter 8 indicates, the evidence is overwhelming that most small growth stocks are very risky and have poor long-term returns. Studies of betting at racetracks and in lotteries have confirmed the propensity of bettors to overplay long shots in the hopes of winning big while ignoring safer bets that promise more moderate returns. This propensity leads many individual investors to take far too much risk and suffer far lower returns than can be had from a fully diversified portfolio of stocks.

Investors who have been burned by picking individual stocks often turn to mutual funds in their search for higher returns. Choosing a mutual fund, however, poses similar obstacles. Hot managers with superior past performance replace hot stocks as the new strategy to beat the market. As a result, many investors end up playing the same game as they had with individual stocks.

Those who finally abandon trying to pick the best funds are

tempted to pursue an even more difficult course. They attempt to beat the market by timing market cycles. Surprisingly, it is often the best-informed investors who fall into this trap. With the abundance of financial news, information, and commentary at our beck and call, it is extraordinarily difficult to stay aloof from market opinion. As a result, one's impulse is to capitulate to fear when the market is plunging or to greed when stocks are soaring.

Many people try to resist this impulse. The intellect may say, "Stay the course!" but this is not easy to do when one hears so many others—including well-respected "experts"—advising investors to beat a hasty retreat. And as John Maynard Keynes aptly stated 60 years ago in *The General Theory*, "Worldly wisdom teaches that it is better for reputation to fail conventionally than to succeed unconventionally."[5] Standing against the crowd is hard because failing with others who are also failing is far easier than failing alone.

Poor investment strategy, whether it is for lack of diversification, pursuing hot stocks, or attempting to time the market, often stems from the belief of investors that it is necessary to beat the market to do well in the market. However, nothing is further from the truth. The principal lesson of this book is that through time, the after-inflation returns on a well-diversified portfolio of common stocks have not only exceeded those of fixed-income assets but also have done so with less risk. Which stocks you own is secondary to whether you own stocks, especially if you maintain a balanced portfolio. Over time, the historical difference between the returns on stocks and the returns on bonds has far exceeded the differences in returns among well-diversified all-stock portfolios.[6]

What does all this mean to the reader of this book? Proper investment strategy is as much a psychological as an intellectual challenge. As with other challenges in life, it is often best to seek professional help to structure and maintain a well-diversified portfolio. If you should decide to seek help, be sure to select a professional investment advisor who agrees with the basic principles of diversification and long-term investing that I have espoused in these chapters. It is within the grasp of all investors to avoid the pitfalls of investing and reap the generous rewards that are only available in equities.

---

[5]Keynes (1965), p. 158.

[6]This is shown first in Gary P. Brinson, L. Randolph Hood, and Gilbert L. Beebower, "Determinants of Portfolio Performance," *Financial Analysts Journal* (July–August 1986):39–44; and extended by William F. Sharpe, "Asset Allocation: Management Style and Performance Measurement," *Journal of Portfolio Management* 18(2)(Winter 1992):7–19.

CONCLUSION

The stock market is exciting. Its daily movements dominate the financial press and record the flows of billions of dollars of investment capital. But the stock market is far more than the quintessential symbol of capitalism or the organization through which investors can stake a claim on the economy's future. It is the driving force behind allocation of the world's capital and the fundamental engine of economic growth and technological change. As the proliferation of stock markets around the world attests, stocks hold the key to enriching the lives of all peoples everywhere.

INDEX

Note: The *n* after a page number refers to footnote; the *i*, to an illustration; and the *q*, to chapter opening quotes.

ABOUT THE AUTHOR

Jeremy J. Siegel, Ph.D., is the Russell E. Palmer Professor of Finance at The Wharton School of the University of Pennsylvania. An advisor to the Federal Reserve and many of Wall Street's leading investment houses, Professor Siegel received his Ph.D. from M.I.T. and taught for four years at the University of Chicago before joining the Wharton faculty in 1976. He has been featured and has written about the economy and financial markets in such noteworthy publications as *The Wall Street Journal* and *The New York Times*, and he is frequently seen on CNBC, CNN, NPR, and national programs such as *Wall Street Week.*